The Psychology of EXERCISE

INTEGRATING THEORY AND PRACTICE

Curt L. Lox
SOUTHERN ILLINOIS UNIVERSITY EDWARDSVILLE

Kathleen A. Martin
MCMASTER UNIVERSITY

Steven J. Petruzzello
UNIVERSITY OF ILLINOIS AT URBANA-CHAMPAIGN

Holcomb Hathaway, Publishers
Scottsdale, Arizona 85250

Library of Congress Cataloging-in-Publication Data

Lox, Curt.
The psychology of exercise : integrating theory and practice / Curt L. Lox, Kathleen A. Martin, Steven J. Petruzzello.
p. cm.
Includes bibliographical references and index.
ISBN 1-890871-47-8
1. Exercise—Psychological aspects. 2. Physical fitness—Psychological aspects. I. Martin, Kathleen Anne. II. Petruzzello, Steven J. III. Title.

GV481.2.L69 2003
613.7'1—dc21

2002191347

Holcomb Hathaway, Publishers, Inc.
6207 North Cattletrack Road
Scottsdale, Arizona 85250
(480) 991-7881
www.hh-pub.com

ISBN 1-890871-47-8

10 9 8 7 6 5 4 3 2

Printed in the United States of America.

Contents

Part II

PSYCHOSOCIAL INFLUENCES AND CONSEQUENCES OF EXERCISE 107

Anxiety/Stress and Exercise 158

Emotional Well-Being and Exercise 180

Preface

Back in the day when the three of us were beginning our careers (which was really not that long ago), no useable undergraduate or graduate course textbooks existed on the topic of exercise psychology. We've come a long way since then. The book you are holding is the resource each of us wished we had, not only when we began our careers, but when we were still students. Our goal when we began writing this book was to produce an upper-level undergraduate/introductory-level graduate textbook that would cover the major topics of interest and research currently thriving in the field of exercise psychology. To this end, we have made great efforts to weave theoretical information with practical application throughout the text. We believe the practical aspect of the book is its strength. Throughout, you will find examples that apply the theories and models discussed to "real world" situations that students are likely to experience.

We feel the content and pedagogy of this text are unique in at least two ways. First, we have limited our inclusion of theories and models to those that appear most prominently in the exercise/rehabilitation psychology literature. Thus, we have chosen not to review theories and models that are not currently being incorporated into research in the field, or that boast little or no systematic exercise research support. Conversely, we have tried to incorporate theories that are just beginning to gain favor in the field of exercise psychology. The second distinguishing characteristic of this text is its range of content. Specifically, we have attempted to present both the "classic" areas of study (e.g., anxiety, depression, personality, self-esteem, emotional well-being) and the emerging topics (e.g., health-related quality of life, body image, social influences) currently dominating the literature. Finally, we feel that certain pedagogical aspects of the book will be very useful for both instructors and students. These include the liberal use of tables, graphs, and figures as well as the questions and activities found at the conclusion of each chapter. An instructor's manual and PowerPoint presentation are available to instructors upon adoption of this book.

The book is divided into two primary sections. Part I is composed of five chapters that will help students to understand and modify exercise behavior (either their own or the behavior of others). Thus, the book opens with a general introduction designed to acquaint the reader with the field of exercise psychology, followed by a chapter that addresses patterns of physical activity participation. The next two chapters discuss the most popular theories of exercise behavior currently accepted by exercise psychology scholars and practitioners. Chapter 5 concludes Part I by introducing students to intervention techniques aimed at modifying exercise behavior.

Part II is devoted to the more commonly promoted and investigated psychosocial influences and consequences of exercise, including the bi-directional relationships between exercise and concepts such as personality and body image. Additionally, this section highlights the impact of exercise on various mental-health states such as depression, anxiety, emotional well-being, self-esteem/self-concept, and health-related quality of life. Finally, we have dedicated an entire chapter to the countless social influences (e.g., group dynamics, leadership) that regularly and significantly affect exercise behavior.

We would like to say a final word about how we have addressed the expanding knowledge of exercise psychology to the many special populations we encounter. Rather than attempting to include information regarding special populations and psychosocial variables in a single chapter, we have incorporated that information, as appropriate, throughout the book. Thus, research related to enhanced quality of life for individuals with HIV-1, for example, will be found in the chapter on health-related quality of life. We applied a similar strategy, where relevant, to discussions of psychophysiology.

Although an extremely arduous task, we have thoroughly enjoyed writing this book and hope that you find it a useful resource for years to come. We welcome any comments, suggestions, or questions you may have in regard to the content or presentation of this text. Please write to us in care of our publisher:

Holcomb Hathaway, Publishers
6207 N. Cattletrack Rd., Ste. 5
Scottsdale, AZ 85250
sales@hh-pub.com

Acknowledgments

Heading the list of people we'd like to thank is our amazing editor, Colette Kelly, whose vision, guidance, and unwavering patience and confidence in the three of us cannot be overstated. We are grateful for all that you have contributed to this book.

We also extend thanks to the following individuals, who devoted their time and energy to review sections of this book at various stages of production: John B. Bartholomew, University of Texas at Austin; Bryan Blissmer, University of Rhode Island; Kerry S. Courneya, University of Alberta; Nicole Culos-Reed, University of Calgary; Caroline Davis, York University; Panteleimon Ekkekakis, Iowa State University; Thelma S. Horne, Miami University; Marc Lochbaum, Texas Tech University; Shannon Mihalko, Wake Forest University; and Karla Kubitz, Towson University. The book is better as a result of their suggestions, and we appreciate their input.

C. L., K. M., S. P.

First and foremost, this book would never have been possible without my two outstanding coauthors, Kathleen and Steve. I cannot thank the two of you enough for your tremendous efforts and teamwork throughout this process. I am indebted to my major academic advisors, Dave Warren, Thelma Horn, and Eddie McAuley. Although you may not realize it, each of you had a significant hand in this effort. Many thanks to Shannon Jackson, who assisted me in countless ways on this project. Finally, an endeavor such as this is never possible without the emotional support provided by immediate and extended family members. A very special thanks to all of you and, in particular, my main sources of inspiration—Shea and Kelsey.

C. L.

I extend my deepest appreciation to Curt Lox for inviting me to be part of this project. I wish to thank Larry Brawley, Mark Leary, and Jack Rejeski; their mentoring influence permeates these pages and for that I am grateful. I also appreciate my students for their enthusiasm and support for this book and, in particular, the insightful suggestions offered by Mary Jung and Amy Latimer. Finally, to Spero Ginis, the one who has given me the most, I need only say: "hey man, thanks!"

K. M.

I would like to extend my gratitude to Curt and Kathleen. Their extreme patience with me was much appreciated. I am especially grateful to Curt for extending the invitation to collaborate on the book in the first place. I am also indebted to the support of my former students, Panteleimon "Paddy" Ekkekakis and Eric Hall. They have been (and continue to be) instrumental in our ongoing examination of the way the field has traditionally looked at exercise and affect and in the advances I think we've made in changing the way we think about the psychological effects of exercise. I like to think that we have motivated and challenged each other and have all benefited as a result. Perhaps the most important collaborations, however, have been those with my family. Wendy, Tony, and Alyssa, you have allowed me to do the work I like to do. Whether you know it or not, you have inspired me. Without you and your support, I certainly couldn't have achieved what I have. Thank you.

S. P.

Part I

Understanding and Modifying Exercise Behavior

8LB

Chapter 1

Introduction to Exercise Psychology

KEY TERMS
acute
adherence
adoption
biopsychosocial approach
chronic
exercise
exercise psychology
exercise science
medical model
noncompliant
physical activity
psychology
rehabilitation psychology

Pretend, for a moment, that you are an exercise/health professional who has been approached by the following three individuals for assistance. After reviewing each scenario, consider what you might do to modify the thoughts, feelings, and behavior of the individuals described. Think of this activity as a proficiency exam to assess how much you already know about the psychology of exercise.

Case A. Individual A leaves for work before the rest of the family wakes up, works all day, and comes home to a husband and children around dinnertime. She reports not having enough time to spend with her family, let alone engage in exercise. She also reports high levels of stress and fatigue.

Case B. Individual B is currently undergoing physical rehabilitation following a complete tear of his anterior cruciate ligament. Although he has always been active, he has never had to cope with such a significant injury, long and (occasionally) painful rehabilitation, and fear with regard to his return to action.

Case C. Individual C knows she should exercise to lose weight but is very self-conscious about her body. She has resisted beginning an exercise regimen because she feels apprehensive about exercising in a public setting. She also reports low self-esteem and generally has a negative attitude toward exercise.

What Is Exercise Psychology?

As you probably realized while thinking about the previous cases, you have already come into contact with principles of exercise psychology without identifying them as such. The individuals described above are fairly typical exercise psychology cases that involve such complex psychological constructs as *adherence, self-esteem, self-efficacy, anxiety,* and *body image* (all of which will be discussed later). But what exactly is exercise psychology? In order to answer this question, we will first need to define exercise as it relates to physical activity. For the purpose of our discussions throughout this book, **physical activity** will refer to all bodily movements that cause increases in physical exertion beyond that which occurs during normal activities of daily living. **Exercise** is a form of *leisure* physical activity (as opposed to occupational or household physical activity) that is undertaken in order to achieve a particular objective (e.g., improved appearance, improved cardiovascular fitness, reduced stress).

physical activity ■

exercise ■

Also crucial to understanding the field of exercise psychology is knowledge about the broader disciplines from which the field has emerged. For the purposes of our discussion, refer to the model in Exhibit 1.1. At the top of the figure are the two parent disciplines from which the field of exercise psychology emerged. The first is **psychology,** which is the field of study concerned with the various mental processes (e.g., perceptions, cognitions, emotions) people experience and utilize in all aspects of their lives. The second is **exercise science,** which is devoted to the study of all aspects of sport, recreation, exercise/fitness, and rehabilitative behavior.

psychology ■

exercise science ■

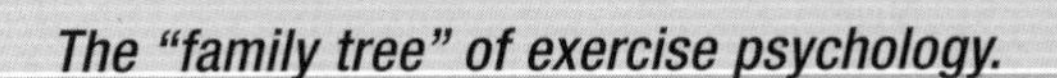

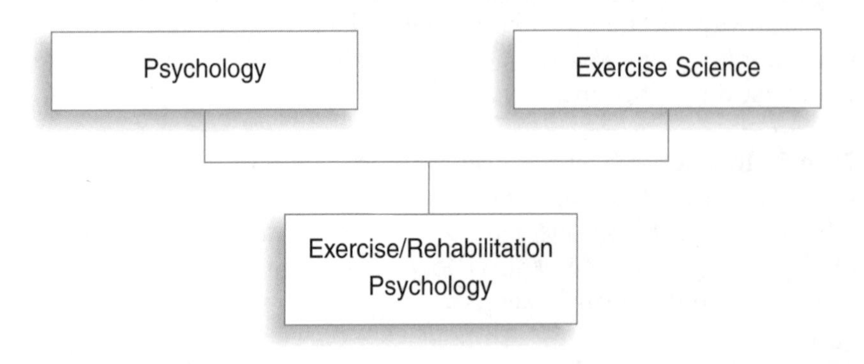

Representing the convergence of exercise science and psychology, the field of **exercise psychology** is concerned with (a) the application of psychological principles to the promotion and maintenance of leisure physical activity (exercise), and (b) the psychological and emotional consequences of leisure physical activity. Consider the individuals described at the beginning of the chapter. As alluded to earlier, each case presents a unique challenge to researchers and practitioners associated with the field of exercise psychology. Case A presents a working woman who perceives multiple barriers (i.e., time, fatigue) that prevent her from adopting exercise as a regular routine. An individual with knowledge of exercise psychology principles might attempt to find an exercise mode and time that she can work into her busy day and point out that properly prescribed exercise can aid in reducing the stress and fatigue that she is experiencing.

■ exercise psychology

In Case B, we find a man beginning the arduous task of physical rehabilitation following a severe injury who is anxious about his return to action and about the entire rehabilitation process. He is also likely struggling with lower than usual confidence in his physical abilities as well as fear of reinjury. As you will learn in more depth later in this book, the health-care practitioner should strive to incorporate exercise psychology concepts into the rehabilitation program. For example, allowing the patient to speak with others who have experienced similar injuries and successful rehabilitation may help to alleviate anxiety and increase confidence concerning his return to action.

Finally, the woman in Case C is apprehensive about exercise because of a negative body image and concern about others viewing her body in a public exercise setting. Although she needs to become physically active, her self-consciousness surrounding her body will likely prevent her from adopting a regimen of exercise. Once again, principles from the field of exercise psychology may help influence the woman's behavior. For instance, we might suggest that she seek out an exercise program geared toward overweight people like herself. This would provide social support and reduce the concern that others (who are not overweight) are viewing her body in a negative fashion.

The reader should note that a "sister" field of exercise psychology is included in Exhibit 1.1. **Rehabilitation psychology** deals with the relationship between psychological factors and the physical rehabilitation process. Thus, this field is concerned with exercise rehabilitation following injury or a cardiac event, as well as the role of physical activity as a complimentary strategy for treating disease and disability. In short, the objective is to employ psychological interventions during physical rehabilitation in order to return the individual to a prior, more

■ rehabilitation psychology

healthy, physical and/or mental state quickly and effectively, and to maximize residual function and health. Given these goals, researchers and practitioners associated with physical rehabilitation might address the following questions:

1. What psychological issues facilitate or hinder the injury rehabilitation process?
2. What forms and amount of exercise provide psychological benefits for cancer, AIDS, spinal cord injury, or cardiac rehabilitation patients?
3. Can exercise improve quality of life for those individuals dealing with injury, disease, or illness?

Readers interested in a more detailed, and somewhat different, approach to defining the boundaries of these fields should consult the seminal article on this topic written by Rejeski and Brawley (1988).

Emergence of Exercise Psychology

Historians have documented widespread physical activity participation as far back as 3,000 years ago when the games of ancient Greece flourished. However, while sporting events have always been central to society, it was not until the Industrial Revolution (late 1700s through the present) that the notion of fitness (and its value to the individual and employer) was first recognized. It was this newfound "philosophy of physical fitness," in fact, that paved the way for what has come to be known in the United States as the "fitness craze" of the 1970s. The birth of exercise psychology came on the heels of this fitness frenzy (during the 1980s) as the population was persuaded to alter its collective behavior in order to extend and improve quality of life. However, the appearance of exercise psychology, at least in the United States, was also a function of several other societal factors that emerged during the 1960s, '70s, and '80s (Rejeski & Thompson, 1993; Sallis & Owen, 1999). One such factor was the increasing emphasis on the physical appearance of the body. During this time, the image of the full-figured woman was ousted in favor of a new body ideal led by the philosophy that "thin is in." On the male front, simply being "big" was no longer the masculine ideal, unless one's girth was made up of muscle as opposed to fat. The ideal body was thus reconstructed to reflect society's preference for a "lean" and "defined" appearance. Not surprisingly, weight training and "aerobics" became popular means to achieve the leanness and strength desired by men and women alike.

Heightened levels of stress experienced by members of society during this time may also have hastened the emergence of the exercise psychology field. Indeed, with men, women, and children facing more domestic, academic, occupational, and social pressures than ever before, the need to reduce the resulting stress became paramount. However, before exercise could be acknowledged as an effective strategy for reducing stress, the scientific community first had to embrace the intimate relationship that exists between the mind and body. For example, reducing mental stress also serves to relax the body, and vice versa. Today, this notion has been expanded to include social context and is now referred to as the **biopsychosocial approach** to studying health behaviors (i.e., the belief that the body, mind, and social environment influence one another and, ultimately, behavior).

- biopsychosocial approach

Finally, the 1960s witnessed a shift in society's perception of who is responsible for maintaining the population's health. Prior to this time, the **medical model,** or the use of traditional forms of medicine (e.g., pharmacology) for improving physical or mental health, dominated health care (and still does to some extent). In the 1960s, however, people began to recognize that health is largely under the control of the individual and that exercise is one strategy that can be undertaken to address health concerns. Thus, individuals do not have to act solely as passive recipients of treatments or interventions prescribed by health-care professionals. Instead, the new philosophy dictated that we could (and should) play an active role in maintaining or improving our own health. This change in philosophy corresponded nicely to an increase in the amount of leisure time available to members of society. Specifically, available leisure time hit an all-time high during the 1980s with people working fewer hours per week than ever before. As a result of this lifestyle change, individuals generally had more time available for physical activity participation.

- medical model

In summary, physical activity became highly valued by society as a means of relieving stress, improving health, and enhancing physical appearance during the 1960s, '70s, and '80s. As a result, the door was open for the emergence of a new field of study that focused on the psychological antecedents and consequences of leisure physical activity. In recognition of this, 1988 saw the first issues of the *Journal of Sport Psychology,* a scientific publication for exercise psychology researchers, appropriately renamed the *Journal of Sport and Exercise Psychology.* Readers interested in learning more about the roots of exercise psychology may wish to consult a special edition of *The Sport Psychologist* (December 1995, Vol. 9, No. 4) devoted specifically to a historical analysis of sport and exercise psychology. With this as a backdrop, we now turn to a discussion of the various means of accessing information related to the field of exercise psychology.

Why Study Exercise Psychology?

If it has not yet become obvious, you may be asking yourself why it is necessary or helpful to study the psychology of exercise in the first place. We feel that such an endeavor is relevant for two primary reasons. First, it can help us to understand the psychological antecedents of exercise behavior given that physical activity adoption and adherence rates are so dismal (see Chapter 2). **Adoption** refers to the beginning stage of an exercise regimen, while **adherence** refers to maintaining an exercise regimen for a prolonged period of time following the initial adoption phase. Central to adherence is the assumption that the individual voluntarily and independently chooses to engage in the activity. Adherence is generally regarded as a largely psychological issue (see Chapters 3 and 4), and given the central role of **noncompliant** behavior (failure to maintain an exercise regimen prescribed by a health-care professional) as it relates to mental and physical health, knowledge of the psychology of exercise becomes paramount in health promotion efforts. The need for this knowledge may be best highlighted by the finding that only one of 13 physical activity and fitness objectives proposed in the federal government's Healthy People 2000 document was actually met (U.S. Department of Health and Human Services, 2000). These points will be further discussed in the next chapter as we review the impact of nonactivity on rates of mortality and morbidity in present-day society.

adoption ■
adherence ■
noncompliant ■

Second, we need to understand the psychological consequences of exercise in order to introduce physical activity interventions capable of reducing **acute** (short-term, temporary) and **chronic** (long-term, relatively permanent) negative psychological/emotional states, and of promoting acute and chronic positive psychological/emotional states. This goal is especially important in light of recent findings described in the U.S. Surgeon General's Report on Mental Health (1999). First, at least one in five persons in the United States has a diagnosed mental disorder (approximately 50 million Americans), the majority of whom are not receiving any form of treatment for the illness. Second, the annual combined direct and estimated indirect costs of mental-health services in the United States are now over $150 billion. Clearly, the promotion of physical activity as an adjunct (complimentary) therapy along with more traditional mental-health interventions (i.e., psychotherapy, pharmacological agents) might enable us to address these staggering statistics.

acute ■
chronic ■

Learning More About Exercise Psychology

We recommend that individuals who wish to obtain information and learn more about exercise psychology contact the prominent professional organizations and peruse applied and theoretical research articles published in the numerous journals devoted to the field. However, because exercise psychology "crosses over" a variety of disciplines (e.g., psychology, nursing/medicine/health, physical education/kinesiology), the task of locating literature related to the field is somewhat challenging. Indeed, it is likely that the student will require a combination of resources in order to gain a complete understanding. Fortunately, in this age of technological innovation, a number of excellent electronic databases (some available via the Internet) exist to help you accomplish this task. Exhibit 1.2 lists some of the most useful databases associated with the field of exercise psychology.

PROFESSIONAL ORGANIZATIONS ASSOCIATED WITH EXERCISE PSYCHOLOGY

The formation of organizations or associations is central to the progress of any field of study or industry. Specifically, such organizations permit individuals with similar interests to come together to share ideas and research related to their particular field. In addition, these organizations also serve as important "links" to the public sector, by

Popular databases utilized in exercise psychology research.* — exhibit 1.2

ERIC (Educational Resource Information Center) (www.eric.ed.gov)

MEDLINE (www.pubmed.com)

PsycINFO (www.psycinfo.com)

PsycLIT (www.psycinfo.com/psyclit.html)

CINAHL (Cumulative Index to Nursing and Allied Health Literature) (www.cinahl.com)

SPORT Discus or SIRC (Sport Information Resource Centre–Canada) (www.silverplatter.com/catalog/spor.htm)

Physical Education Index (www.csa.com/csa/factsheets/pei.shtml)

*Although many readers will access these databases through a library network, we have also provided the website addresses.

publicizing the field and providing information regarding its members to the consumer. Finally, some organizations may be responsible for the development of public policy, guidelines, or standards. A number of organizations currently serve exercise psychology researchers and professionals. The following are a few of the most prominent organizations related to the field of exercise psychology:

Association for the Advancement of Applied Sport Psychology (AAASP). The purpose of this association, founded in 1986, is to promote the development of psychological theory, research, and intervention strategies in the field of sport and exercise psychology. The organization consists of three sections: intervention/performance enhancement, health psychology, and social psychology. **www.aaasponline.org**

American College of Sports Medicine (ACSM). This multidisciplinary organization, founded in 1954, promotes and integrates scientific research, education, and practical applications of sports medicine and exercise science to maintain and enhance physical performance, fitness, health, and quality of life. ACSM is the largest, most respected sports medicine and exercise science organization in the world. **www.acsm.org**

APA Division 47 (Exercise and Sport Psychology). Founded in 1986, this division of the American Psychological Association aims to further the scientific, educational, and clinical foundations of exercise and sport psychology. **www.psyc.unt.edu/apadiv47**

APA Division 38 (Health Psychology). The mission of this division is to facilitate collaboration among psychologists and other health-science and health-care professionals interested in the psychological and behavioral aspects of physical and mental health. **www.health-psych.org**

European Federation of Sport Psychology (FEPSAC). This congress is composed of national societies dealing with sport and exercise psychology in European countries, including the German Association of Sport Psychology (ASP) and British Association of Sport and Exercise Sciences (BASES). **www.psychology.lu.se/fepsac**

International Society of Sport Psychology (ISSP). Founded in 1965, this society is devoted to promoting the study of behavior of individuals and groups associated with sport and physical activity. The ISSP is the only worldwide organization of scholars explicitly concerned with sport and exercise psychology. **www.issponline.org**

North American Society for the Psychology of Sport and Physical Activity (NASPSPA). Founded in 1967, this society is made up of three sections: sport and exercise psychology, motor development, and motor learning/control. **www.naspspa.org**

Society of Behavioral Medicine (SBM). The mission of this society, founded in 1978, is to foster the development and application of knowledge concerning the interrelationships of health, illness, and behavior. The goal of this multidisciplinary society is to form an interactive network for education and collaboration on common research and public policy. **www.sbmweb.org**

The Canadian Society for Psychomotor Learning and Sport Psychology (SCAPPS). Founded in 1977, this society aims to promote the study of motor control, motor learning, motor development, and sport/exercise psychology in Canada and to encourage the exchange of views and scientific information in the fields related to psychomotor learning and sport/exercise psychology. **www.scapps.org**

SCIENTIFIC JOURNALS ASSOCIATED WITH EXERCISE PSYCHOLOGY

In addition to organizations, emerging fields of study also require publication outlets for the research they generate. For exercise psychology researchers, a wide spectrum of both applied and theoretical journals is available, with more publications being introduced every year. Theoretical journals are highly technical in nature and are generally written by scientists for fellow scientists in the field. Applied journals, on the other hand, are written for the practitioner (e.g., rehabilitation specialist, exercise leader) and include useful (and less technical) information often based on research. Exhibit 1.3 lists some of the more popular journals associated with the field of exercise psychology.

TRAINING OPPORTUNITIES IN EXERCISE PSYCHOLOGY

Prior to embarking on a career in exercise psychology, an individual must first learn the skills and knowledge of the field at an institution of higher education that offers a program of exercise psychology–related content. Generally, such content is not found at community/junior college or professional psychology schools. In fact, many four-year colleges and universities do not offer courses in exercise psychology. Nonetheless, those universities that do offer courses or programs that

exhibit 1.3 *Scientific journals containing research from the field of exercise psychology.*

Adapted Physical Activity Quarterly
Annals of Behavioral Medicine
Applied and Preventive Psychology
Australian Journal of Sports Medicine
Basic and Applied Social Psychology
British Journal of Health Psychology
British Journal of Sports Medicine
Health Psychology
International Journal of Behavioral Medicine
International Journal of Rehabilitation and Health
International Journal of Sport Psychology
Journal of Aging and Physical Activity
Journal of Applied Biobehavioral Research
Journal of Applied Social Psychology
Journal of Applied Sport Psychology
Journal of Behavioral Medicine
Journal of Health and Social Behavior
Journal of Health Psychology
Journal of Physical Education, Recreation, and Dance
Journal of Psychosocial Oncology
Journal of Psychosomatic Research
Journal of Sport and Exercise Psychology
Journal of Sport Behavior
Journal of Sports Sciences
Journal of Teaching in Physical Education
Measurement in Physical Education and Exercise Science
Medicine and Science in Sports and Exercise
Mind/Body Medicine
Perceptual and Motor Skills
Psychology and Health
Psychology, Health and Medicine
Psychology of Sport and Exercise
Psychosomatic Medicine
Rehabilitation Psychology
Research Quarterly for Exercise and Sport
The Sport Psychologist

include elements of exercise psychology generally house these courses or programs in one of the departments listed below.

Kinesiology. This is clearly the most likely department to find a course or program. A program would be found only at the graduate level, while courses may be found at both the undergraduate and graduate levels. At the undergraduate level, the fields of sport and exercise psychology are often covered in the same course. Related departments: Physical Education, Movement Studies, Exercise Science, Human Performance, Sport Studies, and many others.

Psychology. Although it is quite rare to find a course focused on exercise psychology in a Psychology department, one is even less likely to find a program of study here. Some Psychology departments offer a health psychology or behavioral medicine program.

Nursing. Students are highly unlikely to find a course (and never a program) in a Nursing department. Related departments such as Health or Medicine, similarly, rarely offer exercise psychology courses and programs.

OCCUPATIONAL OPPORTUNITIES INCORPORATING EXERCISE PSYCHOLOGY

Individuals with background in exercise psychology might be found in positions such as those listed below.

Higher education. This is the primary occupation for individuals trained in the field of exercise psychology. Job responsibilities at the university level generally consist of teaching academic courses and conducting research related to the field of exercise psychology.

Primary/secondary education. Elementary through high school physical education instructors and coaches utilize principles of behavioral modification and group dynamics for teams or physical education classes. Additionally, a background in exercise psychology enables an instructor to increase the self-esteem of a student or provide support for someone experiencing body image concerns.

Fitness and wellness. The fitness and wellness field includes personal trainers as well as directors of corporate fitness and wellness programs. In these positions, the ability to apply motivational and adherence techniques would be particularly valuable.

Rehabilitation. Rehabilitation personnel include athletic trainers, physical therapists, and cardiac rehabilitation staff. The ability to increase confidence and reduce stress in an individual participating in rehabilitation would be extremely useful in this setting.

Business. Consultants and administrators in the business world may employ principles of exercise psychology related to effective leadership and group dynamics to aid in the functioning of a corporate unit. Knowledge of behavioral modification techniques would be beneficial for anyone leading others.

Conclusion

The field of exercise psychology is an inherently interesting and important one: it deals with issues to which most of us can relate and is an invaluable resource in our fight to improve public health. Although it maintains strong theoretical roots, the field is extremely practical in that many thoughts, feelings, and behaviors are sensitive to intervention. This practical focus is not surprising given that exercise psychology emerged from two very applied fields, psychology and exercise science. The psychology of exercise focuses on both the psychosocial antecedents and consequences of exercise behavior. Thus, researchers seek to determine (a) the psychosocial factors that can influence exercise behavior and (b) the psychosocial outcomes of exercise participation. As a "sister" field of exercise psychology, rehabilitation psychology focuses on the relationship between psychological/emotional factors and the physical rehabilitation process.

Given the state of ill health and exceptionally poor rates of physical activity adoption and adherence in society, exercise psychology is poised to contribute mightily to the war against inactivity. Growing out of the "fitness craze" of the 1970s, the field has become a mainstay in the exercise science and behavioral medicine (health psychology) literatures. In addition, the number of higher education courses and training programs offered throughout the world has increased tremendously over the past three decades, and many professional organizations and occupations incorporating exercise psychology now exist.

Although we have barely scratched the surface, we hope that you now have a practical idea of where and how exercise psychology fits into our daily lives, and the central role that it may play in improving the psychological and physical well-being of our society. As you will see in the next chapter on exercise epidemiology, modifying physical activity patterns is no small feat. Based on the contemporary philosophy that the mind and body are inseparable and substantially influence one another, exercise psychology has much to offer fitness professionals, medical personnel, and the mental-health profession. We conclude this introduction with the following quotes from a pair of nineteenth-century writers who lived long before the field of exercise psychology was born. Enjoy the journey!

> "Me thinks that the moment my legs begin to move, my thoughts begin to flow."
>
> *Henry David Thoreau*

> "By too much sitting still the body becomes unhealthy, and soon the mind."
>
> *Henry Wadsworth Longfellow*

What Do You Know?

1. Discuss the parent disciplines from which the field of exercise psychology emerged.
2. Define the fields of exercise psychology and rehabilitation psychology.
3. Why is it important to study the psychology of exercise?
4. What historical/societal factors helped to give rise to the field of exercise psychology?
5. In what university departments are you likely to find courses or programs in exercise psychology?
6. Discuss occupational opportunities incorporating principles of exercise psychology.

Learning Activities

1. Complete the "proficiency exam" provided on the first page of the chapter. Discuss your thoughts with other members of the class.
2. Learn more about the field of exercise psychology by looking up one of the websites listed in the chapter. Alternatively, conduct a search for new sites.
3. Review articles in one or more of the journals listed in Exhibit 1.3 in order to gain a feel for the topics and research methodology in the field of exercise psychology.

References

Rejeski, W. J., & Brawley, L. R. (1988). Defining the boundaries of sport psychology. *The Sport Psychologist, 2*, 231–242.

Rejeski, W. J., & Thompson, A. (1993). Historical and conceptual roots of exercise psychology. In P. Seraganian (Ed.), *Exercise psychology: The influence of physical exercise on psychological processes*. New York: John Wiley & Sons.

Sallis, J. F., & Owen, N. (1999). *Physical activity and behavioral medicine*. Thousand Oaks, CA: Sage.

U.S. Department of Health and Human Services. (2000). *Healthy People 2010*. Washington, DC: U.S. Government Printing Office.

U.S. Public Health Service. (1999). *Mental health: A report of the Surgeon General*. Washington, DC: U.S. Department of Health and Human Services.

Chapter 2

Physical Activity Epidemiology

KEY TERMS
- all-cause mortality rates
- epidemiology
- longitudinal studies
- morbidity
- physical activity epidemiology
- sedentary

Today, the types of physical activity we engage in vary tremendously, from organized sport (e.g., basketball) to playground games (e.g., "tag"), fitness activities (e.g., jogging) to outdoor recreation (e.g., rock climbing). People from all walks of life (both sexes, all age groups, most ethnic groups) engage in exercise and other forms of physical activity for a variety of reasons. Through these activities we rehabilitate, obtain membership status in a socially defined group, improve employee productivity, improve our fitness level, feel better about ourselves, relieve stress, and so forth. Unfortunately, a relatively low percentage of people take advantage of the many benefits of physical activity participation, and the negative consequences of this behavioral choice are becoming painfully clear. The U.S. Centers for Disease Control (CDC) have reported that physical inactivity, along with poor diet, is responsible for at least 300,000 "preventable" deaths per year, a number second only to those caused by smoking.

The epidemic is not limited to the United States—the lack of physical activity is a problem in all industrialized nations (Sallis & Owen, 1999, p. xx). Indeed, the birth of the Industrial Revolution appears to have coincided with the death of widespread involvement in physical activity. Technology, for example, has provided many time- and effort-saving devices (e.g., microwaves, refrigerators, cars, forklifts) as well as means of entertainment (e.g., televisions, cable/satellite/video game systems, video and DVD recorders/players, computers, the Internet). One consequence of this, as reported by the CDC, is that the number of reported trips made by walking or bicycling has declined by more than 40 percent since 1977. Making matters worse, today's occupations rely much more on mental as opposed to physical capacity, thus increasing mental stress and reducing physical fitness. Concern over the inactivity of society has attracted the attention of government agencies, the World Health Organization, and entities such as the task force for the U.S. Healthy People 2010 initiative (see Exhibit 2.1 for a list of Healthy People 2010 objectives). Fortunately, as detailed in Chapter 5, the field of exercise psychology may play a prominent role in improving the rates of physical activity adoption and adherence throughout the world. However, before we discuss how to utilize exercise psychology principles to improve adoption and adherence rates, it is necessary to review current patterns of physical activity participation.

exhibit 2.1 ***Examples of Healthy People 2010 physical activity and fitness objectives.***

- Reduce the proportion of adults who engage in no leisure-time physical activity.
- Increase the proportion of adolescents who engage in moderate physical activity for at least 30 minutes on five or more of the previous seven days.
- Increase the proportion of adolescents who engage in vigorous physical activity that promotes the development and maintenance of cardiorespiratory fitness three or more days per week for 20 or more minutes per occasion.
- Increase the proportion of adults who perform physical activities that enhance and maintain muscular strength and endurance.
- Increase the proportion of adults who perform physical activities that enhance and maintain flexibility.
- Increase the proportion of the nation's public and private schools that require daily physical education for all students.
- Increase the proportion of adolescents who spend at least 50% of school physical education class time being physically active.
- Increase the proportion of worksites offering employer-sponsored physical activity and fitness programs.
- Increase the proportion of trips made by walking.
- Increase the proportion of trips made by bicycling.

Source: USDHHS, 2000.

Physical Activity Participation Patterns: Sampling Across the Globe

One of our goals in this chapter is to document *who* is engaging in *what* forms and "doses" of physical activity and *why* they are, or are not, participating. Such a project falls within the domain of **epidemiology,** which is broadly defined as the study of any epidemic. When applied to physical activity, epidemiology is a field of study devoted to the five "W's": who exercises; where, when, and why they do so; and what they do. Thus, **physical activity epidemiology** may be defined by questions such as, "To what extent are individuals within a particular society physically active?" and "What physical activities are people most engaged in?" Epidemiology of physical activity might also address variations in physical activity patterns across certain groups of individuals (e.g., based on race, age, sex, socioeconomic status), why certain individuals are physically active while others are not, and the links between physical activity, morbidity, and mortality. Such information is paramount as it allows health-care professionals to target specific populations for intervention, determine the impact of the intervention, and highlight public health consequences of current behavioral trends. Clearly then, the fields of exercise psychology and epidemiology share a number of interests and concerns.

- epidemiology
- physical activity epidemiology

As it is beyond the scope of this chapter and textbook to review data from all nations, we focus on those countries that have recently collected (and made available) data from large-scale epidemiological studies. These countries include the United States, Canada, Australia, and the United Kingdom (Scotland and England only). The data reported in this chapter were largely obtained from online documentation of the following reports: the U.S. Surgeon General's report on *Physical Activity and Health* (USDHHS, 1996), *The Health Survey for England* (Teers, 2001), *The Scottish Health Survey* (Nove, 1997), The Canadian Fitness and Lifestyle Research Institute's *Physical Activity Monitor* (1999), and *Physical Activity Patterns of Australian Adults* (Armstrong, Bauman, & Davies, 2000). Before embarking on our discussion, however, we would like to highlight the inherent difficulty in directly comparing the data reported by each of these countries. Specifically, the tremendous variability across nations in definitions of concepts such as "regular activity," "vigorous activity, "minimal activity," and "inactivity" makes comparisons of data between countries somewhat impractical. In addition, variations in the methods used for measuring physical activity (see box on the following page) make any comparisons suspect. Thus, where disparities in activity rates exist, readers should be cautious about drawing conclusions based solely on country membership.

A Primer on Physical Activity Measurement

Related to the issue of variations in activity definitions is concern over the manner in which physical activity is measured. Although a comprehensive review of physical activity measurement is beyond the scope of this text, the issue merits attention as background for our discussion of activity patterns. To begin with, three primary means of assessing physical activity exist:

Self-report. Self-report measures are the most widely used because they provide a great deal of information with relatively little time and financial investment on the part of researchers. Indeed, the data presented throughout the remainder of this chapter are based on self-report measures. These *activity recall* measures may be used for varying periods of time, ranging from one week to an entire lifetime. Obviously, the longer the time frame, the greater the chance of error resulting from memory limitations. The most popular time frame appears to be one week (e.g., Seven Day Recall; see Blair et al., 1985), although a number of three-month and one-year recall measures also exist in the literature. Other measures assess activity as it is performed during a "usual" week (e.g., Godin Leisure Time Questionnaire, Godin, Jobin, & Bouillon, 1986) as opposed to the immediately preceding week.

Objective/technological. The second category of measurement includes the various mechanical and electronic devices currently available. Popular examples include pedometers (which measure distance like the odometer on a car), accelerometers (which sense limb acceleration), and heart rate monitors (which provide constant pulse readings). Although these objective measures are not subject to falsified feedback or memory fade concerns characteristic of self-report tools, they are more expensive (to purchase and maintain), can be somewhat complex to utilize, and do not provide information related to all aspects of the activity (mode, intensity, duration).

Observation. Finally, direct observation (viewing exercise behavior "live" or "in person") and indirect methods of observation (such as viewing behavior on videotape) may be useful for certain populations, such as young children. Observation allows for documentation of the specific activities engaged in and eliminates the issue of memory recall and self-report biases. However, this technique is very costly from a time and financial standpoint and, furthermore, may lead to atypical behavior on the part of the exerciser.

ADULT PATTERNS OF PHYSICAL ACTIVITY

sedentary ■

Not surprisingly, **sedentary** (chronic pattern of inactivity) lifestyles have been consistently identified in all five of these industrialized countries. Generally speaking, 40 to 60 percent of these countries' residents do not achieve the recommended amount of regular physical activity. In fully one-half of the 50 United States, at least 73 percent of adults are not achieving the minimal standard, and significant portions of the population in each of these countries (at least 10 to 25 percent) are not active at all. In the United States, only 20 percent of adults engage in the minimal amount of activity suggested by the American College of Sports Medicine (ACSM, 2000). The corresponding rates of adults engaged in the minimal amount of activity are considerably higher in Canada (40 percent), Scotland (40 percent), and Australia (57 percent), with the rate in England (24 percent) only slightly higher than that of the United States (see Exhibit 2.2).

AGE AND PHYSICAL ACTIVITY

The considerable reduction that occurs in physical activity over the age span is to be expected. In an interesting and informative study of "sitting" and physical activity habits of children, the *Health Survey for England* found that these two behaviors each occupied approximately 10 hours per week in the average life of a three-year-old toddler. By age 15, however, teenagers sat 17 to 18 hours per week and were physically active for only 4 to 8 hours per week. The study is a bit misleading, however, in that sitting is defined as more than simply watching television, for example. Also included were behaviors such as reading and doing homework. Nonetheless, the clear trend toward reduced levels of

Percentage of population engaging in sufficient levels of physical activity. exhibit 2.2

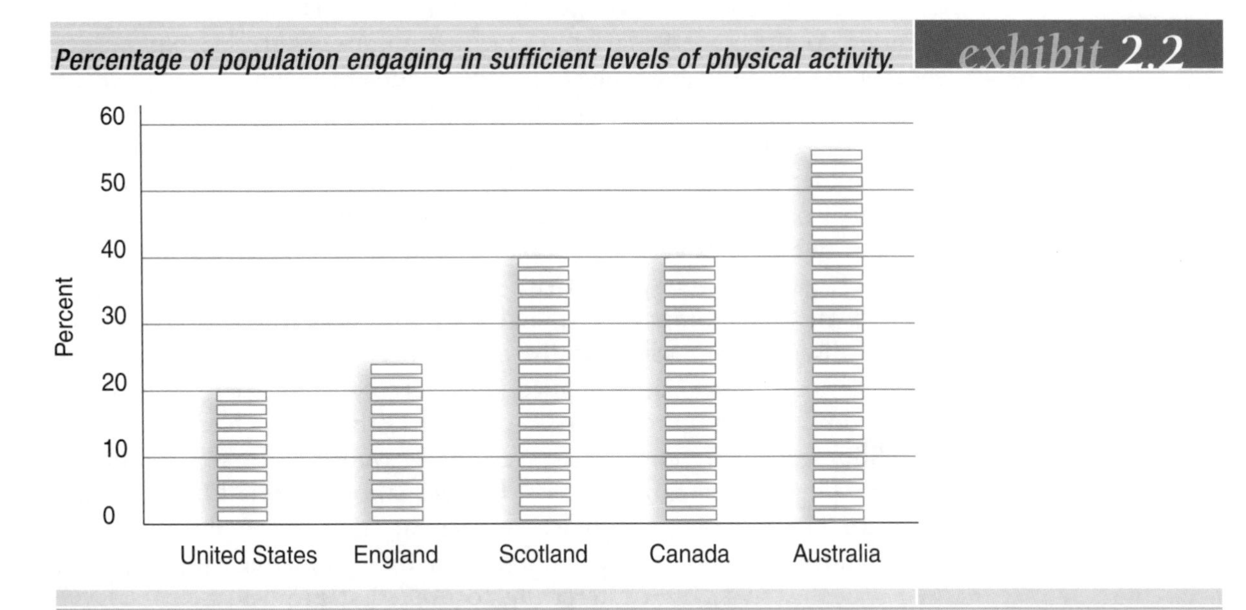

Sources: U.S. Surgeon General's *Report on Physical Activity & Health* (USDHHS, 1996); *Health Survey for England* (2001); *Scottish Health Survey* (Nove, 1997); Canadian Fitness and Lifestyle Research Institute, *Physical Activity Monitor* (1999); *Physical Activity Patterns of Australian Adults* (Armstrong et al., 2000).

The ACSM Definition of Minimal Activity

Because ACSM is considered the foremost authority on fitness in the world, we provide the organization's position concerning the "minimal" amount of cardiovascular and resistance activity suggested for health promotion and disease prevention.

- For *cardiovascular exercise,* individuals should engage in activity three to five days per week with each session lasting approximately 30–45 minutes. The time for each session may be reduced to 10–15 minutes in instances where an individual has chosen to engage in two or three separate bouts of exercise in a given day. Furthermore, although the prescribed intensity will vary substantially across exercisers, it is suggested that activity be maintained within each individual's target heart rate zone of 60 to 90 percent maximum heart rate (MHR).

- For *resistance training,* one set of eight to twelve repetitions should be performed for each exercise. Intensity should be adjusted such that the amount of resistance (e.g., weight) causes the exerciser to experience volitional fatigue upon completing each set. Finally, it is suggested that individuals engage in resistance training twice per week with each session consisting of eight to ten different exercises.

physical activity as one ages is alarming. Similar age trends exist in other countries. Sedentary rates in Australia nearly triple from 6.3 percent in the 18–29 age range to nearly 18 percent in the 60–75 age range. More alarming statistics have been reported in Scotland, where 18 percent of 16- to 24-year-olds, compared with 60 percent of individuals 65 and older, are inactive. In Canada, parents have reported that children aged 1 to 4 spend approximately 28 hours in physically active play each week, while teenagers aged 13 to 17 spend only half that amount of time engaged in physical activity.

Data concerning levels of activity in physical education classes are also disconcerting. Specifically, although enrollment in U.S. physical education classes has remained relatively constant, daily attendance has declined precipitously. As a result, less than 20 percent of all high school students report being physically active for at least 20 minutes in daily physical education classes. Overall, about one-half of Americans 12 to 21 years of age regularly participate in vigorous physical activity, and 25 percent are sedentary. As a final point regarding age and physical activity, it is interesting to note that physical activity levels present during youth are not related to exercise levels in adulthood. In other words, highly active youngsters will not necessarily become physically active adults. Indeed, one of the most significant challenges for researchers and practitioners is to determine how to transfer the enjoyment youngsters appear to experience in sport to the "lifetime" physical activities (e.g., tennis, golf, swimming, bicycling, hiking, dancing) in which active adults characteristically engage.

GENDER AND PHYSICAL ACTIVITY

As alluded to earlier in this chapter, males have historically been more physically active than females and, although the gap in activity levels has lessened, this gender-based pattern of behavior still exists. For example, in Canada more men (41 percent) than women (32 percent) are physically active. For children 5 to 12 years of age, 54 percent of boys, but only 43 percent of girls, meet the recommended levels of physical activity. Gender differences are more pronounced in adolescence, with 50 percent of boys and only 32 percent of girls considered sufficiently active (see Exhibit 2.3).

Gender differences exist not only in the amount of activity but also in the mode of activity performed. Specifically, U.S. males are more likely than females to participate in vigorous physical activities of all sorts as well as strengthening activities, walking, and bicycling. Interesting data have also been reported in Scotland, where, although men are more likely to be sufficiently physically active than women

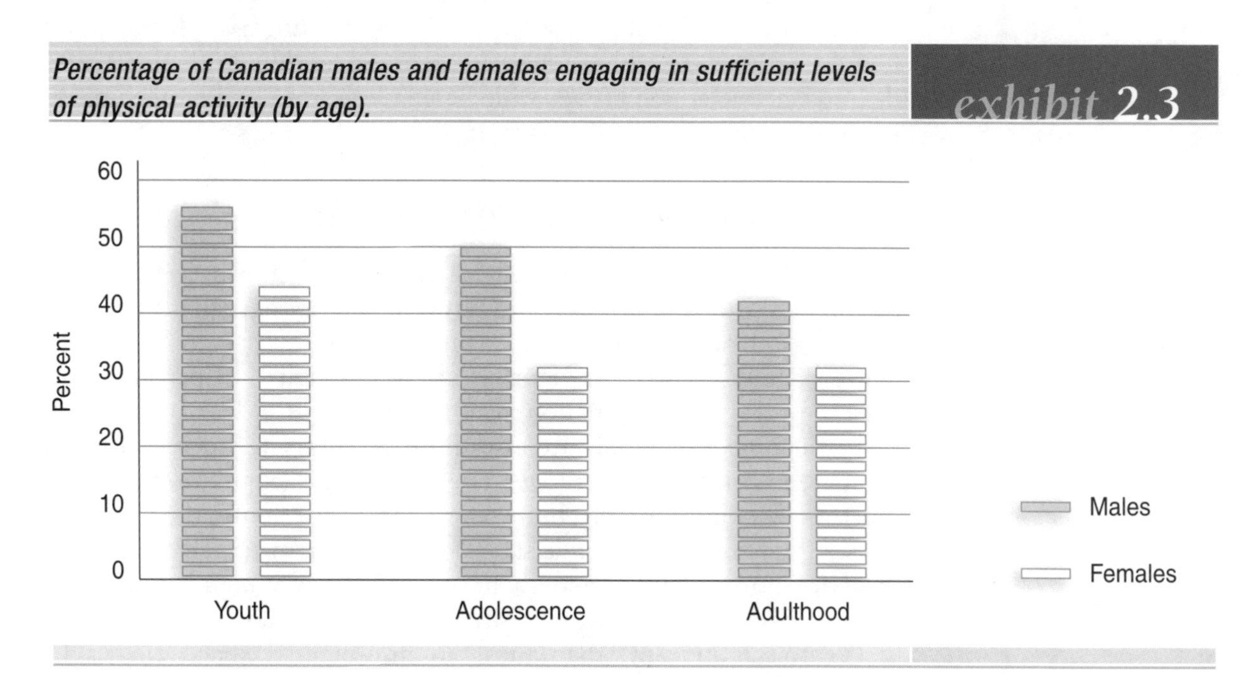

Percentage of Canadian males and females engaging in sufficient levels of physical activity (by age). exhibit 2.3

Source: Canadian Fitness and Lifestyle Research Institute, *Physical Activity Monitor* (1999).

(44 percent vs. 35 percent), activity levels for men decline with age while rates for women remain relatively constant. Although men and women appear to participate fairly equally in sports and exercise modes of activity, women engage in more household-related physical activity, whereas men engage in more work-related physical activity. Additionally, although Scottish men are more likely than women to participate in vigorous activity (37 percent vs. 27 percent), women engage in more moderate-intensity activity (56 percent vs. 41 percent). Finally, men also engage in more frequent bouts of physical activity than do women (average of 4.6 sessions/week for men vs. 3.6 sessions for women).

ETHNICITY AND PHYSICAL ACTIVITY

Data from the United States indicate a trend toward lower physical activity participation in non-Caucasian ethnic groups. Specifically, although the vigorous physical activity rates of African Americans, Hispanics, and the total U.S. population (18 years and older) are relatively similar (ranging from 13 to 16 percent), sedentary rates are higher for African Americans and Hispanics (28 percent and 31 percent, respectively) than for Native Americans and the total U.S. population (23 percent each) (see Exhibit 2.4). Focusing specifically on the health of minority ethnic groups, the *Health Survey for England* (Teers, 2001) found that Black Caribbean men and women residing in England were the most active ethnic group while Bangladeshi men and women residing in England were the least active.

SOCIAL CLASS AND PHYSICAL ACTIVITY

As for ethnicity, scant data exist for the relationship between socioeconomic status (social class) and physical activity participation. Once again, data from the United States indicate that lower-income individuals engage in slightly less vigorous physical activity (14 percent) than does the total U.S. population aged 18 years and older (16 percent). Lower-income individuals are also more sedentary (28 percent) when compared with the overall (over 18 years of age) population (23 percent). In Scotland, among both sexes, those in "non-manual" social classes (higher socioeconomic status) are most likely to achieve a moderate or vigorous level of activity in sports. However, men in "manual" social classes (lower socioeconomic status) are considerably more likely (21 to 26 percent) than those in non-manual social classes (6 percent) to be physically active at work. Women exhibit the opposite

Percentage of American population considered sedentary (by ethnicity).

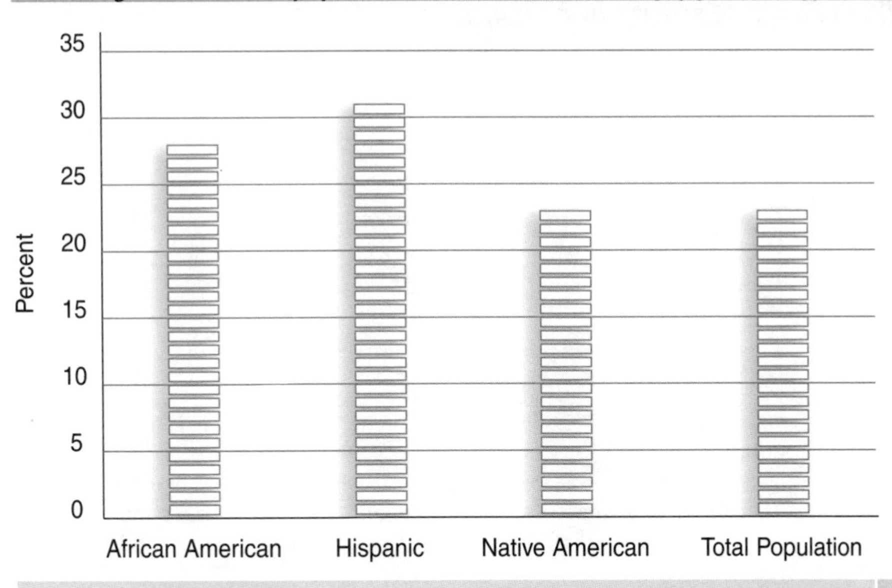

Source: U.S. Surgeon General's *Report on Physical Activity & Health* (USDHHS, 1996).

behavior in that those in manual social classes are the least likely to be active at work (4 percent). Finally, although social class does not correspond to different activity levels of men in the home, women from the manual social classes are more likely to be physically active in the home (71 percent) than are women of non-manual classes (56 percent). In England, a surprisingly different pattern of activity exists: only 26 percent of men from non-manual social classes are likely to engage in moderate or vigorous physical activity (five or more times per week) as compared with 41 percent of men from manual social classes. Little or no difference in activity levels has been found to exist as a function of social class for English women.

EDUCATION LEVEL AND PHYSICAL ACTIVITY

Data from Australia indicate clear trends in levels of "sufficient" physical activity as a function of education. Specifically, only 38.6 percent of individuals with less than 12 years of education are sufficiently active, compared with 47.0 percent of those with a high school certificate (or equivalent) and 52.3 percent of those who continued their education beyond high school (see Exhibit 2.5).

exhibit 2.5 *Percentage of Australian adult population engaging in sufficient levels of physical activity (by education level).*

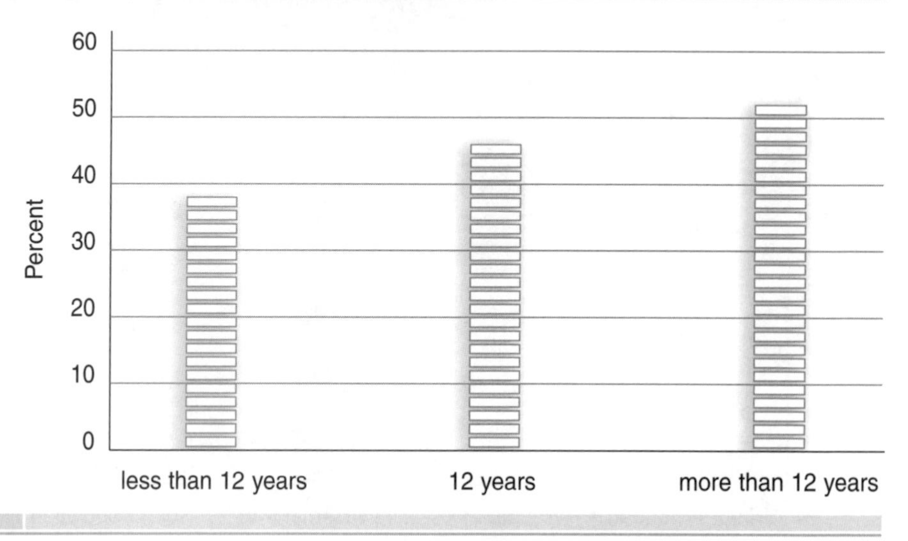

Source: Physical Activity Patterns of Australian Adults (Armstrong et al., 2000).

SUMMARY OF PHYSICAL ACTIVITY PARTICIPATION PATTERNS ACROSS THE GLOBE

Entire university courses are devoted to the study of physical activity epidemiology, and we have barely scratched the surface of this topic in this chapter. The data reviewed above highlight some of the key demographic factors implicated in physical activity behavior patterns across a small sample of industrialized nations. Taken together, the findings reveal the following physical activity participation trends:

- The number of people worldwide who exercise at the minimal level required to achieve physical benefits is extremely low. A conservative estimate is that at least 50 percent of the population in each of the countries reviewed fall into this category. At least 25 percent do not exercise at all.
- The amount of time spent engaged in physical activity declines linearly throughout childhood, and this linear trend continues through the lifespan. Conversely, the amount of time spent in sedentary activities increases linearly.
- Although males are more likely to participate in *vigorous* forms of physical activity, women tend to engage in as much, if not more, *moderate* intensity physical activity.

- Although the differences are relatively small, it appears that low-income groups and ethnic minority groups tend to participate in less leisure physical activity than does the overall population. Low-income individuals, on the other hand, tend to be more physically active at work. For a discussion of physical activity interventions targeting these groups, the reader is referred to an article by Taylor, Baranowski, and Young (1998).
- Education level is directly related to physical activity levels (i.e., the more education, the greater the participation in physical activity).

Consequences of Physical Activity and Inactivity

The previous information simply describes what certain population segments of the world are doing in regard to engagement in physical activity. However, more disconcerting than the poor rates of physical activity participation are the eventual consequences of this widespread inactivity. Next we highlight the positive health outcomes of physical activity as well as the negative consequences of physical inactivity.

PHYSICAL ACTIVITY, MORBIDITY, AND MORTALITY

According to a position paper jointly released by the U.S. Centers for Disease Control and Prevention and the American College of Sports Medicine (Pate et al., 1995), physically active people outlive their sedentary counterparts, as demonstrated by their lower overall **all-cause mortality rates** (i.e., death by any cause) as well as research indicating that a midlife increase in physical activity is associated with a reduced risk of mortality. More specifically, approximately 250,000 deaths per year (12 percent of all deaths) in the United States are linked to sedentary lifestyles. It has been estimated that premature deaths in Canada could be reduced by as much as 20 percent if sedentary and "somewhat active" Canadians became more active.

- all-cause mortality rates

From a **morbidity** (disease) standpoint, although coronary heart disease (CHD) rates have continued to decline in the United States in recent years, approximately 14 million people still suffer from the disease and 1.5 million experience a heart attack each year. An additional 8 million people have adult-onset diabetes, 50 million people have high blood pressure, and more than 60 million people (totaling fully one-third of the population) are overweight. This last statistic is particularly

- morbidity

distressing, as the overweight epidemic has found its way into the country's youth as well. Perhaps the most frustrating aspect of these data is that many of these conditions can be directly and positively affected by the adoption of a physically active lifestyle. Indeed, several large-scale, descriptive, and longitudinal studies of physical activity level and morbidity/mortality rates support this statement. (**Longitudinal studies** allow researchers to monitor changes in behavior over a relatively long period of time, i.e., years, in the same group of people.)

longitudinal studies ■

Two of the most recognized studies were conducted with the help of San Francisco longshoremen and Harvard University alumni. The former study (Paffenbarger, Hale, Brand, & Hyde, 1977) involved literally thousands of longshore workers and a 22-year follow-up assessment in which physical work activity (i.e., energy expenditure), CHD records, and mortality data were obtained. During the 22-year period (1951 to 1972), 11 percent of the longshoremen died of CHD. However, men who expended at least 8,500 kilocalories per week on the job were found to possess a significantly lower CHD mortality risk (at any age) than men who were less physically active on the job.

The Harvard study (Paffenbarger, Hyde, Wing, & Hsieh, 1986) tracked almost 17,000 alumni from 1962 to 1978. As in the longshoremen study, researchers obtained CHD and mortality data. However, unlike the longshoremen study, self-reported *leisure-time* physical activity was the focus of the investigation. Results indicated a 53 percent reduction in all-cause mortality among men who participated in at least three hours of sport activity per week as compared with those who engaged in less than one hour of sport activity per week. Additionally, for those engaged in moderate levels of physical activity (at least 10 miles/16 kilometers walked per week), mortality rates were 33 percent lower than among those who walked less than 3 miles/5 kilometers per week. Generally speaking, active individuals lived more than two years longer than inactive individuals.

In support of the above investigations, a more recent series of studies emanating from the Cooper Institute in the United States (Blair et al., 1995; Blair et al., 1989) has documented the relationship between physical fitness and all-cause mortality among approximately 10,000 men and more than 3,000 women (of ages ranging from the 20s through 80s). Baseline and follow-up assessments several years later indicated that males with the highest levels of fitness had a mortality rate 71 percent lower than that of males with the lowest levels of fitness. Those men who improved their physical fitness levels from "unfit" to "fit" over the course of the study experienced a reduction in mortality risk of 44 percent. The impact of fitness was even greater for females, as evidenced by a 79 percent lower death rate for high-fit versus low-fit individuals. In general, increased mortality rates appear to be associated with decreased levels of physical fitness.

Conclusion

Physical activity epidemiology is a field of study devoted to the *who, what, where, when,* and *why* of exercise behavior. As the epidemic of physical inactivity has spread worldwide, a number of entities have stepped to the forefront in an effort to lead the populace toward a more healthy lifestyle. The poor rates of leisure and general forms of physical activity can be traced to a number of wide-ranging social events and innovations, including the industrial and technological revolutions. In order to document the precise nature of physical activity patterns, we selectively reviewed physical activity and demographic data from several North American and European countries. We noted that two prominent limitations in much of the epidemiological research concern the definition of physical activity and related terminology and the variation in physical activity measurement. Physical activity may be assessed via self-report/survey, mechanical/electronic devices, and observation. The pros and cons of each method should be given careful consideration in the design and evaluation of research investigations. Despite these limitations, data indicate that the majority of individuals in society are either largely or completely inactive. This inactivity increases with age and varies according to a number of factors, including socioeconomic status, race/ethnicity, and education level.

Epidemiology is also concerned with consequences of inactivity, such as the rates of morbidity and mortality. In general, an indirect relationship is said to exist between physical activity and morbidity/mortality: those who engage in the greatest amount of activity tend to achieve longer and more healthy lives. Indeed, several large longitudinal research investigations conducted in the United States provide fairly consistent support for this finding.

What Do You Know?

1. Define the terms *sedentary* and *minimal level of physical activity.*
2. Why are physical activity participation rates so dismal?
3. What are the five "W's" of physical activity epidemiology?

4. Why is the lack of physical activity participation considered an epidemic?
5. What are the general rates of activity and inactivity across the countries listed in the chapter?
6. What is the relationship between age and physical activity?
7. What is the relationship between gender and physical activity?
8. What is the relationship between ethnicity and physical activity?
9. What is the relationship between social class and physical activity?
10. What is the relationship between education level and physical activity?
11. Does physical activity influence morbidity and mortality? Explain your answer.
12. What did you learn from the San Francisco longshoremen, Harvard University alumni, and Cooper Institute research studies?

Learning Activities

1. Gather data from each student in the class regarding exercise behavior (for the purpose of this activity, simply use the number of days per week, on average, each person exercises). Use variables such as age and gender to create graphical representations of your data.
2. Using the data in the chapter and any additional data you can uncover, draft a "position" paper that discusses physical activity in society and what you believe must be done in order to improve activity levels.
3. As a class, design a longitudinal research study incorporating epidemiological data and at least one psychological measure. In other words, devise an investigation similar to the morbidity/mortality studies, but substitute psychological data for death/disease rates.

References

American College of Sports Medicine. (2000). *Guidelines for exercise testing and prescription* (6th ed.). Philadelphia: Lippincott Williams & Wilkins.

Armstrong, T., Bauman, A., & Davies, J. (2000). *Physical activity patterns of Australian adults: Results of the 1999 National Physical Activity Survey.* Canberra, Australia: Australian Institute of Health and Welfare.

Blair, S. N., Haskell, W. L., Ho, P., Paffenbarger, R. S., Jr., Vranizan, K. M., Farquhar, J. W., & Wood, P. D. (1985). Assessment of habitual physical activity by a seven-day recall in a community survey and controlled experiments. *American Journal of Epidemiology, 122,* 794–804.

Blair, S. N., Kohl III, H. W., Barlow, C. E., Paffenbarger, R. S., Jr., Gibbons, L. W., & Macera, C. A. (1995). Changes in physical fitness and all-cause mortality. *Journal of the American Medical Association, 273,* 1093–1098.

Blair, S. N., Kohl III, H. W., Paffenbarger, R. S., Jr., Clark, D. G., Cooper, K. H., & Gibbons, L. W. (1989). Physical fitness and all-cause mortality: A prospective study of healthy men and women. *Journal of the American Medical Association, 262,* 2395–2401.

Canadian Fitness and Lifestyle Research Institute. (1999). *1999 Physical Activity Monitor.* Ottawa, Ontario, Canada: Author.

Godin, G., Jobin, J., & Bouillon, J. (1986). Assessment of leisure time exercise behavior by self-report: A concurrent validity study. *Canadian Journal of Public Health, 77,* 359–361.

Nove, A. (1997). *The Scottish Health Survey.* London: Department of Health.

Paffenbarger, R. S., Jr., Hale, W. E., Brand, R. J., & Hyde, R. T. (1977). Work-energy level, personal characteristics, and fatal heart attack: A birth-cohort effect. *American Journal of Epidemiology, 105,* 200–213.

Paffenbarger, R. S., Jr., Hyde, R. T., Wing, A. L., & Hsieh, C. (1986). Physical activity, all-cause mortality, and longevity of college alumni. *New England Journal of Medicine, 314,* 605–613.

Pate, R. R., Pratt, M., Blair, S. N., Haskell, W. L., Macera, C. A., Bouchard, C., Buchner, D., Ettinger, W., Heath, G. W., King, A. C., Kriska, A., Leon, A. S., Marcus, B. H., Morris, J., Paffenbarger, R. S., Jr., Patrick, K., Pollock, M. L., Rippe, J. M., Sallis, J., & Wilmore, J. H. (1995). Physical activity and public health. *Journal of the American Medical Association, 273,* 402–407.

Sallis, J. F., & Owen, N. (1999). *Physical activity and behavioral medicine.* Thousand Oaks, CA: Sage.

Taylor, W. C., Baranowski, T., & Young, D. R. (1998). Physical activity interventions in low-income, ethnic minority, and populations with disability. *American Journal of Preventive Medicine, 15,* 334–343.

Teers, R. (2001). *Health Survey for England.* London: Department of Health.

U.S. Department of Health and Human Services. (1996). *Physical activity and health: A report of the Surgeon General.* Atlanta, GA: Centers for Disease Control.

U.S. Department of Health and Human Services. (2000). *Healthy People 2010.* Washington, DC: U.S. Government Printing Office.

Chapter 3

Theories and Models of Exercise Behavior I

SOCIAL COGNITIVE APPROACHES

KEY TERMS

amotivation
attitude
contextual motivation
expectancy-value
external regulation
extrinsic
global motivation
identified regulation
integrated regulation
intrinsic
introjected regulation
mastery
model
motivation
past performance accomplishments
perceived behavioral control (PBC)
physiological and affective states
self-determination
self-efficacy
situational motivation
social cognitive approach
social persuasion
subjective norm
theory
vicarious experiences

Students often become uneasy when instructors mention theories and models, perhaps because of a lack of understanding of what a theory or model is. Consider the following case: A woman exercises twice per week, on average, during the course of a calendar year. However, she temporarily reduces (or eliminates completely) her exercise behavior for several weeks at a time at various points throughout the year. Following these brief lapses, she always manages to resume her habitual regimen of exercise. A model of this behavioral phenomenon is depicted in Exhibit 3.1. As you can see, a **model** is simply a visual representation of a phenomenon or behavior. Unfortunately, models do not always indicate *why* the behavior or phenomenon occurs. For example, we might speculate that the woman experiences lapses in her exercise behavior due to seasonal work loads, final exams, or extreme weather patterns. In this way, we are proposing a **theory** to explain *why* a behavior or phenomenon occurs. Thus, although theories may be graphically represented (modeled) to aid in conceptualization, many models do not include a theoretical foundation.

At this point, you may be wondering why theories are so important (and why we've devoted two full chapters to them). We feel that theory is essential to our discussions of exercise psychology for at least two primary reasons. First, theories allow us to better understand and predict physical activity behavior. Second, theories give us a scientifically validated blueprint from which to formulate effective behavioral interventions. If we are to be successful in our intervention efforts, we must understand the relationships among the many variables believed to influence exercise behavior. As you will see throughout this chapter and the next, theory enables us to organize these variables in a coherent manner.

Exhibit 3.1 *Example of a behavioral model of exercise.*

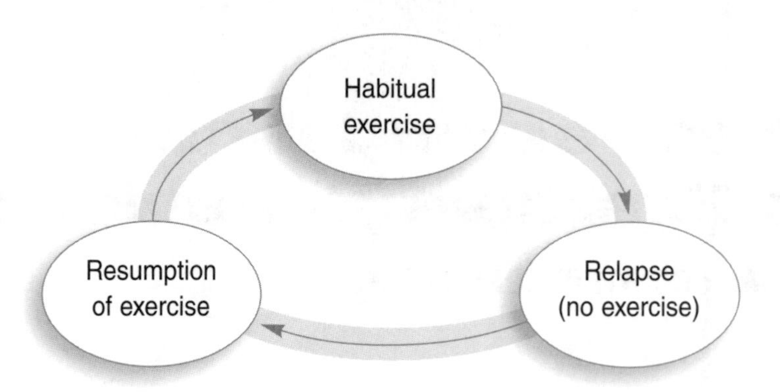

One popular category of theories found throughout the exercise psychology literature incorporates a social cognitive philosophy. From a physical activity standpoint, theories based on a **social cognitive approach** view exercise behavior as being influenced by both human cognition (e.g., expectations, intentions, beliefs, attitudes, feelings) and external stimuli (e.g., social pressures/experiences). Thus, although a person may intend to be physically active, various external forces (e.g., family/occupational commitments) may subjugate the person's efforts to follow through and act on the intention (i.e., prevent the individual from engaging in exercise). Although social pressures to be physically active exist within our society, some individuals choose to engage in exercise while others do not. These examples support the inclusion of both social and cognitive elements within theories of exercise behavior.

social cognitive approach ■

Expectancy-Value Theories: Forerunners to the Social Cognitive Approach

Whether in educational, occupational, sport, health, or exercise environments, theories of behavior have long been rooted in motivation. By **motivation** we mean the degree of determination, drive, or desire with which an individual approaches (or avoids) a behavior. Accordingly, motivation is often defined by the behavior itself. For instance, an individual who is highly motivated would be expected to work exceptionally hard at adopting, changing, or accomplishing a

motivation ■

behavior. We might also expect a highly motivated individual to persist in his or her efforts despite repeated failure and minimal improvement. Simply choosing to engage in one activity instead of another implies an element of motivation.

Although motivation is typically referred to as a singular dimension in general society (ranging from "no motivation" to "high motivation"), researchers and practitioners generally divide motivation into two types based on its origin. Specifically, motivation that emanates from within is termed **intrinsic** while motivation that is induced by a force outside of the individual is labeled **extrinsic.** Although more will be said about these forms of motivation later in the chapter, examples of each are provided in Exhibit 3.2.

- intrinsic
- extrinsic

Early theories of motivation employed what is commonly referred to as an **expectancy-value** approach. Briefly, theorists proposed that motivation (and thus, behavior) was predicated on the individual's expected behavioral outcome and on the value (importance) the individual placed on that predicted outcome. For example, a man desires to begin a regimen of exercise but finds that his motivation, although high, is not strong enough to entice him actually to begin the training. From an expectancy-value standpoint, the man's failure to adopt an exercise regimen may have three explanations. First, although the man may value his prospective exercise habit very highly, he may not believe that he can actually begin and maintain a regular regimen of exercise (expected outcome = inability to maintain exercise) because he failed in a previous attempt (or multiple attempts). Alternatively, he may feel that he just does not have the discipline to maintain *any* behavior change for a prolonged period of time. Second, although the man may believe that he can adopt and adhere to his exercise program (expected outcome = ability to maintain exercise), he may have decided that he just does not value (i.e., place enough importance on) physical fit-

- expectancy-value

exhibit 3.2

Examples of intrinsic and extrinsic motivators for exercise behavior.

INTRINSIC	EXTRINSIC
Fun	Awards (trophy/certificate)
Sense of challenge	Social recognition/praise
Personal improvement	Tangible reinforcers*

*Includes money, t-shirts, water bottles, etc.

exhibit 3.3 ***Expectancy-value approach applied to exercise behavior.***

Value = High	Expected outcome = inability to maintain exercise	→	Failure to adopt
Value = Low	Expected outcome = ability to maintain exercise	→	Failure to adopt
Value = Low	Expected outcome = inability to maintain exercise	→	Failure to adopt
Value = High	Expected outcome = ability to maintain exercise	→	Successful adoption

ness. Although he likely maintains some degree of value for physical fitness (he would not have even considered beginning an exercise regimen if he did not), he probably values an alternative activity (or no activity) to a greater extent. The third explanation is simply a combination of the first two. In other words, the man may not value physical fitness and, furthermore, may not believe that he would successfully adhere to a physical activity regimen (see Exhibit 3.3).

With this discussion as a background, the remainder of this chapter is devoted to a review of the more common theories found in the exercise psychology literature that have grown out of the expectancy-value approach. The presentation of each theory consists of the following information:

1. Name of theory, author(s) credited for introducing the theory, and year the theory was proposed/published
2. Narrative and visual presentation of the theory
3. Example applying the theory
4. A research exemplar
5. Intervention techniques
6. Discussion of the usefulness and limitations of the theory
7. Discussion of potential alternative conceptualizations or future avenues of research employing the theory
8. Summary and conclusions

Self-Efficacy Theory/ Social Cognitive Theory (SCT)

In 1977, Bandura introduced his self-efficacy theory in an effort to describe how individuals form perceptions about their capability to engage in a specific behavior. This "perceived capability," known commonly as self-efficacy, is a construct that has flourished in the field of exercise psychology. **Self-efficacy** is not concerned primarily with an individual's perception of her own abilities, but rather it focuses on the extent to which the individual feels she will be successful in performing the desired behavior, given the abilities she possesses and the unique situation in which she finds herself. Thus, self-efficacy is generally considered to be a situation-specific form of self-confidence. For example, a woman might, in general, consider herself to be an accomplished runner (high self-confidence for running). However, if she is used to running on flat courses, and then must compete on a hilly course, we might find that her self-efficacy for successfully performing on a hilly course is lower than when she competes on a flat course (low self-efficacy for running hills). Similarly, suppose she was scheduled to run on a flat course but had been sick the previous week. Although her overall level of confidence in her running ability likely hasn't subsided, her self-efficacy for the particular race at hand may be low due to the effects of the illness (e.g., fatigue).

■ self-efficacy

Bandura (1977) postulated four primary sources of self-efficacy: past performance accomplishments, vicarious experiences, social persuasion, and physiological arousal (see Exhibit 3.4). The sources are listed in order of their degree of influence. Thus, past performance should prove to exert a greater influence on self-efficacy than do vicarious experiences, and so forth.

Diagram of social cognitive theory. exhibit 3.4

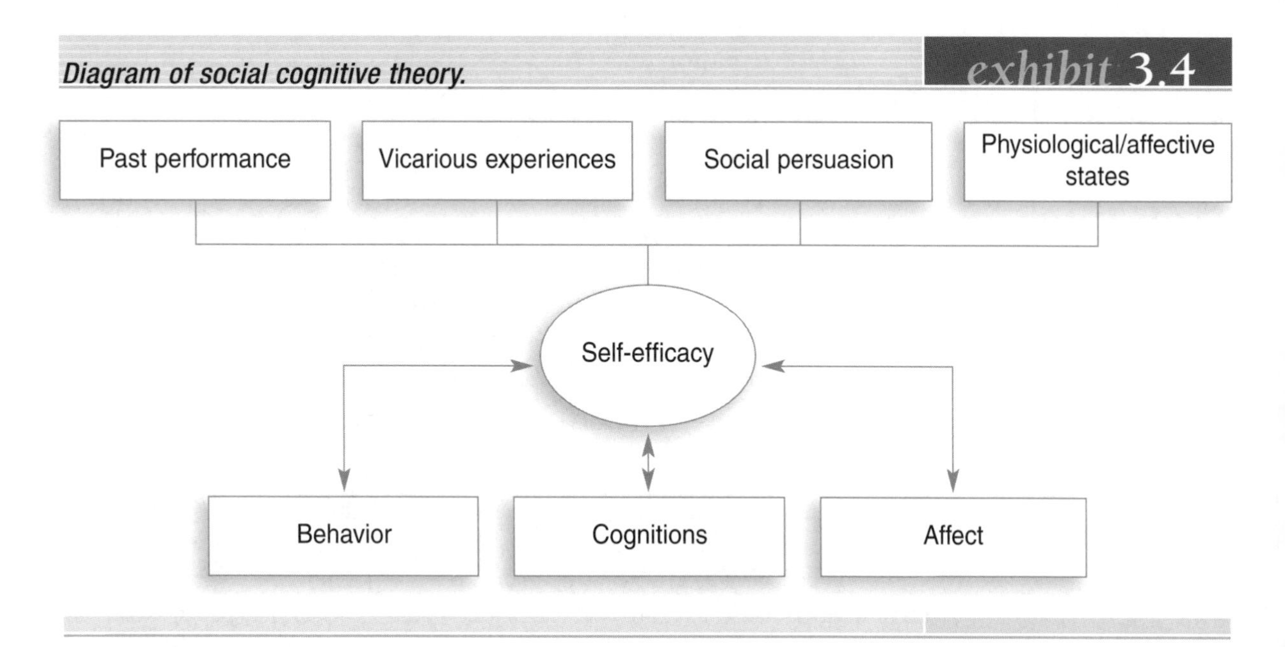

Source: Bandura (1986).

past performance accomplishments

Past performance accomplishments refer to the degree of success perceived by an individual who has previously engaged in activities similar to, or the same as, the current behavior. For example, self-efficacy for running may be derived from an individual's previous experiences with jogging, walking, or even biking. Obviously, the degree of similarity between the previously experienced activity and the current activity determines the strength of this source.

vicarious experiences

Vicarious experiences, also known as *modeling,* are those that involve one individual viewing the performance of a behavior by another individual (the model). The greater the degree of similarity between the model and the viewer, the greater the influence of this source. Additionally, it should be noted that the model need not be a person known to the viewer, although this is preferable. Instead, the person could be a well-known celebrity of the same age who has initiated an exercise regimen. An unfamiliar person on videotape, if perceived as relatively similar to oneself, may also prove to be an effective model. Vicarious experience might be employed as an intervention in an instance where a post-myocardial infarction patient is prescribed exercise but is fearful of engaging in strenuous physical activity. Introducing him or her to an individual who has undergone the same procedure and has successfully completed cardiac rehabilitation without further incidence might serve to increase self-efficacy. Similarly, the use of *imagery*—a behavior performed in the mind using some or all of the body's senses—would be considered a vicarious source.

social persuasion

Social persuasion concerns verbal and nonverbal tactics utilized by others in an attempt to increase a person's self-efficacy. For example, the famous Nike slogan of the 1990s suggested that everyone "Just do it!" Based on this notion, Nike hoped to persuade people that they could, and should, become physically active (in Nike shoes, of course!). Social persuasion is most effective when a knowledgeable or significant other (e.g., spouse, physician, personal trainer) does the persuading.

affective states

The final sources of self-efficacy are physiological and affective states. Physiologically, a rapid heart rate might cause a cardiac rehabilitation patient to doubt whether he is capable of successfully engaging in a bout (or multiple bouts) of exercise. Perceptions of pain and fatigue are further examples of physiological states that might impact efficacy expectations. **Affective** (emotional) **states** can exert both positive and negative influences on self-efficacy. Negative emotionality generally reduces self-efficacy while feelings of positive emotion elevate self-efficacy. For example, a person who is experiencing extremely positive emotions (e.g., happiness, pride) would be expected to view an anticipated exercise bout with higher self-efficacy than would an individual experiencing negative emotions (e.g., sadness, disappointment).

FROM THEORY TO INTERVENTION

To summarize, Bandura's (1977) theory proposes four primary sources of self-efficacy. These sources may work individually or in conjunction with one another to influence an individual's self-efficacy for a specific behavior. Bandura (1986) extended the theory (and renamed it social cognitive theory) by denoting the primary consequences of self-efficacy (see Exhibit 3.4). In order to explore this theory more fully, let us return to the cardiac rehabilitation example presented earlier. Recall that the man had just recovered from myocardial infarction surgery. He is given an exercise rehabilitation prescription but is terrified to begin any form of strenuous activity for fear that physical activity will produce another heart attack. Both he and the physician recognize that his self-efficacy for physical rehabilitation must be increased before he will begin an exercise regimen. Thus, the physician may attempt one or more of the following interventions.

- **Past performance accomplishments.** Obtain the patient's exercise history in an attempt to increase his sense of mastery based on previous exercise experiences. (**Mastery** refers to the process of accomplishing or completing a goal or the thorough learning and performance of a skill, technique, or behavior.)
- **Vicarious experience.** Show him a videotape of a former patient who underwent the same surgery and who is engaging in exercise without incident.
- **Social persuasion.** Strive to be very positive and supportive in conversations with the man and enlist the help of his spouse/family in persuading him to begin and maintain the rehabilitation regimen.
- **Physiological and affective states.** Educate the man in terms of what is a normal physiological response to exercise, so that he does not interpret common exercise symptoms (e.g., heavy breathing, rapid pulse, sweating) as an impending heart attack. This should reduce his anxiety about engaging in physical activity.

■ mastery

As a result of these interventions, the man is likely to perceive a modest level of self-efficacy as he begins his rehabilitation program.

As the man progresses through the rehabilitation (behavior), he begins to realize that he will be capable of doing the things he did before the surgery and becomes satisfied that his life can still be very productive (cognitions). Similarly, the man begins to feel a sense of pride (affect) as a result of his behavior. The bi-directional arrows in Exhibit 3.4 reflect the fact that his behavior, feelings of pride, and sense of life satisfaction all serve to elevate his self-efficacy. The reverse can also occur. For example, a woman with low self-efficacy for maintaining an exercise regimen would not be expected to maintain that regimen. Not only does her self-efficacy affect her behavior, but she also might experience disappointment or shame in herself (affect) and may view herself negatively (as lacking discipline and self-motivation, lazy, etc.). Her unsuccessful behavior, combined with negative affect and cognitions, would further reduce an already low level of self-efficacy.

RESEARCH EXEMPLAR

A considerable literature base demonstrates the relationship between self-efficacy and a variety of psychological, emotional, and behavioral responses to exercise. In a sample of 40 male and female patients diagnosed with chronic obstructive pulmonary disorder (COPD), Lox and Freehill (1999) tracked a number of affective, cognitive, and behavioral responses to a 12-week outpatient pulmonary rehabilitation program. Measures included exercise tolerance (defined as the distance walked in six minutes), walking self-efficacy, quality of life, emotional function, and physical symptoms of dyspnea and fatigue. Results revealed significant improvements over the course of the program in each of these measures, regardless of COPD severity. In addition, improvements in exercise tolerance were significantly associated with increases in self-efficacy which, in turn, were significantly related to improved quality of life. The results support the tenets of social cognitive theory, in that exercise rehabilitation (behavior) was associated with improvements in various components of psychological and emotional well-being.

USEFULNESS, LIMITATIONS, AND FUTURE RESEARCH AVENUES OF SOCIAL COGNITIVE THEORY

It has been said that few things in life are guaranteed, but the central role of self-efficacy as an antecedent and consequence of exercise behavior may be one of those things. Ample research evidence exists to document the impact of self-efficacy on behavior (Hovell et al., 1991) as well as on various affective/cognitive (Treasure & Newbery, 1998) and physiological training outcomes (Ewart, Stewart, Gillilan, & Kelemen, 1986). Furthermore, self-efficacy has been consistently shown to be a prominent exercise outcome itself (McAuley, Lox, and Duncan, 1993). The theory has proven effective in studies employing various forms of physical activity across a wide range of participant samples. It is not, however, without at least one well-acknowledged limitation. As mentioned previously, the theory is predictive of behavior only when the behavior is challenging or novel. Indeed, the influence of the efficacy construct is greatly reduced (or eliminated) as exercise behavior becomes well learned and habitual. This might occur, for example, when an individual moves from the adoption to adherence stage.

Notwithstanding this limitation, the outlook for future research employing social cognitive theory is bright. The substantial literature base might benefit most from investigations that include interventions targeting the key sources of self-efficacy. The results would shed light on the manner in which these sources exert their influence on self-efficacy. Merging social cognitive theory with other theories composed of similar or shared elements may further enhance the predictive utility of this framework. Finally, researchers must revisit the "generality" aspect of self-efficacy proposed by Bandura. In other words, to what extent can enhanced self-efficacy for one activity influence efficacy expectations for another activity?

Theory of Reasoned Action and Theory of Planned Behavior

THEORY OF REASONED ACTION (TRA)

Around the same time Bandura was constructing his self-efficacy theory, Fishbein and Ajzen (1975) were putting the finishing touches on their theory of reasoned action. Although this theory is also based on the social cognitive approach, it is markedly different from self-efficacy theory in its predictive intent. While self-efficacy theory is capable of predicting both acute and chronic behavior, the TRA was originally designed to predict voting behavior, which is a single-instance behavior. Before applying it to an exercise situation, therefore, we will discuss the theory in relation to its original application, voting.

The behavior of voting, as suggested in Exhibit 3.5, is directly related to the individual's *intention* to vote. This intention is determined by two cognitive processes: (1) attitude and (2) sense of subjective norm. **Attitude** simply refers to the individual's positive or negative thoughts concerning the performance of the behavior. Two factors serve to influence attitude. The first is the individual's beliefs about the consequences of carrying out a specific action. The second concerns the individual's evaluation (positive or negative) of the consequences. For example, does the person generally believe that voting is a worthwhile endeavor? Does he feel that his vote is important? Does he care who's running or who wins? If the answers to these questions are yes, we can assume that he possesses a favorable attitude toward voting.

■ attitude

exhibit 3.5 *Diagram of the theory of reasoned action.*

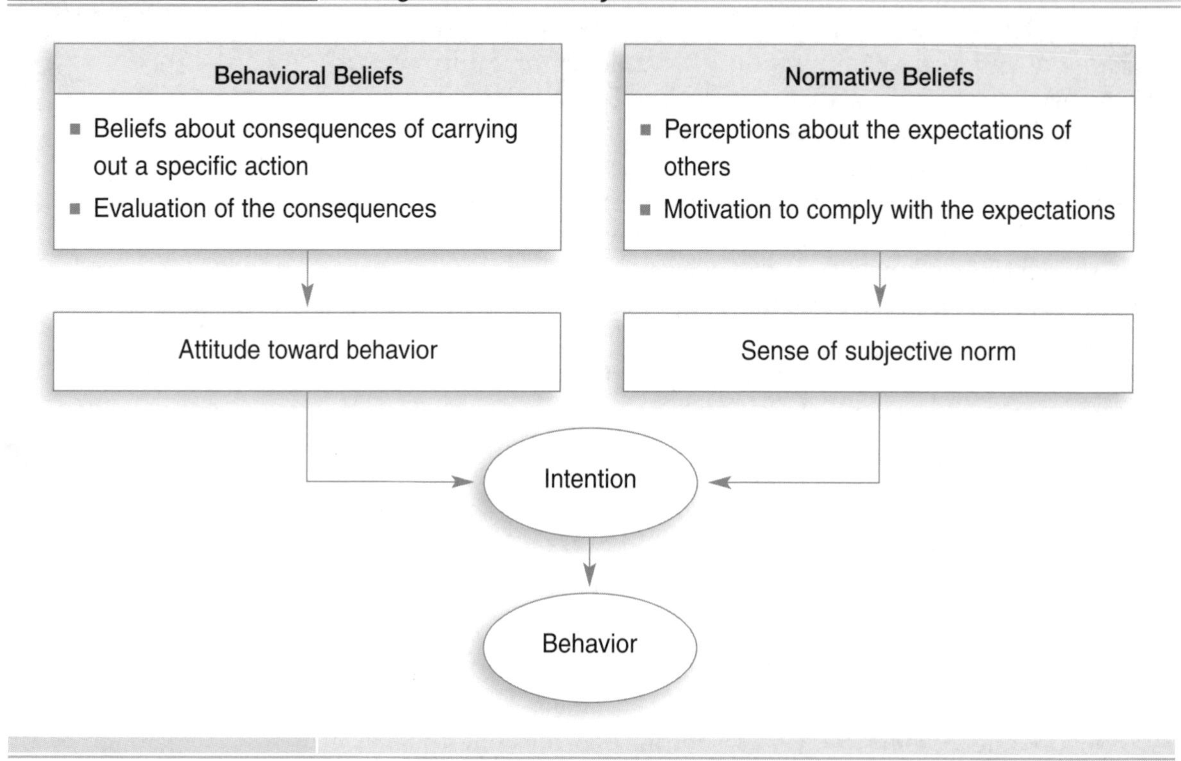

Source: Fishbein & Ajzen (1975).

subjective norm

The second determinant of intention is the individual's sense of **subjective norm.** This construct, which focuses on the degree to which the individual feels social pressure to perform the behavior, is also predicated on two factors. The first concerns perceptions about the expectations of significant others. The second focuses on the individual's motivation to comply with the perceived expectations of others. A person may consider whether or not family, friends, and coworkers will be voting. Will she be perceived as lazy or uninformed if she does not vote? Does she even care what others think in regard to her voting behavior? Thus, the more positive the attitude, and the greater the perceived social pressure (subjective norm), the stronger the intention to vote.

Of course, as the saying goes, "the road to failure is paved with good intentions." In other words, although intention is the single best predictor of behavior within the theory, intentions clearly do not always lead to the behavior intended. This is especially true when we attempt to apply this theory to a repeatable behavior (such as exercise) or to a behavior that is not to be attempted in the immediate future but at some undetermined later time. Thus, intention is the strongest predictor of behavior when that behavior is to be engaged in within a relatively short period of time (i.e., hours). As days, weeks, or months pass, however, the strength of the relationship between intention and behavior progressively weakens. In the previous voting example, the intention to vote would likely be a good predictor if the behavior is to be performed the same day as the acknowledged intent. Conversely, intention would likely not be as good a predictor if election day is a number of months away.

From Theory to Intervention

Let's summarize this theory with a specific exercise example that most people can probably appreciate. With January 1 rapidly approaching, a man contemplates beginning an exercise regimen as his New Year's resolution. His attitude about exercise is mixed—he knows the benefits and wants to do it but, based on prior experiences, is not sure he will enjoy it. He feels a fairly strong social pressure to exercise because family, friends, coworkers, and even the media are discussing "getting back in shape after the holidays." His intention is to exercise two or three times a week for 30 minutes per session from now until the end of time. Unfortunately, in most cases, this intention is really nothing more than a "hope" of maintaining exercise until the end of time. Once again, because intention is an immediately influencing and fleeting judgment, it does not play a significant role in the performance of distant or repeatable behaviors. If we were interested in his intention to exercise today or tomorrow, however, intention would exert a more substantial influence and the theory would, consequently, be more functional. As it stands, his current attitude and sense of subjective norm indicate that he probably maintains a strong intention of exercising on (or shortly after) January 1. This intention is likely to predict his actual behavior at that time. The likelihood that his current intention will accurately predict his long-term exercise behavior (weeks or months in the future), however, is not high.

Interventions based on the TRA must focus on increasing the strength of one's intention to exercise. Not surprisingly, this is best accomplished by techniques that (a) serve to improve one's attitude toward exercise and (b) cause the individual to feel external pressure to engage in exercise. In order to improve attitude, the exercise professional/health-care practitioner could start by heightening awareness of the multiple benefits of exercise (physical, psychological, and social). Oftentimes, individuals have a narrow view of the benefits of exercise (e.g., they are aware only of the physical benefits). If we can help potential exercisers recognize the myriad of additional benefits they might experience (e.g., reduced fatigue), their intentions may be strengthened. This goal may also be accomplished via public service announcements, news stories, research, and simply by word of mouth from significant others (particularly those who are physically active).

Modifying one's concept of social norm is a somewhat more difficult task. Surrounding oneself with others (i.e., creating a reference group) who are physically active is a good start. Ironically, although we tend to extol the virtue of making our own decisions and resisting peer pressure, this is an instance where "doing what others do" appears to be an acceptable philosophy. However, it is likely that adherence to exercise will be greater in instances where the individual is physically active for reasons other than those produced by external expectations.

THEORY OF PLANNED BEHAVIOR (TPB)

perceived behavioral control (PBC)

It has been suggested that the TRA may not be appropriate for predicting behaviors that are continuing or repeatable, such as in the case of exercise. Indeed, it appears that one must investigate factors beyond intention in order to predict chronic exercise behavior. To this end, ten years after the introduction of the TRA, Ajzen (1985) extended the theory by adding the construct of **perceived behavioral control (PBC)**. Similar to the self-efficacy construct discussed earlier, PBC refers to the degree of personal control the individual perceives he or she has over the behavior in question. This concept is significant in that it accounts for the many potential barriers to exercise (work, family, weather, facilities, etc.) that people often perceive. Thus, a woman who believes that she has control over (i.e., the ability to overcome) these potential barriers to exercise will be more likely to perform that behavior than if she believes her exercise behavior is influenced by someone or something else. As indicated in the model (see Exhibit 3.6), attitude, subjective norm, and PBC combine to influence intention. However, while attitude and subjective norm serve to influence behavior via their impact on intention, PBC is proposed to influence behavior by itself (see dotted arrow in Exhibit 3.6) as well as via its effect on intention. Thus, in the TPB, both intention and PBC are hypothesized to be equally influential predictors of behavior.

From Theory to Intervention

Let us assume that a woman exhibits a favorable attitude toward exercise and perceives a high degree of social pressure to exercise. According to the TRA, we estimate that her intentions would be relatively strong and, therefore, the likelihood of her engaging in exercise would be relatively

exhibit 3.6

Diagram of the theory of planned behavior.

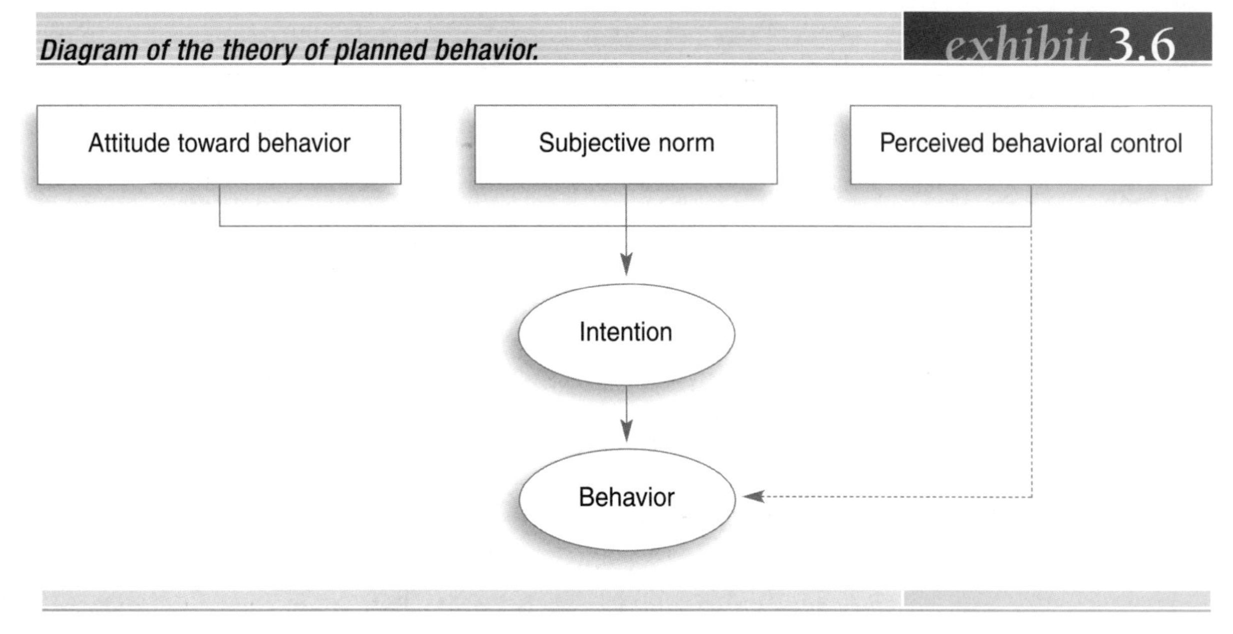

Source: Ajzen (1985).

high. However, if she feels she has little control over her exercise behavior (due to a number of potential barriers), her behavior will be doubly affected in a negative manner. First, low PBC will weaken her intention to exercise, which in turn will reduce the likelihood that she will engage in exercise. Second, low PBC may present itself, for example, as low confidence (self-efficacy) to overcome barriers, thereby also reducing the likelihood that she will engage in exercise (see social cognitive theory).

We have already discussed ways in which we can manipulate attitude and sense of social norm in order to modify intention. Our discussion here will be limited to intervention techniques aimed at enhancing perceived behavioral control. Recall that PBC affects behavior both directly and indirectly (via intention). This would appear to highlight perceived behavioral control as a useful target for producing successful exercise behavior change. Simply put, a strong sense of personal control over one's exercise behavior is essential for adherence. An individual can be helped to develop this sense of control in a number of ways, some of which we identified in our discussion of social cognitive theory. Allowing exercisers some input when designing their physical activity program should increase feelings of personal control. The way in which we teach prospective exercisers to approach perceived barriers to physical activity is also important (see Chapter 5 for a more detailed discussion). For example, if family or occupational responsibilities prevent a person from engaging in regular exercise, physical activity should be scheduled around these times (e.g., early morning, lunch hour, late evening). Similar allowances may be made for difficulties stemming from weather and facility restrictions. For example, inexpensive and portable resistance bands could be purchased for the home when expensive and inconvenient exercise facilities emerge as limiting factors. Purchasing appropriate clothing to permit exercise in inclement weather or joining a facility with aerobic equipment or an indoor track may also reduce the genuine and perceived barriers to exercise. Perhaps most notably, setting a regular time in one's schedule for exercise (and physically displaying a reminder with a sticky note or memo in a daily planner) may facilitate activity participation when time is perceived as a significant barrier.

Research Exemplar

TRA and TPB have achieved widespread use as a theoretical framework for explaining exercise behavior. In a study focused specifically on the TPB, Courneya and Friedenreich (1999) examined motivation to exercise during treatment in a large sample of elderly breast cancer patients. One hundred sixty-four women diagnosed with breast cancer within two years prior to the start of the study were asked to recall their beliefs and exercise behavior during cancer treatment in a self-administered, mailed questionnaire. Results indicated that both attitude and subjective norm were significant determinants of exercise intention during cancer treatment, while both exercise intention and PBC over exercise were significant determinants of exercise behavior. In addition, although PBC did not influence intention beyond that of attitude and subjective norm, it did influence exercise behavior beyond that of intention. Not surprisingly, behavioral, normative, and control beliefs were strongly correlated with attitude, subjective norm, and PBC, respectively. Finally, all three categories of beliefs were strongly associated with intention and exercise behavior. Recognizing the limitations inherent in the retrospective design, the findings of this investigation suggest that the TPB may be a viable framework on which to base interventions designed to promote exercise participation in both clinical and nonclinical samples.

Usefulness, Limitations, and Future Research Avenues of the Theory of Planned Behavior

To summarize the relationships among the various factors incorporated within the TRA and TPB, we turn to several important conclusions of the quantitative literature review conducted by Hausenblas, Carron, and Mack (1997).

1. The TPB appears to be superior to the TRA in its ability consistently to predict exercise behavior (see exception to this rule provided by Yordy & Lent, 1993). This is likely due to the fact that PBC accounts for exercise behavior better than does the intention construct (see exception to this rule provided by Kimiecik, 1992). Additionally, this and previous reviews (Blue, 1995; Godin, 1993) have documented a consistent and significant influence of PBC on intention even after attitude and subjective norm have been accounted for.

2. It appears that it is still too early to make definitive statements regarding the proximal (short-term) and distal (long-term) nature of the intention–behavior relationship. The four studies reviewed by Hausenblas et al. (1997) that included both short-term and long-term intentional assessments did not demonstrate that those assessments differed in their ability to predict exercise behavior.

3. Attitude has proven to be a consistent predictor of intention; subjective norm, however, does not appear to be a stable predictor of intention (Dzewaltowski, 1989; Valois, Desharnais, & Godin, 1988), although support for the role of subjective norm has been documented (Courneya & Friedenrich, 1999).

Both Blue (1995) and Godin (1993) have provided further conclusive evidence. In the former review, perceived barriers to exercise (when operationalized as PBC) were shown to be consistent and significant predictors of behavior. Notably, the author provides insight into the predictive superiority of the TPB (relative to the TRA) by suggesting that exercise may not be seen by all participants to be a completely volitional activity, a view also shared by Godin. In this way, PBC may influence behavior by itself (not only via its influence on intention) in situations where the behavior is not perceived to be under the complete control of the individual.

Although the addition of the PBC construct is significant, the TPB still suffers from the same limitations as its predecessor, the TRA. Specifically, the ability of intention to predict behavior may still be limited by the elapsed time between the intention and the behavior as well as by the repeatability of the behavior. As a result, a relatively distant or chronic behavior would likely be best predicted by the PBC construct. Another potential avenue for exploration might involve redefining the social norm variable. Just as PBC has been modified to reflect self-efficacy, social norm might prove more useful if operationalized as perceptions of *social support* for a behavior as opposed to perceived *pressures* to perform a behavior (see Chapter 12 on social influences).

Self-Determination Theory (SDT)

Much like social cognitive theory, self-determination theory (Deci & Ryan, 1985) was designed to better explain affective, cognitive, and behavioral responses within an achievement domain (e.g., academics, athletics) and has recently begun to draw the attention of exercise psychology researchers. SDT begins with the basic assumption that individuals possess three primary psychosocial needs—namely:

self-determination ■

1. a need for **self-determination** (autonomy, self-dependent behavior)
2. a need to demonstrate competence (experience mastery)
3. a need for relatedness (social interactions)

Thus, individuals seek challenges that serve to satisfy one or more of these needs.

The model further specifies three forms of motivation capable of driving achievement behaviors. On opposite ends of the continuum (see Exhibit 3.7) are intrinsic motivation and amotivation. As defined earlier, intrinsic motivation refers to the mentality of engaging in a behavior for reasons of inherent pleasure or satisfaction (e.g., "I exercise because it's fun"). **Amotivation,** on the other hand, is defined as a relative absence of motivation or lack of intention to engage in a behavior. Individuals may be amotivated in regard to exercise for a number of reasons, such as the belief that they lack the ability to adhere to an exercise regimen (e.g., "I'm not disciplined enough to stick with exercise"), exercise is unimportant or unnecessary (e.g., "I'm perfectly healthy and have no need for exercise"), or exercise will not produce a desired outcome (e.g., reduced fatigue).

amotivation ■

Residing between intrinsic motivation and amotivation are four types of extrinsic motivation. The first (and most self-determined) form of extrinsic motivation is **integrated regulation,** which refers to the process of engaging in a behavior in order to confirm one's sense of self (e.g., "I am an exerciser and this is what I do"). **Identified regulation** occurs when behavior is motivated by personal goals. Although the behavior is initiated autonomously, identified regulation is considered extrinsic since the decision is guided by an external outcome or product (e.g., improved appearance) as opposed to a feeling of enjoyment or sense of accomplishment. Clearly, this form of extrinsic

integrated regulation ■

identified regulation ■

Diagram of self-determination theory, including motives for behavior. exhibit 3.7

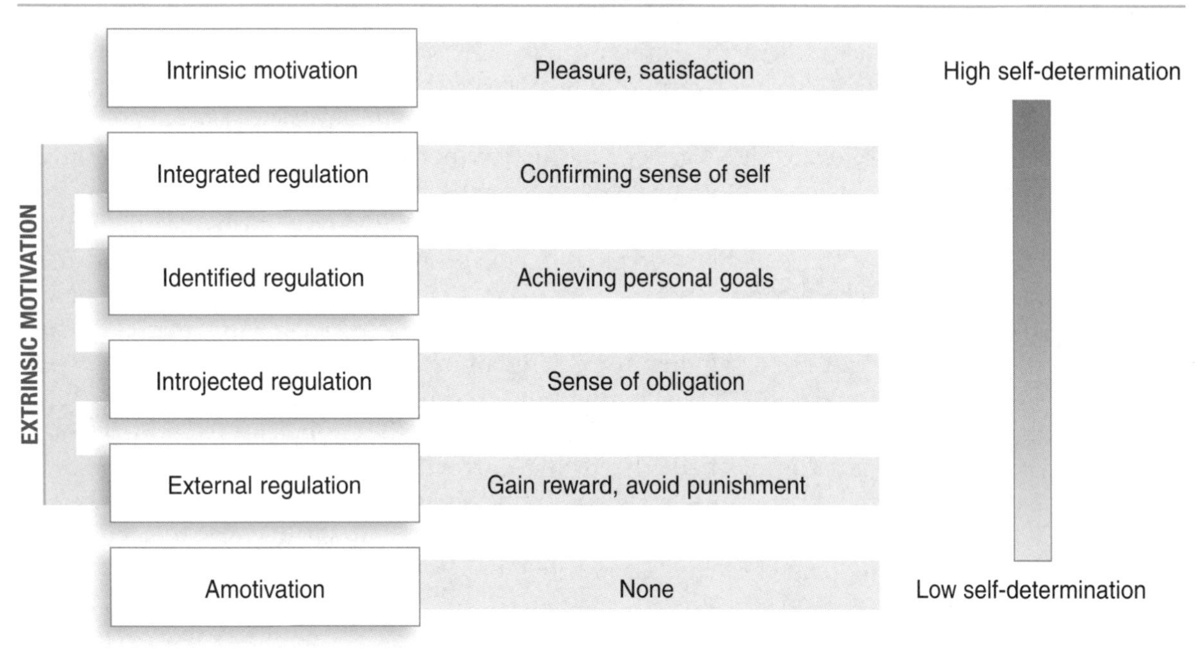

Source: Deci & Ryan (1985).

motivation is one that is commonly employed in the exercise domain. Next on the continuum is **introjected regulation,** which is said to exist when a behavior is dictated by a self-imposed source of pressure (e.g., exercising in order to avoid feelings of guilt). The final (and least self-determining) form of extrinsic motivation is **external regulation,** which refers to the process of engaging in a behavior for the purpose of obtaining an external reward or avoiding an externally applied punishment (e.g., exercising to receive praise from others or because rehabilitation personnel are compelling you to do so).

- introjected regulation
- external regulation

Self-determination is thought to decrease along the continuum from intrinsic motivation to amotivation. Additionally, the order of the various components is relevant, in that those motivational types closest to one another (e.g., intrinsic motivation and integrated regulation) are hypothesized to be more closely related in terms of their motivational qualities than those more distant from one another (e.g., intrinsic motivation and external regulation). This is important because motivation types that are high in autonomy (self-determination) are thought to be associated with the achievement of a number of positive outcomes, including those related to exercise (see the section "Research Exemplar").

The final aspect of the theory concerns the specific versus general nature of motivation. Three levels of motivation are proposed to exist, with all of the three primary motivation types (intrinsic motivation, extrinsic motivation, and amotivation) represented within each level. The first level is **global motivation,** which, similar to a personality trait, refers to the degree of motivation normally experienced by an individual across most behavioral domains. Thus, we might describe someone as being a highly motivated individual based on our observation that he or she is highly motivated to engage in most day-to-day behaviors (e.g., school, work, sport, exercise, etc.). **Contextual motivation** is defined as a relatively stable pattern of motivation experienced in a particular context. Here, we might proclaim an individual to be highly motivated to engage in physical activity but poorly motivated to engage in occupational or academic activities. Finally, **situational motivation** refers to motivation experienced in a particular activity at a specific point in time. For example, you might be highly motivated to engage in exercise today but poorly motivated tomorrow. Similarly, you might be highly motivated to run but poorly motivated to lift weights.

global motivation ■

contextual motivation ■

situational motivation ■

FROM THEORY TO INTERVENTION

Based on the predictions of SDT and preliminary research in the exercise domain (e.g., Chatzisarantis, Biddle, & Meek, 1997; Markland, 1999), we can hypothesize that an individual who exercises for reasons reflective of low self-determination (such as the desire to improve appearance) would be less likely to adhere to the regimen than would someone who exercises for the inherent pleasure involved (high self-determination). To this end, we might expect improvements in intrinsic motivation to result from exercise interventions that are aimed at enhancing an individual's sense of competence and autonomy and conducted in a positive, mutually supportive environment wherein satisfying social interactions can take place. The latter point would certainly seem to highlight group exercise as a potential strategy for achieving the purpose of relatedness. Promoting a sense of ownership or control over the workout routine should serve to enhance a sense of responsibility and autonomy in regard to exercise behavior. Finally, designing a program that leads the individual to feel successful in mastering the activity should help to develop feelings of competence. For example, we might ask novice exercisers to engage in relatively simple, low-intensity, and short-duration movements early in the initiation of their exercise program so that they can experience a sense of accomplishment and concomitant feelings of satisfaction and pride.

RESEARCH EXEMPLAR

In a study designed to explore the relationship between self-determination and exercise behavior, Mullan and Markland (1997) recruited 314 male and female middle-aged adults and asked them to complete a measure of self-determination (autonomy) in regard to exercise as well as an assessment of their level of exercise behavior based on a stages of change model (see discussion of the transtheoretical model in Chapter 4). Briefly, stage models of behavior suggest that individuals pass through a number of sequential steps or "stages" on their way to adopting and maintaining engagement of a particular behavior. These stages range from no consideration of adopting a behavior (the first stage of behavior change) to successful maintenance of the behavior over a period of time (the last stage of behavior change). The results of the Mullan and Markland investigation indicated that those in the latter, more advanced stages of exercise behavior change were significantly more self-determined than those in the early stages. Based on these findings, the authors suggested that enhanced autonomy in regard to exercise should be associated with continued maintenance of the behavior while lower levels of autonomy should be related to relapse to a sedentary lifestyle.

USEFULNESS, LIMITATIONS, AND FUTURE RESEARCH AVENUES OF SELF-DETERMINATION THEORY

SDT is a relative newcomer in the exercise psychology field, and considerable empirical investigation will be required before it may assume the prominence bestowed upon other theories discussed earlier in the chapter. We have included it in this chapter, however, because of its tremendous potential for explaining achievement behavior such as exercise. Throughout this textbook, we discuss the importance of exercise adherence and acknowledge the central role of motivation in its promotion. Furthermore, we highlight the role of motivation in other theories of exercise behavior. Indeed, needs such as competence and autonomy are conceptually similar to constructs offered by other theories, such as self-efficacy and perceived behavioral control. Thus, as discussed earlier, an understanding of the various types of motivation and where they reside on the self-determination continuum can form a useful foundation for developing physical activity interventions. Practicing exercise professionals could certainly benefit from an understanding of the various motivational profiles when attempting to modify their clients' exercise behavior. The three primary needs (autonomy, competence, and relatedness) also appear capable of accounting for why some people might approach exercise while others continue to avoid it.

With these issues in mind, the future for SDT in the exercise domain appears bright. Clearly, a substantial number of research venues remain to be tested and verified. First, the moderating role of self-determination on intrinsic motivation toward exercise must be more fully explored. The relationship between self-determination and the experience of interest and enjoyment in the exercise setting warrants additional empirical investigation. Second, we must demonstrate consistent support for the ability of constructs of SDT to predict exercise behavior. Specifically, the following questions remained to be answered: Can the various SDT constructs predict exercise participation over an extended period of time (i.e., adherence to an exercise regimen)? How do the levels of SDT constructs vary over time as exercise behavior changes? Finally, what interventions are capable of positively or negatively affecting the SDT constructs, and what are the consequences of these interventions to exercise behavior? Not surprisingly, these questions will be best answered as we move beyond cross-sectional designs and toward more longitudinal research methodologies.

Conclusion

The theories and models reviewed in this chapter were designed to help researchers and practitioners better understand and predict physical activity behavior. Theories and models also provide us with a blueprint upon which to base interventions. The expectancy-value and social cognitive philosophies are at the core of each theory presented in this chapter. Bandura's (1977, 1986) self-efficacy/social cognitive theory is, arguably, the most popular theory in the exercise psychology literature and offers tremendous opportunity for intervention. The theory of reasoned action and the theory of planned behavior are also sensitive to various intervention strategies and have gained acceptance in the field of exercise psychology for their ability to predict acute physical activity behavior. The relative newcomer on the block, self-determination theory, offers great potential, as it delineates the various forms of motivation that serve to influence achievement behaviors such as exercise.

The three theories share a common central construct rooted in self-referent thought—namely, self-efficacy (in SCT), perceived behavioral control (in TPB), and the need for autonomy and demonstrating competence (in SDT). This is certainly not surprising given that social cognitive theories typically incorporate such a construct. Indeed, the significance of this self-referencing variable will become clearer when we discuss certain intervention strategies in Chapter 5. As you move through the remainder of this text, try to think in terms of formulating theories in order to gain a more thorough understanding about a particular topic. After all, in the words of noted social psychologist Kurt Lewin, "nothing is so practical as a good theory."

What Do You Know?

1. What is the difference between a model and a theory?
2. Why is theory important?
3. Describe the social cognitive philosophy of human behavior.
4. What is motivation?
5. What factors determine motivation?
6. Compare and contrast intrinsic and extrinsic forms of motivation.
7. Explain the expectancy-value approach to understanding motivation and behavior.
8. What is self-efficacy? How is it different from self-confidence?
9. Discuss the four sources of self-efficacy.
10. What are the primary consequences of self-efficacy?
11. Describe the two constructs that influence intention in both the TRA and TPB.
12. What is the relationship between intention and behavior?
13. What construct distinguishes the TRA from the TPB and why was it added?
14. According to SDT, what are our three primary psychosocial needs?
15. Define "self-determined."
16. What are the three primary categories of motivation in SDT?

Learning Activities

1. Think of a behavior in your life (not related to physical activity) that you feel is a function of both social (learned) experiences and your psychological (cognitive) makeup.

2. Relate a physical activity experience in your life that illustrates one of the theories presented in this chapter.
3. Using the constructs contained in the theories presented in this chapter, construct your own theory or model of exercise psychology/behavior.

References

Ajzen, I. (1985). From intention to actions: A theory of planned behavior. In J. Kuhl & J. Beckman (Eds.), *Action control: From cognition to behavior* (pp. 11–39). Heidelberg, Germany: Springer.

Bandura, A. (1977). Self-efficacy: Toward a unifying theory of behavioral change. *Psychological Review, 84,* 191–215.

Bandura, A. (1986). *Social foundations of thought and action.* Englewood Cliffs, NJ: Prentice Hall.

Blue, C. L. (1995). The predictive capacity of the theory of reasoned action and the theory of planned behavior in exercise research: An integrated literature review. *Research in Nursing and Health, 18,* 105–121.

Chatzisarantis, N., Biddle, S. J. H., & Meek, G. A. (1997). A Self-Determination Theory approach to the study of intentions and the intention–behavior relationship in children's physical activity. *British Journal of Health Psychology, 2,* 342–360.

Courneya, K. S., & Friedenreich, C. M. (1999). Utility of the theory of planned behavior for understanding exercise during breast cancer treatment. *Psycho-Oncology, 8,* 112–122.

Deci, E. L., & Ryan, R. M. (1985). *Intrinsic motivation and self-determination in human behavior.* New York: Plenum Press.

Dzewaltowski, D. A. (1989). Toward a model of exercise motivation. *Journal of Sport and Exercise Psychology, 11,* 251–269.

Ewart, C. K., Stewart, K. J., Gillilan, R. E., & Kelemen, M. H. (1986). Self-efficacy mediates strength gains during circuit weight training in men with coronary artery disease. *Medicine and Science in Sports and Exercise, 18,* 531–540.

Fishbein, M., & Ajzen, I. (1975). *Belief, attitude, intention and behavior.* Don Mills, NY: Addison Wesley.

Godin, G. (1993). The theories of reasoned action and planned behavior: Overview of findings, emerging research problems and usefulness for exercise promotion. *Journal of Applied Sport Psychology, 5,* 141–157.

Hausenblas, H. A., Carron, A. V., & Mack, D. E. (1997). Application of the theories of reasoned action and planned behavior to exercise behavior: A meta-analysis. *Journal of Sport and Exercise Psychology, 19,* 36–51.

Hovell, M., Sallis, J., Hofstetter, R., Barrington, E., Hackley, M., Elder, J., Castro, F., & Kilbourne, K. (1991). Identification of correlates of physical activity among Latino adults. *Journal of Community Health, 16,* 23–36.

Kimiecik, J. (1992). Predicting vigorous physical activity of corporate employees: Comparing the theories of reasoned action and planned behavior. *Journal of Sport and Exercise Psychology, 14,* 192–206.

Lox, C. L., & Freehill, A. J. (1999). The impact of pulmonary rehabilitation on self-efficacy, quality of life, and exercise tolerance. *Rehabilitation Psychology, 44,* 1–14.

Markland, D. (1999). Self-determination moderates the effects of perceived competence on intrinsic motivation in an exercise setting. *Journal of Sport and Exercise Psychology, 21,* 351–361.

McAuley, E., Lox, C., & Duncan, T. E. (1993). Long-term maintenance of exercise, self-efficacy, and physiological change in older adults. *Journal of Gerontology, 48,* P218–P224.

Mullan, E., & Markland, D. (1997). Variations in self-determination across the stages of change for exercise in adults. *Motivation and Emotion, 21,* 349–362.

Treasure, D. C., & Newbery, D. M. (1998). Relationship between self-efficacy, exercise intensity, and feeling states in a sedentary population during and following an acute bout of exercise. *Journal of Sport and Exercise Psychology, 20,* 1–12.

Valois, P., Desharnais, R., & Godin, G. (1988). A comparison of the Fishbein and Ajzen and the Triandis attitudinal models for the prediction of exercise intention and behavior. *Journal of Behavioral Medicine, 11,* 459–472.

Yordy, G. A., & Lent, R. W. (1993). Predicting aerobics exercise participation: Social cognitive, reasoned action, and planned behavior models. *Perceptual and Motor Skills, 76,* 287–292.

Chapter 4

Theories and Models of Exercise Behavior II

STIMULUS–RESPONSE THEORY AND INTEGRATIVE APPROACHES

Social cognitive theories and models assume that people's decisions to exercise are based on a rational decision-making process whereby their thoughts and feelings (e.g., attitudes, self-efficacy beliefs) factor in to their decisions. For instance, the theory of reasoned action holds that people's exercise attitudes and subjective norms influence their decisions or intentions to exercise. Likewise, self-determination theory proposes that the decision to exercise is based on the belief that exercise will satisfy one's psychosocial needs. Other theories, however, do not consider thoughts and feelings about exercise, or even rational decision making, to be necessary determinants of exercise behavior. For example, consider a child who hates to do any type of physical activity, but who loves to collect stickers. The child's parents influence him to be physically active by providing a packet of stickers for every 30 minutes he spends in active play. Although the child's thoughts and feelings toward exercise may remain negative, his behavior changes. This phenomenon can be explained by the principle of *reinforcement.*

In the first part of this chapter, we look at reinforcement and other principles of stimulus–response theory as an alternative to the social cognitive approach for explaining exercise behavior. In the second part, we examine two models—the transtheoretical model and a preliminary social ecological model of exercise—that have attempted to explain exercise by integrating social cognitive approaches with approaches that look beyond the individual's thoughts, feelings, and decision-making processes.

KEY TERMS

action stage
antecedent cue
behavioral processes
classical conditioning
consciousness raising
consequent reinforcement
contemplation stage
decisional balance
descriptive studies
experiential processes
extinction
extrinsic reinforcers
instrumental conditioning
intervention studies
intrinsic reinforcers
learning theory
maintenance stage
negative reinforcer
positive reinforcer
precontemplation stage
predictive studies
preparation stage
punishment
reinforcement management
self-reevaluation
social ecological models
stimulus control

Stimulus–Response Theory (SRT)

B. F. Skinner's (1953) stimulus–response theory (SRT) suggests an explanation for how people learn new behaviors. SRT grew out of the principles of classical conditioning (Pavlov, 1928) and instrumental conditioning (Thorndike, 1898). **Classical conditioning** principles state that a reflexive behavior (e.g., salivating, eye blinking) can be elicited through repeated pairings of the behavior with an **antecedent cue** (i.e., a cue that precedes the behavior). For example, in his famous experiments, Pavlov observed that after repeated pairings of a ringing bell with the delivery of food, dogs would start to salivate whenever the bell rang, even if there was no food present. The dogs salivated because they had learned to associate the ringing bell with the delivery of food (a stimulus that naturally elicits the salivary reflex). **Instrumental conditioning** principles state that a voluntary (i.e., non-reflexive) behavior can be learned by pairing the behavior with **consequent reinforcement** (i.e., a reward that follows the behavior). For example, a dog can learn to sit on command if he is given a cookie every time he responds successfully to the command.

classical conditioning ■

antecedent cue ■

instrumental conditioning ■

consequent reinforcement ■

According to Skinner (1953), although a behavior can be learned through repeated pairings of that behavior with antecedent cues or consequent reinforcers, consequences have a greater impact on behavior than do antecedents. Thus, SRT identifies events that can follow a behavior and the effects these events will have on future behavior. According to SRT, there are four types of events—positive reinforcement, negative reinforcement, punishment, and extinction—that can follow a behavior and that will alter the likelihood of that behavior occurring again in the future (Exhibit 4.1 summarizes information about these events). Let's look at each of these events within the context of exercise behavior.

exhibit 4.1 *Predictions of stimulus–response theory.*

EVENTS THAT CAN FOLLOW A BEHAVIOR	DESCRIPTION OF EVENTS	EFFECTS ON FUTURE EXERCISE BEHAVIOR
1. Positive reinforcement	Adding something positive (e.g. money, praise)	Increases exercise
2. Negative reinforcement	Taking away something negative (e.g. pain, depression)	Increases exercise
3. Punishment	Adding something negative (e.g. injury, embarrassment)	Decreases exercise
4. Extinction	Taking away something positive (e.g. opportunities to socialize)	Decreases exercise

POSITIVE REINFORCEMENT

Reinforcement is the key element of stimulus–response theory. A positive reinforcer is an enjoyable or pleasant outcome that makes a person feel good, and that strengthens a particular behavior. Within the context of exercise, a **positive reinforcer** is any intrinsic or extrinsic reward that increases the likelihood of a person exercising in the future.

■ positive reinforcer

Intrinsic reinforcers are rewards that come from within the self, such as feeling good about one's body, feeling a sense of accomplishment at the end of a workout, or simply experiencing the physical and emotional sense of well-being that accompanies exercise. **Extrinsic reinforcers** are rewards that come from other people, such as verbal praise from a fitness instructor, t-shirts awarded for perfect attendance at an exercise class, or compliments from friends and family about one's improved physique. According to the principles of SRT, when individuals receive positive reinforcement after exercising, they will be more likely to exercise again in the future.

■ intrinsic reinforcers

■ extrinsic reinforcers

Although extrinsic reinforcers have been shown to increase exercise behavior (Noland, 1989), there are dangers to using them. For instance, if a parent extrinsically rewards a child every time she is physically active, then the child may not choose to be active in situations when the parent is not around to give reinforcement (e.g., when she is playing at a friend's house). In addition, if the child becomes accustomed to receiving some type of reward in return for being active, she may start to think of physical activity as work or a chore—something she does in order to get something that she wants. Another danger with extrinsic rewards is that they can prevent the individual from learning about the intrinsic rewards associated with exercise. The child who is given rewards may be so focused on attaining the extrinsic reinforcement that she never comes to realize the intrinsic rewards associated with being physically active, such as having fun, learning new skills, and making new friends. Moreover, people with intrinsic reasons for exercise tend to adhere better over the long term than do those with extrinsic reasons. It is crucial, therefore, that people of all ages—not just children—realize the intrinsic benefits of physical activity participation.

NEGATIVE REINFORCEMENT

Negative reinforcers are generally unpleasant or aversive stimuli that, when withdrawn after a behavior, will *increase* the frequency of that behavior in the future. (Note that negative reinforcement is not the same as punishment, which is discussed in the next section). For example, Jacob is a 50-year-old man with arthritis of the knees. He finds

■ negative reinforcer

that after a long day at work, sitting in front of a computer, his knees ache and become very stiff. However, at the end of each day, Jacob rides his bicycle for half an hour because he finds that this activity significantly reduces his knee discomfort. Thus, for Jacob, knee pain serves as a negative reinforcer for exercise. When he exercises, the knee pain is withdrawn, and this increases the likelihood that he will continue to exercise in the future.

Both positive and negative reinforcement will have their greatest effects when people are able to see the relationship between their behavior and the reinforcing outcome. Thus, reinforcement is most effective when it is delivered *frequently* and *immediately* after exercise. This means that outcomes that occur often and soon after an exercise bout (e.g., feelings of satisfaction, changes in pain) will have a bigger effect on future exercise behavior than will outcomes that occur only occasionally or that are accumulated after many exercise sessions (e.g., changes in body composition or cardiovascular fitness). This latter point may explain why so many people who start an exercise program for the purpose of weight loss drop out so quickly. Of course, weight loss does not occur immediately after exercising. Because it may take months for new exercisers to see significant weight loss, weight reduction is a poor reinforcer for exercise. People who exercise only to lose weight often become discouraged and drop out because they fail to derive any immediate reinforcement from their workouts.

PUNISHMENT

punishment ■

Punishment usually involves presenting an unpleasant or uncomfortable stimulus after a behavior in order to decrease the probability of that behavior happening in the future. If Jacob were to experience even greater pain after cycling, it is unlikely that he would continue to cycle regularly. Under these conditions, pain would be considered a punishment that decreases exercise.

Although pain would likely be considered a punishment by virtually anyone, other exercise consequences that some people consider punishment may be surprising. For example, some older women report that they don't want to exercise because they don't like the feeling of being sweaty. For these women, sweat is a punishing stimulus—an uncomfortable consequence of exercise that actually deters them from being physically active. Other consequences—having to go outside with wet hair after a swim or do additional laundry to clean workout clothing—may not seem particularly unpleasant to many people, but for others they are sufficiently aversive to function as a punishment that deters exercise.

EXTINCTION

Extinction involves withholding a positive stimulus after a behavior in order to decrease the likelihood of that behavior happening in the future. According to the principle of extinction, people will decrease their exercise behavior if they stop attaining the positive benefits/reinforcers that they associate with exercise (e.g., losing weight, feeling better physically and psychologically, having an opportunity to socialize). For instance, a woman who starts an exercise program with the sole purpose of losing weight will exercise less or may even quit altogether once she stops losing weight.

■ extinction

FROM THEORY TO INTERVENTION

In real-world exercise settings, trainers, therapists, and others often use the principles of SRT to develop interventions to increase people's exercise behavior. For instance, gyms and fitness classes frequently offer t-shirts, water bottles, and other rewards as a form of positive reinforcement for adherent exercisers. Likewise, many people motivate themselves to exercise by promising themselves a reward at the end of the exercise session (e.g., a trip to the frozen yogurt shop) or after several months of exercise adherence (e.g., a new outfit). These rewards function as positive reinforcement and are relatively easy to apply as an intervention strategy. Negative reinforcement, however, requires some creativity in its application. One intervention approach is to make exercisers aware of decreases in negative symptoms (e.g., pain) and feelings (e.g., depression) over the course of their exercise program. Like Jacob, people who recognize that exercise causes a decrease in negative sensations may be more likely to continue exercising.

Because punishment is an intervention technique used only to *decrease* behaviors, by definition it cannot be applied to *increase* physical activity. It can, however, be used to decrease sedentary activity, which may, in turn, cause people to increase their physical activity. When people decrease their time spent in sedentary activities, they often fill their spare time with more physically active pursuits (Epstein, Saelens, Myers, & Vito, 1997). Parents who want their children to be more physically active might use punishment to decrease the amount of time the children spend on sedentary activities such as watching television or playing on the computer. For example, parents may assign additional chores (the punishment) to a child who watches too much television. It is important to note that physical activity should *never* be used as a punishment. Children who are punished with exercise may come to see physical activity as something that they only do when they are bad, and thus, something that is highly aversive.

Finally, the principal of extinction occurs all too often in fitness settings. When people stop deriving pleasure from exercise, they often quit. For instance, if one's friends leave the exercise group, or a favorite fitness instructor quits, an exerciser may stop exercising if she perceives that she is no longer having fun and deriving the social benefits of exercise that she formerly enjoyed. Fitness professionals can intervene to prevent extinction, however, by helping people to identify what it is that they value and enjoy about exercise, or by pointing out additional benefits that they may not have previously considered (see Chapter 5 for a more detailed discussion of this intervention strategy). When valued benefits have been identified, the fitness professional can introduce the exerciser to the types of exercise activities and programs that lead to those benefits.

RESEARCH EXEMPLAR

In comparison to the social cognitive theories discussed in Chapter 3, relatively little research has applied SRT to the study of exercise behavior. The lack of such research probably reflects exercise psychologists' recognition of the importance of thoughts and feelings in determining exercise behavior. SRT does not take these factors into account, so it tends not to be the theory of choice for many researchers. Nonetheless, some studies have demonstrated the utility of SRT principles for altering exercise activity.

For instance, in one study (Epstein et al., 1997), 34 obese children came to a laboratory that offered equipment for four physical activities (a stationary bicycle, a climbing machine, a speed-skating slide, and a cross-country skiing machine) and four sedentary activities (a VCR with children's movies, video games, books, and coloring materials). On the first day of the experiment, children were given free access to all of the activities for 45 minutes and were then randomized to one of four conditions: children in the *reinforcement condition* were told that they would earn one point for each minute that they did not spend doing their two favorite sedentary activities. Children in the *punishment condition* were instructed that they would lose a point for each minute they spent doing their two favorite sedentary activities. Children in these two conditions could redeem their points for reinforcers such as tickets to a baseball game, passes to the zoo, and video arcade tokens. In the *restriction* condition, the children's two favorite sedentary activities were removed from the lab. In the *control condition,* children were given access to all activities. Children in these latter two conditions were not given any information about gaining or losing points. Each child returned to the lab for three more days. On the fifth day of the experiment, the contingencies (i.e., rewards, punishment, restricted access) were removed and children were given free access to all eight activities.

When the data were analyzed, it was found that on Days 1 and 5, children in all four conditions engaged in similar amounts of physical activity—on average, only about 5 or 6 minutes. However, on Days 2, 3, and 4 of the experiment (the days on which the contingencies were in effect), children in the reinforcement and punishment conditions were significantly more physically active than were children in the control condition. On average, they were active for about 15 minutes. Children in the restricted access condition were only slightly more physically active (about 10 minutes of activity per session) than those in the control condition (about 5 minutes of activity per session). These results show that reinforcement and punishment are more effective strategies for increasing physical activity than is restricting sedentary activity.

USEFULNESS, LIMITATIONS, AND FUTURE RESEARCH AVENUES OF STIMULUS–RESPONSE THEORY

Stimulus–response theory provides a simple and useful framework for understanding the effects of exercise consequences on future exercise behavior. Both reinforcement and punishment have been shown to alter subsequent exercise behavior (Epstein, Saelens, & O'Brien, 1995, Epstein et al., 1997; Noland, 1989). Yet, to date, no experiments have investigated the effects of negative reinforcement or withdrawal on exercise behavior. Whether these events can be manipulated to affect exercise behavior remains to be determined in future research.

A major limitation of SRT is that it does not consider the important role of cognition. In SRT, the major role of cognition is to interpret exercise-related outcomes as either positive or negative. Although the theory proposes that these interpretations will determine subsequent exercise behavior (e.g., an outcome interpreted as positive will increase behavior whereas an outcome interpreted as negative will decrease behavior), in reality the relationship between outcomes and exercise behavior is not that simple. If it were, then beginner exercisers would never continue working out beyond the first few painful sessions, and people who felt good after working out would never quit. Of course, many beginners do persist despite the initial discomfort, and many seasoned exercisers quit despite seeing considerable positive outcomes associated with exercise. Clearly, other cognitions pertaining to the outcome—not merely whether it is positive or negative—are involved in determining future exercise behavior. These other cognitions may include *expectations* of deriving a particular outcome again, *perceived control* over attaining that outcome, and the *perceived value* of that outcome (cognitions that were discussed in the previous chapter). Although considerable research has demonstrated the importance of these cognitions in determining exercise behavior, they are not included in the SRT. Consequently, the SRT is limited in its ability to predict and explain exercise behavior.

Another limitation of the SRT in exercise settings is that although reinforcement has proven to be a very useful principle in altering exercise behavior, the other three principles are difficult to manipulate in exercise interventions (e.g., it is difficult and generally unethical to punish people if they miss a workout). The SRT also fails to provide information that can be used to develop interventions to change exercisers' perceptions of a particular outcome as reinforcing or punishing. It has been observed, for example, that some older women can eventually come to see sweating as a reinforcement rather than a punishment. This shift occurs when the women change their beliefs and attitudes toward sweating, yet beliefs and attitudes are cognitions not included in the SRT. In short, the SRT has limited use for predicting future exercise behavior and developing exercise interventions because it ignores the important role of cognition. (For an approach that attempts to integrate SRT with cognition, see the box on the following page.)

Integrative Approaches

Integrative approaches pull together concepts from a variety of theories and models in order to explain exercise behavior. They include the transtheoretical model and social ecological models.

TRANSTHEORETICAL MODEL (TM)

The transtheoretical model (TM), developed at the University of Rhode Island Cancer Prevention Research Center, was the result of years of studying and observing how people quit smoking (Prochaska & DiClemente, 1983; Prochaska, DiClemente, & Norcross, 1992; Prochaska & Velicer, 1997). The prefix *trans* means across. The TM was given its name because it integrates elements from *across* a variety of theories and models of behavior, some of which are social-cognitive in nature and some of which are not.

According to the TM, behavior change is not a quick process—people do not suddenly *decide* to quit smoking or to start exercising and then immediately change their behavior. Rather, behavior change is a gradual progress whereby the individual progresses through a

Behavioral Economics

AN ALTERNATIVE TO STIMULUS–RESPONSE THEORY

Behavioral economic theory involves the integration of stimulus–response theory with basic research on cognitive psychology and decision making in order to explain how people allocate time and effort to various options. When individuals are trying to become more physically active, they are often forced to decide whether they will spend their time exercising or performing highly reinforcing, sedentary activities (e.g., watching movies may be reinforced by evoking fun and relaxation). In an exercise context, an understanding of behavioral economics can reveal ways to make highly reinforcing sedentary activities less attractive (Epstein, 1998). Specifically, when the cost of performing sedentary activities increases, people may be less inclined to do them. For example, children may come to see video and computer games less attractive, and consequently spend less time with them, if access to these activities is contingent on the performance of household chores. In contrast, if parents provide noncontingent or "free" access to physical activities, children may see these as less costly and more attractive options than sedentary activities.

Behavioral economics would suggest that information about the reinforcing aspects of *sedentary* activities can be used to identify *physical* activities that may provide the individual with similar reinforcements. For example, consider a group of neighbors who get together to play cards every Wednesday evening. Upon questioning these individuals, an exercise psychologist discovers that the most reinforcing aspect of their card games is the opportunity to socialize with one another. Recognizing the importance of socializing, the exercise psychologist might suggest that the group go for a walk before starting their card game. This extra time together will allow more time to talk with one another and to enjoy one another's company.

Behavioral economics seems to be a promising approach for understanding and promoting physical activity. By understanding factors that alter the reinforcing value of certain activities, exercise psychologists may help people make more healthful choices regarding the ways in which they spend their leisure time.

series of stages. Because TM conceptualizes behavior change in this way, it is considered a stage model.

1. Precontemplation. In the **precontemplation stage,** people have no intention to start exercising in the foreseeable future (the next six months or so). People in this stage consider the cons (disadvantages) of exercising to be greater than the pros (advantages), perhaps because of a lack of information about the health consequences of a sedentary lifestyle or because they have failed at attempts to exercise in the past and have completely given up. Precontemplators are often very defensive when other people try to convince them to change their ways, so

■ precontemplation stage

it can be difficult for people to provide them with information regarding the benefits of exercise, or strategies for starting an exercise program. Consequently, the precontemplation stage is very stable, meaning that without intervention, people tend to stay here for very long periods of time before moving on to the next stage.

contemplation stage ■

2. Contemplation. People in the **contemplation stage** have intentions to start exercising within the next six months. At this stage, they are aware of the pros of exercising, but they are also equally aware of the cons. These are people who know that exercise is good for them, and may feel that they should be exercising, but are not yet ready to make a commitment to change. Because people in this stage have ambivalent feelings about exercise, unless there is some form of intervention, they may remain in this stage for long periods of time.

preparation stage ■

3. Preparation. In the **preparation stage,** people intend to start exercising in the immediate future (i.e., the next month). People in this stage consider the pros of exercising to be greater than the cons. During this stage, people are performing tasks that will prepare them for starting an exercise program, such as getting medical clearance to exercise, obtaining information about local exercise facilities and programs, or buying exercise equipment. They may also be making small changes to their current level of physical activity, such as taking the stairs in a building instead of the elevator. Preparation is considered an unstable stage, meaning that once people start taking these small steps, even without intervention it is highly likely that they will progress to the next stage within a few months.

action stage ■

4. Action. In the **action stage,** people are exercising at optimal levels for health and fitness (usually defined as exercise on most days of the week at a moderate intensity for at least 30 minutes duration). Although for people in this stage the pros of exercise outweigh the cons, this is a very unstable stage. In fact, of the five stages, the action stage is the least stable, because people find it so difficult to maintain their new exercise routine. Individuals in the action stage must work hard to avoid falling back into their old sedentary lifestyle.

maintenance stage ■

5. Maintenance. The **maintenance stage** is achieved when people have been exercising at optimal levels for six months. Of course, for maintainers, the pros of exercising continue to outweigh the cons. Maintainers still must work to prevent lapsing into a sedentary lifestyle, but they don't find exercise as difficult to maintain as they did during the action stage. Overall, they are less tempted to relapse and are highly confident that they can continue their exercise program.

How Do People Move Through the Stages?

Movement through the stages involves changing:

a. how people think about exercise
b. how people think about themselves
c. aspects of the environment that influence exercise behavior.

According to the TM, these changes occur through a combination of 10 basic experiential and behavioral processes. These 10 processes are defined in Exhibit 4.2, which also provides examples of interventions that can help people apply each of the processes.

- experiential processes
- self-reevaluation
- consciousness raising

Experiential processes are typically directed toward increasing people's awareness of, and changing their thoughts and feelings about, both themselves and their exercise behavior. For example, the process of **self-reevaluation** involves people's carefully considering how they feel about themselves as "couch potatoes," and deciding whether that is an identity they want to maintain. The process of **consciousness raising** involves increasing one's awareness and memory of the benefits of physical activity. Ways to achieve this include providing people with educational literature on physical activity and having them talk with someone who used to be sedentary, but who has since become active and who now recognizes the advantages of exercising.

- behavioral processes
- stimulus control
- reinforcement management

Behavioral processes generally consist of behaviors that a person undertakes in order to change aspects of the environment that can affect exercise participation. For instance, **stimulus control** involves placing cues in the environment that will remind people to be more physically active (e.g., putting your workout clothes by your door) and removing cues that tempt them to be inactive (e.g., taking the batteries out of the television remote control). The process of **reinforcement management** involves developing strategies for rewarding or reinforcing oneself when exercise goals are achieved.

Studies of smoking cessation have shown that people use different types of processes at different stages of change (Prochaska et al., 1992). Specifically, experiential processes are used more during the earlier stages of smoking cessation and behavioral processes are used more in the later stages. Yet, for exercise, there does not seem to be a shift across the stages from the use of experiential to behavioral processes (Marshall & Biddle, 2001). Rather, behavioral processes tend to be used just as often as experiential processes across all the stages of physical activity behavior change. It is not known, however, just how important it is for a person to use each of these processes in order to move through the stages.

exhibit 4.2 *Definitions and examples of interventions associated with each of the processes of change in the TM.*

PROCESS	DEFINITION	INTERVENTION EXAMPLE
Experiential Processes		
Consciousness raising	Seeking new information and a better understanding of exercise	Read pamphlets, talk to a health-care professional about the benefits of exercise
Self-reevaluation	Assessing how one thinks and feels about oneself as an inactive person	Consider whether being inactive is truly in line with the person's values
Environmental reevaluation	Considering how inactivity affects the physical and social environment	Find out the costs of inactivity to the health-care system
Dramatic relief	Experiencing and expressing feelings about becoming more active or remaining inactive	Imagine the feelings of regret and loss for not having prevented the loss of health through exercise
Social liberation	Increasing awareness of the social and environmental factors that support physical activity	Seek out information about exercise groups and resources in the community, workplace, etc.
Behavioral Processes		
Self-liberation	Activities that strengthen one's commitment to change and the belief that one can change	Announce one's commitment to exercise to family and friends; stay positive and remind oneself "I can do it!"
Counterconditioning	Substituting physical activities for sedentary activities	Go for a walk after dinner rather than watch television
Stimulus control	Controlling situations and cues that trigger inactivity and skipped workouts	Plan ahead for a busy period at work/school and schedule exercise on a calendar
Reinforcement management	Rewarding oneself for being active	Establish goals and reward oneself for achieving them
Helping relationships	Utilizing support from others during attempts to change	Buddy up with a friend who is also trying to start an exercise regimen

Indications That People Are Moving Through the Stages

According to the TM, we can determine whether people are moving through the stages by looking for shifts in their decisional balance and an increase in their self-efficacy to overcome the temptation to skip exercise sessions.

Decisional balance in the TM model. **exhibit 4.3**

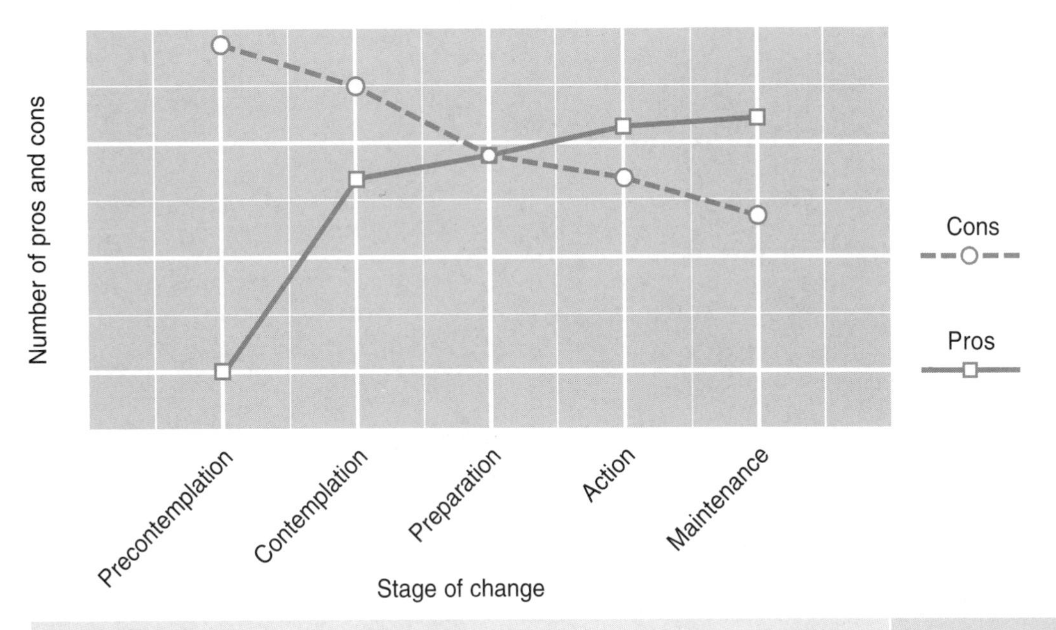

Shift in decisional balance. The **decisional balance** construct was borrowed from Janis and Mann's (1977) model of decision making. It reflects how people perceive the pros and cons of changing their behavior. We can tell if people are moving through the stages by looking for differences in the number of pros versus cons that they list for exercise. In the precontemplation stage, the cons of exercising will far outweigh the pros. In the contemplation stage, pros and cons will be more equal. In the advanced stages, the pros will outweigh the cons. This relationship is shown in Exhibit 4.3.

■ decisional balance

Increased self-efficacy to overcome temptations. The self-efficacy construct was borrowed from Bandura's self-efficacy theory (see Chapter 3). In the TM, self-efficacy represents the situation-specific confidence people have in their ability to deal with high-risk situations that might tempt them to lapse into their old sedentary ways. Situations that might tempt an exerciser to skip a workout include rainy days, a busy work or school schedule, and fatigue. According to the TM, self-efficacy increases as people move through the five stages. Thus, we can tell whether people are moving through the stages by looking for an increase in their self-efficacy.

exhibit 4.4 *Change in self-efficacy for exercising in all situations across the five stages of the TM.*

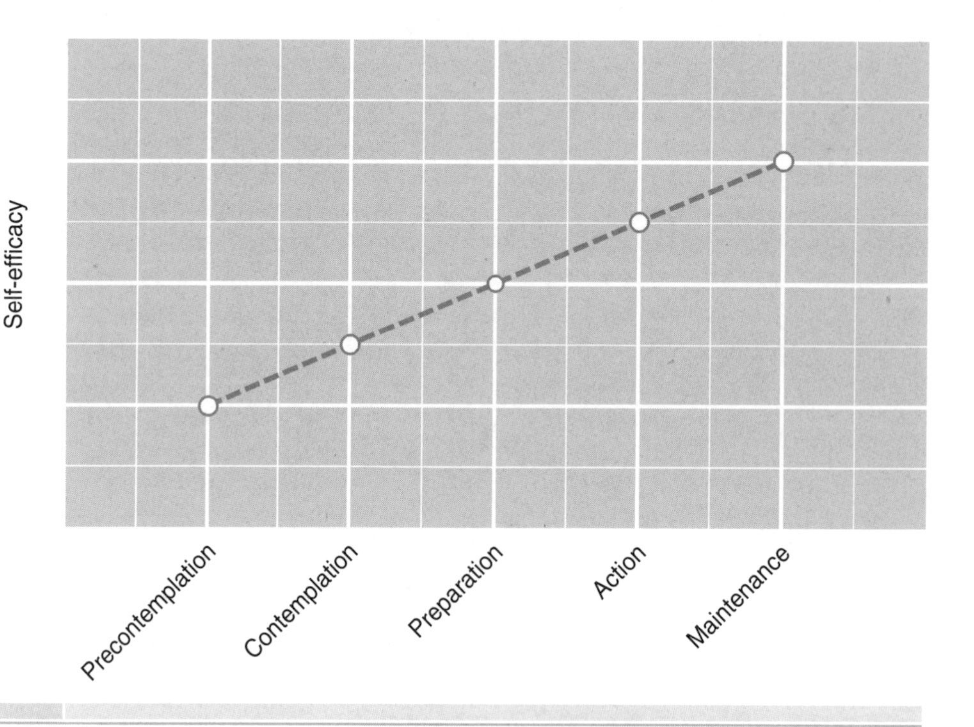

Exhibit 4.4 shows levels of self-efficacy that are typically found among people in each of the five stages. In the precontemplation stage, people have virtually no confidence in their ability to overcome temptation. By the time they reach the action stage and are exercising at optimal levels, their efficacy has increased dramatically. The high level of self-efficacy in the maintenance stage indicates that people are confident that they can resist the temptation to skip a workout in most situations, most of the time.

From Theory to Intervention

The TM is very useful for guiding exercise interventions. It provides a framework for identifying the interventions that are most appropriate for a person at a particular stage. Exhibit 4.5 shows an example of a simple questionnaire that can be used to determine which exercise stage a person is in. Once a person's exercise stage has been identified, the interventionist can then introduce strategies that are most likely to help that person progress to the next stage. The Cancer Prevention Research Consortium (1995) has suggested the following interventions for people in the various stages of the TM:

Precontemplation stage. Recall that people in this stage underestimate the benefits of changing (the pros) and overestimate the costs (the cons). To move to the next stage, precontemplators need to become more informed of the benefits of exercise. This may be accomplished by providing them with factual information about the connection between exercise and well-being through media resources (e.g., pamphlets or videos) or through consultations with a health-care professional.

Contemplation stage. People in the contemplation stage are still not yet fully convinced of the pros of exercise. In addition to providing more information about the advantages of regular physical activity, another

What exercise stage are you in? — exhibit 4.5

"Regular exercise" is any planned physical activity (e.g., brisk walking, aerobics, jogging, bicycling, swimming, rowing, etc.) performed to increase physical fitness. Such activity should be performed three to five times per week for 20 to 60 minutes per session.

Do you exercise regularly according to that definition?

- ☐ 1. Yes, I have been exercising regularly for MORE than six months.
- ☐ 2. Yes, I have been exercising regularly for LESS than six months.
- ☐ 3. No, but I intend to start exercising regularly in the next 30 days.
- ☐ 4. No, but I intend to start exercising regularly in the next six months.
- ☐ 5. No, and I do NOT intend to start exercising regularly in the next six months.

RESULTS

If you checked the last box, you are in the precontemplation stage.

If you checked the fourth box, you are in the contemplation stage.

If you checked the third box, you are in the preparation stage.

If you checked the second box, you are in the action stage.

If you checked the first box, congratulations! You are in the maintenance stage.

useful intervention is to have contemplators ponder how they feel about themselves as "couch potatoes" and whether they can really feel good about themselves if they continue to be sedentary. These questions can spur the contemplator to identify more pros for becoming physically active.

Preparation stage. People in the preparation stage are ready to change soon, but they are concerned about failing. Thus, their self-efficacy for exercising is still relatively low. Interventionists can help these people progress through the preparation stage by encouraging them to get organized and start planning for a new physically active lifestyle (e.g., investigate the cost to join a fitness club, decide how exercise will be worked into a busy schedule, identify walking trails) and to seek out support from others (e.g., find an exercise buddy). These strategies provide people with some of the tools and information they will need to change their behavior, which, in turn, can decrease their doubts about their ability to change.

Action stage. People in the action stage are already doing some physical activity, but they can benefit from information that will keep them in the action stage and prevent them from backsliding. Helpful interventions include providing tips on overcoming barriers that might prevent them from adhering, and introducing strategies to help maintain their motivation, such as establishing a contract or setting goals (see Chapter 5 for a discussion of these strategies).

Maintenance stage. People in the maintenance stage have been exercising regularly for at least six months. Interventions that are most useful to maintainers are those that prevent them from slipping back into a sedentary lifestyle. For example, it is particularly valuable for maintainers to plan ahead and to identify situations that might cause them to lapse, such as going on vacation or being busy at work or school. Strategies can then be developed to deal with these situations, if and when they occur. In Chapter 5, we provide an in-depth description of an intervention to prevent lapses.

It is important to note that these are only a few of the intervention techniques that can be used at each of the TM stages. Refer also to Exhibit 4.2 and Chapter 5, where we discuss some other interventions that are useful for helping people move through the stages of the TM.

Research Exemplar

Most exercise research involving the TM can be classified as:

1. **Descriptive studies**—studies that *describe* differences between people in the different TM stages
2. **Predictive studies**—studies that attempt to *predict* future exercise behavior
3. **Intervention studies**—studies that use the TM to develop exercise *interventions*

- descriptive studies
- predictive studies
- intervention studies

Descriptive studies. Considerable research has shown that people in different stages of the TM differ in reliable ways in terms of:

- exercise self-efficacy
- attitudes toward exercise
- the use of the processes of change
- exercise behavior.

For example, a study of 819 Canadian high school students found that students who were in the maintenance and action stages of physical activity had greater exercise self-efficacy, perceived more benefits of exercise, and were more likely to use processes of change than were students in any other stage (Nigg & Courneya, 1998). (For a quantitative review of other descriptive studies, see Marshall & Biddle, 2001.)

Predictive studies. In a study of the predictive capabilities of the TM, Nigg (2001) found that students' use of the processes of change did not predict their exercise behavior or stage of exercise three years later. He also failed to find support for the TM prediction that an increase in exercise self-efficacy and a shift in decision balance cause increased exercise behavior and movement across the stages. These results suggest that the TM constructs may not allow researchers accurately to predict an increase in exercise participation and movement from one stage to the next.

Intervention studies. Research has demonstrated the benefits of matching self-help manuals and other motivational materials to a person's stage of change (Marcus, Bock, et al., 1998; Marcus, Emmons, et al., 1998; Marcus et al., 1992). For example, in one study, 194 sedentary men and women received self-help materials and feedback reports throughout the study (Marcus, Bock, et al., 1998). These materials were either individually tailored to correspond with the problems and processes typically associated with the individual's stage of change, or standard, generic materials that did not provide information unique to any particular stage of change. At the end of the six-month intervention, participants who received the individually tailored, stage-matched materials were engaging in more minutes of physical activity per week and were more likely to have reached the action stage of the TM than were participants who received the standard intervention.

Usefulness, Limitations, and Future Research Avenues of the Transtheoretical Model

The TM has proven to be very useful for matching specific interventions to specific groups of individuals (Marcus et al., 1992; Marcus, Bock, et al., 1998; Marcus, Emmons, et al., 1998). Exercise interventions seem to be most effective when they are matched with a person's stage of change. The TM recognizes that when it comes to exercise interventions, one size does not fit all.

A major limitation of the TM, however, is that although it is useful for *describing* differences between people in different stages (Marshall & Biddle, 2001), measures of the TM constructs (e.g., processes of change, self-efficacy, decision balance) cannot reliably *predict* who will increase exercise behavior and when (Nigg, 2001). In addition, it seems that some people move backward through the stages, regressing rather than progressing (e.g., Cole, Leonard, Hammond, & Fridinger, 1998). The TM is unable to predict who will *backslide* and when.

In an attempt to improve the predictive capabilities of the TM in exercise settings, future research may identify subgroups of individuals within a particular stage, who are most likely to move on to the next stage by the end of an intervention (e.g., Gorely & Bruce, 2000). Presumably, people within a particular stage who have higher efficacy, perceive more exercise pros, and are more active at the start of an intervention will be more likely to advance to the next TM stage than will people who are less efficacious, perceive fewer pros, and are less active. For example, in one study of more than 1,000 adults, some people in the preparation stage were *almost* sufficiently active to be classified as in the action stage, but not quite (Cole et al., 1998). The researchers categorized this subgroup of people in a substage that they labeled "late preparation." After an intervention, people in this group were more likely to move forward to the action stage than were the rest of the people in the preparation stage. Thus, it seems that within the five stages of the TM, there are subgroups of people who are more likely to move forward than are others. Further research is needed to determine whether the creation of subcategories or substages improves the predictive power of the TM.

SOCIAL ECOLOGICAL MODELS

Stimulus-response theory, the transtheoretical model, and the social cognitive approaches discussed in Chapter 3 emphasize that physical activity participation is largely determined by the *individual*. In other words, how the *individual* thinks and feels about exercise and how the *individual* chooses to respond to exercise consequences (e.g., reinforcement) and antecedents (e.g., cues to action) will have a potent effect on future exercise behavior. In contrast, **social ecological models** take the approach that these individual-level factors are only one of multiple levels of influence on behavior (McLeroy, Bibeau, Steckler, & Glanz, 1988). Social ecological models of health recognize that individuals bear responsibility for engaging in healthful behaviors, but the models also recognize other levels of influence on health behavior, including the physical environment, the community, society, and the government (Stokols, 1996; Green, Richard, & Potvin, 1996).

■ social ecological models

Social ecological models can be considered an integrative approach because they pull together a variety of models and theories. That is, at each level of influence (e.g., the individual level, the community level, government level), different models and theories may be used to explain health behavior and to bring about health behavior change. For instance, at the individual level, self-efficacy theory may be used to explain, in part, why so many people have difficulty being physically active. Interventions can then be developed to increase self-efficacy as a means of ultimately increasing physical activity. At higher levels, theories of community organization and government policy may be used to understand some of the barriers people may have to becoming more physically active (e.g., a lack of affordable exercise facilities). These community- and government-level theories can then be applied to bring about environmental and policy changes that will help to remove barriers and ultimately increase physical activity.

An Ecological Model for Physical Activity

Exercise participation can be influenced by a wide array of factors that are potentially beyond the individual's control (e.g., availability of equipment and public facilities). Because social ecological models take these factors into consideration, it makes intuitive sense that a social ecological approach would be very useful for understanding and predicting exercise behavior. Unfortunately, such models are not yet well developed, largely because there has been so little research examining the effects of policy and environmental interventions on physical activity. A group of Australian and American researchers, however, has created a preliminary social ecological model for physical activity that might provide a basis for further research that could ultimately lead to a more complete model (New South Wales Physical Activity Task Force, 1997; Sallis, Bauman, & Pratt, 1998). As illustrated in Exhibit 4.6, their exhibit 4.6 *A preliminary social ecological model of exercise.*

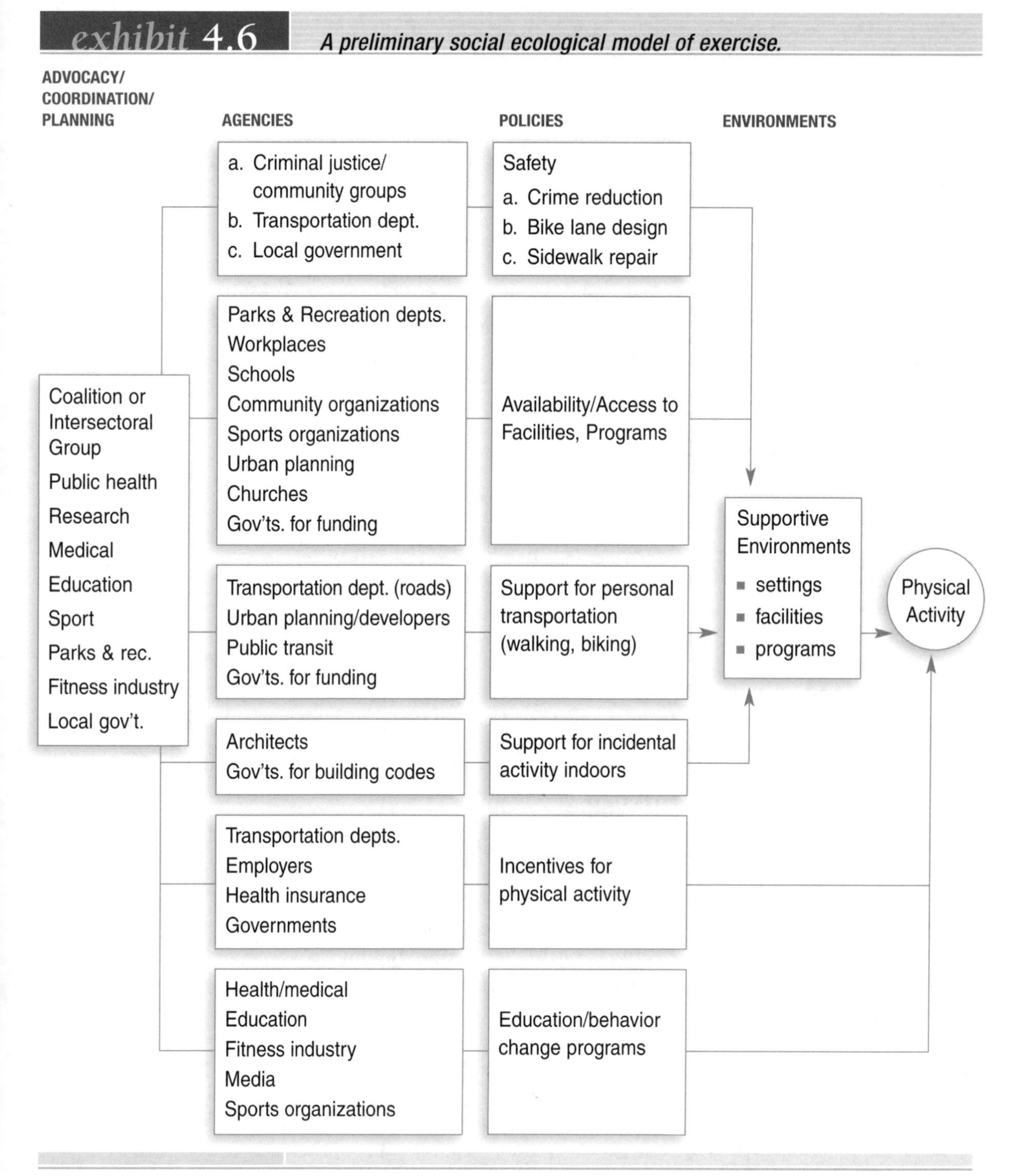

Source: Reprinted by permission of Elsevier Science from Environmental and policy interventions to promote physical activity by Sallis et al. *American Journal of Preventive Medicine,* Vol. 15, No. 4, p. 388, copyright © 1998 by *American Journal of Preventive Medicine.*

model suggests several ways in which community agencies and groups can influence policies that will provide supportive physical activity environments. According to the social ecological approach, more supportive environments will lead to greater physical activity among community members. To illustrate this chain of events, let's look at two ways in which the model suggests that physical activity can be increased.

1. *Improve availability of and access to facilities and programs.* A social ecological model would predict that if people do not have places where they can be active (e.g., parks, community centers, fitness clubs), then they won't be active. Indeed, the presence of accessible facilities has been shown to correlate positively with physical activity participation. Among both adults (Sallis et al., 1990) and children (Sallis et al., 1993), those who are more physically active have more facilities for exercise or play near their homes than do those who are less active.

2. *Support active transportation (walking, biking).* Social ecological models highlight the importance of the physical aspects of home, school, and work environments in influencing physically active forms of transportation. For example, because many suburban developments are now built without sidewalks and beyond walking distance of shops, schools, and workplaces, people are often compelled to use sedentary forms of transportation (e.g., buses, automobiles) because it is inconvenient and often unsafe to walk or bike (Sallis & Owen, 1999). The social ecological model predicts that physical activity can be increased if agencies develop policies that provide supportive environments for active forms of transportation.

From Theory to Intervention

The social ecological model can be applied in numerous ways to develop interventions that enhance availability and access to facilities and programs, and increase active forms of personal transportation. As shown in the model, various agencies can implement policies in the form of organizational statements, rules, or laws that can help to increase facility availability and accessibility. For example, governments could provide funding for more walking and biking trails. Workplaces could subsidize health club memberships for employees. Churches and other houses of worship could make their basements and meeting halls available for community exercise programs. According to the model, improved availability and accessibility will foster a more supportive exercise environment, and ultimately greater physical activity participation.

The Ecological Model at Work

COPENHAGEN'S CITY BIKE PROGRAM

An ingenious example of an ecological intervention to enhance active transportation comes from Copenhagen, Denmark. Copenhagen's City Bike Program is a public/private partnership that placed 1,100 specially designed bicycles throughout downtown for public use. To use a City Bike, the user deposits a coin into a slot on the handlebar, which unlocks it from a rack. The user can then ride the City Bike throughout the city center, for as long as desired, and return it by locking it into any of the city bike racks. At that time, the user's coin is returned, making the bike rental free. Although the City Bike program was largely initiated to solve pollution and traffic problems in the city, just imagine the exercise-related benefits that users are gaining! (City Bike Foundation of Copenhagen, 2000.)

The model also predicts that physical activity will increase if agencies develop policies that provide supportive environments for active forms of transportation. For example, urban planners could incorporate plans to construct sidewalks and bicycle paths and lanes in new suburban developments. Public transit organizations could provide more bike carriers on buses. Schools and workplaces could offer further encouragement by providing secure bicycle racks and facilities for showering and changing. The model suggests that these changes to the environment will encourage people to become more physically active through the use of active forms of transportation.

Research Exemplar

To date, very little exercise research has been based on social ecological models. In a 1998 review paper, researchers were able to identify only seven published studies that examined the effects of environmental and policy interventions to promote physical activity (Sallis et al., 1998). One of these studies took place at a San Diego naval air station where several environmental and policy changes were made with the goal of increasing physical activity among personnel living on the base (Linenger, Chesson, & Nice, 1991). Environmental changes included opening a women's fitness center, building bicycle trails, purchasing new exercise equipment for the gymnasium, and organizing running and cycling clubs. Policy changes included obtaining financial support for the environmental changes and instituting release time for personnel on the base to be physically active. Comparisons of preintervention and postintervention fitness tests indicated that Navy personnel who lived at the San Diego station had greater improvements in fitness over a one-year period than did Navy personnel living in other communities that did not receive the interventions.

Usefulness, Limitations, and Future Research Avenues of Ecological Models

The major utility of ecological models is that they recognize multiple levels of influence on physical activity, and multiple levels of intervention opportunities for increasing physical activity. In other words, an individual's physical activity participation is not solely influenced by that person's thoughts, feelings, and behavior. His or her participation can also be influenced by environmental and policy-related factors beyond the individual's control. As researchers, we can better understand physical activity by understanding the impact of these factors. As interventionists, we can also improve physical activity participation rates by focusing our interventions not just on the individual (e.g., improving attitudes toward exercise or increasing self-efficacy for exercise), but also on the environment (e.g., removing environmental barriers to activity such as unsafe streets) and on public policy (e.g., pressuring city planners to build designated traffic lanes for cyclists). By looking at this "big picture" of variables that can influence physical activity, we increase our ability to understand existing levels of participation and our ability to improve these levels (Stokols, 1996).

Of course, a social ecological approach does have limitations. Environmental and policy changes can take a long time and a lot of money to implement. It is also important to note that social ecological approaches are not intended to be "stand-alone" interventions, with the idea that "if we build it, they will come." Simply building fitness facilities does not mean that people will automatically become more physically active. Rather, social ecological approaches recognize the importance of community-wide educational and incentive programs to motivate individuals to take advantage of activity-promoting environments and policies. These programs themselves can be very expensive and time-consuming.

Yet despite these limitations, social ecological approaches appear to be garnering interest among researchers and interventionists. Given that the Centers for Disease Control and Prevention (2001) have "strongly recommended" environmental and policy approaches to increasing physical activity, we expect that a growing number of exercise psychologists will begin considering ecological factors in their research. For instance, researchers could investigate how the social cognitions that affect physical activity—such as self-efficacy or perceived behavioral control—are influenced by changes in the environment, such as the construction of bicycle and walking paths. They might also examine whether changes in public policy—for example, legislation that limits the use of private automobiles along downtown streets—affect attitudes and perceived benefits of physically active commuting.

Conclusion

In this chapter, we have presented stimulus response theory (SRT), the transtheoretical model (TM), and a social ecological model of exercise behavior. Unlike the social cognitive approaches discussed in Chapter 3, SRT does not consider the individual's thoughts and feelings to be significant determinants of exercise behavior. Instead, SRT suggests that exercise behavior is contingent on the pairings of exercise with reinforcers and punishers, and that future exercise behavior depends primarily on whether the exerciser has experienced positive or negative outcomes following previous exercise bouts. Although SRT does have merit, its applicability and explanatory power are reduced by the absence of social cognitions. As demonstrated in Chapter 3, social cognitive variables play a very important role in explaining exercise behavior.

The transtheoretical model represents an attempt to merge some of the best predictors of behavior (e.g., self-efficacy, outcome expectancies) into a single model. Perhaps by integrating theoretical constructs, researchers will be more likely to capture the variety of factors that explain exercise behavior than they would by relying on any single theory. Social ecological models go one step further toward integration. The ecological approach emphasizes the importance of integrating theory, research, and interventions aimed at the individual, with theory, research, and interventions aimed at various other levels of influence including the community, society, and the government.

What Do You Know?

1. What is the key difference between social cognitive theories and models and SRT?
2. Identify and describe two types of events that can follow a behavior and will increase the likelihood of the behavior occurring again in the future.

3. What is the difference between negative reinforcement and punishment?
4. Describe two limitations of SRT.
5. Describe how people are believed to move through the stages of the TM.
6. What is meant by the term "decisional balance," and how does decisional balance change as one moves through the stages?
7. Define and provide examples of experiential processes and behavioral processes.
8. How does self-efficacy change as one moves through the stages?
9. Describe two strategies that could help people move through the preparation stage.
10. Describe one benefit and one limitation of the TM.
11. What sets apart social ecological models from all of the other theories and models discussed in Chapters 3 and 4?
12. Identify two levels of influence in social ecological models and describe how each of these levels can influence physical activity.
13. What types of difficulties might be encountered when using a social ecological approach to change physical activity?

Learning Activities

1. Visit a fitness center, gym, or exercise rehabilitation facility and identify situations in which reinforcement, punishment, negative reinforcement, and extinction occur.
2. Choose one stage in the transtheoretical model and develop a pamphlet that would provide useful exercise-related information for people currently in that stage.
3. Imagine that you have been hired to increase physical activity within your community. You will be given all of the money and all of the resources that you need. Using an ecological approach, develop a plan for increasing physical activity that will target multiple levels of influence.
4. Make a list of all of the constructs presented in the theories and models in Chapters 3 and 4. Which constructs occur the most often? Which constructs occur the least often? Which constructs would you be most likely to include if you were to develop your own model or theory of exercise behavior and why?

References

Cancer Prevention Research Consortium. (1995). *Pathways to health.* Kingston, RI: Author.

Centers for Disease Control and Prevention. (2001, October). *Increasing physical activity: A report on recommendations of the task force on community preventive services* (No. RR-18). Atlanta, GA: Author.

City Bike Foundation of Copenhagen. (2000). The history of the Copenhagen City Bike. Retrieved April 12, 2002, from www.bycyklen.dk/frameset_uk.html

Cole, G., Leonard, B., Hammond, S., & Fridinger, F. (1998). Using "stages of behavioural change" constructs to measure the short-term effects of a worksite-based intervention to increase moderate physical activity. *Psychological Reports, 82,* 615–618.

Epstein, L. H. (1998). Integrating theoretical approaches to promote physical activity. *American Journal of Preventive Medicine, 15,* 257–265.

Epstein, L. H., Saelens, B. E., Myers, M. D., & Vito, D. (1997). Effects of decreasing sedentary behaviours on activity choice in obese children. *Health Psychology, 16,* 107–113.

Epstein, L. H., Saelens, B. E., & O'Brien, J. G. (1995). Effects of reinforcing increases in active versus decreases in sedentary behaviour for obese children. *International Journal of Behavioural Medicine, 2,* 41–50.

Gorely, T., & Bruce, D. (2000). A 6-month investigation of exercise adoption from the contemplation stage of the transtheoretical model. *Psychology of Sport and Exercise, 1,* 89–101.

Green, L. W., Richard, L., & Potvin, L. (1996). Ecological foundations of health promotion. *American Journal of Health Promotion, 10,* 270–281.

Janis, I. L., & Mann, L. (1977). *Decision making.* New York: Macmillan.

Linenger, J. M., Chesson, C. V., & Nice, D. S. (1991). Physical fitness gains following simple environmental change. *American Journal of Preventive Medicine, 7,* 298–310.

Marcus, B. H., Bock, B. C., Pinto, B. M., Forsyth, L. H., Roberts, M. B., & Traficante, R. M. (1998). Efficacy of an individualized, motivationally-tailored physical activity intervention. *Annals of Behavioral Medicine, 20,* 174–180.

Marcus, B. H., Emmons, K. M., Simkin-Silverman, L., Linnan, L. A., Taylor, E. R., Bock, B. C., Roberts, M. B., Rossi, J. S., & Abrams, D. B. (1998). Evaluation of motivationally-tailored versus standard self-help physical activity interventions at the workplace. *American Journal of Health Promotion, 12,* 138–146.

Marcus, B. H., Rossi, J. S., Selby, V. C., Niaura, R. S., & Abrams, D. B. (1992). The stages and processes of exercise adoption and maintenance in a worksite sample. *Health Psychology, 11,* 386–395.

Marshall, S. J., & Biddle, J. H. (2001). The Transtheoretical Model of Behavior Change: A meta-analysis of applications to physical activity and exercise. *Annals of Behavioral Medicine, 23,* 229–246.

McLeroy, K. R., Bibeau, D., Steckler, A., & Glanz, K. (1988). An ecological perspective on health promotion programs. *Health Education Quarterly, 15,* 351–377.

New South Wales Physical Activity Task Force. (1997). *Simply active every day: A discussion document from the NSW Physical Activity Task Force on proposals to promote physical activity in NSW, 1997–2002.* Summary report. Sydney, Australia: New South Wales Health Department.

Nigg, C. R. (2001). Explaining adolescent exercise behavior change: A longitudinal application of the transtheoretical model. *Annals of Behavioural Medicine, 23,* 11–20.

Nigg, C. R., & Courneya, K. S. (1998). Transtheoretical model: Examining adolescent exercise behaviour. *Journal of Adolescent Health, 22,* 214–224.

Noland, M. P. (1989). The effects of self-monitoring and reinforcement on exercise adherence. *Research Quarterly for Exercise and Sport, 60,* 216–224.

Pavlov, I. V. (1928). *Lectures on conditioned reflexes.* (W. H. Gantt, Trans.). New York: International.

Prochaska, J. O., & DiClemente, C. C. (1983). Stages and processes of self-change in smoking: Towards an integrative model of change. *Journal of Consulting and Clinical Psychology, 51,* 390–395.

Prochaska, J. O., DiClemente, C. C., & Norcross, J. C. (1992). In search of how people change: Applications to addictive behaviors. *American Psychologist, 47,* 1102–1114.

Prochaska, J. O., & Velicer, W. F. (1997). The transtheoretical model of behaviour change. *American Journal of Health Promotion, 12,* 38–48.

Sallis, J. F., Bauman, A., & Pratt, M. (1998). Environmental and policy interventions to promote physical activity. *American Journal of Preventive Medicine, 15,* 379–397.

Sallis, J. F., Hovell, M. F., Hofstetter, C. S., Elder, J. P., Hackley, M., Caspersen, C. J., & Powell, K. E. (1990). Distance between homes and exercise facilities related to frequency of exercise among San Diego residents. *Public Health Reports, 105,* 179–185.

Sallis, J. F., Nader, P. R., Broyles, S. L., Berry, C. C., Elder, J. P., McKenzie, T. L., & Nelson, J. A. (1993). Correlates of physical activity at home in Mexican-American and Anglo-American preschool children. *Healthy Psychology, 12,* 390–398.

Sallis, J. F., & Owen, N. (1999). *Physical activity and behavioural medicine.* Thousand Oaks, CA: Sage.

Skinner, B. F. (1953). *Science and human behavior.* New York: Macmillan.

Stokols, D. (1996). Translating social ecological theory into guidelines for community health promotion. *American Journal of Health Promotion, 10,* 282–298.

Thorndike, E. L. (1898). Some experiments in animal intelligence. *Science, 8,* 818–824.

Chapter 5

Physical Activity Interventions

KEY TERMS

abstinence violation effect
cognitive restructuring
cues-to-action
cues-to-decision
exertion scale
lapse
rating of perceived exertion scale
relapse

In light of the poor rates of participation reviewed in Chapter 2, the reader is left to ponder what to do in order to increase the number of people who begin and maintain a regular regimen of physical activity. In Chapters 3 and 4, we described several theories of exercise and provided some examples of how knowledge of these theories can be used to influence exercise behavior. Theories, thus, may be used as a blueprint for developing interventions. In this chapter, we provide an overview of several theoretically based interventions and also discuss other interventions that are not necessarily tied to any particular theoretical construct but have proven useful for modifying physical activity behavior. Individuals interested in learning more about exercise behavior interventions should consult more in-depth narrative and quantitative reviews of the topic (e.g., Baranowski, Anderson, & Carmack, 1998; Dishman & Buckworth, 1996; Dishman & Sallis, 1994; Epstein, 1998; King, Rejeski, & Buchner, 1998). Nonetheless, the interventions described in this chapter should provide exercise/health professionals with concrete ideas for improving their clients' exercise behavior.

Interventions Based on Exercise Behavior Theories

In the first part of this chapter, we present interventions that can be used to change activity participation by altering specific constructs (i.e., attitude, personal control) discussed earlier in the theory chapters.

CHANGING PEOPLE'S PERCEPTIONS ABOUT EXERCISE: WEIGHING THE PROS AND CONS

In Chapter 3, we highlighted the prominent role played by cognitions in various theories of exercise behavior. One category of cognitions often included in these theories is that related to perceived benefits and barriers to physical activity. As mentioned previously, these judgments are theorized to influence constructs such as self-efficacy and attitude, as well as exercise behavior itself. (See Chapter 4 for a discussion of the importance placed on shifting the balance of "pros and cons" for exercise behavior in the transtheoretical model.) Consequently, intervention strategies that serve to increase perceived benefits (pros) or decrease genuine or perceived barriers (cons) should lead to greater exercise participation.

Altering Perceptions of Perceived Benefits

The unfortunate reality is that, despite the best efforts of science, government, educational institutions, and the media, many people still are not aware of the benefits of exercise or why they should value physical activity. Recognizing and understanding the primary benefits associated with exercise is helpful when attempting to modify exercise behavior. By determining the primary benefits sought out by the client, the exercise leader can tailor the program to meet those outcomes. The exercise leader may also educate the client about certain benefits of physical activity that the client had not previously considered. The result of this interaction should be enhanced levels of commitment, motivation and, ultimately, adherence. The studies reviewed in Chapter 2 provided clear evidence of the benefit of physical activity to morbidity and mortality. However, physical activity offers a number of additional benefits. Although any list is likely to be incomplete, Exhibit 5.1 features a number of the more commonly acknowledged benefits of physical activity. In general, the benefits can be categorized under the following four headings:

1. *Improved physiological health/physical fitness.* As indicated earlier, physical activity provides a number of physiological health benefits, including improvements in cardiovascular endurance (fitness), muscle strength/endurance, bone strength, flexibility, lean weight percentage, and resting heart rate. Indeed, participants often choose to engage in exercise for the purposes of preventing or treating poor physical health (fitness). Relatedly, an increasing number of participants have chosen to embark on an exercise regimen in order to increase sensations of vigor (energy), improve sleep patterns, or reduce levels of pain or fatigue.

exhibit 5.1

Common benefits of physical activity.

Lowers morbidity and mortality rates
Reduces risk of developing diabetes, hypertension, colon cancer, and heart disease
Helps reduce blood pressure in those with hypertension
Reduces feelings of depression, anxiety, and general negative mood
Enhances general positive mood
Improves body image and self-esteem
Helps control weight
Helps build and maintain healthy bones, muscles, and joints
Enhances ability to perform activities of daily living
Provides opportunity to develop social contacts, relationships, and support

2. *Enhanced physical appearance.* Exercise produces body composition changes considered desirable in today's society. For example, long-term engagement in aerobic modes of exercise (e.g., walking, running, biking) is associated with body fat reduction. Similarly, chronic resistance training is associated with increased muscle mass. Taken together, reduced body fat and increased lean muscle tissue produce a "toned" body which is currently portrayed as "ideal" and, more important, attractive for both men and women (see Chapter 13 for a discussion of body image). Enhancing one's physical appearance may also serve to improve elements of psychological health such as self-concept and self-esteem.

3. *Improved psychological/emotional health.* Improvements in psychological and emotional health are no longer considered secondary benefits of physical activity. Indeed, as discussed throughout the remainder of this book, exercise may play a primary role in reducing negative psychological and emotional states (e.g., poor body image and depression). Exercise can also induce positive psychological and emotional responses (e.g., self-esteem and positive mood). Perhaps most important, the impact of exercise on psychological and emotional health may be both acute (immediate, short-term) and chronic (distant, long-term) in nature. In other words, while a single bout of exercise may produce immediate temporary benefits, a regular regimen of physical activity may provide enduring benefits. It should also

be pointed out that, contrary to popular opinion, individuals do exercise for reasons of enjoyment.

4. *Improved social relations.* An often overlooked reason for engaging in physical activity is the social benefits it provides. Exercisers representing all ages and both genders report engaging in physical activity for reasons of social support and camaraderie. For certain segments of society, the social reasons are particularly salient. How often have you seen a small group of elderly individuals walking through a mall early in the morning? Pregnant women also particularly enjoy group exercise as it allows them an opportunity to support each other through emotionally and physically challenging times.

How, then, do we promote these benefits so that the prospective exerciser becomes aware of them? From a mass marketing standpoint (see Marcus, Owen, Forsyth, Cavill, & Fridlinger, 1998, for a review of physical activity interventions using mass media and information technology), we could introduce a number of educational strategies (e.g., pamphlets, videos) in an effort to enhance the public's knowledge of the benefits of physical activity. Such attempts have been made by the government (e.g., President's Council on Physical Fitness and Sport), recognized organizations devoted to the study of fitness (e.g., American College of Sports Medicine), and consumer-based corporations (see Nike's media campaigns). On an individual level, a valuable approach would be to gear messages about the benefits of exercise to the specific values of a particular population. For instance, messages that highlight the benefits of physical activity for maintaining a level of physical fitness that allows people to play with their grandchildren might be particularly meaningful to older adults, whereas messages that highlight the benefits of physical activity for weight loss might be particularly meaningful to obese people. Presumably, messages that target a valued aspect of one's life (e.g., playing with one's grandchildren, losing weight) will have a greater effect than those that target less valued aspects of one's life. The effectiveness of population-geared messages about exercise benefits has been demonstrated in a sample of sedentary healthy adults (Brawley, Rodgers, & Horne, 1990) who reported improvements in attitudes toward exercise after watching a brief videotaped program that conveyed information about the benefits of regular physical activity for healthy adults.

Altering Perceptions of Perceived Barriers

It is a law of physics that for every action, there is an equal and opposite reaction. When it comes to the benefits and barriers of exercise, this law seems often to apply. Thus, while many individuals perceive substantial benefits to adopting a regular exercise regimen, these "pros" are generally balanced (or even overmatched) by the numerous "cons," or barriers to exercise. Simply put, barriers are those things that prevent an individual from exercising. Barriers may be categorized as either *genuine* (e.g., inaccessible facilities for persons who use a wheelchair) or *perceived* (e.g., lack of time).

Genuine barriers. The following are some common genuine barriers to physical activity:

1. *Convenience/availability.* Inaccessible transportation, lack of facilities (or inconvenient location), and lack of equipment are a few of the more popular reasons why people fail to engage in regular physical activity. For example, the elderly often face the barrier of inaccessible transportation when attempting to adopt exercise into their lifestyles. However, although these factors clearly limit activity mode and, perhaps, the setting in which the activity takes place, a study of Southern California residents indicated that both sedentary and active people have an equivalent number of exercise facilities within a two- to five-kilometer radius of their homes (Sallis, Hovell, Hofstetter, Elder, Hackley, et al., 1990). Interestingly, this same study found that *perceived* convenience of exercise facilities was completely unrelated to the *actual* proximity of these facilities. Thus, it appears that convenience and availability of facilities are often "excuses" for failing to be physically active (see review by Brawley, Martin, & Gyurcsik, 1998). To overcome this barrier, fitness/health professionals must work with the prospective exerciser to identify a time and location for regular exercise. Options should also be discussed in relation to equipment and transportation needs.

2. *Environmental/ecological factors.* Aspects of geographical location, climate, and neighborhood may all serve as genuine barriers to exercise. For example, rain and snowfall, as well as extreme temperatures, may preclude some individuals from engaging in certain outdoor activities. Individuals residing in Colorado might not find exercise enjoyable because of the high altitude and its effect on the respiratory system. Finally, an individual who would enjoy running through his neighborhood may not want to do so for safety reasons (e.g., poor lighting, crime). Thus, exercising indoors and/or with others may aid in overcoming these barriers.

3. *Physical limitations.* Physical limitations such as injury, disease, and fatigue are real and significant causes of inactivity. Clearly, exer-

cise should be avoided in certain stages or phases of disease or when a body part required for activity is injured. On the other hand, exercise has become a prominent treatment strategy for various diseases (e.g., cancer, HIV/AIDS, diabetes, arthritis, obesity) as well as for combating fatigue and pain. Additionally, arm ergometers may be used by individuals who do not have use of their legs.

Perceived barriers. As mentioned earlier, people often fail to exercise because of perceived barriers—things that we think are insurmountable obstacles to exercise. In contrast to many genuine barriers, perceived barriers may be overcome through an effective intervention. Two of the most frequently cited perceived barriers to exercise and strategies for overcoming them are presented below.

1. *Lack of time.* In most cases, if you ask nonexercisers why they do not engage in physical activity, they will tell you that they do not have time to do so. We can certainly all appreciate such sentiment. However, a survey of nearly 20,000 Canadians (Shaw, Bonen, & McCabe, 1991) found that people who cited lack of time as a barrier to physical activity actually performed more hours of physical activity per week than did those who did not consider lack of time to be a barrier! This suggests that regular exercisers are employing time-management strategies that nonexercisers are not and, further, that they have made exercise a priority in their lives. The following strategies have proven useful in combating the "no time for exercise" epidemic:

    - *Scheduling physical activity into your daily planner and exercising at the same time each day.* These behaviors help to establish exercise as part of your routine, which can promote adherence by reducing the complexity of planning each exercise session. If you have already planned when, where, and how you are going to exercise, you are more likely to follow through with your exercise intentions than if you must make each of these decisions every time you contemplate exercise (cf. Maddux, 1993). Scheduling exercise into your daily agenda will also help prevent you from making other commitments during times when you would like to exercise.
    - *Planning ahead for potential time-crunches* (e.g., final exams, seasonal work loads, holidays) and learning how to deal with them in the future in order to preserve time for physical activity. These types of stressful situations frequently cause people to lapse back into their previously sedentary ways. As you will see later in this chapter, relapse prevention training is one technique

that has been documented to be effective for preventing people from backsliding.

- *Making exercise a priority rather than a luxury.* This may be done by formulating a "contract" that specifically describes the amount of exercise a person will commit to and may also include the promise of positive reinforcement for engaging in the behavior (see Exhibit 5.2). The contract imparts a feeling of commitment to exercise (importance) and, further, serves as a reminder and motivator to exercise. The effects of exercise contracts have been demonstrated in a study of patients in a cardiac rehabilitation exercise program (Oldridge & Jones, 1983). Patients were randomly assigned to either an experimental (contract) or control (no-contract) condition. At the end of the six-month study period, participants who signed the contract had attended more exercise sessions than had those in the control condition. In addition, contract participants attended more sessions than did those who were asked to sign a contract but refused to do so (see Exhibit 5.3).

Sample exercise contract. exhibit 5.2

EXERCISE CONTRACT

Contract start date: 1/3/03 Award date: 6/1/03

In order to obtain my goal of improving my cardiovascular endurance (increase $\dot{V}O_2$max by 10%) and lose weight (10 pounds), I will

(a) walk one mile through my neighborhood daily after dinner and

(b) ride the stationary bike three times per week (30 mins, 70% heart rate).

As a reward for accomplishing this goal by the award date shown above, I will be entitled to a shopping spree to purchase all-new exercise attire and equipment (e.g., winter outdoor exercise wear, electronic pedometer, stationary bicycle for home).

Signed Kevin Kelly Date 1/2/03

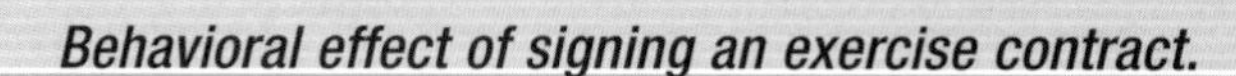

exhibit 5.3 *Behavioral effect of signing an exercise contract.*

Percentage of exercise classes attended over a six-month period by cardiac rehabilitation patients who signed an exercise contract (Experimental—signed), refused to sign an exercise contract (Experimental—refused to sign), and were not asked to sign a contract (Control).

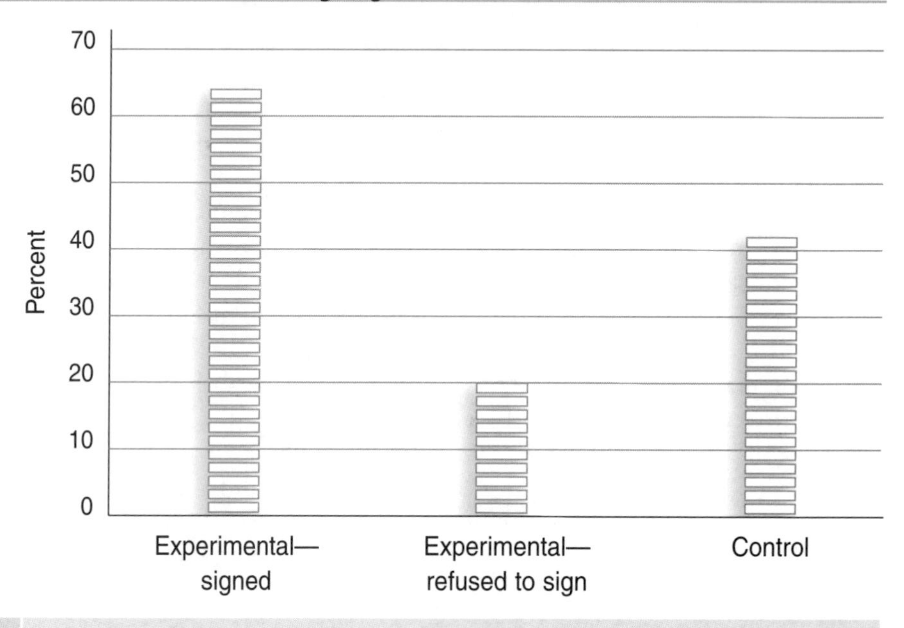

Source: Oldridge & Jones (1983).

2. *Boredom/lack of enjoyment.* A prominent barrier for many people is the mentality that "physical activity" means running or aerobics—highly vigorous activities that they find unappealing. This barrier may be best overcome by exposing people to other forms of leisure activity, such as dancing, hiking, gardening, or swimming. The following techniques may also be considered:

- *Participating in a variety of enjoyable modes of activity.* As we have just identified "boredom" as a prominent barrier of exercise, it would be logical to suggest that exercise/health professionals engage their clients in a variety of activities. Exhibit 5.4 lists the most popular modes of physical activity in Canada. Clearly, one may accomplish physical activity goals by utilizing a variety of different activities. Although this principle of "cross-training" has been promoted for the physiological training benefits it provides, its most significant consequences may be the reduction in exercise monotony and corresponding increase in adherence. Indeed, it has been shown that people are less likely to quit exercising, and more likely to report greater enjoyment of their exercise sessions, when

exhibit 5.4

Popular modes of physical activity in Canada.

(Activities are listed in order of popularity.)

Walking	Skating	Cross-country skiing
Gardening/yardwork	Baseball/softball	Ice hockey
Swimming	Exercise class/aerobics	Yoga/tai-chi
Social dancing	Basketball	Football
Bicycling	Alpine skiing	Ballet/modern dance
Weight training	Volleyball	Snowboarding
Bowling	Badminton	Squash
Golf	Soccer	Racquetball
Jogging/running	Tennis	

they participate in a program that permits a variety of exercise modes rather than a program that prescribes just a single mode of exercise (Glaros & Janelle, 2001).

- *Exercising to music.* Many novice and experienced exercisers do not consider exercise enjoyable and, thus, are best served by occupying their minds with something other than the exercise stimuli. Listening to music (and, to a lesser extent, watching television) has become a popular form of exercise distractor, and it appears that qualities such as the type, tempo, and volume of music may lead to variations in physical, psychological, and behavioral responses during exercise (Karageorghis & Terry, 1997). For example, performing exercise while watching an exercise video has been shown to influence both affective and physiological responses to the exercise experience, and may motivate exercisers to push themselves harder than they would without the distraction (Robergs, Bereket, & Knight, 1998).

- *Exercising with a group.* As detailed in Chapter 12, exercise performed among a group of supportive, enthusiastic individuals can increase exercise enjoyment and bolster one's future intentions to exercise (Fox, Rejeski, & Gauvin, 2000). Furthermore, the presence of others can help to reduce boredom by providing a distraction from exercise. Group activity is also an excellent opportunity to form new friendships, which can be an important incentive and source of enjoyment for some exercisers (Poole, 2001). Finally, adherence is generally greater when two or more participants exercise together, as exercise buddies and exercise groups can provide social support and help one another through periods when their exercise motivation may be waning.

- *Exercising with an enthusiastic leader.* Students tend to be more motivated and put forth greater effort in class when they are led by an enthusiastic instructor. The same principle applies in the exercise setting. Fitness leaders are often cited as the single most important determinant of an exerciser's continued participation in an exercise program (Franklin, 1988). An enthusiastic and supportive exercise leader has been shown to have significant positive effects on exercisers' enjoyment of an exercise class, their affective responses to the class, and their future intentions to exercise (Fox et al., 2000). The importance of the fitness leader is discussed in further detail in Chapter 12.

INCREASING CONFIDENCE AND CONTROL IN THE EXERCISE SETTING

Another factor repeatedly highlighted in social cognitive theories and research in the field of exercise psychology is the notion of personal control or mastery regarding one's physical activity behavior (e.g., self-efficacy in SCT, perceived behavioral control in TPB). Perceived control is an important variable to consider, because people who perceive that they have control over their physical activity behavior are more likely to be physically active than are those who do not believe that they have control over their behavior. The mechanism behind this relationship is probably the enhanced commitment and motivation generated by perceptions of control. A heightened sense of personal control will also serve gradually to reduce exercisers' dependency on others to motivate their behavior, thus allowing the individual to assume the responsibility for engaging in physical activity. Most important, as previously mentioned, people are considerably more likely to exercise if they believe that they can. The following techniques are suggested to enhance perceptions of personal control and mastery (self-efficacy):

Goal-Setting

As described in Chapter 3, master experiences can greatly enhance self-efficacy. In other words, exercisers' self-efficacy will typically increase as they accumulate successful exercise experiences (i.e., they see themselves making progress). However, in order to produce these desirable outcomes, exercisers must know what constitutes a successful exercise experience, and they must know the level at which they started in order to recognize progress over time. One popular and proven method for meeting these requirements is goal-setting. In regard to exercise, goal-setting involves the process of assessing one's current level of fitness/performance, creating a specific, measurable, realistic, and challenging goal, and most important, detailing the actions to be taken in order to achieve the goal. An example of a goal-setting sheet is provided in Exhibit 5.5.

Sample goal-setting sheet. exhibit 5.5

GOAL-SETTING SHEET

Contract set date: 1/2/03 Target date: 6/1/03

Goal defined: To improve my cardiovascular endurance ($\dot{V}O_2$ max) by 10% and lose weight (10 pounds)

Strategies to achieve goals: (a) walk neighborhood daily after dinner (1 mi.) (b) ride stationary bike three times per week (30 mins, 70% max heart rate)

Daily progress notes: 1/4/03 - walked after dinner, no bike today, weighed myself at 7:00 a.m. - no change from 2 days ago
1/6/03 - walked after dinner yesterday and today, biked during lunch hour but only made it 20 mins, heart rate around 80% max, lost a pound

Although a helpful strategy for even the most advanced exerciser, goal-setting is particularly important during the early adoption stage of exercise. This is because, while the "costs" associated with exercise are often experienced immediately or soon after commencement of a physical activity regimen (e.g., soreness, fatigue, negative affect), many of the desired benefits (e.g., enhanced fitness and appearance) typically are not realized until weeks or even months later. Therefore, it is suggested that exercisers also divide their long-term goals into short-term (days) and intermediate (weeks) checkpoints that can be met along the way to attaining their ultimate objectives. This will maintain or increase commitment and motivation until the final goal is met. For example, one of the goals in Exhibit 5.5 is a loss of 10 pounds in five months. A short-term goal might be to lose one pound after two weeks and an intermediate goal might be to lose five pounds in two months. Additionally, the fitness professional should strive to promote additional benefits that may be realized in a shorter time frame (e.g., improvements in mood, sleeping patterns, etc.) and to set goals for these as well.

Activity Logs

As you might expect, the use of activity logs (see Exhibit 5.6) goes hand in hand with goal-setting. These logs are essential for self-monitoring one's exercise behavior and charting improvements in fitness over time. A typical activity log would contain information about each exercise session such as the amount of time spent on a particular activity (e.g., strength training, jogging), one's level of performance on that activity (e.g., amount of weight lifted, distance run), and ratings of affect or perceived exertion (see discussion below) following the workout. When completed regularly, these become invaluable sources of self-efficacy information as the exerciser can refer to the log to measure progress. In a test of the effects of activity logs, adults who were asked to monitor all of their exercise activities over an 18-week period showed significantly greater improvements in cardiovascular fitness, and reported a significantly higher frequency of exercise per week, than did adults who did not log their physical activity (Noland, 1989).

Negotiated Prescriptions

As mentioned earlier, people are more likely to adhere to their health regimens if they are given the opportunity to participate in the decision-making process (Meichenbaum & Turk, 1987). A survey of more than 400 patients in a medical clinic revealed that patients felt they would be more willing to comply with a doctor's recommendation to

Sample seven-day activity log. **exhibit 5.6**

DATE	MODE	DISTANCE	TIME	MY HEART RATE	MY RPE
7/19	Jog	2.0 mi.	16:20	156	14
7/20	Jog	2.0 mi.	15:47	154	14
	Swim	15 lengths	7:19	161	15
7/21	Rest				
7/22	Jog	2.5 mi.	21:08	165	17
7/23	Jog	2.0 mi.	16:53	159	15
	Swim	20 lengths	10:22	164	17
7/24	Rest				
7/25	Jog	3.0 mi.	26:59	164	16

exercise if the doctor allowed them to negotiate the exercise prescription (Harsha, Saywell, Thygerson, & Panozzo, 1996). These findings suggest that allowing people to negotiate their exercise prescription could increase their level of adherence. For instance, an individual who is told to exercise 120 minutes per week could be given the opportunity to negotiate how the prescription is carried out (i.e., as either three 40-minute bouts per week or as five 25-minute bouts per week). Although the mechanism is not certain, it is likely that individuals experience enhanced personal control over, and are more motivated and committed to, their exercise routine under active (self-defined) versus passive (leader-defined) prescriptions.

Exercise Monitoring

For many novice exercisers, high-intensity physical activity should be avoided. If nothing ensures continued behavior like success, then nothing ensures exercise dropout like the immediate experiences of muscle

exhibit 5.7

Beginning with an easy level of exercise helps reduce muscle soreness, fatigue, and injury, and allows the exerciser to feel a sense of accomplishment.

soreness, fatigue, and injury, all of which may be avoided by starting the exerciser out at a relatively low intensity. Beginning easy will not only help to reduce or eliminate these immediate costs, but will also allow exercisers to feel a sense of accomplishment. Both consequences should increase the likelihood that participants will maintain their exercise routines. Similarly, instructing exercisers on the proper method of determining their heart and respiration rates further promotes a sense of control over their exercise behavior and may help to prevent overexertion and injury.

In addition to these objective measures, participants should also be instructed on the proper use of subjective measures of intensity such as the **rating of perceived exertion scale** (RPE; Borg, 1998). This scale ranges from 6 to 20; each value multiplied by 10 would approximate one's heart rate at that particular point in time during or immediately following the exercise bout. For example, if we ask an individual to indicate the value, according to the RPE scale, that she feels best describes her current exercise exertion level (i.e., how hard she feels she is working), and she reports it to be 14, we would theorize that she is exercising at approximately 140 beats per minute ($14 \times 10 = 140$). Although the ability of the RPE scale accurately to reflect heart rate in this manner has been questioned, the scale is, nonetheless, a valid and reliable means of determining a person's subjective rating of exertion level. Furthermore, after training clients on the proper use of the scale, we can utilize an RPE value or range of values to designate the intensity at which a client or group of clients should be active. [For correct usage of the Borg scale the user must go to the instruction and administration given by Borg. See Borg, G. (1998). *Borg's Perceived Exertion and Pain Scales,* Champaign, IL: Human Kinetics.]

rating of perceived exertion scale ■

AN INTERVENTION MODEL APPROACH TO IMPROVING EXERCISE BEHAVIOR

The relapse prevention model (RPM; Marlatt & George, 1984) is based on the theories and models described in Chapters 3 and 4. In Chapter

4, we discussed the importance of preventing relapses in regular physical activity in conjunction with the transtheoretical model. **Relapse** describes an individual's failure to resume regular exercise following a **lapse** in activity. Lapses themselves appear to be quite common, even among regular exercisers. In one study (Sallis, Hovell, Hofstetter, Elder, Faucher, et al., 1990), 1,800 Southern California residents were asked to report the number of times over the course of their lives that they had exercised vigorously for at least six months prior to becoming inactive for at least three months. Results indicated that approximately 40 percent of respondents had relapsed on at least one occasion.

■ relapse

■ lapse

Although the periodical lapse is almost expected, lapses can become a cause of concern when they lead to relapse back to a previously sedentary lifestyle. When a single lapse leads an individual to believe that all hope of behavior change is lost (the "all or nothing" approach) and, subsequently, to give up trying to change the behavior, the result is a full relapse, and the entire process is termed the **abstinence violation effect.** Because of the difficulty in maintaining behavior change such as exercise, there is a need to better understand the factors that cause people to relapse, as well as the factors that may prevent relapse. It was this need that led to the development of the RPM. Specifically, this model was designed to teach individuals who are attempting to change their behavior how to anticipate and cope with the issue of relapse. The RPM was initially derived from observations of relapse among people suffering from a variety of substance addictions (e.g., alcohol, cigarettes, drugs).

■ abstinence violation effect

At the core of the model is the notion that relapse is triggered by high-risk situations—those instances that challenge an individual's ability to maintain his or her behavioral regimen (see Exhibit 5.8). The individual's coping response to the high-risk situation (i.e., how he or she psychologically/emotionally responds to the situation) dictates the flow of the model. Specifically, a negative coping response would lead to decreases in exercise self-efficacy and the anticipation of positive consequences of inactivity (e.g., the feeling of relief from both not having to exercise and the fact that the activity will cease to encroach on the individual's time). The initial lapse then leads to the abstinence violation effect, a negative emotional response (e.g., guilt), and self-blame. The combination of these, in turn, leads to an increased probability of relapse. When the individual demonstrates a positive coping response, exercise self-efficacy is increased and the probability of relapse is reduced.

Based on the components of the model, the following relapse prevention strategies may be readily applied to the exercise setting (Knapp, 1988; Marlatt & Gordon, 1985):

1. *Identify high-risk situations that might prompt a relapse.* For example, a beginning exerciser might be encouraged to keep a diary of her exercise behavior, noting thoughts, feelings, and situations that tempt her to skip a workout or that actually prevent her from working out. High-risk thoughts might include worries about not having enough time to exercise, or thoughts about substituting alternative, sedentary activities that might be more appealing than exercise (e.g., going to a movie with

exhibit 5.8 ***The relapse prevention model in the exercise domain.***

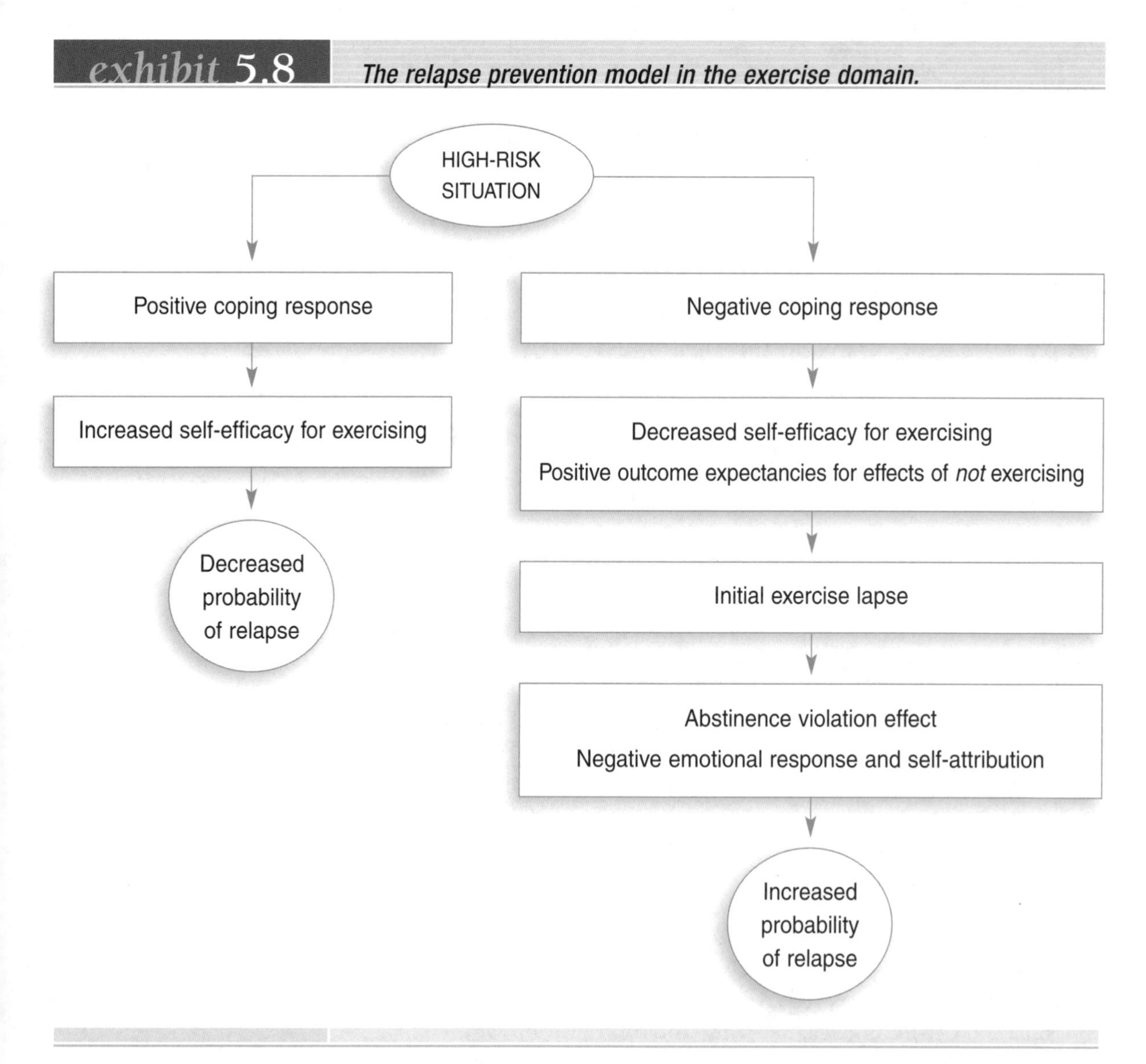

Source: Marlatt & George (1984).

friends). High-risk feelings include the sense that one is too tired to exercise or the experience of boredom with one's exercise routine. Situations that might be considered high-risk for a relapse include being on vacation and away from one's normal exercise location, and experiencing a spell of bad weather. By identifying high-risk situations, the exerciser can then focus on trying to avoid those situations and developing strategies to deal with them as they arise, so that they do not prevent exercise in the future.

2. *Plan for lapses.* It is not always possible to overcome high-risk situations, and it is inevitable that sometimes these situations will cause a lapse in exercise. However, people can be trained to cope with lapses *before* they occur, so as to increase their self-efficacy for returning to exercise after the lapse (thereby preventing a complete relapse). For example, a novice exerciser might plan ahead for a lapse by identifying an "exercise buddy" who can be called after a lapse and who will help the exerciser to "get back on track" by taking her for a walk, bike ride, etc.

3. *Minimize the abstinence violation effect.* Exercisers can be given strategies to cope with the despair they experience when they violate their intention to exercise regularly. One strategy involves **cognitive restructuring** (changing how one thinks about a lapse). For example, rather than considering a lapse to be a catastrophe, exercisers should be taught to think of lapses as a normal and inevitable part of the exercise process, and something that they can learn from and plan to deal with in the future. Likewise, "all or nothing" thinkers might be encouraged to be more flexible with their exercise goals. For instance, if the exerciser skips an exercise session, he could allow himself to "make up" the missed session by adding a day the following week or by adding time to the next session.

■ cognitive restructuring

Practical Interventions: Cueing it Up

The first part of the chapter was devoted to a discussion of intervention techniques based on theories reviewed in Chapters 3 and 4. However, some behavioral modification strategies known to influence exercise behavior do not arise from a theoretical foundation. One such strategy involves the use of cues-to-action and cues-to-decision. **Cues-to-action** are stimuli in the environment (e.g., posters, television advertisements) or within the person (e.g., symptoms, memories) that prompt the performance of exercise (see Exhibit 5.9). Placing your running shoes by the front door to ensure that you will see them upon arriving home later in the day would be a cue-to-action (i.e., the shoes serve as a physical prompt to exercise). **Cues-to-decision** are stimuli that initiate a process

■ cues-to-action

■ cues-to-decision

exhibit 5.9 *Examples of desired exercise cues and competing cues.*

EXERCISE CUES	COMPETING CUES
Purchase home exercise equipment	TV
Lay out workout clothes on bed	Telephone
Indicate workout in daily scheduling device	Work (home, office)
Join fitness facility conveniently located along daily commute	Family*

**Note:* This cue is listed simply as an example of a prominent competing cue. We suggest that you attempt to decrease the other competing cues listed.

of deciding whether or not to perform the behavior. Although they do not elicit the behavior itself, they do elicit the social cognitive factors involved in deciding and intending to perform the behavior.

In a classic study, a cue-to-decision was shown significantly to increase stair use in public places (Brownell, Stunkard, & Albaum, 1980). For 15 days, researchers placed a cue-to-decision at the point where people had to decide whether to take the stairs or the escalator. The cue consisted of a poster that showed a cartoon healthy heart running up the stairs, an unhealthy heart riding an escalator, and the statement: "Your heart needs exercise, here's your chance." While the cue was posted, the proportion of people who took the stairs (instead of the escalator) increased from 11.6 percent to 18.3 percent. One month after the poster was removed, 15.6 percent of people were still taking the stairs, but three months after the poster was removed, stair use had returned to baseline levels (11.9 percent). Thus, the long-term effectiveness of cues-to-decision warrants further empirical investigation.

Cues to physical activity should be incorporated into one's life, and cues that distract the individual from the exercise routine should be removed. Whether at home or at work/school, we are constantly bombarded by cues enticing us to engage in certain behaviors, oftentimes at the expense of exercise behavior (see Exhibit 5.9). Thus, it is imperative that we work to reduce or eliminate the myriad of cues we experience for competing behaviors. Simply bringing work home from the office can serve as a competing cue that forces the individual to weigh the importance of completing the work versus the importance of engaging in physical activity. In this instance, the individual would benefit most from either working exercise into his or her day before returning home or, alternatively, leaving work at the office. Purchasing a piece of exercise equipment for the home that allows you to work while being physically active (e.g., recumbent stationary bicycle) may prove to be an effective compromise. Similarly, to combat competing cues such as television viewing and intruding phone calls, one might employ strategies such as hiding the television remote control or "screening" phone calls. As you might expect, the lifestyle of sedentary individuals is particularly high-risk in that they tend to perceive few natural cues for exercise behavior and many cues for competing behaviors.

Conclusion

The epidemic of inactivity is well documented, and it is becoming clear that any efforts to reverse this trend must incorporate principles from the fields of behavioral medicine, health psychology, and most notably, exercise psychology. Indeed, the strength of the exercise psychology field is the vast potential for successful intervention that it offers. To this end, this chapter was devoted to an analysis of various intervention strategies aimed at modifying perceptions about physical activity, perceptions of confidence and control in the exercise setting, and exercise behavior.

Although practical intervention techniques are useful, we submit that intervention strategies based on a sound theoretical framework offer the greatest potential for altering physical activity behavior. Accordingly, a model intervention approach (relapse prevention model) was advanced as one example of a comprehensive strategy aimed at enhancing exercise adherence. For the exercise/health professional, the importance of effectively utilizing these techniques to improve adherence can be summarized in one simple statement: It doesn't matter what you know, or how capable you are of helping your clients meet their fitness objectives, if you cannot ensure their continued attendance.

What Do You Know?

1. Describe the four categories of physical activity benefits.
2. What are three genuine barriers to physical activity?
3. What are two perceived barriers to physical activity?
4. Discuss four intervention strategies for increasing confidence in, and control over, one's physical activity behavior.
5. What are cues-to-action and cues-to-decision? Give examples of each.

6. What is the abstinence violation effect?
7. Discuss three intervention strategies based on the concept of relapse prevention.
8. Provide examples of how specific strategies presented in this chapter can be used to alter one or more of the theoretical constructs reviewed in Chapters 3 and 4.

Learning Activities

1. Test an intervention strategy on yourself to modify some aspect of your exercise behavior.
2. Pretend you are the owner of a fitness facility. The employees who work with the clients (and you too for that matter!) will make money as long as the clients keep returning. What intervention strategies will you require your employees to learn and incorporate into their training sessions with clients to ensure high rates of adherence?
3. Design your own unique activity log and goal-setting sheet. Be as creative as possible and be sure to incorporate a motivational aspect into each.

References

Baranowski, T., Anderson, C., & Carmack, C. (1998). Mediating variable framework in physical activity interventions: How are we doing? How might we do better? *American Journal of Preventive Medicine, 15,* 266–297.

Borg, G. (1998). *Borg's perceived exertion and pain scales.* Champaign, IL: Human Kinetics.

Brawley, L. R., Martin, K. A., & Gyurcsik, N. C. (1998). Conceptualizing and measuring perceived barriers to exercise. In J. Duda (Ed.), *Advances in sport and exercise psychology measurement* (pp. 312–334). Morgantown, WV: Fitness Information Technology.

Brawley, L. R., Rodgers, W. M., & Horne, T. E. (1990). Evaluating fitness promotion messages: A social cognition approach. *Report to the Ontario Ministry of Tourism and Recreation.*

Brownell, K. D., Stunkard, A. J., & Albaum, J. M. (1980). Evaluation and modification of exercise patterns in the natural environment. *American Journal of Psychiatry, 137,* 1540–1545.

Dishman, R. K., & Buckworth, J. (1996). Increasing physical activity: A quantitative synthesis. *Medicine and Science in Sports and Exercise, 28,* 706–719.

Dishman, R. K., & Sallis, J. F. (1994). Determinants and interventions for physical activity and exercise. In C. Bouchard, R. J. Shepard, & T. Stephens (Eds.), *Physical activity, fitness, and health: International proceedings and consensus statement* (pp. 214–238). Champaign, IL: Human Kinetics.

Epstein, L. H. (1998). Integrating theoretical approaches to promote physical activity.

American Journal of Preventive Medicine, 15, 257–265.

Fox, L. D., Rejeski, W. J., & Gauvin, L. (2000). Effects of leadership style and group dynamics on enjoyment of physical activity. *American Journal of Health Promotion, 14,* 277–283.

Franklin, B. A. (1988). Program factors that influence exercise adherence: Practical adherence skills for the clinical staff. In R. K. Dishman (Ed.), *Exercise adherence: Its impact on public health* (pp. 237–258). Champaign, IL: Human Kinetics.

Glaros, N. M., & Janelle, C. M. (2001). Varying the mode of cardiovascular exercise to increase adherence. *Journal of Sport Behavior, 24,* 42–62.

Harsha, D. M., Saywell, R. M., Thygerson, S., & Panozzo, J. (1996). Physician factors affecting patient willingness to comply with exercise recommendations. *Clinical Journal of Sports Medicine, 6,* 112–118.

Karageorghis, C. I., & Terry, P. C. (1997). The psychophysical effects of music in sport and exercise: A review. *Journal of Sport Behavior, 20,* 54–68.

King, A. C., Rejeski, W. J., & Buchner, D. M. (1998). Physical activity interventions targeting older adults: A critical review and recommendations. *American Journal of Preventive Medicine, 15,* 316–333.

Knapp, D. N. (1988). Behavioral management techniques and exercise promotion. In R. K. Dishman (Ed.), *Exercise adherence: Its impact on public health* (pp. 203–235). Champaign, IL: Human Kinetics.

Maddux, J. E. (1993). Social cognitive models of health and exercise behaviour: An introduction and review of conceptual issues. *Journal of Applied Sport Psychology, 5,* 116–140.

Marcus, B. H., Owen, N., Forsyth, L. H., Cavill, N. A., & Fridlinger, F. (1998). Physical activity interventions using mass media, print media, and information technology. *American Journal of Preventive Medicine, 15,* 362–378.

Marlatt, G. A., & George, W. H. (1984). Relapse prevention: Introduction and overview of the model. *British Journal of Addiction, 79,* 261–273.

Marlatt, G. A., & Gordon, J. R. (1985). *Relapse prevention: Maintenance strategies in the treatment of addictive behaviors.* New York: Guilford Press.

Meichenbaum, D., & Turk, D. C. (1987). *Facilitating treatment adherence: A practitioner's guidebook.* New York: Plenum Press.

Noland, M. P. (1989). The effects of self-monitoring and reinforcement on exercise adherence. *Research Quarterly for Exercise and Sport, 60,* 216–224.

Oldridge, N. B., & Jones, N. L. (1983). Improving patient compliance in cardiac exercise rehabilitation: Effects of written agreement and self-monitoring. *Journal of Cardiac Rehabilitation, 3,* 257–262.

Poole, M. (2001). Fit for life: Older women's commitment to exercise. *Journal of Aging and Physical Activity, 9,* 300–312.

Robergs, R. A., Bereket, S., & Knight, M. A. (1998). Video-assisted cycling alters perception of effort and increases self-selected exercise intensity. *Perceptual and Motor Skills, 86,* 915–927.

Sallis, J. F., Hovell, M. F., Hofstetter, C. S., Elder, J. P., Faucher, P., Spry, V. M., Barrington, E., & Hackley, M. (1990). Lifetime history of relapse from exercise. *Addictive Behaviours, 15,* 573–579.

Sallis, J. F., Hovell, M. F., Hofstetter, C. S., Elder, J. P., Hackley, M., Caspersen, C. J., & Powell, K. E. (1990). Distance between homes and exercise facilities related to frequency of exercise among San Diego residents. *Public Health Reports, 105,* 179–185.

Shaw, S. M., Bonen, A., & McCabe, J. F. (1991). Do more constraints mean less leisure? Examining the relationship between constraints and participation. *Journal of Leisure Research, 21,* 286–300.

Part II

Psychosocial Influences and Consequences of Exercise

Chapter 6

Personality and Exercise

KEY TERMS

agreeableness
androgynous
autonomic nervous system
cerebrotonia
conscientiousness
dispositional
ectomorph
endomorph
expressive personality
extraversion–introversion
extraverts
hardiness
instrumental personality
interactionist perspective
introverts
learning
mesomorph
limbic system
neuroticism
neuroticism–stability
openness to experience
personality
personality core
psycho-biological model
psychoticism–superego
role-related behaviors
self-motivation
somatotonic
type A behavior pattern
typical responses
visceratonia

Jenny is a rather tense person. She always seems to be worrying about something and becomes upset fairly easily. She has a tendency to be suspicious of things and is also timid and apprehensive. Her friend Sarah, who has taken some courses in exercise psychology, suggests to Jenny that she might try beginning a regular exercise program. Sarah has learned that even something as relatively simple as going for a walk can increase energy and, more important for Jenny, reduce feelings of tension and promote relaxation. Sarah is also smart enough to realize that because of Jenny's timid approach to things, it will be worthwhile for her to have a supervised exercise routine, at least until she becomes comfortable with the process. After about six weeks of exercising three to four days per week, Sarah notices that Jenny seems to be more relaxed and that she doesn't get as agitated over the "little things" as she did before she began her exercise program.

As discussed in Chapter 1, exercise psychology has enjoyed a tremendous surge of interest since the 1980s, although the importance of the relationship between bodily movement and the mind has been "known" for centuries. The ancient Greeks espoused exercise as an important component of both physical and mental health. This philosophy carried over into the sixteenth century, when Mendez wrote the *Book of Bodily Exercise,* which discussed the effects of exercise on the mind (Mendez, 1553/1960). Noted psychologist and philosopher William James (1899) spoke of the importance of physical activity when he addressed the American Association for the Advancement of Physical Education, saying,

> Everyone knows the effect of physical exercise on the mood: how much more cheerful and courageous one feels when the body has been

> toned up, than when it is 'run down.' . . . Those feelings are sometimes of worry, breathlessness, anxiety, tension; sometimes of peace and repose. It is certain that physical exercise will tend to train the body toward the latter feelings. The latter feelings are certainly an essential ingredient in all perfect human character.

Although our ancestors recognized the intimate link between body and mind, it wasn't until the late 1960s to early 1970s that any systematic investigation of issues relevant to the psychology of exercise began to emerge. Since its "revival" at that time, exercise psychology has had two primary research objectives that relate to exercise and personality:

1. Determination of the psychological *antecedents* of participation in physical activity
2. Determination of the psychological *consequences* of participation in physical activity.

Examples of the first objective would include research that attempts to determine what personality (or individual difference) factors might lead someone to participate in physical activity. The second objective would be represented by research that examines how an exercise-training program might influence individual difference factors—for example, whether regular exercise might lead one to become less emotional or more emotionally stable.

Defining Personality

Historically, the study of personality has been one of the most popular topics in exercise psychology. In keeping with the aforementioned primary objectives, this study has most often involved attempts at determining whether certain personality attributes are important *antecedents* to physical activity/exercise participation and whether certain personality attributes are developed as the *consequence* of such participation.

personality ■

Personality can be defined as the underlying, relatively stable, psychological structures and processes that organize human experience and shape a person's actions and reactions to the environment. More simply, personality is the individual's unique, but consistent, psychological makeup. Personality is consistent in that it is relatively stable over time and across situations. Hollander (1967) described the structure of personality as being composed of:

personality core ■

1. The **personality core,** which is developed from early environmental interactions and includes things like our perceptions of the

external world, perceptions of self, basic attitudes, values, interests, and motives, our self-concept. The core is a reflection of who we are.

2. **Typical responses,** which characterize our fairly predictable behaviors and ways of reacting to our environment. For example, an outgoing person might be very engaging, introducing himself to people when sitting in a classroom prior to the beginning of a class.

■ typical responses

3. **Role-related behaviors,** which are more variable, daily behaviors influenced by the particular context in which we find ourselves. For example, the same outgoing, engaging person may be quiet and attentive during the class, likely becoming involved in class discussions or giving input when it is asked for by the instructor, but otherwise fulfilling the role of the "typical" student.

■ role-related behaviors

The core is least amenable to change; role-related behaviors are most easily changed.

Approaches to the Study of Personality

Personality has been studied from a variety of perspectives. The two most prominent approaches have been the **learning** and **dispositional** approaches, with the emphasis of the latter being on the person while the emphasis of the former has been on the environment. Both approaches essentially endorse what has been termed an **interactionist perspective** to studying personality (see box on the following page). Such a perspective essentially views both the individual and the situation in which he finds himself (i.e., the *interaction* of the person with the environment) as important in determining behavior. Learning approaches include conditioning or behaviorist theories and social learning theories (see Chapters 3 and 4). Dispositional approaches include biological theories and the trait theories. Of primary importance for the field of exercise psychology are the dispositional/biological approaches.

■ learning
■ dispositional

■ interactionist perspective

BIOLOGICAL THEORIES

Early biological theories of personality related personality to various biological processes. The ancient Greeks focused on body "humors" or fluids. They posited that a preponderance of one of the four basic body fluids (humors) was manifested in discernible personalities. A prepon-

The Person–Situation Debate

The interactionist perspective arose from the debate in the study of personality about whether it was most effective to place the primary focus on the person or on the environment. This was termed the *person–situation debate* and dates to the late 1960s. The person perspective, usually referred to as the *trait approach,* places primary emphasis on the notion that personality is derived from stable, enduring attributes of the individual that lead to consistent responses over time and across situations. The *situation approach,* on the other hand, emphasizes that behavior is best explained by examining the environment and the individual's reaction to that environment. Extreme adherents of either approach basically give no credence to the other position. Over time, a more moderate position, one that considers both the person and the situation and, more important, the interaction between them, has been shown to offer the most utility for understanding the influence of personality on behavior.

derance of blood predisposed one to be "sanguine" or cheerful and optimistic; yellow bile was related to a "choleric" or irritable disposition; black bile predisposed one to be "melancholic" or sad and depressed; and phlegm was thought to make one "phlegmatic" or calm and indifferent. This approach clearly reflects the thinking at that time that mind and body were closely related to one another.

A much more recent biological theory of personality, developed by Sheldon (1942), is referred to as constitutional theory. According to Sheldon, individuals possess certain body types, or somatotypes. These somatotypes are largely genetically determined, and they predispose the individual toward behavioral consistency. Sheldon's formulation defines three major somatotypes (see Exhibit 6.1). The **ectomorph** has a body type that is characterized by linearity, tallness, and leanness. Sheldon proposed that such a body type was associated with what he referred to as **cerebrotonia.** Individuals possessing such a body type were characterized, Sheldon suggested, by tense, introverted, socially restrained, inhibited personalities. The **endomorph** body type is characterized by plumpness, fatness, and roundness and was purported to be linked with the **visceratonia** personality. This type of individual was characterized by affection, sociability, relaxation, and joviality. Finally, the **mesomorph** is characterized by the classic inverted triangle—wide muscular shoulders and narrower hips. Sheldon referred to this as the classic athletic body type. These individuals have **somatotonic** personalities that predispose them to be adventurous, risk-taking, dominant, and aggressive, and to take charge (i.e., be leaders). Sheldon's initial work with this framework resulted in correlations on the order of .7 or

ectomorph ■
cerebrotonia ■
endomorph ■
visceratonia ■
mesomorph ■
somatotonic ■

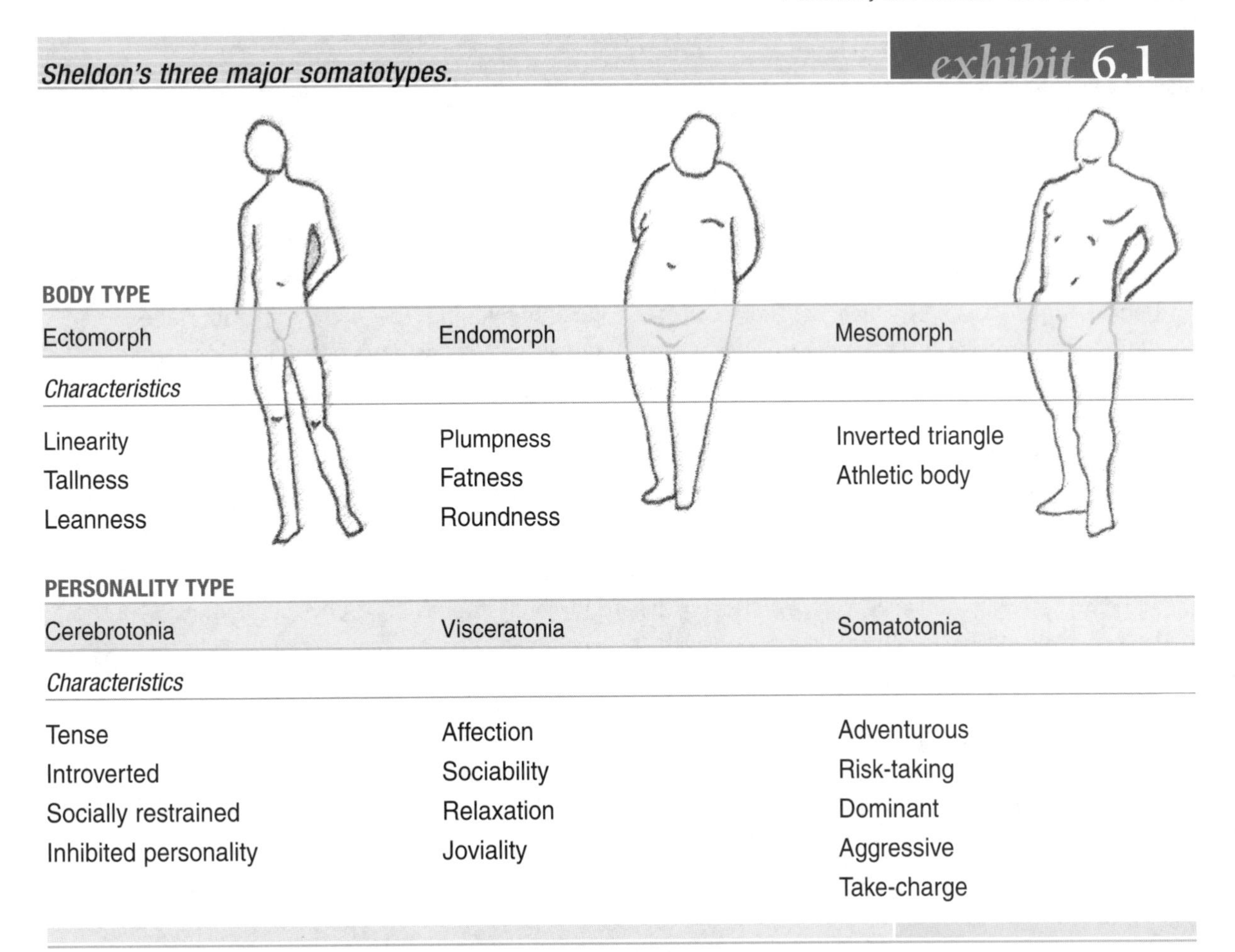

	Ectomorph	Endomorph	Mesomorph
BODY TYPE	Ectomorph	Endomorph	Mesomorph
Characteristics	Linearity Tallness Leanness	Plumpness Fatness Roundness	Inverted triangle Athletic body
PERSONALITY TYPE	Cerebrotonia	Visceratonia	Somatotonia
Characteristics	Tense Introverted Socially restrained Inhibited personality	Affection Sociability Relaxation Joviality	Adventurous Risk-taking Dominant Aggressive Take-charge

exhibit 6.1 *Sheldon's three major somatotypes.*

better between the body types and associated personality characteristics. Such strong relationships have not held up in subsequent work. It is worth noting, however, that relationships between body types and personality have been shown to be small to moderate in nature, on the order of approximately .3 to .4. This suggests that there might be a meaningful association between body type and personality.

TRAIT THEORIES

Perhaps the most predominant theoretical approach of the "modern" era has involved the examination of **traits,** defined as relatively enduring, highly consistent internal attributes. Traits are thought to reflect motivational systems that increase adaptation to positive or negative stimuli. Approaches centered on the examination of traits

Traits vs. States

The distinction between *traits* and *states* is an important issue in personality research. As noted previously, traits are seen as relatively enduring dispositions that exert a consistent influence on behavior in a variety of situations. States, on the other hand, are viewed as the psychological reaction to the situation in which the individual finds herself, consistent with the individual's traits.

For example, a highly trait anxious person would tend to be a worrisome, nervous individual regardless of the situation in which she finds herself. When placed in a stressful situation such as standing before an audience to give a speech, this individual would be expected to respond with a high amount of state anxiety. This typically manifests itself cognitively as extreme nervousness or tension and somatically with sweaty palms, tense muscles, and an unsettled stomach.

Carron, in 1980, noted that skeptics had called for abandoning the trait approach altogether because of its failure to account for physical activity behavior. This prompted some scientists to argue that instead of abandoning the trait approach, the approach should be more adequately utilized. Theorists like Eysenck and Cattell wouldn't necessarily expect broad personality characteristics (i.e., traits) accurately to predict an individual's behavior in physical activity. Coupling such traits with situational factors like psychological states would more accurately predict behavior.

have been referred to as trait theories. The emphasis in such theories is placed on the person as opposed to the situation or the environment (see box above).

Eysenck's Personality Theory

Trait theories have dominated recent work in the area of personality, and the individual perhaps most responsible for their prominence has been Hans Eysenck (see Eysenck, Nias, & Cox, 1982). Eysenck proposed that it was the relationships between traits that generated second-order, what he referred to as superordinate, trait dimensions. Within his framework, there were three superordinate dimensions: Extraversion–Introversion (***E***), Neuroticism (Emotionality)–Stability (***N***), and Psychoticism–Superego (***P***). One of the unique aspects of Eysenck's personality framework is that he proposed a biological basis for each of the three dimensions.

extraversion–introversion ■

Extraversion–introversion. Eysenck proposed that **extraversion–introversion** was driven by level of arousal in the cortex of the brain. More specifically, he proposed that the reticular formation mediates cortical arousal: if the reticular formation is functioning at a high level, the individual feels alert; if it is functioning at a low level, the individual feels drowsy. According to the theory, **introverts** have *higher* base levels of activation, that is, their cortical arousal tends to be higher than the "normal" individual. Because of this greater arousal at rest, introverts tend to augment incoming stimulation and thus they *avoid* further stimulation that might increase arousal. **Extraverts,** on the other hand, have *lower* base levels of activation, that is, lower cortical arousal. This lower arousal results in a reduction of incoming stimulation, thus the extravert tends to *seek* opportunities and situations that might provide additional stimulation. Additionally, because of this augmentation or reduction of incoming stimulation, introverts tend to have lower pain tolerance whereas extraverts have greater tolerance for painful stimuli.

- introverts
- extraverts

Neuroticism–stability. Eysenck proposed that the **neuroticism–stability** dimension was associated with activity of the **limbic system,** sometimes referred to as the emotional brain, and the **autonomic nervous system** (ANS). The ANS is often cited as driving the fight-or-flight response seen when a stressful stimulus is encountered. High **neuroticism** individuals tend to have more labile and longer-lasting autonomic reactions than do low *N* individuals. For example, if asked to give a short speech (i.e., a stressor) in front of a large group, the high *N* person might respond with a large increase in heart rate and blood pressure, which would remain elevated during and following the speech. Even when the stressor was over, the high *N* person would take longer to return to the prestressor resting heart rate and blood pressure. In essence, he continues to process the stressor even when it is no longer present.

- neuroticism–stability
- limbic system
- autonomic nervous system
- neuroticism

Psychoticism–superego. Finally, the **psychoticism–superego** dimension is hypothesized to be driven by hormonal function, more specifically by androgens and the relative absence of serotonin (neurotransmitter) metabolites. Such hormonal function is thought to lead to heightened aggressiveness, impersonal attitudes, and antisocial behavior. Such traits can be advantageous in certain sporting situations, but it should be pointed out that this last dimension has received relatively little attention in the exercise domain. It is somewhat difficult to imagine situations where an impersonal attitude would be advantageous in the exercise context.

- psychoticism–superego

Eysenck's framework and exercise. With this theoretical basis, specific predictions for physical activity/exercise can be made regarding extraversion–introversion and neuroticism–stability. As mentioned previously, low arousal leads the extravert to seek sensory stimulation through physical activity. Eysenck hypothesized that physical activity/exercise might be one such avenue for increased stimulation. As a result, extraverts would be more likely to adopt and adhere to a physical activity/exercise regimen than would introverts. This could be manifested in terms of greater-intensity activity and activity for longer durations. Additionally, the extraverts' higher tolerance of pain serves them in such activities.

Although Eysenck does not make specific predictions regarding the Neuroticism dimension, because of its basis in the autonomic nervous system one could surmise that activities that modify ANS function might also affect this personality dimension. Given that exercise training typically results in reductions in heart rate, blood pressure, and numerous other factors, it would seem reasonable to propose that exercise training could also result in a change toward a more stable/less neurotic personality.

In spite of its theoretical foundation and relative simplicity, theories like Eysenck's have received precious little examination in the exercise domain. (More recent formulations, most notably the five-factor model, have added other dimensions to personality, yet the most prominent all contain extraversion–introversion and neuroticism–stability.) In general, individuals involved in physical activity tend to be more extraverted than nonparticipants and also to be more likely to adhere to exercise programs (Courneya & Hellsten, 1998). It has been shown that extraversion is related to a preference for a higher level of exercise intensity (Morgan, 1973). Morgan has also shown that extraversion is associated with lower ratings of perceived exertion during an actual exercise bout, but this finding has not always been demonstrated. Again consistent with the theoretical predictions, Shiomi (1980) found that extraverts have greater persistence while exercising.

More recently, Schnurr, Vaillant, and Vaillant (1990), in a prospective study, found that those individuals possessing vital, well-adjusted personalities as young adults were more likely to engage in frequent exercise 40 years later. Conversely, those with more sensitive, anxious (high *N*) personalities as young adults were likely to exercise less frequently 40 years later. It has also been consistently demonstrated that extraversion is associated with involvement in physical activity (Eysenck et al., 1982; Furnham, 1981; Kirkcaldy & Furnham, 1991), although this is not inviolate. For example, Arai and Hisamichi (1998) noted in a study of more than 22,000 40- to 64-year-old Japanese residents that extraversion was positively related, whereas neuroticism was inversely related, to exercise frequency, although Yeung and Helmsley (1997) found that extraversion was actually inversely related to attendance in an eight-week exercise program.

Extraversion and neuroticism can also influence the behaviors people might engage in to regulate mood. Thayer, Newman, and McClain (1984), in a study examining behaviors that would increase energy and decrease tension, found that extraverts were more likely to exercise to improve energy. Hsiao and Thayer (1998), in a similar study, found that those scoring high on neuroticism reported valuing exercise for its ability to improve mood. Consistent with Eysenck's theoretical tenets, Hsiao and Thayer recommended the following as a way to increase exercise behavior and adherence in those who score high on neuroticism:

> First, the energizing and tension-releasing effects of exercise should be emphasized because these effects are likely to be extremely reinforcing and appealing to the target population. Secondly, exercise regimens should be structured so as to result in minimum physical discomfort. Painful bodily sensation (e.g., soreness of muscle, shortness of breath) could be easily magnified and interpreted as disease symptoms by individuals high on Neuroticism, who then could cease from physical activity altogether. Obviously, the general population can also benefit from following these guidelines. (p. 835)

A fairly substantial body of work has also shown that long-term exercise programs often result in reductions in trait anxiety or neuroticism (see Landers & Petruzzello, 1994; Petruzzello, Landers, Hatfield, Kubitz, & Salazar, 1991; also see next section detailing work on emotional stability). This work clearly demonstrates the fact that personality can change. It is possible, over a period of weeks, months, or years, for personality to change as a result of regular physical activity. This change is usually in the direction of reduced negative factors (neuroticism) and enhanced positive factors (extraversion), changes that are quite consistent with the theoretical predictions drawn from Eysenck's model.

Cattell's Personality Theory

Cattell, a contemporary of Eysenck, likewise proposed a theory of personality based on traits. Personality in this conceptualization was composed of 16 factors, derived through the statistical technique of factor analysis. From the many available personality traits, Cattell isolated 16 that he felt described the essence of personality (see Exhibit 6.2 for a list of the factors). From this conceptualization, Cattell developed what he called the 16 Personality Factor questionnaire (16PF) to assess these factors. The 16PF enjoyed widespread use in sport personality studies and has been used to some extent in exercise studies as well. Following are a few sample questions from the 16PF.

- I consider myself a very sociable, outgoing person.
  a. yes b. in between c. no
- People say I'm impatient.
  a. true b. uncertain c. false
- I prefer friends who are:
  a. quiet b. in between c. lively
- When I get upset, I try hard to hide my feelings from others.
  a. true b. in between c. false

Cattell's model and exercise. As with Eysenck's model, Cattell's model has not received much attention in the exercise domain. This is particularly curious given the fact that Cattell specifically discussed a possible relationship between fitness and personality (Cattell, 1960). Cattell suggested that fitness would be related to personality in that individuals

exhibit 6.2 *Cattell's 16 primary personality factors.*

A	Warm, sociable	vs.	Aloof, stiff
B	Intelligent, bright	vs.	Unintelligent, dull
C	Emotionally stable, mature	vs.	Emotional, immature
E	Dominant, ascendant	vs.	Submissive, mild
F	Happy-go-lucky, enthusiastic	vs.	Sober, glum
G	Conscientious, persistent	vs.	Casual, undependable
H	Adventurous, outgoing	vs.	Shy, timid
I	Tender-minded, sensitive	vs.	Tough, realistic
L	Trusting, accepting	vs.	Suspicious, jealous
M	Imaginative, unconventional	vs.	Practical, conventional
N	Naïve, unpretentious	vs.	Shrewd, sophisticated
O	Confident, self-secure	vs.	Timid, apprehensive
Q_1	Radical, experimenting	vs.	Conservative, moralizing
Q_2	Self-sufficient, resourceful	vs.	Group-dependent, conventional
Q_3	Controlled, disciplined	vs.	Uncontrolled, undisciplined
Q_4	Relaxed, composed	vs.	Tense, excitable

with high levels of fitness would be likely to have lower anxiety and neuroticism. Furthermore, he hypothesized that individuals with lower levels of anxiety and neuroticism (i.e., those with greater emotional stability) would respond favorably to intense physical training.

Dienstbier (1984) summarized the results of a number of studies from the mid-1970s to early 1980s that examined the relationship between exercise and personality change using the 16PF. Upon examination of the dimensions thought to be associated with emotionality (conceptually analogous to neuroticism), Dienstbier found support for a link between fitness and emotional stability, did not find support for changes in fitness being associated with greater emotional stability, and did find support for exercise programs leading to greater placidity or relaxation. He speculated that the increased physiological capacity that accompanies physical training might be the reason for the reduced emotional tension (i.e., neuroticism).

One of the major conceptual problems with research using the 16PF has been the difficulty of interpreting the complicated findings. Cattell has also described second-order factors, derived through the combination of various primary factors. For example, the second-order factor termed "emotionality" (sometimes referred to as "anxiety") is derived through the combination of the primary factors C, H, L, O, Q_3, and Q_4 (see Exhibit 6.2). Additionally, the primary factors A, E, F, H, and Q_2 can be combined to derive the second-order factor labeled "extraversion–introversion." It is interesting that Eysenck has also asserted (as well as demonstrated empirically) that the 16 factors can often be simplified into the two major dimensions of his model (extraversion–introversion, neuroticism–stability) and thus explain the data more parsimoniously. Morgan (1980), perhaps echoing the sentiments of Eysenck, noted that more sophisticated analysis of data using the 16PF might clarify relationships between exercise and personality. In particular, Morgan suggested more emphasis on the second-order factors.

The Five-Factor Model (FFM)

The five-factor model (FFM) (Costa & McCrae, 1992; McCrae & John, 1992) has developed relatively recently into the dominant framework for the study of personality. This is also a trait theory that proposes personality to be composed of five dimensions: neuroticism (N), extraversion (E), openness to experience (O), agreeableness (A), and conscientiousness (C). Neuroticism and extraversion are similar to the same constructs presented in the earlier models (see Eysenck, Cattell). **Openness to experience** refers to a willingness to adjust ideas and activities when presented with new ideas or situations. **Agreeableness** refers to compatibility with

- openness to experience
- agreeableness

conscientiousness ■

others, and **conscientiousness** refers to the number of goals an individual is focused on and the level of self-discipline to accomplish those goals. Conscientiousness has been further defined as being determined, strong-willed, and systematic in conducting designated jobs.

The five-factor model and exercise. Because of its relatively recent development, the FFM has not received a great deal of research attention in the exercise domain, with some notable exceptions. Courneya and Hellsten (1998) found E, N, and C to be significantly related to exercise behavior and adherence. Specifically, E and C were positively related to both moderate (e.g., fast walking) and strenuous (e.g., jogging) exercise behavior, and N was a significant predictor of exercise adherence, with greater levels of N predicting lower levels of adherence. Courneya, Bobick, and Schinke (1999) reported that E, N, and C were again all related to exercise behavior in two samples of female undergraduates. E and C were positively related to self-reported exercise (calculated from both intensity and duration of activity in a typical week in the first sample, determined based on attendance in aerobic classes over an 11-week span in the second sample), while N was negatively related. Even more recently, Rhodes, Courneya, and Bobick (2001) showed again that E, N, and C were important personality dimensions in examining exercise participation in female breast cancer survivors. Again, E and C were associated with adaptive exercise patterns and more advanced exercise stages, whereas N was associated with maladaptive exercise patterns and less advanced exercise stages (see Exhibit 6.3).

exhibit 6.3 *The five-factor model and exercise behavior.*

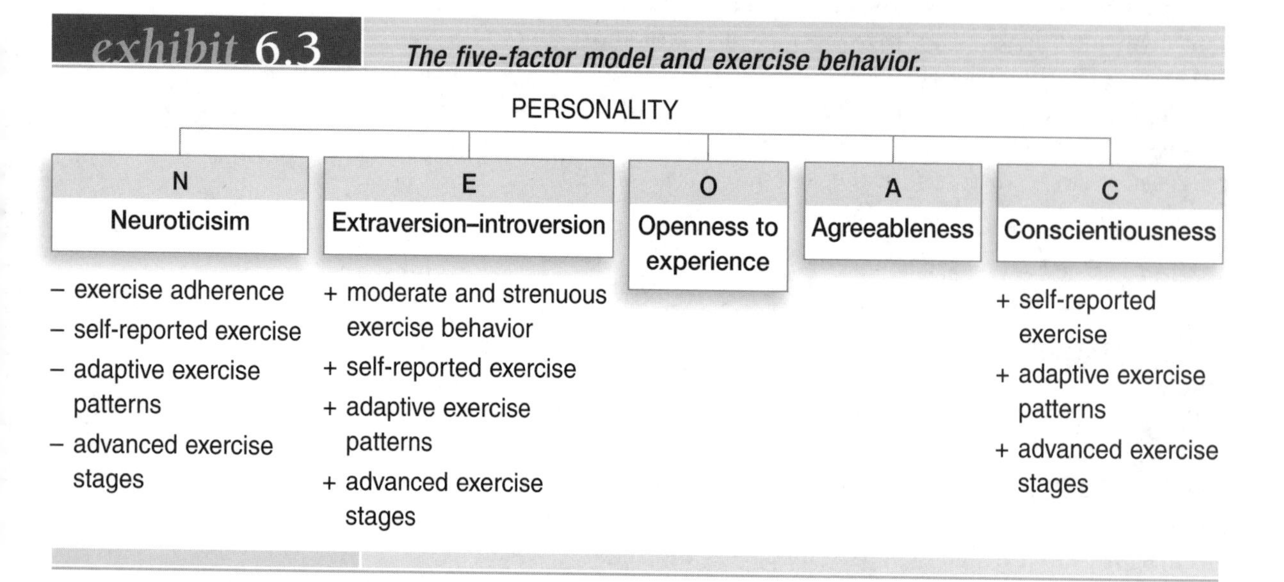

OTHER PERSONALITY FACTORS EXAMINED IN EXERCISE RESEARCH

Sex-Role Orientation

Although the body of literature on sex-role orientations and their role in the exercise domain is not large, the dimensions of masculinity (M) and femininity (F; Bem, 1974; Spence & Helmreich, 1978) as personality constructs may have important implications for exercise behavior and exercise prescription. Both M and F are conceived of as positive, desirable traits that are possessed by both males and females. It is somewhat unfortunate that these constructs were given the labels they were, because the tendency is to relate them directly to biological sex, when in fact they are not sex-linked. In fact, some formulations have taken to referring to M as "instrumental" and F as "expressive" as a way of avoiding the confusion with biological sex. In essence, the **instrumental personality** is characterized by traits like risk-taking, independence, aggressiveness, and competitiveness. The **expressive personality** is characterized by traits like understanding, sympathy, affection, and compassion. Because the two dimensions are viewed as orthogonal to one another, an individual can possess each to varying degrees. Individuals who score high on the instrumental dimension and low on the expressive dimension are classified as masculine/instrumental; those who score high on the expressive and low on the instrumental dimension are classified as feminine/expressive. Individuals who score high on both dimensions are classified as **androgynous.**

- instrumental personality
- expressive personality
- androgynous

Sex roles and exercise. Such sex-role personality characteristics have implications for exercise behavior. Cross-gender activities are generally avoided by gender-typed individuals. When cross-gender activities are performed, greater psychological discomfort is often reported. For example, feminine-typed individuals avoid masculine activities when given a choice. If forced to engage in such an activity, they often have more negative feelings and debilitating perceptions while involved in the activity.

To examine whether gender roles do in fact mediate the perception of strenuous exercise, Rejeski, Best, Griffith, and Kenney (1987) conducted a study with 42 college-aged males. Noting that exercise is typically stereotyped as a masculine task, Rejeski et al. hypothesized that feminine-typed males would respond with greater distress to strenuous exercise than would either androgynous or masculine-typed males. Ratings of perceived exertion (RPE) and affective responses were examined to a six-minute exercise bout on a cycle ergometer at an intensity equivalent to 85 percent of each individual's estimated aerobic capacity. The results revealed the following: Feminine-typed males had significantly higher ratings of perceived exertion than either masculine-typed or androgynous males, even though the work load was physiologically equivalent for each group. Feminine-typed males also had significantly greater negative affect compared with the androgynous males, and the trend was in the right direction for the masculine-typed males. Furthermore, immediately following completion of the six-minute exercise bout, subjects were asked to continue exercising at a supramaximal intensity (approximately 110 percent of estimated aerobic capacity) for as long as they could. This behavioral measure indicated that the feminine-typed males, now having the opportunity to withdraw from a potentially uncomfortable activity, exercised for half as long (about 20 seconds) as the masculine-typed males (about 46 seconds) and only about 30 percent as long as the androgynous males (about 67 seconds).

Clearly, such personality traits and the psychological discomfort that accompanies the performance of cross-typed activities might predispose one either to avoid exercise altogether or to have negative experiences during the activity. Such findings certainly require further study. However, it is possible that if this pattern of findings is reliable, exercise professionals could intervene to help, particularly with feminine-typed individuals. This could involve structuring exercise protocols that would not create such negative psychological effects (e.g., lower intensities).

Type A Behavior Pattern

type A behavior pattern ■

The majority of research examining the **type A behavior pattern (TABP)** has focused primarily on its role in cardiovascular disease. Indeed, it has sometimes been referred to as the *coronary-prone* personality. Originally proposed by Friedman and Rosenman (1974), the TABP has been shown to be prevalent in those with heart disease and to place one at greater risk for developing cardiovascular disease. Friedman and Rosenman had initially posited that it was the sense of time urgency that distinguished the TABP, but more recent investigations have implicated the anger or hostility components of the TABP as the most important features for increased risk of cardiovascular disease. Some researchers have even speculated that it is not just cardiovascular disease, but disease in general for which the TABP places one at greater risk (Friedman & Booth-Kewley, 1987). Because of the beneficial effects of exercise programs for those suffering from cardiovascular disease, it has been suspected that exercise could also be beneficial for the type A individual.

TABP and exercise. Exercise has been shown to be effective in reducing the TABP (e.g., Blumenthal, Williams, Williams, & Wallace, 1980), but studies have not produced uniform results. For example, Roskies et al. (1986) showed exercise to be less effective than a cognitive–behavioral treatment in reducing heart rate and blood pressure reactivity to stress-inducing laboratory tasks. In contrast, Blumenthal et al. (1988) showed that a 12-week aerobic exercise program did successfully reduce cardiovascular reactivity to psychosocial stressors compared to a strength and flexibility intervention.

There is, however, reason to believe that the TABP might have important implications for individual differences regarding exercise in social contexts. It has been noted that type A individuals tend to have lower adherence rates to exercise programs than do type B individuals (e.g., Oldridge, 1982) and type As also have higher rates of exercise-related injuries (Fields, Delaney, & Hinkle, 1990). One aspect of the TABP that might explain such findings is the tendency toward involvement in more intense and competitive exercise for type As (e.g., Hinkle, Lyons, & Burke, 1989). Type As have also been shown to exert greater effort, causing greater levels of physiological activation during exercise. However, they also tend to estimate their perceived exertion and discomfort at lower levels during low to moderate levels of exercise intensity (Hassmen, Stahl, & Borg, 1993). Finally, compared to type Bs, type A individuals have greater stress responses at higher exercise intensities (McMurray, Hardy, Roberts, Forsythe, & Mar, 1989) and more negative affective responses (Hardy, McMurray, & Roberts, 1989) (see Exhibit 6.4).

Type A and B behavior patterns and exercise. exhibit 6.4

TYPE A	TYPE B
↑ Risk of cardiovascular disease	↓ Risk of cardiovascular disease
↓ Adherence rates	↑ Adherence rates
↑ Effort	↓ Effort
↑ Intensity	↓ Intensity
↑ Physiological activation	↓ Physiological activation
↓ RPE	↑ RPE
↑ Stress responses	↓ Stress responses
↑ Negative affective responses	↓ Negative affective responses

Hardiness

hardiness ■

Whereas the TABP is thought to place one at greater risk for disease, the personality construct of *hardiness* is proposed to be stress buffering. Originally delineated by Kobasa (1979), **hardiness** is theorized to comprise:

1. a sense of control over events
2. commitment, dedication, or involvement in everyday life
3. a tendency to perceive life events as challenges and opportunities rather than as stressors.

This particular constellation of characteristics is thought to protect against the deleterious effects of stress and to serve as a buffer against illness. Initial studies by Kobasa, Maddi, and Puccetti (1982) and Kobasa, Maddi, Puccetti, and Zola (1985) were supportive of this notion, largely because of the additive effects of the hardiness personality coupled with exercise behavior. In other words, those higher in hardiness are able to transform stressful events to decrease their stressfulness (e.g., obtaining information, taking action, learning from experience), and exercise serves to buffer against the strain of stressful events.

Hardiness and exercise. Other research examining the link between hardiness and exercise in the stress–illness relationship has been somewhat mixed. Roth, Wiebe, Fillingim, and Shay (1989) found that although fitness and hardiness were negatively related to illness, neither fitness nor hardiness moderated the stress effect. They suggested that, consistent with Kobasa's formulation, hardiness might indirectly affect either the occurrence or interpretation of stressful events. Furthermore, exercise serves to increase fitness, which is indirectly associated with reduced illness. Carson (1993) demonstrated that in long-term AIDS survivors, hardiness was positively associated with, among other things, exercise participation.

At present it appears that hardiness is related to a tendency to engage in more healthful behaviors. Exercise can certainly be included among such behaviors. It should be noted, however, that the majority of research in this area has been correlational in nature. It is not clear whether a hardy personality leads one to engage in exercise or whether exercise participation leads to a hardy personality. This certainly has implications for the impact that exercise might have on reactivity to stress and illness.

Self-Motivation

psycho-biological model ■

Dishman undertook one attempt at the development of an exercise-specific theory that incorporated personality. He proposed a **psycho-**

biological model as an attempt to explain exercise adherence (Dishman, 1981). The model specifically advocates consideration of both biological factors (i.e., body composition, body mass) and a psychological factor. The specific psychological factor espoused by Dishman was the construct of **self-motivation** (which is conceptually analogous to the conscientiousness factor from the FFM), defined as a generalized, nonspecific tendency to persist in the absence of extrinsic reinforcement. The Self-Motivation Inventory (Dishman & Ickes, 1981), a questionnaire developed to assess self-motivation, includes statements that reflect

■ self-motivation

1. low self-motivation (e.g., I'm not very good at committing myself to do things; I never force myself to do things I don't feel like doing) and
2. high self-motivation (e.g., I'm really concerned about developing and maintaining self-discipline; I like to set my goals and work toward them).

Initial work with this model predicted that percentage of body fat and body mass would negatively affect adherence whereas self-motivation would positively affect adherence [it is interesting to note that Courneya et al.'s (1999) work with the FFM has also shown conscientiousness to be related to adherence]. As with so many other attempts, the initial work was fairly positive, but subsequent research has not supported the model nearly as well. Thus, while the psychobiological model holds appeal, much more work is needed in this area.

PRACTICAL RECOMMENDATIONS

In general, because we currently have such a vague understanding of which personality factors are important for exercise behavior, it is difficult to make straightforward practical recommendations. Given what research has shown, however, it seems reasonable to propose at least a few suggestions. Individuals who seem to be more emotional (i.e., neurotic) may be encouraged to begin a regular exercise program. The beautiful thing about such a suggestion is that it doesn't have to be made for the psychological benefits. The current state of fitness for most individuals would allow such a suggestion to be made for the physical benefits, but it seems apparent that the psychological benefits (reduced emotionality in this case) would occur as well. Essentially, the recommended "exercise dose" could be the same as what would be given for improving fitness or encouraging weight loss in terms of frequency, duration, and intensity. The key would appear to be to start slowly, with the realization that improvements will take some time. It also seems reasonable to propose that any exercise program have some type of aerobic activity as a primary component. Although time may well show that resistance activities also influence personality factors, such effects have already been shown for aerobic activities.

Conclusion

It is worth pointing out that the study of personality or individual differences is important for exercise psychology. While regular exercise can clearly be important in both the prevention of chronic diseases and the treatment of such diseases, one of the most vexing problems for the field continues to be an inability to accurately predict those who will adhere to exercise programs and those who will drop out. Certainly, knowledge of factors such as an individual's level of extraversion or neuroticism or whether the person is more instrumental or expressive can be helpful in prescribing exercise programs. It also seems fairly apparent that an individual's participation in a regular program of exercise can be important in the development of a more emotionally stable, extraverted personality.

What Do You Know?

1. What are the three main aspects of an individual's personality?
2. What is the main feature of constitutional theory thought to determine personality?
3. What are the three major dimensions of Eysenck's theory?
4. What predictions can be made about Eysenck's personality dimensions with respect to exercise/physical activity?
5. Describe the relationship between fitness and emotionality.
6. What kind of psychological reactions might a feminine-typed individual have to a strenuous bout of exercise?
7. What are the three factors that seem to make up the hardiness personality constellation?
8. What is self-motivation and is it important in understanding exercise behavior?

Learning Activities

1. A personal trainer needs to design exercise programs for many different kinds of clients. Based on what you have learned from this chapter, describe a program for an individual who is not particularly self-motivated and who is also overweight. What if the client is feminine-typed? What if the client displays a number of type A behaviors?
2. Return to the opening scenario of the chapter. If you were Sarah, what kind of exercise program might you have designed for Jenny? Be more specific than the scenario indicated (i.e., more specific than exercising three days per week). What activity or activities would you recommend to Jenny? How often, how hard, and for how long would you have her do them?
3. Assuming that Sheldon's constitutional theory of personality can be put into practice, what kinds of exercise might be most useful for the ectomorph? Endomorph? Mesomorph?

References

Arai, Y., & Hisamichi, S. (1998). Self-reported exercise frequency and personality: A population-based study in Japan. *Perceptual and Motor Skills, 87,* 1371–1375.

Bem, S. L. (1974). The measurement of psychological androgyny. *Journal of Consulting and Clinical Psychology, 42,* 155–162.

Blumenthal, J. A., Emery, C. F., Walsh, M. A., Cox, D. K., Kuhn, C. M., Williams, R. B., & Williams, R. S. (1988). Exercise training in healthy type A middle aged men: Effects on behavioral and cardiovascular responses. *Psychosomatic Medicine, 50,* 418–433.

Blumenthal, J. A., Williams, R. S., Williams, R. B., & Wallace, A. G. (1980). Effects of exercise on the type A (coronary prone) behavior pattern. *Psychosomatic Medicine, 42,* 289–296.

Carron, A. V. 1980. *Social psychology of sport.* Ithaca, NY: Mouvement Publications.

Carson, V. B. (1993). Prayer, meditation, exercise, and special diets: Behaviors of the hardy person with HIV/AIDS. *Journal of Associated Nurses AIDS Care, 4*(3), 18–28.

Cattell, R. B. (1960). Some psychological correlates of physical fitness and physique. In S. C. Staley (Ed.), *Exercise and fitness* (pp. 138–151). Chicago: Athletic Institute.

Costa, P. T., & McCrae, R. R. (1992). *The NEO Personality Inventory R: Professional Manual.* Odessa, FL: Psychological Assessment Resources.

Courneya, K. S., Bobick, T. M., & Schinke, R. J. (1999). Does the theory of planned behavior mediate the relation between personality and exercise behavior? *Basic and Applied Social Psychology, 21,* 317–324.

Courneya, K. S., & Hellsten, L. M. (1998). Personality correlates of exercise behavior, motives, barriers and preferences: An application of the five-factor model. *Personality and Individual Differences, 24,* 625–633.

Dienstbier, R. A. (1984). The effect of exercise on personality. In M. L. Sachs, & G. W. Buffone (Eds.), *Running as therapy* (pp. 253–272). Lincoln, NE: University of Nebraska Press.

Dishman, R. K. (1981). Biologic influences on exercise adherence. *Research Quarterly for Exercise and Sport, 52,* 143–189.

Dishman, R. K., & Ickes, W. (1981). Self-motivation and adherence to therapeutic exercise. *Journal of Behavioral Medicine, 4,* 421–438.

Eysenck, H. J., Nias, D. K., & Cox, D. N. (1982). Sport and personality. *Advances in Behaviour Research and Therapy, 4,* 1–56.

Fields, K. B., Delaney, M., & Hinkle, J. S. (1990). A prospective study of type A behavior and running injuries. *Journal of Family Practice, 30,* 425–429.

Friedman, H. S., & Booth-Kewley, S. (1987). Personality, type A behavior, and coronary heart disease: The role of emotional expression. *Journal of Personality and Social Psychology, 53,* 783–792.

Friedman, M., & Rosenman, R. H. (1974). *Type A behavior and your heart.* New York: Knopf.

Furnham, A. (1981). Personality and activity preference. *British Journal of Social Psychology, 20,* 57–68.

Hardy, C. J., McMurray, R. G., & Roberts, S. (1989). A/B types and psychophysiological responses to exercise stress. *Journal of Sport and Exercise Psychology, 11,* 141–151.

Hassmen, P., Stahl, R., & Borg, G. (1993). Psychophysiological responses to exercise in type A/B men. *Psychosomatic Medicine, 55*(2), 178–184.

Hinkle, J. S., Lyons, B., & Burke, K. L. (1989). Manifestation of type A behavior pattern among aerobic runners. *Journal of Sport Behavior, 12,* 131–138.

Hollander, E. P. (1967). *Principles and methods of social psychology.* New York: Holt.

Hsiao, E. T., & Thayer, R. E. (1998). Exercising for mood regulation: The importance of experience. *Personality and Individual Differences, 24,* 829–836.

James, W. (1899). Physical training in the educational curriculum. *American Physical Education Review, 4,* 220–221.

Kirkcaldy, B., & Furnham, A. (1991). Extraversion, neuroticism, psychoticism and recreational choice. *Personality and Individual Differences, 12,* 737–745.

Kobasa, S. C. (1979). Stressful life events, personality and health: An inquiry into hardiness. *Journal of Personality and Social Psychology, 37,* 1–11.

Kobasa, S. C., Maddi, S. R., & Puccetti, M. C. (1982). Personality and exercise as buffers in the stress-illness relationship. *Journal of Behavioral Medicine, 5,* 391–404.

Kobasa, S. C., Maddi, S. R., Puccetti, M. C., & Zola, M. A. (1985). Effectiveness of hardiness, exercise and social support as resources against illness. *Journal of Psychosomatic Research, 29,* 525–533.

Landers, D. M., & Petruzzello, S. J. (1994). Physical activity, fitness, and anxiety. In C. Bouchard, R. J. Shephard, & T. Stephens (Eds.), *Physical activity, fitness, and health: International proceedings and consensus statement* (pp. 868–882). Champaign, IL: Human Kinetics.

McCrae, R. R., & John, O. P. (1992). An introduction to the five-factor model and its applications. *Journal of Personality, 60,* 175–215.

McMurray, R. G., Hardy, C. J., Roberts, S., Forsythe, W. A., & Mar, M. H. (1989). Neuroendocrine responses of type A individuals to exercise. *Behavioral Medicine, 15,* 84–92.

Mendez, C. (1553/1960). *Book of bodily exercise.* Translated by F. Guerra. New Haven, CT: Elizabeth Licht.

Morgan, W. P. (1973). Psychological factors influencing perceived exertion. *Medicine and Science in Sports, 5,* 97–103.

Morgan, W. P. (1980). The trait psychology controversy. *Research Quarterly for Exercise and Sport, 51,* 50–76.

Oldridge, N. B. (1982). Compliance and exercise in primary and secondary prevention of coronary heart disease: A review. *Preventive Medicine, 11,* 56–70.

Petruzzello, S. J., Landers, D. M., Hatfield, B. D., Kubitz, K. A., & Salazar, W. (1991). A meta-analysis on the anxiety reducing effects of acute and chronic exercise: Outcomes and mechanisms. *Sports Medicine, 11,* 143–182.

Rejeski, W. J., Best, D. L., Griffith, P., & Kenney, E. (1987). Sex-role orientation and the responses of men to exercise stress. *Research Quarterly for Exercise and Sport, 58,* 260–264.

Rhodes, R. E., Courneya, K. S., & Bobick, T. M. (2001). Personality and exercise participation across the breast cancer experience. *Psycho-Oncology, 10,* 380–388.

Roskies, E., Seraganian, P., Oseasohn, R., Hanley, J. A., Collu, R., Martin, N., & Smilga, C. (1986). The Montreal Type A intervention project: Major findings. *Health Psychology, 5,* 45–69.

Roth, D. L., Wiebe, D. J., Fillingim, R. B., & Shay, K. A. (1989). Life events, fitness, hardiness, and health: A simultaneous analysis of proposed stress-resistance effects. *Journal of Personality and Social Psychology, 57,* 136–142.

Schnurr, P. P., Vaillant, C. O., & Vaillant, G. E. (1990). Predicting exercise in late midlife from young adult personality characteristics. *International Journal of Aging and Human Development, 30*(2), 153–160.

Sheldon, W. H. (1942). *The varieties of temperament: A psychology of constitutional differences.* New York: Harper.

Shiomi, K. (1980). Performance differences between extraverts and introverts on exercise using an ergometer. *Perceptual and Motor Skills, 50,* 356–358.

Spence, J. T., & Helmreich, R. L. (1978). *Masculinity and femininity: Their psychological dimensions, correlates, and antecedents.* Austin: University of Texas Press.

Thayer, R. E., Newman, R., & McClain, T. M. (1994). Self-regulation of mood: Strategies for changing a bad mood, raising energy, and reducing tension. *Journal of Personality and Social Psychology, 67,* 910–925.

Yeung, R. R., & Helmsley, D. R. (1997). Exercise behaviour in an aerobics class: The impact of personality traits and efficacy cognitions. *Personality and Individual Differences, 23,* 425–431.

Chapter 7

Depression and Exercise

John retired from his job as a professor at the university in May. By the end of August, he is rather despondent. His wife Mary doesn't know what to do anymore. He frequently rises at 2:00 or 3:00 in the morning and often sleeps two or three hours during the day. John has loads of free time to putter in his workshop, something he had always wanted to do but didn't have the time, but even this doesn't bring him any happiness. Finally, in a last effort to help, Mary makes an appointment for John to see a clinical psychologist. The psychologist is a firm believer in the value of exercise for helping those with depression, and she sees John as a perfect candidate. He hasn't been involved in any regular physical activity since his days as a college athlete. Susan, the psychologist, suggests that John begin walking with Mary every night after dinner. Susan suggests this for two reasons: one, John will get started on an exercise program; two, he will be able to spend some time with Mary, who Susan senses is a supportive spouse who could be helpful in this transition period for John. John is initially skeptical, but takes the daily walk more to satisfy Mary than anything else. After the first few nights, however, John initiates the walk. Their walks become longer and then more vigorous, and within a few weeks, John and Mary are walking for an hour at a time. Both start losing weight and John's despondency abates. They become a regular fixture around the neighborhood during the late afternoons and early evenings.

> "In all of my years on the trails and roadways, I have never seen depressed walkers."
>
> —Keith W. Johnsgard (1989, p. 166)

KEY TERMS

- anthropological hypothesis
- bipolar disorder
- cyclothymia
- depressive disorder
- disability adjusted life years (DALYs)
- distraction/time-out hypothesis
- dysthymia
- effect size
- endorphin hypothesis
- mastery hypothesis
- mental disorders
- mental health
- mental health problems
- mental illness
- meta-analyses
- moderating factors
- monoamine hypothesis
- social interaction hypothesis

"I would like to suggest that running should be viewed as a wonder drug, analogous to penicillin, morphine, and the tricyclics. It has a profound potential in preventing mental and physical disease and in rehabilitation after various diseases have occurred."

—William P. Morgan (cited in Johnsgard, 1989, p. 119)

Mental Health Versus Mental Illness

mental health ■

mental illness ■

mental disorders ■

mental health problems ■

Mental health is defined in the Surgeon General's report as "a state of successful performance of mental function, resulting in productive activities, fulfilling relationships with other people, and the ability to adapt to change and to cope with adversity" (USDHHS, 1999, p. 4). **Mental illness,** on the other hand, is the term used to refer collectively to all diagnosable mental disorders (p. 5). **Mental disorders** "are health conditions that are characterized by alterations in thinking, mood, or behavior (or some combination thereof) associated with distress and/or impaired functioning" (USDHHS, 1999, p. 4). Depression is a mental disorder characterized primarily by altered mood. Mental illnesses are distinguished from "mental health problems" based on the criterion that **mental health problems** refer to signs and symptoms of insufficient intensity or duration to meet the criteria for any mental disorders, but sufficient enough potentially to warrant active efforts in health promotion, prevention, and treatment. In other words, a person with mental health problems may display some signs or symptoms of a mental illness, for example, depression, but would not be considered sufficiently ill to receive a diagnosis of a particular mental disorder.

Defining Depression

depressive disorder ■

bipolar disorder ■

dysthymia ■

cyclothymia ■

According to the *Diagnostic and Statistical Manual of Mental Disorders,* 4th Edition (DSM-IV), depression falls under a category of mental disorders that the DSM classifies as "mood disturbances" and includes disorders that influence mood regulation *beyond the usual variations between sadness and happiness/excitement.* Four major mood disorders are covered in the first Surgeon General's Report on Mental Health, released at the end of the twentieth century (USDHHS, 1999). The four major disorders are **depressive disorder** (unipolar major depression), **bipolar disorder, dysthymia,** and **cyclothymia** (see Exhibit 7.1).

Definitions of depression can vary widely, "from episodes of unhappiness that affect most people from time to time, to persistent

exhibit 7.1

Characteristics of main depressive disorders.

Major Depressive Disorder

- Depressed mood, loss of interest or pleasure are primary symptoms
  - Not driven by physiological causes (e.g., drugs) or medical condition (e.g., hypothyroidism)
- Other symptoms can vary widely
- Episodes last approximately nine months if untreated
  - 80 to 90 percent remit within two years of first episode
  - 50 percent will recur
- Symptoms cause significant impairment in social, work, or other important areas

Dysthymia

- Chronic form of depression
- Fewer than five persistent symptoms
- Duration of approximately two years for adults, approximately one year for children
- Increased susceptibility to major depression
- Seldom remits spontaneously
- Women twice as likely to be diagnosed than men

Bipolar Disorder

- One or more episodes of mania or mixed episodes of mania and depression
  - Mania can range from pure euphoria/elation to irritability
  - Thoughts are grandiose or delusional
  - Decreased need for sleep
  - Easily distracted, with racing thoughts
  - Excessive involvement in pleasurable activities that are likely to have painful consequences (e.g., unrestrained shopping spree, sexual indiscretions)
- Higher familial prevalence (i.e., stronger genetic component)

Cyclothymia

- Marked by manic and depressive states, but of insufficient intensity/duration to diagnose as bipolar or major depressive
- Increased risk of developing bipolar disorder

Source: USDHHS (1999, p. 247).

low mood and inability to find enjoyment" (Biddle & Mutrie, 2001, p. 207). Depression is often characterized by the presence of one or more of the following (see Exhibit 7.2 also):

- sustained feelings of sadness or elation
- feelings of guilt or worthlessness
- disturbances in appetite
- disturbances in sleep patterns
- lack of energy
- difficulty concentrating
- loss of interest in all or most activities
- problems with memory
- thoughts of suicide
- hallucinations

A student might be depressed upon receiving the results of an exam on which he did very poorly, but this usually subsides and motivates the student to study harder, take better notes, or be better prepared for

exhibit 7.2 ***DSM–IV criteria for major depressive disorders.***

1. Depressed mood most of the day, nearly every day, as indexed by self-report or observations made by others
2. Diminished interest/pleasure in all or most activities, as indexed by self-report or observations of others
3. Significant weight loss when not dieting or weight gain (change of greater than 5 percent body weight in a month), decreased or increased appetite nearly every day
4. Insomnia or hypersomnia
5. Psychomotor agitation or retardation, observable by others
6. Fatigue or loss of energy when no physical work has been performed
7. Feelings of worthlessness or excessive/inappropriate guilt
8. Inability to think or concentrate
9. Recurrent thoughts of death or suicide

Note: Major depression may be diagnosed when five or more of the symptoms have been present during the same two-week period and represent a change from previous functioning. At least one of the symptoms is either depressed mood or loss of interest or pleasure.

Source: USDHHS (1999, p. 247).

the next exam. More severe depression might take the form of an unexplainably depressed mood. A student might be unable to concentrate sufficiently to work on an assignment, lacking the motivation to begin or continue, and experience feelings of worthlessness because of this. Or, as in the case of John in the chapter-opening scenario, a lack of interest in previously pleasurable activities.

PREVALENCE OF DEPRESSION

The Surgeon General's Report on Mental Health noted that mental illness is relatively prevalent in the United States. The disease burden that such disorders create has been seriously underestimated. **Disability adjusted life years (DALYs)** provides a measure of the disease burden (Murray & Lopez, 1996). DALYs estimates the years of healthy life lost due to premature death and years lived with a disability of specified severity and duration. Using DALYs, mental illnesses rank second only to cardiovascular problems in disease burden within industrialized nations. As noted in the Surgeon General's report, a number of mental illnesses (e.g., bipolar disorder, panic disorder, post-traumatic stress disorder, schizophrenia, obsessive–compulsive disorder) contribute significantly to the disease and disability burden attributed to these kinds of illnesses. Of the mental illnesses, major depression, when compared with different disease conditions, was second only to ischemic heart disease and ranked ahead of cardiovascular disease, alcohol use, and traffic accidents in disease and disability burden.

■ disability adjusted life years (DALYs)

It has been repeatedly estimated that every year approximately 20 to 25 percent of adults in the United States suffer from some diagnosable form of mental health problem, including severe and disabling mental disorders (Centers for Disease Control & Prevention, 1998). In adults, mood disorders (e.g., major depression, bipolar disorder) rank within the top 10 causes of disability worldwide (Murray & Lopez, 1996).

Two large, nationwide probability surveys published in the mid-1990s highlight the prevalence of such disabling mental conditions. The National Comorbidity Survey (Kessler et al., 1994) estimated a 23.4 percent one-year prevalence rate for any mental disorder, which means that within a given year, 23.4 percent of the U.S. adult population will have a diagnosable mental disorder. This translates to approximately 44 million people. This included an 11.1 percent one-year prevalence rate for any of the mood disorders. The Epidemiological Catchment Area Study (Regier et al., 1993) estimated a 19.5 percent one-year prevalence rate for any mental disorder, including a 7.1 percent one-year prevalence rate for any mood disorder. From these studies, best estimates of the one-year prevalence rates have been calculated to be 7.1 percent for any mood disorder and 21.0 percent for any mental disorder (USDHHS, 1999). It is worth pointing out that similar estimates obtained from the mid-1980s (Robins et al., 1984) were notably lower (approximately 4 percent one-year prevalence), which prompted Thayer (2001) to speculate that an even greater increase may have occurred for mild to moderate depression.

The prevalence of these disabling conditions creates an economic burden in terms of both treatment and lost productivity. Conservative estimates of the indirect costs of all mental illness totaled nearly $80 billion in the United States in 1990 (Rice & Miller, 1996), most of which is reflective of the loss of normal productivity due to the illness. In 1996, $69 billion was spent in direct costs for the treatment of mental disorders (USDHHS, 1999). Beyond the immeasurable human suffering, costs associated with depression have been estimated to be about $44 billion per year (Greenberg, Stiglin, Finkelstein, & Berndt, 1993), with $12 billion in direct costs of treatment and another $31 billion in indirect costs due to premature death, absenteeism, and reduced work productivity. These figures say nothing about the burdens created on the individuals and their families in decreased quality of life.

SYMPTOMOLOGY

As indicated earlier, depression can be either a mental problem or a mental illness, and nonclinical or clinical depending on the severity and duration of symptoms. Clearly, not all forms of depression reach clinical levels. It is quite normal to experience sadness, distress, or grief in times of stress and during tragedy (e.g., death of a loved one, severe illness, job loss). Such instances of dysphoria (negative or aversive mood) are usually not as pervasive or as long lasting as when such symptoms reach clinical levels. As with clinical manifestations, symptoms of mild to moderate depression can include difficulty concentrating, disturbed sleep, changes in appetite, and fatigue or loss of energy (see Exhibit 7.2).

CAUSES

The causes of depression are not well understood. Both physiological and psychosocial factors interact, often in response to some stressful event in the person's life (e.g., death of a loved one, divorce, or retirement as in John's case in the chapter-opening scenario). As noted in the Surgeon General's report, there is tremendous individual variation in such responses. Factors such as heredity, coping skills, and social support influence the degree to which depression is manifested, or if it is manifested at all (USDHHS, 1999).

Investigations of the causes of depression have focused on biological factors like neurotransmitter deficiencies. For example, the monoamine hypothesis proposes that the cause for depression is depleted levels of the monamines (the main neurotransmitters): serotonin, dopamine, norepinephrine, and epinephrine. The functions of neurotransmitters result in brain states like the level of arousal, attention, and coloring of information with emotion (USDHHS, 1999). Ultimately, the monoamine hypothesis has been found to be an insufficient explanation for depression because a complicated mental disorder like depression is a result of interactions between neurotransmitter levels, genetics, information from the environment, experience, gender, and social support. Certainly, understanding the causes of depression will be important in developing and refining the most appropriate and effective treatments, but there appears to be a long way to go before such discoveries are made.

TREATMENT

Although depression has been linked with mortality and morbidity worldwide (Lawlor & Hopker, 2001), it often goes untreated. When depressed individuals do seek help from a physician, it is often not for their depression. This reluctance to seek treatment is partly due to the stigma that is still associated with mental illness in this country (USDHHS, 1999). When the depression is treated, this is often done through pharmacological means (e.g., sertraline, imipramine). Often there is a lack of compliance when such drug treatments are prescribed (see Lawlor & Hopker). In addition, traditional treatment protocols (e.g., medication, psychotherapy) are often expensive; the costs include both the expense of the direct treatment and indirect costs such as lost productivity and reduced quality of life. For example, medications can often have unwanted side effects (e.g., drowsiness, weight gain), which can result in difficulty concentrating at work and an inability to perform normal functions effectively. Clearly, if other treatments can be shown to have utility in the management of mental disorders, at the very least these would provide additional options in the treatment toolbox for the therapist.

It has been suspected for quite some time, at least within the exercise science community, that physical activity may be a useful tool in both the prevention and treatment of depression. Much of the impetus for the work that has been done over the past 30 years could be traced back to the pioneering efforts of William P. Morgan. His early work noting the lower fitness levels in depressed patients compared with nonhospitalized controls (Morgan, 1968, 1969, 1970) is probably the earliest work in the modern era to demonstrate the potential utility of exercise in dealing with mental health problems. Before examining further the research that has utilized exercise in both the prevention and treatment of mental health problems, it would be instructive to discuss their assessment.

Measurement of Depression

In exercise depression research, depression is measured in two ways: (1) using standard classification criteria and (2) using self-report measures.

STANDARD CLASSIFICATION CRITERIA

Easily the major tool in the diagnosis of mental disorders is the *Diagnostic and Statistical Manual of Mental Disorders,* 4th edition (DSM–IV). The DSM–IV provides extensive guidelines for psychologists and psychiatrists to use in diagnosing and classifying nearly 400 mental disorders. The current diagnostic system allows for a detailed assessment, incorporating different aspects (mental, emotional, physical) of an individual's life, to provide the most complete context possible for making a proper diagnosis. The Research Diagnostic Criteria (RDC; Spitzer, Endicott, & Robins, 1978) and the International Classification of Diseases (ICD-10; World Health Organization, 1993) provide other standard classification criteria.

SELF-REPORT MEASURES

Studies of clinical and mild to moderate depression employ a number of standardized self-report measures (i.e., questionnaires). Perhaps the two most common and well validated are the Beck Depression Inventory (BDI) and the Zung Self-Rating Depression Scale. Other commonly used instruments include the Hamilton Depression Rating Scale (Hamilton, 1960), the Symptom Rating Test (Kellner & Sheffield, 1973), the Center for Epidemiologic Studies–Depression (CES-D) scale, and the Depression subscale of the Profile of Mood States (POMS).

Sample items from the 20-item CES-D include

- I was bothered by things that usually don't bother me.
- I felt that I could not shake off the blues even with help from my family or friends.
- I felt depressed.
- I felt lonely.
- I felt sad.

The individual is asked to indicate how frequently he or she experienced the events over the past seven days, using a rating from 0 (rarely or none of the time, less than one day) to 3 (most or all of the time, five to seven days). All of these measures essentially derive a "level" of depression, with higher scores indicating greater levels of depression. For example, on the CES-D, scores could range from 0 to 60. A score of 16 or more indicates that the individual experienced some level of depression over the past week. It is important to note that a qualified mental health professional should be consulted to make a reliable clinical diagnosis of depression.

In many exercise studies, the depression score obtained on the questionnaire of choice is usually examined before and after a single bout of exercise or, more commonly, before and after some type of exercise intervention.

Research on Exercise and Depression

Systematic research has been conducted to examine the relationship between exercise and mental health since the late 1960s. This section presents evidence for the beneficial effects of exercise on depression, from mild to moderate levels of depression to clinical manifestations of the disorder.

Physical activity/exercise has been shown to be a useful tool in the treatment of such mental disorders/disabilities, whether mild/moderate or severe, and may be a useful treatment strategy when the goal is to return those who suffer from such debilitating mental problems to a more productive, independent lifestyle. There is even some evidence that physicians use exercise as at least part of the treatment for depressive disorders. A survey published in *The Physician and Sportsmedicine* (albeit a survey of physicians who read this particular publication, which may introduce at least some bias) revealed that of the 1,750 physicians who participated in the survey, 85 percent prescribed exercise for patients suffering from depression (Ryan, 1983). Perhaps more important, evidence from epidemiological surveys indicates that a lifestyle of regular physical activity may be influential in preventing such debilitating mental disorders from developing or at least reducing the risk of such disorders. This has particular importance, because as Morgan (1994) pointed out, the widespread nature of depression makes both pharmacological and psychotherapeutic treatments less desirable owing to the time, money, and potential side effects involved.

EVIDENCE FOR PREVENTIVE EFFECTS

A number of cross-sectional epidemiological studies have examined the role of exercise in promoting and maintaining mental health (preventing mental illness). Stephens (1988), in four separate samples ranging in size from 3,025 to 23,791, found self-reported physical activity to be associated with better mental health, which included fewer symptoms of anxiety and depression. Weyerer (1992), using a community sample of 1,536 individuals from Bavaria, showed that those who were physically inactive were over three times more likely to have depressive symptoms than those who were regularly active. In another international sample, Hassmen, Koivula, and Uutela (2000) noted that those who exercised less frequently had greater reporting of depressive symptoms on the Beck Depression Inventory discussed earlier, a commonly used tool for assessing such symptoms.

A number of prospective studies have provided further evidence for a link between physical activity and depression prevention. Prospective studies are able to examine how the risk of developing depression plays out over a period of time. Farmer et al. (1988) found that women who were sedentary or engaged in little activity were twice as likely to develop depression [measured as symptoms using the Center for Epidemiologic Studies–Depression (CES-D) scale] over an eight-year follow-up period as those who were at least moderately active. Furthermore, inactivity at baseline was a strong predictor of continued depression at follow-up. In the Alameda County Study, Camacho, Roberts, Lazarus, Kaplan, and Cohen (1991) found an association between inactivity and incidence of depression from 1965 to 1983. The relative risk of developing depression was significantly greater for men and women at both follow-up periods (1974, 1983) if they were inactive in 1965. Those who were inactive at baseline but became active (at either moderate or high levels) by one of the follow-up periods were at no greater risk than were those who were active at baseline, highlighting the potential importance of physical activity in warding off depression. Similarly, Paffenbarger, Lee, and Leung (1994), in a sample of more than 21,000 college alumni, found that physical activity at baseline was negatively associated with depression 25 years later (i.e., more activity predicted lower depression). Finally, Mobily, Rubenstein, Lemke, O'Hara, and Wallace (1996), in a sample of 2,084 older male and females, found that of individuals who reported (using the CES-D) greater numbers of depressive symptoms at baseline, those who subsequently became daily walkers had a greater likelihood of reduced depressive symptoms at the three-year follow-up.

All together, these cross-sectional and prospective studies show an association between (lack of) activity and depression. Specifically, people who are less active or sedentary are at greater risk for depression than are people who are more active. Perhaps not surprisingly, the connection between the growing lack of physical activity and increasing incidence and prevalence of mental health problems in industrialized nations has led numerous investigators to suggest that the decline of physical activity is largely responsible for the rise of the mental health problems (Johnsgard, 1989; Martinsen, 2002; Thayer, 2001). The consistent finding has been that the least active have the greatest incidence of mental health problems. Thus, regular physical activity can be useful in preventing mental disorders or in reducing their risk of occurrence.

EVIDENCE FOR USE OF EXERCISE AS TREATMENT

Although the evidence for preventive effects of exercise on depression is noteworthy, we are still investigating whether exercise can be a useful treatment once mental disorders, and in particular severely disabling forms of such disorders, have manifested themselves. The exercise–depression literature includes studies examining exercise effects on those with mild to moderate levels of depression and on clinical samples. Although not as much research has been done with clinical as with nonclinical populations, there has been a more concerted effort of late to examine the utility of exercise in treating clinical manifestations of depression. Clearly, some evidence suggests that exercise can be useful in the treatment of clinical as well as nonclinical depression. In his book *The Exercise Prescription for Depression and Anxiety,* clinical psychologist Keith Johnsgard (1989) cites numerous case study examples of how exercise has been useful in the treatment of both anxiety and mood disorders in his patients. The box on the following page presents a synopsis of one of the cases.

Other, more carefully controlled studies have highlighted the utility of such an "exercise prescription." Research summaries of the exercise–depression literature have taken the form of both the more traditional "narrative" reviews and the more recently used "quantitative" reviews, more commonly referred to as **meta-analyses** (see box on page 143). In the following sections, we examine the evidence found in some of these studies for the effectiveness of exercise in treating non-clinical and clinical samples.

■ meta-analyses

Nonclinical Depression

One of the more oft-cited and comprehensive reviews of the exercise–depression literature is a meta-analysis conducted by North, McCullagh, and Tran (1990). Using data from 80 studies, North et al. calculated 290 effect sizes that represent the amount of impact exercise

Sample Case Study Synopsis

One case involved a man who had lost his wife to suicide and who was struggling with a great deal of depression and guilt. Johnsgard prescribed a two-pronged approach to treatment: symptom prescription and exercise therapy. The symptom prescription involved requiring the patient to ruminate for an hour each day on nothing but his guilt feelings. The exercise therapy involved walking/jogging for the same hour each day. Johnsgard is convinced that the two treatments had a substantive interaction effect. The patient "recovered" fairly quickly, with Johnsgard noting that the patient came to realize that he had control over his guilt ruminations. The exercise had an effect of its own as well. Johnsgard speculated that the exercise might have resulted in greater activation of the antidepressant neurotransmitters in the patient's brain, that the tranquilizing effect of the exercise allowed the individual to sleep better, and that the patient had more energy.

Source: Johnsgard (1989).

had on depression in each of the studies. From these effect sizes a number of primary findings were found, including:

1. Exercise resulted in decreased depression.
2. Certain factors moderated exercise treatment effects while others did not.
3. Exercise was as effective as and sometimes more effective than, traditional therapies.

Decreased depression. Perhaps the most important finding was that exercise results in decreased depression, yielding an effect size of 0.53. This is interpreted to mean that depression is reduced fairly sizably as a result of exercise of some sort.

moderating factors ■

Moderating factors. Moderating factors are variables that could influence or "moderate" the treatment effects. In North et al.'s (1990) meta-analysis the moderating factors considered were (1) exercise variables and (2) subject variables.

EXERCISE VARIABLES

- *Mode of exercise.* One factor of importance was whether the kind of exercise matters. North et al. (1990) found no differences among various modes of exercise. Whether people engaged in weight training, walking, jogging, or various other aerobic activities, the reduction of depression was similar.

Defining Meta-Analysis

Meta-analysis is a technique for statistically synthesizing a body of literature. As noted by North et al. (1990), meta-analytic methodology has the following primary purposes:

1. Increasing statistical power, or the ability to find differences when they exist, for example, whether levels of depression differ between a group that exercises and a group that doesn't
2. Resolution of conflicting studies
3. Better estimates of magnitude of an effect (referred to as an **effect size**), for example, how big the difference in depression is between those who exercise and those who don't
4. Allowing questions to be addressed that may not have been posed in the original studies, because gaps in the knowledge base can now be more readily seen.

One advantage of meta-analysis is that it allows the quantification of the effects of a treatment, exercise in this case, across a variety of moderating factors. It is worth pointing out that not all exercise scientists are impressed by the advantages offered by meta-analytic techniques (see Morgan, 1994), but the conclusions from the different kinds of reviews (narrative vs. quantitative) seem to converge to the same points regardless.

- *Length of exercise program.* In studies examining exercise training, the length of the exercise program was apparently not as important as "just doing it." On examining programs ranging in length from less than four weeks to greater than 24 weeks, no particular length resulted in greater reductions in depression than any other. It is of interest to note that it appears from the effect sizes presented that as the length of the program increases, the degree of depression reduction also increases. However, because so few studies have examined longer exercise programs, the apparently greater reduction in depression seen in longer exercise programs is not significantly different from that of shorter programs.
- *Exercise intensity.* Results for other important exercise variables were not as consistent as were mode and the length of the exercise program. Exercise intensity, a factor important to developing the most effective exercise prescription, was not examined consistently enough (or, more likely, reported consistently enough in the 80 studies included in this review) for any comparisons to be made.
- *Duration or frequency.* As for duration or frequency of exercise bouts, neither had any systematic influence on degree of depression reduction. Clearly, much work remains to be done to uncover any systematic influences of the exercise "dose."

- effect size

- *Acute versus chronic.* Another factor of interest in the meta-analysis was whether the exercise was acute or chronic. The depression reduction occurred for both *acute* and *chronic* exercise; in other words, depression was reduced following single bouts of exercise and following longer-term programs of physical activity.

SUBJECT VARIABLES

In addition to studying exercise variables, North et al. (1990) were able to examine a variety of subject variables that may have served as moderating factors, including age, gender, and initial level of depression.

- *Age.* It didn't matter whether subjects were young (under 18 years old), college-aged (18 to 24 years old), or middle-aged (25 to 64 years or age): exercise decreased depression for all ages. The effect was larger for middle-aged adults, but not significantly so.
- *Gender.* The anti-depressant effect was similar for males and females.
- *Initial level.* A final subject variable of interest was whether initial level of depression had an influence on the degree of depression reduction. The meta-analytic findings indicated that both depressed *and* nondepressed subjects showed similar decreases in depression following exercise.

Effectiveness of exercise versus traditional treatments. North et al. (1990) also examined the effectiveness of exercise compared to other typical treatments for depression. They noted that exercise reduced depression better than did no treatment, a waiting list control treatment (designed to control for expectancy effects; see box on the following page), and other enjoyable activities (i.e., nonexercise activities of choice). Exercise was shown to be as effective as more traditional therapies such as relaxation, psychotherapy, and in some instances medication (see below for more extended discussion of this issue).

Finally, exercise in conjunction with psychotherapy yielded the best depression-reducing effects. Perhaps the strongest conclusion to be taken from the North et al. (1990) meta-analysis is that exercise can apparently be a cost-effective treatment for depression. Exercise also has the added benefit of improved physical health, which can of course help in the prevention of an ever-expanding list of physical maladies. Although reviews are no substitute for original research, they do provide answers to questions and highlight deficiencies in the literature (see also Biddle & Mutrie, 2001).

Waiting List Control

In a waiting list control, individuals are recruited to a study with the understanding that there is currently no room for them in the treatment protocol, but that as soon as there is room, they will be included. Thus, the individual has an expectancy of being a participant in the study protocol and should respond in ways that the actual participants would, with the exception of any actual treatment effects. Ethically, at the conclusion of the experimental protocol, these waiting list control subjects should be offered the opportunity to receive the actual treatment protocol.

Clinical Depression

As pointed out in the meta-analytic review of exercise effects on clinical depression by Craft and Landers (1998), the recent changes in the health-care climate with respect to limits on treatment therapies (in terms of both time and money) highlight the need for examination of other, less costly treatment options. As with nonclinical levels of depression, exercise has been used, and is being examined more frequently, as a viable option for the treatment of clinical levels of depression (Dunn, Trivedi, & O'Neal, 2001; O'Neal, Dunn, & Martinsen; 2000). Below we examine the literature on such effects.

In perhaps the classic exercise–depression study, Greist et al. (1979) examined the effects of running compared to time-limited and time-unlimited psychotherapy in patients with minor clinical depression as defined by Research Diagnostic Criteria (RDC). Time-limited psychotherapy involves receiving therapy for a specific amount of time (e.g., 16 weeks), whereas time-unlimited psychotherapy does not put time constraints on the therapy. The running treatment (three times per week for 12 weeks) was shown to be as effective as both forms of psychotherapy, with continued improvement at a three-week follow-up.

Martinsen and colleagues have also contributed greatly to our knowledge regarding exercise effects in patients suffering from anxiety and depressive disorders. Martinsen, Medhus, and Sandvik (1985) studied the effects of aerobic exercise in 43 hospitalized psychiatric patients diagnosed with major depression (classified according to DSM–III criteria). Individuals were randomly assigned to either exercise or occupational therapy (control) groups in addition to standard psychotherapy and pharmacotherapy for nine weeks. The exercise group patients had significant reductions in depressive symptoms relative to the control group. Interestingly, patients rated exercise as the most important component of the comprehensive treatment they received. This information was obtained one to two years after the patients were discharged. More than 90 percent of the subjects continued to exercise regularly on their own, with 65 percent exercising aerobically for two or more hours per week.

Martinsen, Hoffart, and Solberg (1989) demonstrated that both aerobic and nonaerobic (muscular strength, flexibility) exercise resulted in significant psychological improvements in 99 clinically depressed in-patients who met DSM–III-R criteria for major depression, dysthymic disorder, or nonspecified depressive disorders. A third intervention study was conducted by Martinsen, Sandvik, and Kolbjornsrud (1989) with 92 nonpsychotic in-patients. The intervention consisted of eight weeks of at least one hour of aerobic exercise five times per week. All patients showed significant increases in physical fitness, as demonstrated by increased physical work capacity, with alcohol abuse or dependence patients showing the largest reductions in symptom scores (assessed via the Symptom Rating Test). Patients with unipolar depressive and anxiety disorders (generalized anxiety disorder and agoraphobia) also showed significant symptom reduction. In 84 percent of the patients who responded to a one-year follow-up, regular exercise habits were strongly associated with low symptom scores; in other words, those who exercised more regularly had fewer symptoms than did those who did not exercise.

Singh, Clements, and Fiatarone (1997) conducted a randomized, controlled trial with 32 individuals (71.3 years old) diagnosed with major or minor depression or dysthymia (DSM-IV). A randomized controlled trial is the best experimental design, because individuals are selected to represent accurately the population from which they are drawn, and then these individuals are randomly assigned to either the treatment or to a control condition. In this study, the exercise involved a 10-week program of supervised progressive resistance training (three times per week). An attention-control group, designed to prevent expectancy effects, met twice a week and received lectures and videos on health education. Exercise patients had significant reductions in depression, as measured by the BDI and Hamilton Rating Scale, compared with controls after the 10-week intervention. A significant increase in strength was seen in the exercise group, with intensity of training serving as a significant predictor of depression reduction. In other words, people who trained harder had greater reductions in depression.

Singh, Clements, and Fiatarone Singh (2001) reported in a follow-up study that the 10 weeks of supervised weight lifting was followed by 10 weeks of unsupervised exercise. Exercise patients had significant reductions in BDI depression compared with controls at both 20 weeks and 26 months of follow-up.

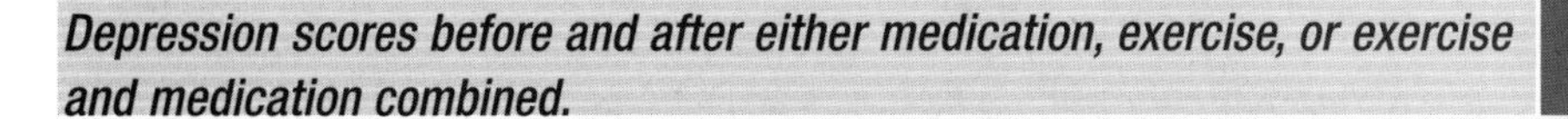

exhibit 7.3

Depression scores before and after either medication, exercise, or exercise and medication combined.

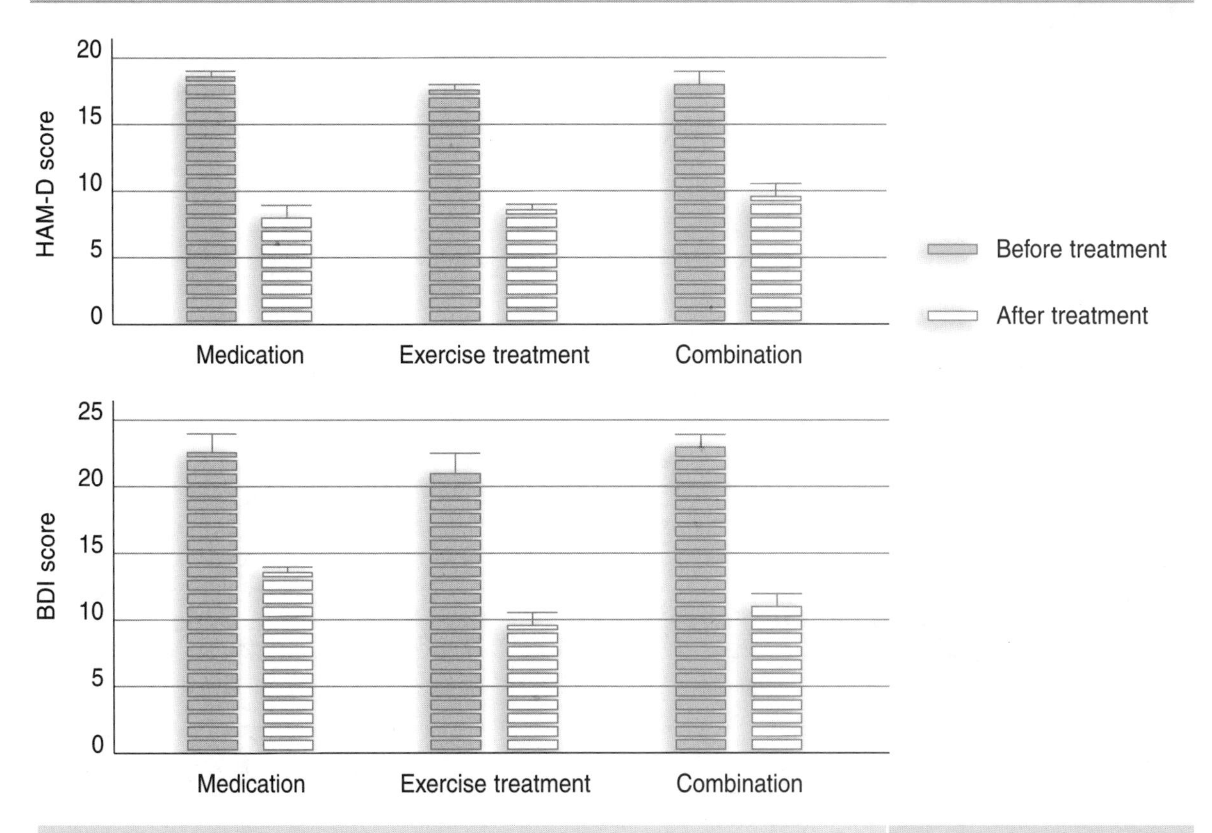

Source: Blumenthal, J. A., et al. (1999). Effects of exercise training on older patients with major depression. *Archives of Internal Medicine, 159,* 2349–2356. Copyright © 1999, American Medical Association.

Blumenthal et al. (1999), in their Standardized Medical Intervention and Long-term Exercise (SMILE) study, randomly placed 156 patients with major depressive disorder in one of three 16-week treatments:

1. exercise training (three times per week at 70 to 85 percent of maximum heart rate)
2. pharmacotherapy (sertraline)
3. combined exercise and pharmacotherapy.

All three treatment groups showed reduced depressive symptoms, with no clinically or statistically significant differences among them (see Exhibit 7.3). In other words, the exercise treatment was *as effective as* both the drug and the combined drug and exercise treatments. Six months

Percentage of patients whose depression had returned eight months following either exercise, medication, or exercise and medication treatments.

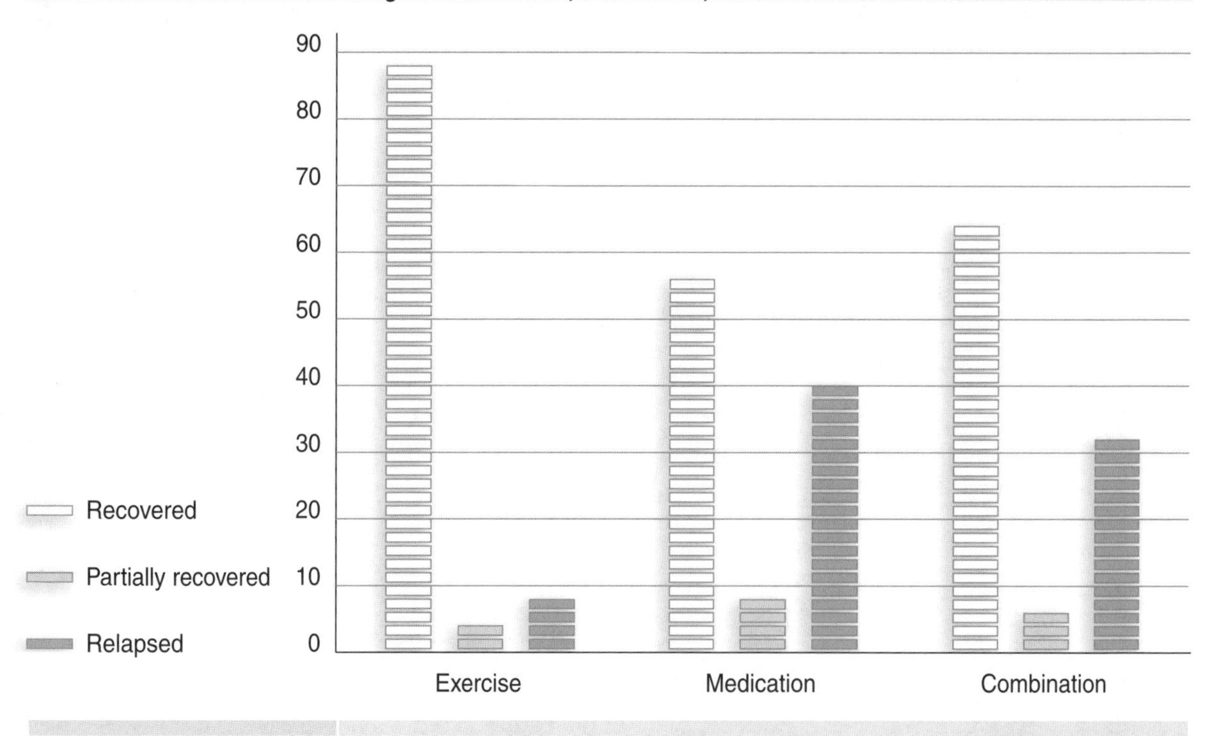

Source: Babyak et al. (2000). Exercise treatment for major depression: Maintenance of therapeutic benefit at 10 months. *Psychosomatic Medicine, 62(5),* 633–638. Reprinted with permission of Lippincott, Williams, & Wilkins.

after completion of the formal treatment phase, a follow-up with the same sample (Babyak et al., 2000) found that fewer individuals had relapsed in the exercise treatment group (i.e., had recurrences of depression) than in the medication group (see Exhibit 7.4). Babyak et al. noted that continuing to exercise on one's own was related to a reduced likelihood of being diagnosed as depressed even after formal treatment had stopped.

In light of findings like those presented above, Tkachuk and Martin (1999) noted in their review of the literature that significant improvements could be obtained in those who are clinically depressed. Such improvements were seen with exercise training of:

1. at least five weeks duration
2. three times per week of supervised aerobic or nonaerobic activity
3. low to moderate intensity (50 percent maximum heart rate)
4. durations of 20 to 60 minutes.

Consensus statements regarding exercise and depression. **exhibit 7.5**

1. Exercise can be associated with a decreased level of mild to moderate depression.
2. Exercise may be an adjunct to the professional treatment of severe depression.

Source: Adapted from Morgan & Goldston (1987).

Follow-up assessments have shown maintenance of improvements up to one year post-treatment, particularly when some level of activity is continued. Finally, Tkachuk and Martin concluded that exercise could be more cost effective than traditional treatments. In other words, exercise can be a cheaper alternative than medication, and, when used in conjunction with other traditional treatments, it might reduce the level of medication, the length of time medication is needed, and perhaps even the need for medication at all.

Before turning to a discussion of the mechanisms proposed to explain the effect of exercise on depression, we provide a summary of consensus statements regarding exercise and depression in Exhibit 7.5.

MECHANISMS OF CHANGE

As the research discussed in the preceding section shows, a primary interest of the work examining the effects of exercise on depression is "simply" to demonstrate that there is an effect. Equally important is the interest in understanding why such changes occur. Pursuing this understanding often involves the search for the mechanisms underlying such effects. In the domain of exercise and depression reduction, a number of plausible mechanisms have been discussed, although relatively little research has been done to date to systematically examine such possibilities. Among these mechanisms are those that are primarily physiological in nature on the one hand, and those that are primarily psychological on the other. The ultimate explanation will likely not be one or the other, but rather a combination of biopsychosocial explanations. (Many of these same explanations are also posited to explain the reductions in anxiety associated with exercise; see Chapter 8.)

Anthropological Hypothesis

Recently labeled the **anthropological hypothesis** (Martinsen, 2002), one potential explanation for the link between physical activity and depression reflects an evolutionary perspective. As Martinsen recent-

■ anthropological hypothesis

ly pointed out, humans spent the vast majority of their existence in lifestyles that emphasized physical activity. Whether as hunter–gatherers or even as recently as in the early twentieth century, when manual labor still predominated, our lifestyles typically required large amounts of physical activity on a daily basis. Only within the last 50 years or so has technology progressed to the point that such vigorous forms of activity are no longer necessary for our survival. Interestingly, it is also within the past 50 years or so that incidences of depression have increased dramatically. It seems highly unlikely that this has been coincidental. Given the epidemiological evidence linking physical activity with decreased depression, it may very well be that we are "violating our genetic warranty" (Johnsgard, 1989) by not engaging in more regular physical activity. In other words, the anthropological hypothesis suggests that human beings are genetically designed to be physically active. If we violate this genetic predisposition by being sedentary, then perhaps it is not surprising that we subsequently face a host of health problems, including depression.

Endorphin Hypothesis

endorphin hypothesis ■

The explanation for the depression-reducing effects of exercise that clearly has been the most popular with the media is the **endorphin hypothesis** (see Hoffmann, 1997). This hypothesis has been discussed as a possible explanation in nearly every exercise–depression literature review. The essence of the hypothesis is that during stress (e.g., exercise) the body produces endorphins. Endorphins are neuropeptides—"informational substances" (Pert, 1997) that make communication between neurons possible—and are thought to be analogous to the drug morphine. The name *endorphin* is derived from the combination of the terms "endogenous" (naturally occurring) and "morphine." Endorphins are the body's own natural painkillers. Thus, if endorphins are released during exercise and exercise makes us feel better (e.g., less depressed), then the increased endorphins could be the reason why. At this point, however, it appears that for every solid study that has supported the endorphin hypothesis, there is an equally solid study that refutes it. Clearly, more work is needed before any firm conclusions can be reached.

Monamine Hypothesis

monoamine hypothesis ■

The **monoamine hypothesis** has been proposed as another mechanism to explain the depression-reducing effects of exercise. This hypothesis has been divided into more specific hypotheses in recent years, evolving into the serotonin hypothesis (Chaouloff, 1997) and the norepinephrine hypothesis (Dishman, 1997). In essence, these hypotheses attempt to explain the effects of exercise on depression through the alteration of brain neurotransmitters like serotonin, norepinephrine, and dopamine. All of these neurotransmitters have been implicated in the regulation of emotion, variously enhancing or inhibiting emotion, and are also altered through exercise (e.g., increased release, increased uptake, etc.). In other words, exercise can increase the rate at which neurotransmitters are produced, released into the spaces between neurons (allowing communication between neurons), or taken up by neurons (again resulting in either a facilitation or inhibition of the neuronal action). Much of the evidence for these hypotheses is based on animal research, largely because it is rather difficult to assess levels of these neurotransmitters in intact humans. It remains to be seen to what extent they will ultimately help explain the effects of exercise on depression; undoubtedly they will.

Mastery Hypothesis

A psychological explanation for the depression-reducing effects of exercise is the **mastery hypothesis** (see Biddle & Mutrie, 2001). This hypothesis posits that the psychological effects of exercise are derived from the sense of accomplishment or mastery that is felt upon completion of a task. This is thought to give the individual a sense of greater self-worth or personal control over the environment. (See Chapter 10 for more information.)

- mastery hypothesis

Social Interaction Hypothesis

The **social interaction hypothesis,** quite simply, proposes that the reason exercise reduces depression is that it provides an opportunity for the individual to interact with others. Certainly, some (perhaps many) people enjoy exercising in a social setting (e.g., aerobics class, running with a partner). It is quite clear, however, that while this explanation may account, in part, for the depression reduction following exercise, it cannot be the sole explanation. The social interaction idea completely fails when data from laboratory studies and more ecologically valid settings show that exercising alone also results in reduced levels of depression. The Blumenthal et al. (1999) study with older depressives showed significant reductions in depression following 16 weeks of aerobic exercise, effects that are not accounted for by any social interaction influences.

- social interaction hypothesis

Distraction/Time-Out Hypothesis

distraction/time-out hypothesis ■

The **distraction/time-out hypothesis** grew out of the findings from the Bahrke and Morgan (1978) study described in Chapter 8, wherein 20 minutes of either treadmill exercise, noncultic meditation, or sitting quietly in a sound-dampened chamber reading a *Reader's Digest* magazine (which has come to be known as the "quiet rest" condition) were compared from pre-treatment to post-treatment and 10 minutes post-treatment. There were essentially no differences across the three conditions. This particular hypothesis, stated simply, says that the anxiety-reducing effects seen with exercise are due to the distraction it provides from the normal routine. It allows the depressed, anxious, stressed person to "leave behind" or take a time-out from his or her cares and worries. Other distraction "therapies" have also been shown to reduce depression and anxiety (e.g., meditation, relaxation, quiet rest). As noted earlier, however, the effect of exercise may be qualitatively different from other cognitively based therapies because the exercise effect lasts longer. The distraction hypothesis remains a possible explanation for depression and anxiety reduction; however, it appears that the exercise-related depression and anxiety reduction is the consequence of more than simply taking time away from one's daily routine, given the evidence available.

As noted earlier, any of these proposed mechanisms may be operating to drive the changes in depression typically seen with exercise. It remains to be determined to what extent these (or others) might actually explain the effects.

Practical Recommendations

As noted by Johnsgard (1989), research consistently "shows that 30 minutes of aerobic exercise three times a week will significantly reduce depression" (p. 280). The "minimal" level of exercise activity (i.e., frequency, duration, intensity) is currently unknown, but it seems clear that exercise done on a regular basis can be useful in the treatment of depression as well as in protecting against depression that we might ordinarily succumb to if we remained sedentary. The type of exercise does not seem to matter, as both aerobic and nonaerobic (e.g., weight training) forms of exercise seem to be effective in reducing depression.

Those suffering from more severe forms of depression can also find relief in exercise therapies. As demonstrated by Susan, the psychologist in the chapter-opening scenario, mental health professionals clearly need to be educated as to the value of exercise as another tool at their

Risk categories for medical exams before beginning an aerobic training program.

exhibit 7.6

LEVEL OF RISK	POPULATION		RISK FACTORS	TYPE OF PROGRAM	PRIOR PHYSICAL EXAM
Low	men < 45 yrs. women < 55 yrs.	No more than one	Family history of coronary artery disease, cigarette smoking, hypertension	Moderate Vigorous	No No
Moderate	men ≥ 45 yrs. women ≥ 55 yrs.	Two or more	Hypercholesterolemia, impaired fasting glucose, obesity, sedentary lifestyle	Moderate Vigorous	No Yes
High	All	One or more	Known cardiovascular, pulmonary, or metabolic disease, ischemia, dizziness/syncope, orthopnea/paroxysmal nocturnal dyspnea, ankle edema, palpitations/tachycardia, intermittent claudication, known heart murmur, unusual fatigue	All	Yes

Source: Housh, Housh, & DeVries (2003), *Applied Exercise and Sport Physiology* (Scottsdale, AZ: Holcomb Hathaway).

disposal in helping patients suffering from subclinical and clinical levels of depression. Obviously, medical clearance from a physician should be obtained before any exercise program is prescribed (Tkachuk & Martin, 1999, outline three classes of individuals with varying levels of risk factors and the attendant cautions associated with exercise for each; see Exhibit 7.6). Tkachuk and Martin also provide guidelines for the use of exercise therapy that should prove useful. Included among their recommendations are the following:

1. Obtain information about the individual's past experiences with exercise to determine enjoyable/disliked activities as a way of enhancing adherence to the exercise program.
2. Exercise with the individual for support and to provide a model of correct behavior.
3. Help to make the exercise adaptable to the individual's lifestyle (e.g., walking to work, including household activities).
4. Utilize the individual's environment to foster activity (e.g., parks, home equipment).

5. Monitor exercise dosage (i.e., frequency, intensity, duration), modifying as the individual's level of fitness changes.
6. Help the individual to understand that setbacks may occur and to devise strategies for dealing with them (discussed in Chapter 4).

Conclusion

Given the information presented herein, it would seem reasonable to promote the value of regular physical activity. The evidence from epidemiological/prospective studies fairly clearly links lack of physical activity with increased risk for and prevalence of mental disorders. It also seems reasonable to propose that physical activity be carefully considered as an important part of any treatment regimen for depression. We may certainly make the case that exercise can indeed be a valuable tool in the treatment "toolbox" for those suffering from mental disorders and disabilities. At the very least, the consensus statements regarding exercise and depression that appear in Exhibit 7.5 seem to be warranted. Beyond the positive mental health effects, physical activity concomitantly leads to the improvement of physical health as well, further reducing the risks of debilitating chronic disease conditions.

What Do You Know?

1. What is the difference between mental health and mental illness?
2. What percentage of adults in the United States suffer from some type of mental health problem in a given year?
3. What are some of the symptoms associated with mild to moderate depression?
4. What is the major tool used in the diagnosis of mental disorders?
5. What is known from the cross-sectional and prospective studies regarding the association between (lack of) activity and depression?
6. How long do exercise programs need to be to result in reductions in depression?
7. What is the optimal "dosage" in terms of type, frequency, intensity, and duration needed for depression reduction?
8. Can exercise be useful in the treatment of clinical levels of depression? What evidence is there to support this answer?
9. What is the basis for the anthropological hypothesis as a mechanism to explain the exercise–depression relationship?

10. Which hypothesis for explaining the exercise–depression relationship relies on changes in neuropeptides?

Learning Activities

1. Imagine that your help as an expert in exercise psychology has been solicited by a clinical psychologist who is designing an exercise program as part of the treatment plan for a patient suffering from depression. Utilizing the guidelines outlined by Tkachuk and Martin (1999), describe the exercise therapy that you would recommend.
2. Develop an argument that you would use in trying to convince an individual suffering from mild to moderate depression that he should consider beginning an exercise program as a way of helping to deal with the depression. You will need to be as convincing as you can, so you should incorporate reasons for exercising from many different approaches (e.g., both physical and psychological).

References

American Psychiatric Association. (1994). *Diagnostic and statistical manual of mental disorders* (4th ed.). Washington, DC: American Psychiatric Association.

Babyak, M. A., Blumenthal, J. A., Herman, S., Khatri, P., Doraiswamy, P. M., Moore, K. A., Craighead, W. E., Baldewicz, T. T., & Krishnan, K. R. (2000). Exercise treatment for major depression: Maintenance of therapeutic benefit at 10 months. *Psychosomatic Medicine, 62*(5), 633–638.

Bahrke, M. S., & Morgan, W. P. (1978). Anxiety reduction following exercise and meditation. *Cognitive Therapy and Research, 2*, 323–333.

Biddle, S. J. H., & Mutrie, N. (2001). Depression and other mental illnesses. In S. J. H. Biddle & N. Mutrie, Eds., *Psychology of physical activity: Determinants, well-being and interventions* (pp. 202–235). London: Routledge.

Blumenthal, J. A., Babyak, M. A., Moore, K. A., Craighead, W. E., Herman, S., Khatri, P., Waugh, R., Napolitano, M. A., Forman, L. M., Appelbaum, M., Doraiswamy, P. M., & Krishnan, K. R. (1999). Effects of exercise training on older patients with major depression. *Archives of Internal Medicine, 159*, 2349–2356.

Camacho, T. C., Roberts, R. E., Lazarus, N. B., Kaplan, G. A., & Cohen, R. D. (1991). Physical activity and depression: Evidence from the Alameda County Study. *American Journal of Epidemiology, 134*, 220–231.

Centers for Disease Control and Prevention. (1998). Self-reported frequent mental distress among adults: United States, 1993–1996. *Morbidity and Mortality Weekly Report, 47*(16), 325–331.

Chaouloff, F. (1997). The serotonin hypothesis. In W. P. Morgan (Ed.), *Physical activity and mental health* (pp. 179–198). Washington, DC: Taylor & Francis.

Craft, L. L., & Landers, D. M. (1998). The effect of exercise on clinical depression and depression resulting from mental illness: A meta-analysis. *Journal of Sport and Exercise Psychology, 20*, 339–357.

Dishman, R. K. (1997). The norepinephrine hypothesis. In W. P. Morgan (Ed.), *Physical activity and mental health* (pp. 199–212). Washington, DC: Taylor & Francis.

Dunn, A. L., Trivedi, M. H., & O'Neal, H. A. (2001). Physical activity dose-response effects on outcomes of depression and anxiety. *Medicine and Science in Sports and Exercise, 33* (Supplement), S587–S597.

Farmer, M. E., Locke, B. Z., Moscicki, E. K., Dannenberg, A. L., Larson, D. B., & Radloff, L. S. (1988). Physical activity and depressive symptoms: The NHANES I epidemiological follow-up study. *American Journal of Epidemiology, 128,* 1340–1351.

Greenberg, P. E., Stiglin, L. E., Finkelstein, S. N., & Berndt, E. R. (1993). The economic burden of depression in 1990. *Journal of Clinical Psychiatry, 54*(11), 405–418.

Greist, J. H., Klein, M. H., Eischens, R. R., Faris, J. W., Gurman, A. S., & Morgan, W. P. (1979). Running as a treatment for depression. *Comprehensive Psychiatry, 20,* 41–54.

Hamilton, M. (1960). A rating scale for depression. *Journal of Neurology, Neurosurgery and Psychiatry, 23,* 56–62.

Hassmen, P., Koivula, N., & Uutela, A. (2000). Physical exercise and psychological well-being: A population study. *Preventive Medicine, 30,* 17–25.

Hoffmann, P. (1997). The endorphin hypothesis. In W. P. Morgan (Ed.), *Physical activity and mental health* (pp. 163-177). Washington, DC: Taylor & Francis.

Johnsgard, K. W. (1989). *The exercise prescription for depression and anxiety.* New York: Plenum.

Kellner, R., & Sheffield, B. F. (1973). A self-rating scale of distress. *Psychological Medicine, 3,* 88–100.

Kessler, R. C., McGonagle, K. A., Zhao, S., Nelson, C. B., Hughes, M., Eshleman, S., Wittchen, H. U., & Kendler, K. S. (1994). Lifetime and 12-month prevalence of DSM-III-R psychiatric disorders in the United States: Results from the National Comorbidity Survey. *Archives of General Psychiatry, 51,* 8–18.

Lawlor, D. A., & Hopker, S. W. (2001). The effectiveness of exercise as an intervention in the management of depression: Systematic review and meta-regression analysis of randomized controlled trials. *British Medical Journal, 322,* 1–8.

Martinsen, E. W. (2002). The role of exercise in the management of depression. In D. L. Mostofsky & L. D. Zaichowsky (Eds.), *Medical and psychological aspects of sport and exercise* (pp. 205–214). Morgantown, WV: Fitness Information Technology.

Martinsen, E. W., Hoffart, A., & Solberg, O. Y. (1989). Comparing aerobic with anaerobic forms of exercise in the treatment of clinical depression: A randomized trial. *Comprehensive Psychiatry, 30,* 324–331.

Martinsen, E. W., Medhus, A., & Sandvik, L. (1985). Effects of aerobic exercise on depression: A controlled study. *British Medical Journal, 291,* 109.

Martinsen, E. W., Sandvik, L., & Kolbjornsrud, O. B. (1989). Aerobic exercise in the treatment of nonpsychotic mental disorders: An exploratory study. *Nordic Journal of Psychiatry, 43,* 521–529.

Mobily, K. E., Rubenstein, L. M., Lemke, J. H., O'Hara, M. W., & Wallace, R. B. (1996). Walking and depression in a cohort of older adults: The Iowa 65+ Rural Health Study. *Journal of Aging and Physical Activity, 4,* 119–135.

Morgan, W. P. (1968). Selected physiological and psychomotor correlates of depression in psychiatric patients. *Research Quarterly, 39,* 1037–1043.

Morgan, W. P. (1969). A pilot investigation of physical working capacity in depressed and nondepressed psychiatric males. *Research Quarterly, 40,* 859–861.

Morgan, W. P. (1970). Physical working capacity in depressed and non-depressed psychiatric females: A preliminary study. *American Corrective Therapy Journal, 24,* 14–16.

Morgan, W. P. (1994). Physical activity, fitness, and depression. In C. Bouchard, R. J. Shephard, & T. Stephens (Eds.), *Physical activity, fitness, and health: International proceedings and consen-*

sus statement (pp. 851–867). Champaign, IL: Human Kinetics.

Morgan, W. P., & Goldston, S. E. (Eds.). (1987). *Exercise and mental health.* Washington, DC: Hemisphere.

Murray, C. J. L., & Lopez, A. D. (1996). *The global burden of disease: A comprehensive assessment of mortality and disability from diseases, injuries, and risk factors in 1990 and projected to 2020.* Cambridge, MA: Harvard School of Public Health.

North, T. C., McCullagh, P., & Tran, Z. V. (1990). Effect of exercise on depression. *Exercise & Sport Sciences Reviews, 18,* 379–415.

O'Neal, H. A., Dunn, A. L., & Martinsen, E. W. (2000). Depression and exercise. *International Journal of Sport Psychology, 31*(2), 110–135.

Paffenbarger, R. S., Lee, I. M., & Leung, R. (1994). Physical activity and personal characteristics associated with depression and suicide in American college men. *Acta Psychiatrica Scandinavica, Suppl. 377,* 16–22.

Pert, C. B. (1997). *Molecules of emotion.* New York: Scribner.

Regier, D. A., Narrow, W. E., Rae, D. S., Manderscheid, R. W., Locke, B. Z., & Goodwin, F. K. (1993). The de facto U.S. mental and addictive disorders service system: Epidemiologic Catchment Area prospective 1-year prevalence rates of disorders and services. *Archives of General Psychiatry, 50,* 85–94.

Rice, D. P., & Miller, L. S. (1996). The economic burden of schizophrenia: Conceptual and methodological issues and cost estimates. In M. Moscarelli, A. Rupp, & N. Sartorious (Eds.), *Handbook of mental health economics and health policy. Vol. 1: Schizophrenia* (pp. 321–324). New York: Wiley.

Robins, L. N., Helzer, J. E., Weissman, M. M., Orvaschel, H., Gruenberg, E., Burke, J. D., Jr., & Regier, D. A. (1984). Lifetime prevalence of specific psychiatric disorders in three sites. *Archives of General Psychiatry, 41*(10), 949–958.

Ryan, A. J. (1983). Exercise is medicine. *Physician & Sportsmedicine, 11,* 10.

Singh, N. A., Clements, K. M., & Fiatarone Singh, M. A. (2001).The efficacy of exercise as a long-term antidepressant in elderly subjects: A randomized, controlled trial. *Journal of Gerontology: Medical Sciences, 56A*(1), M497–M504.

Singh, N. A., Clements, K. M., & Fiatarone, M. A. (1997). A randomized controlled trial of progressive resistance training in depressed elders. *Journal of Gerontology, 52A*(1), M27–M35.

Spitzer, R. L., Endicott, J., & Robins, E. (1978). Research diagnostic criteria: Rationale and reliability. *Archives of General Psychiatry, 35,* 773–782.

Stephens, T. (1988). Physical activity and mental health in the United States and Canada: Evidence from four population surveys. *Preventive Medicine, 17,* 35–47.

Thayer, R. E. (2001). *Calm energy: How people regulate mood with food and exercise.* New York: Oxford.

Tkachuk, G. A., & Martin, G. L. (1999). Exercise therapy for patients with psychiatric disorders: Research and clinical implications. *Professional Psychology: Research and Practice, 30*(3), 275–282.

U.S. Department of Health and Human Services. (1999). *Mental health: A report of the Surgeon General.* Rockville, MD: U.S. Department of Health and Human Services, Substance Abuse and Mental Health Services Administration, Center for Mental Health Services, National Institutes of Health, National Institute of Mental Health.

Weyerer, S. (1992). Physical inactivity and depression in the community: Evidence from the Upper Bavarian Field Study. *International Journal of Sports Medicine, 13*(6), 492–496.

World Health Organization (1993). *The ICD-10 classification of mental and behavioral disorders: Diagnostic criteria for research.* Geneva: World Health Organization.

Chapter 8

Anxiety/Stress and Exercise

Jim has begun his first semester at the university as a pre-med student. His first class every Monday and Wednesday is a very challenging anatomy and physiology class. Jim gets the feeling from the very first day that his instructor doesn't like him, and this creates a lot of stress for Jim. He is at the point that he dreads going to lectures and the mere thought of those lectures makes his heart race and blood pressure skyrocket. Jim begins to get physically ill on the mornings of his class and his grades start to suffer as a result. He finally seeks help at the student health center and is fortunate enough to get an appointment with a physician who is an avid exerciser. She suggests that Jim get up an hour earlier on the days of his lectures and go for a 20-minute run, preceded by and followed up with some stretching. She suggests that he start at a very easy pace, but that he gradually build up to whatever pace he feels comfortable with. Jim begins the next day and within two weeks he is running for 35 minutes every other day. On the days of his anatomy and physiology class, he still gets nervous before class, but he somehow feels better able to handle the stress of the course. He even begins to view it as a challenge rather than an obstacle. The morning run becomes almost ritualistic for Jim, and he is certain it is the most important thing he ever did to help him prepare for the challenges of the day.

> "Exercise has the effect of defusing anger and rage, fear and anxiety. Like music, it soothes the savage in us that lies so close to the surface. It is the ultimate tranquilizer."
>
> —George Sheehan, *How to Feel Great 24 Hours a Day*

KEY TERMS

- anxiety disorders
- anxiolytic
- clinical anxiety
- double blind
- generalized anxiety disorder
- obsessive–compulsive disorder
- panic disorder
- phobias
- physiological toughness
- post-traumatic stress disorder
- state anxiety
- stress
- thermogenic hypothesis
- trait anxiety

Defining Stress and Anxiety

We live in a world that has become very fast paced. As a result, many experience an increasing level of stress in their daily lives. Simply defined, **stress** is what we experience when we face challenges in our lives as Jim experienced when he began his anatomy and physiology class. These challenges are referred to as *stressors,* and they can be external (e.g., physical threats) or internal (e.g., fear of speaking in public). Stress can result from

stress ■

- biological sources—substance abuse (alcohol, drugs)
- nutritional excess (caffeine, food, sugar)
- psychological sources (attitudes such as perfectionism, obsessiveness, compulsiveness, need for control, neurosis)
- social sources (lack of social skills, shyness, insecurity, loneliness, environmental strain such as noise or temperature).

When a person encounters a stressor (e.g., threat of injury, embarrassment or potential loss), the initial reaction is often referred to as "arousal and alarm." This initial reaction is often followed by feelings of anxiety, irritability, and vulnerability until the stressor is resolved. If the stressor continues, a stage of resistance ensues, characterized by strain, worry, cynicism, and difficulty sleeping. If the stressor is prolonged, with no resolution, the individual becomes overloaded. Continuing strain causes fatigue, anxiety, depression, and numerous, insidious stress-related disorders.

Because of ever-increasing stressors in our lives, depression (see Chapter 7), and anxiety and anxiety disorders have become increasingly prevalent problems in our society. Because anxiety is a prominent consequence of stress and exercise has been studied as a way of influencing anxiety, this chapter focuses on the exercise–anxiety relationship. As noted in the Surgeon General's report, the anxiety disorders are the most prevalent of the mental disorders (Regier et al., 1990). **Anxiety disorders** include **panic disorder, phobias, generalized anxiety disorder, obsessive–compulsive disorder,** and **post-traumatic stress disorder.** They, like depression, contribute significantly to the disease and disability burden of the nation. See Exhibit 8.1 for a description of these disorders.

anxiety disorders ■
panic disorder ■
phobias ■
generalized anxiety disorder ■
obsessive–compulsive disorder ■
post-traumatic stress disorder ■

PREVALENCE

Two nationwide probability surveys published in the mid-1990s highlight the prevalence of such disabling mental conditions. The 23.4

percent one-year prevalence rate for any mental disorder in the National Comorbidity Survey (Kessler et al., 1994) included an 18.7 percent one-year prevalence rate for any anxiety disorder, which means that within a given year, 18.7 percent of the U.S. adult population will have a diagnosable anxiety disorder. The Epidemiological Catchment Area Study (Regier et al., 1993) estimated a 19.5 percent one-year prevalence rate for any mental disorder, including 13.1 percent for any anxiety disorder. From these studies, best estimates of the one-year prevalence rates have been calculated to be 16.4 percent for any anxiety disorder (USDHHS, 1999).

The prevalence of these disabling conditions creates an economic burden both in terms of treatment and in terms of lost productivity. Conservative estimates of the indirect costs of all mental illness totaled nearly $80 billion in the United States in 1990 (Rice & Miller, 1996), most of which is reflective of the loss of normal productivity due to illness. In 1996, $69 billion was spent in direct costs for the treatment of mental disorders (USDHHS, 1999). Beyond the immeasurable human suffering, it has been estimated that annual costs associated with anxiety disorders are around $47 billion (DuPont et al., 1996). This accounts for 31.5 percent of the total for *all* mental illness, with about 75 percent of the total attributed to lost or reduced productivity and about 25 percent to direct medical treatment.

SYMPTOMOLOGY

Anxiety can be manifested both psychologically and physiologically, and is characterized by one or more of the following:

1. unpleasant feelings, (e.g., uncertainty over what to do, feeling overwhelmed)
2. bodily symptoms resulting from activation of the autonomic nervous system (e.g., muscle tension, autonomic hyperactivity)
3. changes in cognitions (e.g., recurrent obsessions or compulsions; irrational fear of objects, activities, or situations)
4. changes in behavior (e.g., avoidance of situations)
5. vigilance (e.g., being on the lookout for danger or a problem).

Patients with **clinical anxiety** are often distinguished from those with "normal" anxiety on the basis of the number and intensity of symptoms, degree of suffering, and degree of dysfunction.

■ clinical anxiety

Anxiety need not, however, manifest itself to the extent that it becomes clinical. Often, when we perceive that a situation exceeds our capabilities for effectively coping with it or feel uncertain of our control

exhibit 8.1 *Characteristics of main anxiety disorders.*

Panic Disorder

- Intense fear and discomfort associated with physical and mental symptoms, including:
  - Sweating, trembling, shortness of breath, chest pain, nausea
  - Fear of dying or loss of control of emotions
- Induces urge to escape or run away, and often results in seeking emergency help (e.g., hospital)
- Frequently accompanied by major depressive disorder
- Twice as common in women as in men

Agoraphobia

- Severe, pervasive anxiety when in situations perceived to be difficult to escape from, or complete avoidance of certain situations (e.g., crowded areas, alone outside of home, travel in bus or plane)
- Often seen after onset of panic disorder
- Twice as common in women as in men

Social Phobia (Social Anxiety Disorder)

- Marked, persistent anxiety in social situations (e.g., public speaking)
  - Possibility of embarrassment or ridicule is crucial factor
  - Individual is preoccupied with concern that others will notice the anxiety symptoms (e.g., trembling, sweating, halting/rapid speech)
- Accompanied by anticipatory anxiety days or weeks prior to feared event
- More common in women than in men

Obsessive–Compulsive Disorder

- Obsessions, such as recurrent thoughts or images perceived as inappropriate or forbidden, elicit anxiety
- Individual perceives loss of control, thus acts on impulses or thoughts
- Compulsions, including behaviors or thoughts, reduce anxiety associated with obsessions
  - Includes overt behavior (e.g., hand washing) and mental acts (e.g., counting, praying)
  - Take long periods of time to complete
- Equally common in women and men
- Disorder has fluctuating course, including periods of increased symptoms, usually linked with life stressors

(continued)

Continued. **exhibit 8.1**

Generalized Anxiety Disorder

- Defined by worry lasting more than six months, along with multiple symptoms (e.g., muscle tension, poor concentration, insomnia, irritability)
- Anxiety and worry not attributable to other conditions (e.g., panic disorder, phobias)
- Twice as common in women as in men
- Disorder has fluctuating course, including periods of increased symptoms, usually linked with life stressors

Post-Traumatic Stress Disorder

- Anxiety and behavioral disturbances following exposure to extreme trauma (e.g., combat, physical assault) that persist for more than one month
- Dissociation, symptom involving perceived detachment from emotional state or body, is critical feature
- Symptoms also include generalized anxiety, hyperarousal, avoidance of situations that trigger memories of trauma, recurrent thoughts
- Occurs in about 9 percent of those exposed to extreme trauma

Source: USDHHS (1999), pp. 234–237.

over the situation, we experience stress. When our appraisal becomes negative, anxiety is often the result. This is a state characterized by worry, self-doubt, nervousness, and tension, but a state that also disrupts thought processes and behavior, and alters physiological functioning. When anxiety affects these processes to such an extent that normal behavior is disrupted, it becomes clinical.

TREATMENT

Traditional treatment protocols for anxiety (e.g., medication, psychotherapy), while readily available and generally effective, are often expensive and time consuming as is the case with depression. Medications, such as tranquilizers and antidepressants, are often used. Benzodiazepines, drugs that inhibit neurotransmitter systems (e.g., diazepam), have sedative effects. Antidepressants (e.g., clomipramine, a tricyclic antidepressant, or specific serotonin reuptake inhibitors such as sertraline and fluoxetine) are also used to treat anxiety because of their anti-anxiety properties. Both classes of medication often require that they be taken for extended periods of time, often up to four to six months. Furthermore, pharmacological treatments often cause numerous side effects (e.g., withdrawal symptoms when medication is stopped). Psychotherapy, while certainly helpful, can also be problematic, primarily in terms of the length of the treatment (which also means greater financial cost). Cognitive-behavioral therapies help to (a) determine the cause-and-effect relationships between the person's thoughts, feelings, and behaviors and (b) develop strategies for attenuating symptoms and reducing avoidant behaviors (USDHHS, 1999). Time-limited therapies (i.e., therapy conducted within a finite time frame, for example, 12 weeks) are often used to assist the individual in directly coping with the anxiety and its symptoms.

For quite some time, the use of physical activity (e.g., exercise) has been examined as a potential tool in both the prevention and the treatment of anxiety. Indeed, the National Institute of Mental Health identified examination of the **anxiolytic** (i.e., anxiety-reducing) effects of exercise as an important topic (Morgan & Goldston, 1987). Some of the anxiety disorders (e.g., phobias) are thought to be unaffected by exercise because they are linked to specific situations or objects (Dunn, Trivedi, & O'Neal, 2001). This view, however, is not uniformly accepted (Johnsgard, 1989). A fairly extensive body of literature examining the relationship between exercise and anxiety has developed over the past 40 years. This chapter presents the major findings of this work, both for normal anxiety and for anxiety sufficient to be considered clinical. Before examining the research on exercise and anxiety, we first examine the ways in which anxiety is assessed.

anxiolytic ■

Measurement

An understanding of the difference between state and trait forms of anxiety is necessary as background to the ways in which anxiety is measured. **State anxiety** is a noticeable but *transient* emotional state characterized by feelings of apprehension and heightened autonomic nervous system activity, such as increased heart rate, sweaty palms, increased breathing rate, and increased muscle tension. Thus, state anxiety is assessed by asking the subject to respond based on how he feels "right now, at this moment." For example, respondents are asked to indicate the extent to which they "feel calm," "feel relaxed," or "are presently worrying over possible misfortunes."

state anxiety ■

Conversely, **trait anxiety** reflects a more general predisposition to respond with apprehension, worry, and nervousness across many situations. For example, a person with high trait anxiety would respond

trait anxiety ■

with increased restlessness, lack of confidence, difficulty in making decisions, and a feeling of inadequacy in most of the situations she finds herself in. Thus, trait anxiety is assessed by asking subjects to respond based on how they "generally feel." So, for example, they are asked the extent to which they "generally feel this way, that is, how they feel on average" to items like "I feel satisfied with myself," "I feel like a failure," "I wish I could be as happy as others seem to be," and "I take disappointments so keenly that I can't put them out of my mind." Finally, because measures of trait anxiety are conceptually analogous to the personality construct of neuroticism (see Chapter 6), some studies have utilized measures that assess this construct (see examples from Chapter 6). Because trait anxiety is a general feeling of anxiety, it makes sense to assess trait anxiety before and after *chronic* exercise programs rather than before and after *single* bouts of exercise. Anxiety in pre–post studies of single bouts of exercise is primarily assessed by using state anxiety measures because the goal is to assess the currently experienced level of anxiety.

PSYCHOLOGICAL MEASURES

As stated earlier, anxiety can be manifested both psychologically and physiologically, and therefore it can be assessed in a variety of ways. The most common method for the psychological assessment of anxiety in exercise studies is through the use of self-report inventories. Easily the most popular inventory has been the Spielberger State–Trait Anxiety Inventory (STAI; Spielberger, 1983), followed by the Tension subscale of the Profile of Mood States (McNair, Droppleman, & Lorr, 1981), and the anxiety subscale of the Multiple Affect Adjective Check List (MAACL; Zuckerman & Lubin, 1965).

PHYSIOLOGICAL MEASURES

In addition to psychological measures for assessing anxiety, numerous measures of physiological activation or arousal (e.g., increased heart rate, muscle tension, feelings of being jittery or shaky) have been used. Because anxiety often occurs along with increased tension in skeletal muscles, measures of muscle tension, via electromyography (EMG), have been used to index anxiety. Notable in this regard is the work of Herbert deVries (e.g., deVries & Adams, 1972; see example of this research in the "Exercise Versus Other Treatments" section).

Anxiety can also be detected in the cardiovascular system through measures of blood pressure and heart rate, through the electrodermal system (skin responses—Galvanic skin response, palmar sweating, skin temperature), and through the central nervous system (e.g., electroencephalography or EEG—measure of electrical activity in the brain). Although anxiety responses are likely to have neurochemical components (e.g., increases in catecholamines and cortisol), measures of these components have not been used much in the exercise–anxiety literature. This is largely because of the expense involved in collecting and analyzing these kinds of variables and a general lack of knowledge of how to collect and analyze these variables in the exercise psychology domain.

Research on Exercise and Anxiety

In the exercise–anxiety literature, exercise can be classified as either *acute* or *chronic* in nature. As defined in Chapter 1, acute exercise involves single bouts of exercise at some level of intensity or duration. Chronic exercise, on the other hand, typically involves a regular program lasting for weeks or months and is usually designed to improve aerobic capacity, although increases in strength can be seen from chronic resistance programs. More than 100 studies have been documented in this literature (including both the acute and chronic exercise studies). As with depression, physical activity/exercise is believed to be a useful tool in alleviating anxiety and anxiety disorders. Physicians, at least to some extent, prescribe exercise to their patients. A survey in *Physician and Sportsmedicine* indicated that 60 percent of the 1,750 physicians surveyed prescribed exercise for those suffering from anxiety (Ryan, 1983). We now turn to a summary of the evidence accumulated on the anxiety–exercise relationship to date.

EVIDENCE FOR PREVENTIVE EFFECTS

Various studies have indicated that exercise can play a role in preventing anxiety; however, to date, only one cross-sectional epidemiological study has examined the link between exercise and anxiety. Stephens (1988), in four separate large adult samples (ranging in size from 3,025 to 23,791), found greater self-reported physical activity to be associated with better mental health, including fewer symptoms of anxiety (and fewer symptoms of depression).

In addition, studies have consistently shown that individuals who are physically fit have less anxiety than do their unfit counterparts. A review by Landers and Petruzzello (1994) concluded that physically fit individuals have less anxiety than those who are unfit. This could be the result of fitter individuals leading healthier lifestyles (e.g., more activity, better nutrition). For example, when they reviewed studies examining the effects of exercise training programs (which often lead to increased fitness), Landers and Petruzzello concluded that, in addition to an increase in fitness, trait (i.e., more general) levels of anxiety decrease following such activity protocols. In studies that have examined levels of neuroticism, neuroticism has been seen to decline over the length of a training program. This effect seems to be more pronounced as the length of the training program is increased (Petruzzello, Landers, Hatfield, Kubitz, & Salazar, 1991). There could, of course, also be other explanations for this relationship independent of fitness.

EVIDENCE FOR USE AS TREATMENT

The preventive effects of exercise are clearly important, but it is also important to determine the extent to which exercise can be useful as a treatment for anxiety problems once they have manifested themselves. Although the literature has not focused exclusively on clinical samples, some evidence does suggest that exercise can be useful in the treatment of mental disorders. As discussed in Chapter 7, Johnsgard (1989) cites numerous case study examples in *The Exercise Prescription for Depression and Anxiety* of how exercise has been useful in the treatment of both anxiety and mood disorders in his patients. For example, he presents the case of a woman suffering from agoraphobia (fear of public places) wherein he was able to help treat her phobia with brief but ever-increasing durations of exercise. Other, more carefully controlled studies conducted with clinically depressed and anxious samples highlight the utility of such an "exercise prescription." Some of these studies are presented below.

Whereas a fair amount of research has examined the utility of exercise for those with depression, less research has examined the efficacy of exercise in treating the anxiety disorders. Some studies have suggested that initially low-fit and highly anxious individuals have the most to gain from exercise training from a psychological perspective. Martinsen, Hoffart, and Solberg (1989) demonstrated that both aerobic (walk/jog) and nonaerobic (muscular strength, flexibility) exercise resulted in significant psychological improvements in 79 in-patients with anxiety disorders. The treatment protocol involved 60 minutes of exercise three times per week over the course of eight weeks. As noted in Chapter 7, Martinsen, Sandvik, and Kolbjornsrud (1989) conducted an intervention study with 92 nonpsychotic in-patients. The intervention consisted of eight weeks of at least one hour of aerobic exercise five times per week. All patients showed significant increases in physical fitness, as demonstrated by increased physical work capacity, with alcohol abuse or dependence patients showing the largest reductions in symptom scores (number of anxiety symptoms). Patients with unipolar depressive and anxiety disorders (generalized anxiety disorder and agoraphobia) also showed significant symptom reduction. In 84 percent of the patients who responded to a one-year follow-up, regular exercise habits were strongly associated with low symptom scores.

Sexton, Maere, and Dahl (1989) examined the effects of an eight-week exercise program (walking, jogging) in 52 symptomatic neurotics with a follow-up six months post-program. Participants were patients with a nonpsychotic diagnosis using the DSM–III (the precursor to the currently used DSM–IV). Both walking and jogging significantly reduced anxiety and depression, with these changes being maintained at follow-up. In fact, at follow-up a significant relationship was noted between aerobic capacity and anxiety levels, with greater fitness levels related to lower anxiety. This finding provides evidence that an increase in fitness and not just in physical activity level is associated with anxiety reduction. Sexton et al. noted the importance of the finding that vigorous exercise was not necessary for improvements in the psychological variables, with walking and running yielding equivalent effects. The study further reinforces the point made earlier that moderate-intensity exercise is sufficient to decrease anxiety even in clinical populations. These researchers also noted that the patients rated exercise as more important than medication and psychotherapy in their improvement.

Meyer, Broocks, Bandelow, Hillmer-Vogel, and Ruther (1998) examined the influence of 45 to 60 minutes of running three times per week over the course of 10 weeks in patients with DSM–III-Revised diagnosed panic disorder with or without agoraphobia compared to pharmacotherapy (clomipramine) or control. After the 10 weeks of treatment, the exercise group showed significant clinical improvement in their anxiety relative to the control condition and similar levels of improvement to the clomipramine group.

Broocks et al. (1998), in a randomized, placebo-controlled clinical trial, assigned 46 outpatients diagnosed with moderate to severe panic disorder to either a 10-week exercise treatment (running three times per week), pharmacotherapy (112.5 mg/d of clomipramine), or placebo treatment. Results revealed the drug treatment was most effective, but the exercise treatment also resulted in significant clinical improvement in anxiety symptoms. The drug treatment improved symptoms earlier and more effectively than did exercise, but exercise was superior to placebo in alleviating anxiety symptoms. This is particularly salient given the call by Salmon (2001) for more studies examining the utility of exercise in dealing with panic disorder. Some have proposed that exercise might actually induce panic attacks in panic-prone individuals, but this is based more on flawed logic than on experimental evidence. O'Connor, Smith, and Morgan (2000b) point out that exercise, both acute and chronic, is safe for panic disorder patients and that generally, panic patients show anxiety reductions following exercise similar to those seen in nonanxious individuals. O'Connor, Raglin, and Martinsen (2000a) do note, however, that more work is needed to examine the effect of exercise on generalized anxiety disorder.

THE RELATIONSHIP BETWEEN EXERCISE AND ANXIETY

In perhaps the most comprehensive review of the exercise–anxiety literature to date, Petruzzello et al. (1991) conducted a meta-analysis of more than 100 studies that had examined the exercise–anxiety relationship. This review actually included three meta-analyses: one each for the acute exercise–state anxiety research, for the chronic exercise–trait anxiety research, and for studies utilizing psychophysiological concomitants of anxiety (e.g., EMG, cardiovascular measures). A number of other meta-analyses have appeared since 1991 (Long & van Stavel, 1995; McDonald & Hodgdon, 1991; Schlicht, 1994), but none has been as comprehensive or shown any striking differences from the Petruzzello et al. review.

Aerobic exercise and anxiety. Easily the most noteworthy finding from the Petruzzello et al. (1991) meta-analysis was that anxiety is reduced following exercise, but only exercise of an aerobic nature. Importantly, no consistent differences have been found among the various modes of aerobic exercise (e.g., walking, jogging, running, swimming, cycling, aerobics). These reductions occur for *state* anxiety following *acute* exercise and for *trait* anxiety following *chronic* exercise. Anxiety reductions occur regardless of how the anxiety is *operationalized*:

1. Reductions are seen in self-report measures (questionnaires).
2. Reductions are seen in measures of muscular tension (EMG).
3. Reductions are seen in cardiovascular measures (heart rate, blood pressure).
4. Alterations consistent with reduced anxiety are seen in central nervous system measures (e.g., EEG alpha activity).

Anaerobic exercise and anxiety. In contrast to the findings regarding aerobic exercise and anxiety, Petruzzello et al. (1991) found that anaerobic or resistance exercise seems to result in slight *increases* in anxiety. These findings contrast with the effects of this form of exercise on depression (see Chapter 7). A number of studies that have appeared since 1991 support the conclusion that resistance training slightly increases anxiety. A review of these more recent studies involving resistance exercises (Raglin, 1997) indicates that the picture hasn't really changed—reductions in state anxiety are not consistently seen following resistance exercise. Speculation about the reasons for the lack of change in anxiety, and even increase in some cases, revolves around issues related to subject (in)experience with the activity and exercise intensity. At least some support has been shown for the intensity explanation; Bartholomew and Linder (1998) showed reductions in anxiety following low-intensity weight training, but increases following high-intensity activity.

It is also possible that the unchanged/increased anxiety may result from measurement problems. As articulated by Ekkekakis, Hall, and Petruzzello (1999), studies using the STAI to measure anxiety (which includes the vast majority of all exercise studies) may be erroneously reflecting increased "anxiety" that may be little more than increased activation or arousal (e.g., increased heart rate). The STAI includes numerous items that were designed to reflect perceived activation based on the notion that changes in such perceptions of activation would be related to changes in anxiety (e.g., jitteriness). With exercise, however, such changed perceptions may be more reflective of actual changes in autonomic activity consistent with the demands of the exercise. Thus, an individual might respond that he is more "jittery" following exercise, particularly resistance exercise, which is a normal outcome of the exertion of the activity, but the STAI reflects this as increased anxiety.

Acute exercise and anxiety. In the acute exercise studies, the anxiolytic effect seen following exercise is transient. Studies examining the anxiety responses for an extended period suggest that the effect seems to last for about two to four hours following acute exercise. In other words, anxiety reduction does not last indefinitely, but anxiety instead returns to pre-exercise levels after some period of time (Petruzzello et al., 1991). Interestingly, this psychological change parallels some physiological changes that occur following exercise (e.g., post-exercise hypotension or reduced blood pressure). Many studies have shown reductions in blood pressure following exercise and numerous studies have also shown reductions in anxiety, leading to speculation that the two might be linked. Given that participants in chronic exercise programs also show reduced trait anxiety, it is possible that over time pre-exercise levels become reduced, that is, a new baseline is achieved. Anxiety reduction, however, does take place following a single bout of aerobic activity. For example, a baseline level of anxiety prior to an acute exercise session might be a score of 35. Following the exercise bout, this anxiety level might drop to 28. The next day, prior to an exercise session, the anxiety level might again be 35. However, over a period of 12 to 16 weeks of consistent exercise, the baseline level of anxiety might drop to 30. With this reduction in baseline anxiety, anxiety following a single exercise bout might fall to 25, but return to the pre-exercise level of 30 before the next exercise session.

Exercise vs. other treatments. An important question that has been asked in the exercise–anxiety literature is: To what extent does exercise reduce anxiety as well as, or better than, other common treatments for anxiety (e.g., meditation, relaxation, or quiet rest—or not doing anything)? Exercise has been shown to be better at reducing anxiety than not doing anything and has also been shown to be as effective as other known anxiety-reducing treatments. A study conducted by Bahrke and Morgan (1978) shows this quite nicely. In this work, 75 males were randomly assigned to 20 minutes of either treadmill exercise, noncultic meditation, or sitting quietly in a sound-dampened chamber reading a *Reader's Digest* magazine (which has come to be known as the "quiet rest" condition). Comparisons were made of pre-treatment to post-treatment and 10 minutes post-treatment. State anxiety was reduced across all three conditions, and there were no differences among the three. The pessimist might view this as evidence that exercise isn't necessary for anxiety reduction. The optimist, however, would suggest that while exercise is perhaps no better than other anxiety-reducing treatments, it is just as good. Furthermore, numerous physiological benefits accrue from physical activity that wouldn't be achieved from other treatments. Another beneficial aspect of exercise over other treatments is that the anxiety-reducing effects seem to last longer following exercise. For example, Raglin and Morgan (1987) showed that anxiety was still reduced below pre-treatment levels three hours following exercise but not quiet rest.

Another common treatment for anxiety is pharmacotherapy (i.e., medication). Limited evidence shows that exercise may be more effective than anti-anxiety drugs (e.g., diazepam). In a classic study, deVries and Adams (1972) recruited 10 elderly adults (52 to 70 years old) with anxiety/tension problems (e.g., difficulty concentrating, excessive muscle tension, nervousness). Each of these individuals performed five different treatment conditions three separate times:

1. 400 mg capsule containing meprobamate, a commonly used anti-anxiety drug at the time,
2. 400 mg placebo capsule containing lactose (a sugar pill),

3. 15 minutes of walking at an intensity to elicit a heart rate (HR) of 100 bpm (about 67 percent of the individual's maximal heart rate),
4. 15 minutes of walking at an intensity to elicit a HR of 120 bpm (about 80 percent of the individual's maximal heart rate),
5. a control condition (sat quietly and read).

double blind ■

As is often done in drug studies, conditions (1) and (2) were done in **double blind** fashion (i.e., neither the subjects nor the experimenters interacting with the subjects knew whether the subjects were receiving the drug or the placebo) to reduce expectancy effects. DeVries and Adams assessed anxiety through EMG measures taken before and after each treatment condition. Of the five conditions, only the exercise at the lower intensity (i.e., 100 bpm) elicited a significant reduction in muscle tension (although it is worth noting that the higher-intensity exercise condition nearly achieved significance as well). The control, drug, and placebo conditions were essentially the same and did not reduce muscle tension. Clearly more work is needed in this area, but these results suggest that exercise may be more effective than anti-anxiety drugs. Indeed, deVries consistently referred to the "tranquilizer effect of exercise" (1981). Given the widespread use of anti-anxiety (i.e., tranquilizer) medications, more research in this area is needed (see Martinsen & Stanghelle, 1997).

Before turning to a discussion about what we don't know about exercise and anxiety, we provide a summary of what we do know in Exhibit 8.2.

What we don't know. Although we have learned a great deal regarding exercise and anxiety reduction, much, unfortunately, remains unknown. This is particularly true with respect to dose–response issues (i.e., intensity, duration).

It has been suggested that thresholds exist for the achievement of anxiety reduction. For example, Dishman (1986) proposed that exercise

exhibit 8.2 *Consensus statements regarding exercise and anxiety.*

1. Exercise can be associated with reduced state anxiety.
2. Long-term exercise is usually associated with reductions in neuroticism and anxiety.
3. Exercise can result in the reduction of various stress indices.
4. Exercise can have beneficial emotional effects across all ages and both genders.

Source: Adapted from Morgan & Goldston (1987).

of at least 70 percent of aerobic capacity sustained for at least 20 minutes would yield anxiety reduction. Raglin and Morgan (1987) suggested that a more moderate intensity (greater than 60 percent of maximum) was sufficient. The minimum intensity needed for anxiety reduction, however, has been poorly investigated. Ekkekakis and Petruzzello (1999), summarizing studies that specifically examined dose–response issues, concluded that evidence shows state anxiety and tension (measured via the Profile of Mood States (POMS), which is discussed in Chapter 9) are sensitive to exercise intensity effects. They found that higher intensities led to increases in anxiety/tension and lower intensities resulted in no change or decreases (but remember the caveat raised earlier regarding the potential problems with measuring anxiety in the exercise context). Clearly more work is needed before any firm conclusions can be made and certainly before any recommendations about minimal exercise intensity levels can be made.

As for the issue of minimum duration of exercise needed to achieve anxiety-reducing effects, the meta-analysis by Petruzzello et al. (1991) noted that exercise durations of less than 20 minutes were as effective as durations of greater than 20 minutes for reducing anxiety. Thus, research at this point shows that the anxiety-reducing effect that is achieved by exercise is present regardless of the duration of that exercise. Recommendations like those made by Dishman for a minimum duration of 20 minutes are thus sufficient but not necessarily accurate. More research is clearly needed for a definitive answer, but reductions in anxiety can apparently be realized simply by exercising.

MECHANISMS OF CHANGE

We do not yet have a definitive picture of the mechanisms responsible for the anxiety-reducing effect of exercise. Many of the mechanisms that have been proposed to explain the anxiolytic effect are the same as those proposed to explain depression reduction. Thus, the interested reader can return to Chapter 7 to review the discussion of the mastery, endorphin, monoamine, social interaction, and distraction/time-out hypotheses. Two additional mechanisms, the thermogenic hypothesis and the physiological toughness model, have also been proposed as explanations for anxiety reduction with exercise.

Thermogenic Hypothesis

Derived from research showing that treatments that elevate body temperature (e.g., sauna bathing, warm showers) produce therapeutic benefits (e.g., reduced muscle tension), the **thermogenic hypothesis** states that the

■ thermogenic hypothesis

elevated body temperature resulting from exercise may also lead to the observed psychological changes, such as reduced anxiety. In essence, exercise is thought to result in elevated body temperature. This temperature increase is sensed by the brain, a muscular relaxation response is triggered, and this relaxation is fed back to the brain and interpreted as relaxation or reduced anxiety. This is probably the most systematically studied of the proposed mechanisms. At present, research seems to indicate that the elevated body temperature is probably not directly responsible for the psychological changes (Koltyn, Shake, & Morgan, 1993; Petruzzello, Landers, & Salazar, 1993; Youngstedt, Dishman, Cureton, & Peacock, 1993). The thermogenic hypothesis remains tenable, however, in part because it could very well be that brain temperature and not body temperature is what drives the affective response and decrease in anxiety. Some evidence shows that the temperature of the brain is regulated independently from the body, although this independence is not completely accepted, and researchers have not yet been able to measure exercise-related increases in brain temperature. Thus more work is needed to determine the effects of exercise on brain temperature before the thermogenic hypothesis can be accepted or ruled out.

Physiological Toughness Model

physiological toughness ■

A final explanation, referred to as the **physiological toughness** model (Dienstbier, 1989), offers a psychophysiological framework for explaining both the state and trait anxiety changes seen with exercise. In essence, the model postulates that exposure to stressors (e.g., exercise) can lead to psychological coping and emotional stability (e.g., reduced anxiety). The basic premise is that regular (although not constant) experiences with stressors results in reduced basal sympathetic nervous system (SNS) arousal.

In a "physiologically tough" individual who is confronted with a challenge or a threat, the SNS response, in conjunction with the adrenal medulla, is fast and strong. For example, epinephrine is proposed to be released in response to a challenge, with a fast, large outpouring of the catecholamines occurring fairly quickly after the onset of the challenge. Importantly, this arousal response quickly returns to baseline when the stressor is removed. Catecholamines dissipate fairly quickly from the system once they are released. The "physiologically tough" individual thus has a more adaptive response to stress than does the "untough" individual, particularly as the latter avoids or does not engage the less adaptive stress response, which activates the hypothalamic-pituitary-axis arousal response with its concomitant adrenal cortical outpouring of cortisol. This response is much more indicative of the "untough" individual, who responds with a large amount of cortisol. Whereas catecholamines act quickly, cortisol takes much longer to reach its peak, and it stays in the system much longer as well. In other words, the untough response is similar to continuing to react to the stressor even after the stressor itself has stopped. This model, while certainly attractive, has not received the kind of attention it probably deserves as a way of better understanding the anxiety/stress response in the exercise paradigm.

Practical Recommendations

As is the case with depression, the "minimal" level of exercise activity is currently unknown, but it seems clear that exercise done on a regular basis can be useful in the treatment of anxiety as well as in protecting against anxiety that we might ordinarily succumb to as a result of our busy, stressful lives if we remained sedentary. As Jim discovered in the chapter-opening scenario, a running regime can reduce the stress of everyday life. The type of exercise *does* seem to matter, as only aerobic forms of exercise seem to be effective in reducing anxiety. Those suffering from more severe forms of anxiety can also find relief in exercise therapies, but these individuals should certainly consult with a mental health–care provider before beginning an exercise program.

Those who use exercise as a way of dealing with the daily stressors that challenge us should try to arrange to work out when it will be most helpful. Thus, a morning workout might help some to "get ready" to take on the day's challenges; a noontime workout might provide a much-needed break in the day to recharge the batteries; or some might find a workout later in the day helpful for "purging" the tensions and worries of the day. Each person should find his or her own best time to exercise.

Conclusion

As with exercise and depression, it seems reasonable to propose that exercise can be helpful in reducing anxiety in the short term and in reducing general tension, nervousness, and worry, thus increasing emotional stability over the longer term. Exercise can also be successful in treating clinical manifestations of anxiety, such as panic disorder, phobias, and generalized anxiety disorder. The current state of research is summarized in Exhibit 8.2. Much remains to be done, however, not the least of which is determining what causes this reduced level of emotionality and determining what "doses" of exercise reliably yield such effects.

What Do You Know?

1. What percentage of adults in the United States suffer from some type of anxiety disorder in a given year?
2. What are some of the symptoms associated with panic disorder?
3. What is known from cross-sectional and prospective studies regarding the association between (lack of) activity and anxiety?
4. To reduce anxiety, how long must exercise programs be?
5. What is the optimal "dosage" in terms of type, frequency, intensity, and duration needed for anxiety reduction?
6. What kind of exercise is best for anxiety reduction?
7. Can exercise be useful in the treatment of clinical manifestations of anxiety? What evidence is there to support this answer?
8. Which hypothesis for explaining the exercise–anxiety relationship relies on changes in temperature?

Learning Activities

1. Imagine two groups of individuals. Group 1 scores relatively high on trait anxiety and Group 2 scores relatively low on trait anxiety. Based on what you know from the chapter, describe these different groups in terms of the levels of physical activity you suspect they have.
2. Take a day when your perceived stress level is reasonably high. Go for a 15-minute brisk walk. Before you go and after you finish, answer each of the following items based on how you feel at that time:

	NOT AT ALL	SOMEWHAT	MODERATELY SO	VERY MUCH SO
I am tense	1	2	3	4
I am upset	1	2	3	4
I am nervous	1	2	3	4
I am worried	1	2	3	4

After completing the items after the walk, do the following:

a. Add the four items together for both the pre-walk and the post-walk. The result should be a number between 4 and 16.
b. Compare the two totals. Is there any change?

c. Based on the results, how would you rate the walk in terms of its ability to affect your anxiety level? Why did the score change (or not change)?

References

Bahrke, M. S., & Morgan, W. P. (1978). Anxiety reduction following exercise and meditation. *Cognitive Therapy and Research, 4,* 323–333.

Bartholomew, J. B., & Linder, D. E. (1998). State anxiety following resistance exercise: The role of gender and exercise intensity. *Journal of Behavioral Medicine, 21,* 205–219.

Broocks, A., Bandelow, B., Pekrun, G., George, A., Meyer, T., Bartmann, U., Hillmer-Vogel, U., & Ruther, E. (1998). Comparison of aerobic exercise, chloripramine, and placebo in the treatment of panic disorder. *American Journal of Psychiatry, 155,* 603–609.

DeVries, H. A. (1981). Tranquilizer effect of exercise: A critical review. *Physician and Sportsmedicine, 9*(11), 47–54.

DeVries, H. A., & Adams, G. M. (1972). Electromyographic comparison of single doses of exercise and meprobamate as to effects on muscular relaxation. *American Journal of Physical Medicine, 51,* 130–141.

Dienstbier, R. A. (1989). Arousal and physiological toughness: Implications for mental and physical health. *Psychological Bulletin, 96,* 84–100.

Dishman, R. K. (1986). Mental health. In V. Seefeldt (Ed.), *Physical activity and well-being* (pp. 303–341). Reston, VA: American Association for Health, Physical Education, Recreation and Dance.

Dunn, A. L., Trivedi, M. H., & O'Neal, H. A. (2001). Physical activity dose–response effects on outcomes of depression and anxiety. *Medicine and Science in Sports and Exercise, 33* (Supplement), S587–S597.

DuPont, R. L., Rice, D. P., Miller, L. S., Shiraki, S. S., Rowland, C. R., & Harwood, H. J. (1996). Economic cost of anxiety disorders. *Anxiety, 2,* 167–172.

Ekkekakis, P., Hall, E. E., & Petruzzello, S. J. (1999). Measuring state anxiety in the context of acute exercise using the State Anxiety Inventory: An attempt to resolve the brouhaha. *Journal of Sport and Exercise Psychology, 21,* 205–229.

Ekkekakis, P., & Petruzzello, S. J. (1999). Acute aerobic exercise and affect: Current status, problems and prospects regarding dose–response. *Sports Medicine, 28,* 337–374.

Johnsgard, K. W. (1989). *The exercise prescription for depression and anxiety.* New York: Plenum.

Kessler, R. C., McGonagle, K. A., Zhao, S., Nelson, C. B., Hughes, M., Eshleman, S., Wittchen, H. U., & Kendler, K. S. (1994). Lifetime and 12-month prevalence of DSM-III-R psychiatric disorders in the United States: Results from the National Comorbidity Survey. *Archives of General Psychiatry, 51,* 8–18.

Koltyn, K. F., Shake, C. L., & Morgan, W. P. (1993). Interaction of exercise, water temperature and protective apparel on body awareness and anxiety. *International Journal of Sport Psychology, 24,* 297–305.

Landers, D. M., & Petruzzello, S. J. (1994). Physical activity, fitness, and anxiety. In C. Bouchard, R. J. Shephard, & T. Stephens (Eds.), *Physical activity, fitness, and health: International proceedings and consensus statement* (pp. 868–882). Champaign, IL: Human Kinetics.

Long, B. C., & van Stavel, R. (1995). Effects of exercise training on anxiety: A meta-analysis. *Journal of Applied Sport Psychology, 7,* 167–189.

Martinsen, E. W., Hoffart, A., & Solberg, O. Y. (1989). Aerobic and non-aerobic forms of exercise in the treatment of anxiety disorders. *Stress Medicine, 5,* 115–120.

Martinsen, E. W., Sandvik, L., & Kolbjornsrud, O. B. (1989). Aerobic exercise in the treatment of nonpsychotic mental disorders: An exploratory study. *Nordic Journal of Psychiatry, 43,* 521–529.

Martinsen, E. W., & Stanghelle, J. K. (1997). Drug therapy and physical activity. In W. P. Morgan (Ed.), *Physical activity and mental health* (pp. 81–90). Washington, DC: Taylor & Francis.

McDonald, D. G., & Hodgdon, J. A. (1991). *Psychological effects of aerobic fitness training: Research and theory.* New York: Springer-Verlag.

McNair, D. M., Droppleman, L. F., & Lorr, M. (1981). *Manual for the Profile of Mood States.* San Diego, CA: Educational and Industrial Testing Service.

Meyer, T., Broocks, A., Bandelow, B., Hillmer-Vogel, U., & Ruther, E. (1998). Endurance training in panic patients: Spiroergometric and clinical effects. *International Journal of Sports Medicine, 19,* 496–502.

Morgan, W. P., & Goldston, S. E. (Eds.). (1987). *Exercise and mental health.* Washington, DC: Hemisphere.

O'Connor, P. J., Raglin, J. S., & Martinsen, E. W. (2000a). Physical activity, anxiety and anxiety disorders. *International Journal of Sport Psychology, 31*(2), 136–155.

O'Connor, P. J., Smith, J. C., & Morgan, W. P. (2000b). Physical activity does not provoke panic attacks in patients with panic disorder: A review of the evidence. *Anxiety, Stress and Coping, 13,* 333–353.

Petruzzello, S. J., Landers, D. M., Hatfield, B. D., Kubitz, K. A., & Salazar, W. (1991). A meta-analysis on the anxiety-reducing effects of acute and chronic exercise: Outcomes and mechanisms. *Sports Medicine, 11,* 143–182.

Petruzzello, S. J., Landers, D. M., & Salazar, W. (1993). Exercise and anxiety reduction: Examination of temperature as an explanation for affective change. *Journal of Sport and Exercise Psychology, 15,* 63–76.

Raglin, J. S. (1997). Anxiolytic effects of physical activity. In W. P. Morgan (Ed.), *Physical activity and mental health* (pp. 107–126). Washington, DC: Taylor & Francis.

Raglin, J. S., & Morgan, W. P. (1987). Influence of exercise and quiet rest on state anxiety and blood pressure. *Medicine and Science in Sports and Exercise, 19,* 456–463.

Regier, D. A., Farmer, M. E., Rae, D. S., Locke, B. Z., Keith, S. J., Judd, L. L., & Goodwin, F. K. (1990). Comorbidity of mental disorders with alcohol and other drug abuse: Results from the Epidemiologic Catchment Area (ECA) Study. *Journal of the American Medical Association, 264,* 2511–2518.

Regier, D. A., Narrow, W. E., Rae, D. S., Manderscheid, R. W., Locke, B. Z., & Goodwin, F. K. (1993). The de facto U.S. mental and addictive disorders service system: Epidemiologic Catchment Area prospective 1-year prevalence rates of disorders and services. *Archives of General Psychiatry, 50,* 85–94.

Rice, D. P., & Miller, L. S. (1996). The economic burden of schizophrenia: Conceptual and methodological issues, and cost estimates. In M. Moscarelli, A. Rupp, & N. Sartorious (Eds.), *Handbook of mental health economics and health policy. Vol. 1: Schizophrenia* (pp. 321–324). New York: Wiley.

Ryan, A. J. (1983). Exercise is medicine. *Physician and Sportsmedicine, 11,* 10.

Salmon, P. (2001). Effects of physical exercise on anxiety, depression, and sensitivity to stress: A unifying theory. *Clinical Psychology Review, 21*(1), 33–61.

Schlicht, W. (1994). Does physical exercise reduce anxious emotions? A meta-analysis. *Anxiety, Stress and Coping, 6,* 275–288.

Sexton, H., Maere, A., & Dahl, N. H. (1989). Exercise intensity and reduction in neurotic symptoms. *Acta Psychiatrica Scandinavica, 80,* 231–235.

Spielberger, C. D. (1983). *Manual for the State-Trait Anxiety Inventory (Form Y).* Palo Alto, CA: Consulting Psychologists Press.

Stephens, T. (1988). Physical activity and mental health in the United States and Canada: Evidence from four population surveys. *Preventive Medicine, 17,* 35–47.

U.S. Department of Health and Human Services. (1999). *Mental health: A report of the Surgeon General.* Rockville, MD: U.S. Department of Health and Human Services, Substance Abuse and Mental Health Services Administration, Center for Mental Health Services, National Institutes of Health, National Institute of Mental Health.

Youngstedt, S. D., Dishman, R. K., Cureton, K. J., & Peacock, L. J. (1993). Does body temperature mediate anxiolytic effect of acute exercise? *Journal of Applied Physiology, 74,* 825–831.

Zuckerman, M., & Lubin, B. (1965). *Manual for the Multiple Affect Adjective Checklist.* San Diego, CA: Educational and Industrial Testing Service.

Chapter 9

Emotional Well-Being and Exercise

KEY TERMS

affect
categorical approach
circumplex model
dimensional approach
emotional well-being
emotions
energetic arousal
exercise dependence syndrome
iceberg profile
lactate threshold
moods
primary exercise dependence
secondary exercise dependence
staleness syndrome
tense arousal
ventilatory threshold

Nick and Stephanie both turned 40 in the past year. They have two kids, ages 11 and 13, who are both very involved in school and sports activities. Nick and Steph find themselves so busy with working, carpooling kids to practices, games, and social functions, and household chores that they have no time for themselves. At the end of the day, they both collapse onto the couch, usually with a glass of wine or beer, and vegetate in front of the television until it is time for bed (if they don't fall asleep on the couch first!). They usually sleep later than they had planned, yet wake up tired and immediately stressed out at the prospect of yet another crazy day.

This kind of schedule goes on for quite a while until Steph runs across a book at the local bookstore that catches her attention. Written by Robert Thayer, a psychologist from the California State University at Long Beach, it is titled *Calm Energy.* It sounds interesting, so Steph buys it and begins reading it at her first opportunity. To her surprise, she has a hard time putting it down, largely because so much of what she reads strikes a chord with her. She is particularly taken by the sections of the book dealing with the energizing effects of exercise and its mood-improving capabilities.

Steph formulates a plan: she and Nick will get up 45 minutes earlier than usual and take their golden retriever for a 30-minute walk around the neighborhood. This will accomplish two major goals—she and Nick can spend some time together at the beginning of the day to discuss the day's activities and to just talk to each other without being interrupted by phone calls and kids. It will also get them some much-needed exercise. It takes some getting used to the earlier wake-up time, but before too long Nick and Steph find themselves looking forward to their early morning walks. They feel like they have much more energy during the day and much less tension, all of which make the daily activities much easier to deal with. Within two months, Nick and Steph have begun incorporating some running into their exercise routines. It seems like the more exercise they incorporate, the better they feel. They sleep better, handle stress much better, and are generally just a lot more pleasant to be around. They marvel at how something like exercise can actually leave them feeling energized.

> "Everyone knows the effect of physical exercise on the mood: how much more cheerful and courageous one feels when the body has been toned up, than when it is 'run down.' . . . Our moods are determined by the feelings which come up from our body. Those feelings are sometimes of worry, breathlessness, anxiety; sometimes of peace and repose. It is certain that physical exercise will tend to train the body toward the latter feelings. The latter feelings are certainly an essential ingredient in all perfect human character."
>
> —William James (1899, pp. 220–221)

The vast majority of research examining psychological changes associated with exercise and physical activity has traditionally focused on reductions in negative emotions like anxiety and depression (see Chapters 7 and 8). Given the prevalence of such mental-health problems, this is certainly an important endeavor. Yet, when it comes to recommending exercise and physical activity, the focus tends to be on making the activity more enjoyable or more tolerable rather than on the mental-health benefits. For example, the National Institutes of Health Consensus Development Panel on Physical Activity and Cardiovascular Health (1996) suggested that activities such as walking and other moderate-intensity activities would likely improve adherence rates over more strenuous activities. The assumption of recommending moderate-intensity exercise seems to be that if the activity is more enjoyable or less aversive, then rates of exercise adherence might improve and the benefits of physical activity can be more readily experienced. This is likely true; however, an approach that focuses on benefits may be effective as well. Consider that one of the most consistently reported effects from exercise of even mild intensities is an increase in feelings of energy, such as experienced by Nick and Stephanie in the chapter-opening scenario. For example, Thayer has consistently shown that a 10-minute walk is more effective, not only at increasing energy but also at reducing tension, than eating a candy bar or smoking cigarettes (1987). It has also been shown that people tend to do what makes them feel good (Emmons & Diener, 1986). Thus, if exercise can be shown to have the ability to improve psychological states, exercise programs might be developed to capitalize on such effects so that people not only begin exercise programs but stick with them.

Defining Emotional Well-Being

The concept of emotional well-being is an aspect of mental health, related to anxiety and depression yet also distinct from them, that has recently gained more research attention in the exercise domain. Simply put, **emotional well-being** is a greater amount of positive affect than negative affect, along with favorable thoughts such as satisfaction with life. It should be easy to see that if exercise reduces negative emotions like anxiety and depression, and increases positive emotions like energy and vigor, then it should also result in better emotional well-being. Exercise and physical activity have also been shown to result in greater self-confidence, self-esteem, and improved cognitive function (see Chapter 10; see also McAuley & Rudolph, 1995), which serve to bolster well-being.

■ emotional well-being

Unfortunately, a number of issues involved in the examination of such psychological states continue to be problematic in the exercise literature. These issues include how such states are conceptualized, how they are measured, and when they are measured, and issues related to what is often called the "dose–response" relationship.

CONCEPTUALIZATION ISSUES: AFFECT, EMOTIONS, OR MOODS?

It has been noted that an unfortunate tendency in the exercise psychology literature has been to equate the terms *affect, emotion*, and *mood* as if they all refer to the same thing (see Ekkekakis & Petruzzello, 2000). This has led to a great deal of confusion and messiness in the literature. It is a reasonable and defensible position to claim that these terms represent distinct constructs and should thus not be used as synonyms. Affect, emotion, and mood can be viewed as related to one another, yet each has important differences from the others.

Emotions (e.g., fear, guilt, pride) are states of feeling elicited following an appraisal wherein an object, person, or event is determined to impact the well-being of the individual. An emotion is an immediate response to a specific stimulus (e.g., an impending speech elicits anxiety, winning a race elicits joy) that requires some level of cognitive input. Perhaps more simply, emotions occur following mental processing that attaches some meaning to an event.

■ emotions

moods ■ Like emotions, **moods** (e.g., irritation, cheerfulness) are subjective states of feeling rather than thinking, have a cognitive basis, and can enhance or interfere with purposive behavior. Moods can be distinguished from emotions in at least three important ways:

1. Moods usually imply a longer course of time, whereas emotions are rather short-lived.
2. Antecedents or causes of emotions can usually be identified, whereas moods come and go with sometimes unidentifiable causes.
3. Emotions are usually more intense and variable than moods.

affect ■ Unlike emotions and moods, **affect** (e.g., tension, calmness) is a more general "valenced" response, that is, a good–bad/pleasure–displeasure feeling. Thus, all emotions and moods are subsumed under affect. Affect is thought to be more basic than emotion for at least two reasons: affect is evolutionarily more primitive, and affect does not require thought processes to precede it. Understanding the more primitive nature of affect is valuable because basic affective responses can be elicited through "hard-wired" mechanisms, very similar to eliciting a reflexive response. For example, consider the feeling of unpleasantness in response to pain. The immediate response to pain does not require a detailed cognitive analysis before the feeling can be labeled as pain and indeed, such "cognitive elaboration" could be dangerous to the individual. Any valenced response is an affect, but not necessarily an emotion, because, as stated previously, cognitive elaboration is not needed for affect. For example, affect is present when an infant cries because it feels distress, but the infant cannot feel sadness because it has not yet developed the cognitive appraisal capacity necessary to determine sadness (Ekkekakis & Petruzzello, 2000).

Measurement

In this section, we discuss various measures used to assess affective states, including generalized and exercise-specific measures.

GENERALIZED MEASURES

Generalized measures are measures of mood or affect not specific to any context. They include the Profile of Mood States (POMS), the Positive and Negative Affect Schedule (PANAS), and the Activation Deactivation Adjective Check List (AD ACL).

Profile of Mood States (POMS). The POMS (McNair, Lorr, & Droppleman, 1981) has been one of the most popular self-report instruments used in the exercise (and sport) psychology literature. Originally developed for use in psychiatric populations, the POMS has been employed to examine mood changes occurring in response to various exercise manipulations for nearly 30 years. The POMS is a 65-item adjective rating scale that yields scores on six different mood subscales:

- tension–anxiety
- depression–dejection
- anger–hostility
- vigor–activity
- fatigue–inertia
- confusion–bewilderment

Respondents rate each of the 65 adjectives (e.g., exhausted, alert, terrified, ready to go, miserable, tense, confused, uneasy, fatigued) along a 5-point scale ranging from 0 (not at all) to 4 (extremely) according to how they feel. The response set, which is essentially the instructions given to respondents for making their assessments, can be varied to reflect how the individual feels "right now," "today," "over the past week," "over the past month," or "over the past year" or "lifetime." The problem with using an instrument like the POMS is that it assumes that only the six moods that it measures are affected by an exercise manipulation when other moods could also be affected, such as excitement or boredom. It is also worth noting that because of its length, the POMS poses problems when a researcher wants to measure mood multiple times in a single exercise session. Because of concerns about its length, the original 65-item measure has been modified, and shorter versions and alternative versions are now available.

Positive and Negative Affect Schedule (PANAS). The PANAS (Watson, Clark, & Tellegen, 1988), another relatively popular measure in the exercise domain, is a 20-item self-report instrument based on the two-dimensional (positive affect, negative affect) model proposed by Watson and Tellegen (1985). As such, it provides measures of the two orthogonal (i.e., conceptually perpendicular) dimensions of positive affect (PA) and negative affect (NA). See Exhibit 9.1. As with the POMS, respondents rate each of the 20 adjectives (e.g., interested, distressed, excited, jittery, ashamed) along a 5-point scale ranging from 1 (very slightly or not at all) to 5 (extremely) according to how they feel.

exhibit 9.1 *The dimensions of positive affect and negative affect as assessed by the PANAS.*

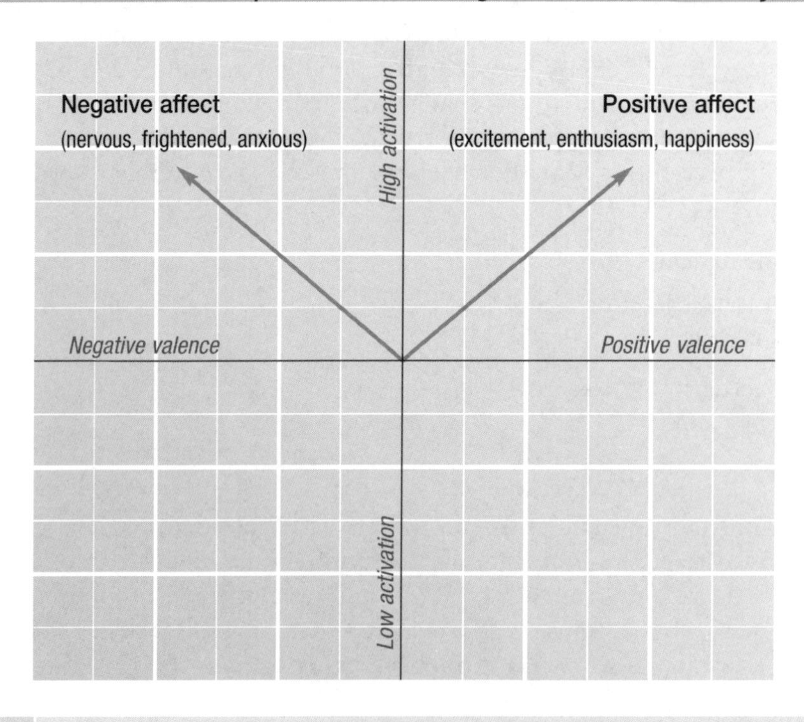

Possible time frames for these assessments range from "you feel this way right now, that is, at the present moment" to "you generally feel this way, that is, how you feel on the average." One of the problems with the PANAS is that it measures only the high-activation ends of PA and NA and not the low-activation ends (see Exhibit 9.1). Thus, it is useful for measuring high-activation states like excitement or enthusiasm (PA) and nervous or scared (NA), but not low-activation states like relaxation or calmness (PA) and sadness or tiredness (NA).

Activation Deactivation Adjective Check List (AD ACL). The AD ACL (Thayer, 1986, 1989) was developed based on a theoretical framework incorporating two bipolar dimensions of activation/arousal. The first dimension, termed **energetic arousal (EA)**, is characterized by energy–sleep and refers to feelings ranging from energy, vigor, and liveliness to feelings of fatigue and tiredness. EA is proposed to follow a circadian rhythm and, importantly for the exercise domain, to reflect changes in gross physical activity. The second dimension, termed **tense arousal (TA)**, is characterized by tension–placidity and refers to feelings rang-

energetic arousal ■

tense arousal ■

A diagram of the relationships between EA and TA. exhibit 9.2

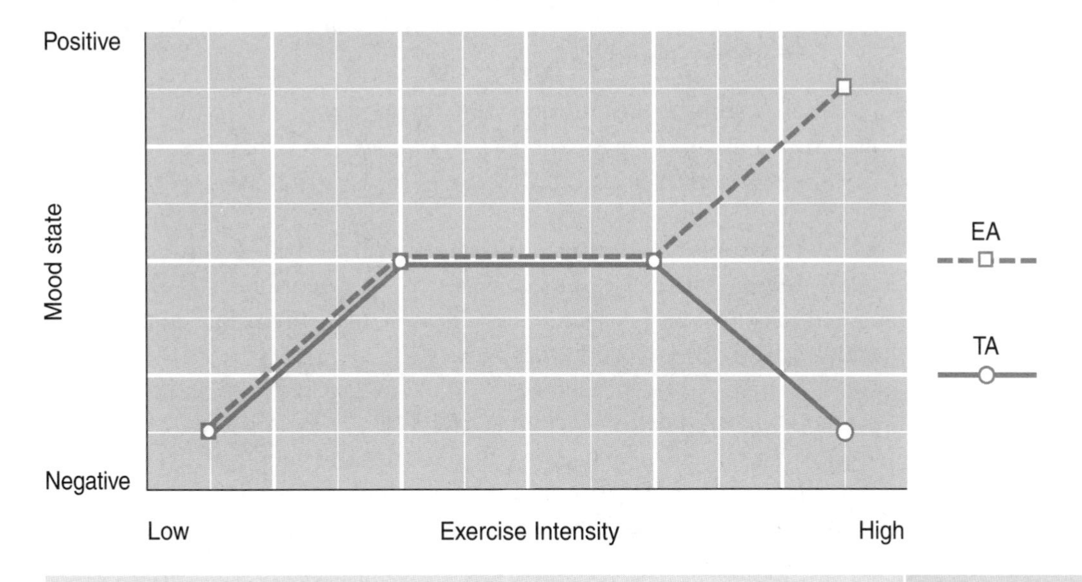

Source: Thayer (2001).

ing from subjective tension to placidity, quietness, and stillness. Thayer (1989) proposed that the relationship between the two dimensions varies as a function of energy expenditure, so that they are positively correlated from low to moderate levels of energy expenditure, and negatively correlated from moderate to high levels. In other words, EA and TA will both be either increased or decreased at low/moderate levels of energy expenditure, but as the level of energy expenditure is increased, EA will increase while TA decreases (See Exhibit 9.2). From this model, the AD ACL was developed to provide a measure of the various feelings characterized in the model. The AD ACL is a 20-item measure, in which respondents rate their feelings on a 4-point scale ranging from "definitely feel" to "definitely do not feel," thus providing scores for both EA and TA, as well as the component subscales of energy and tiredness (EA) and tension and calmness (TA).

EXERCISE-SPECIFIC MEASURES

Among exercise researchers, a growing dissatisfaction with more general self-report instruments led to a movement in the early 1990s toward the development of exercise-specific scales. This dissatisfaction arose from two concerns:

1. that measures like the POMS and the PANAS were either not sensitive enough to exercise stimuli (i.e., the existing measures had irrelevant items or items that didn't seem to change in response to exercise manipulations) and

2. that exercise has unique and distinct properties (i.e., affect is somehow changed in the exercise context in ways that are not seen in other contexts) that existing measures failed to detect.

Out of this dissatisfaction, three multi-item scales—Exercise-induced Feeling Inventory (EFI), Subjective Exercise Experiences Scale (SEES), and Physical Activity Affect Scale (PAAS)—and one single-item scale—Feeling Scale (FS)—were developed.

Exercise-induced Feeling Inventory (EFI). The EFI (Gauvin & Rejeski, 1993) is a 12-item measure of exercise-induced feeling states. It comprises four subscales (positive engagement, revitalization, physical exhaustion, and tranquility) thought to reflect aspects of the affective experience associated with exercise that were not available with other instruments. These subscales are supposedly analogous to enthusiasm, energy, fatigue, and calmness (Gauvin & Spence, 1998). Responses are made on a 5-point scale ranging from 0 (do not feel) to 4 (feel very strongly).

Subjective Exercise Experiences Scale (SEES). The SEES (McAuley & Courneya, 1994) is also a 12-item scale designed to measure the subjective experiences unique to exercise, with specific attention to the positive dimensions of affect in response to exercise. The SEES is composed of three subscales, namely positive well-being, psychological distress, and fatigue. Psychological well-being is analogous to positive affect, whereas psychological distress is analogous to negative affect. Ratings are made along a 7-point scale ranging from 1 (not at all) to 7 (very much so). Among other things (see extensive discussion of EFI by Ekkekakis & Petruzzello, 2001a and the SEES by Ekkekakis & Petruzzello, 2001b), it has been noted that some potential redundancy exists within and between the EFI and SEES (Lox, Jackson, Tuholski, Wasley, & Treasure, 2000).

Physical Activity Affect Scale (PAAS). In an effort to capitalize on the unique aspects of both the EFI and the SEES while at the same time reducing the overlap between them, Lox et al. (2001) developed the PAAS, an instrument consisting of the Psychological Distress subscale of the SEES and the subscales of the EFI. This resulted in another 12-item exercise-specific measure utilizing the same response format as the EFI (a 5-point scale of 0 to 4 ranging from "do not feel" to "feel very strongly"). This relatively new instrument has not been used very extensively in the literature to this point.

Feeling Scale (FS). Finally, the FS (Hardy & Rejeski, 1989) is a single-item measure of valence or hedonic tone (good–bad/pleasant–unpleasant), with responses made along an 11-point continuum ranging from –5 (very bad) to +5 (very good) with 0 as a neutral midpoint. It was designed for use as an in-task (i.e., during exercise) measure of affect and has been used in numerous studies to measure affect during acute exercise bouts. Perhaps the biggest drawback of all four of the exercise-specific scales is the fact that each was developed in the absence of a guiding theoretical framework (see Ekkekakis & Petruzzello, 2000, 2001a, 2001b for extensive critiques).

Research Issues

Before examining the research, we first look at the following important issues related to the study of exercise-related affect: categorical versus dimensional approaches, temporal dynamics of affective response, and dose–response issues.

CATEGORICAL VERSUS DIMENSIONAL APPROACHES

One of the underlying assumptions of the vast majority of research examining the affective/emotional/mood responses to exercise is that exercise influences certain affect/emotions/moods. Thus, the field is rife with studies examining anxiety and depression responses to exercise and with studies all using the same measure (e.g., POMS). This tendency seems to reflect a **categorical approach,** an approach that assumes that affective states (be they emotions, moods, or affect) are distinct and have unique properties and antecedents. Thus, the implicit assumption is that exercise can reduce anxiety or depression, but does not have any other influence on affective states. For example, this approach implicitly assumes that exercise can't improve energy or increase relaxation or minimize fatigue. In contrast is the less-often used **dimensional approach,** which assumes that affective states are interrelated and can be accurately captured by a small number of dimensions (as few as two). For example, using the dimensions of activation and valence, a much more informative picture of the affective dynamics accompanying a bout of exercise might emerge. Each approach has its advantages and

- categorical approach
- dimensional approach

disadvantages. The main advantages attributed to dimensional models are their broader, more encompassing scope and their parsimony. Thus, with as little as two dimensions, exercise might be shown to result in increased energy during and immediately following activity and increased relaxation during the recovery from activity.

Little is actually known about the nature of the affective changes that occur in response to bouts of exercise (e.g., how affect might change over time, the kind of affect actually being experienced). Given the limited knowledge, dimensional models provide a desirable approach to studying such affective phenomena (see Biddle & Mutrie, 2001; Ekkekakis & Petruzzello, 2002).

Consider the following, which indicates the utility in using a dimensional approach to study affect in the exercise domain:

> [The dimensional] approach seems better suited to the understanding of exercise and affect because the models stemming from it are intended to be broad, encompassing conceptualizations of affective experience. Because the affective experience that accompanies exercise has not been thoroughly described, a model of affect that has a wider breadth is more likely to capture the essence of exercise-induced affect than a model that, at the outset, limits the focus of investigation to specific emotions. (Gauvin & Brawley, 1993, p. 152)

A potentially useful dimensional model is the two-dimensional circumplex model of affect, which has been described extensively by Russell (1980, 1997) and Ekkekakis and Petruzzello (1999, 2002). The **circumplex model** describes affective states along the perimeter of a circle defined by the dimensions of affective valence (pleasure–displeasure) and activation. These two dimensions form four quadrants that can be characterized by the various combinations of valence and activation:

circumplex model

1. pleasant–activated, reflecting excitement, enthusiasm, energy
2. pleasant–unactivated, reflecting relaxation and calmness
3. unpleasant–unactivated, reflecting boredom, fatigue, depression
4. unpleasant–activated, reflecting anxiety, tension, distress (see Exhibit 9.3).

Researchers have only recently begun to examine affective responses to exercise from this framework (see the following section), but it has the potential to handle the problematic issues in the area. It provides a more general representation of affect, allows for both positive and negative affective states, and is a more parsimonious approach to studying affect in the exercise domain. The AD ACL provides measures of affect that can be used within such a dimensional framework (see Exhibit 9.3).

exhibit 9.3

The circumplex model of affect.

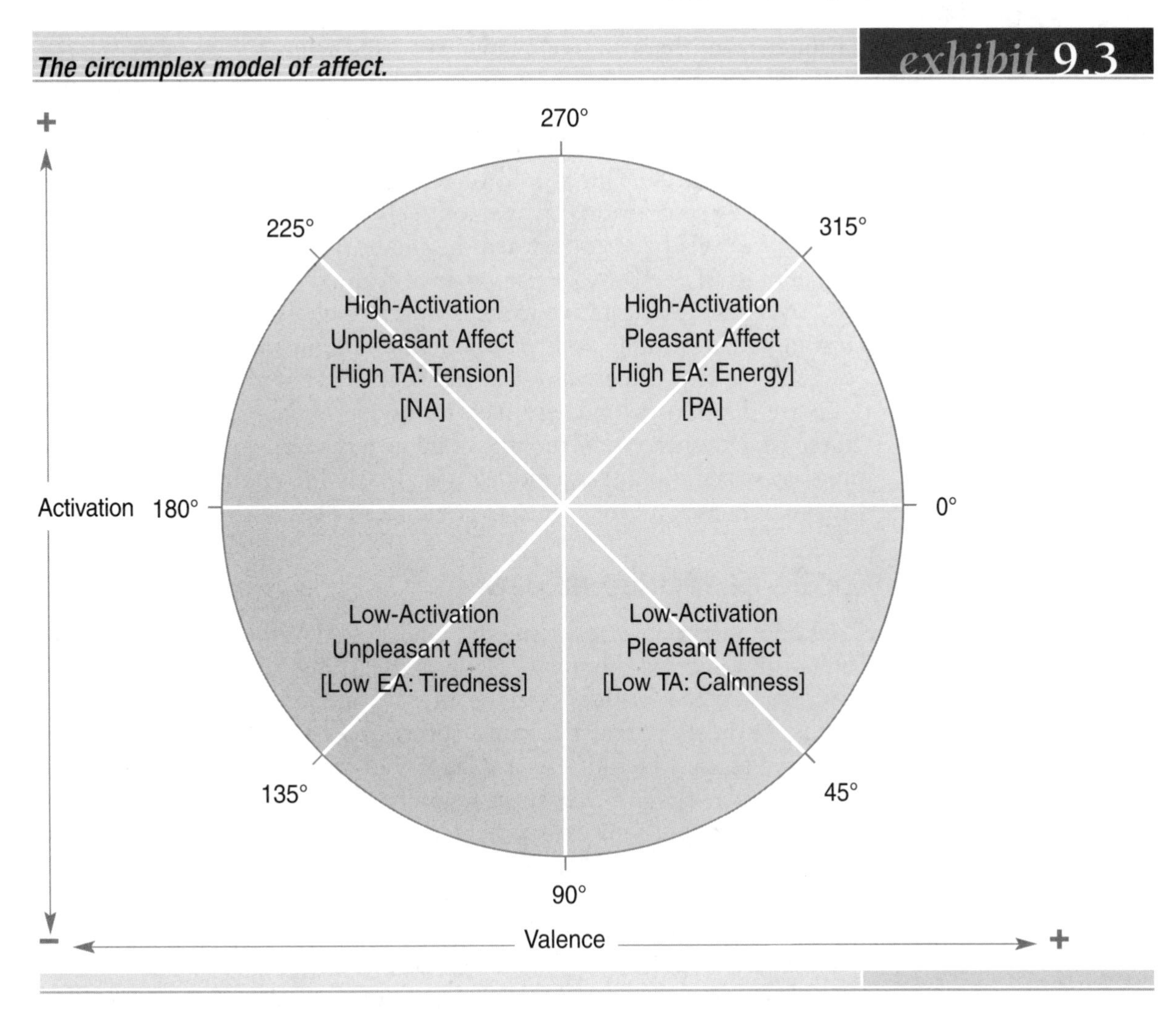

Source: Ekkakakis and Petruzzello (2002, p. 39). Reprinted from *Psychology of Sport and Exercise, 3,* Ekkekakis, P. and Petruzzello, S. J., Analysis of the affect measurement conundrum in exercise psychology, IV. A conceptual case for the affect circumplex, 35–63, 2002, with permission from Elsevier Science.

TEMPORAL DYNAMICS OF AFFECTIVE RESPONSES

Another extremely important issue in the study of exercise-related affect is the timing of the measurement of affective responses. The vast majority of the literature has been content to study responses before and after an acute bout of exercise. Only recently has there been any systematic investigation into the responses *during* a bout of exercise. This distinction is potentially very important for understanding the temporal dynamics associated with affective responses to exercise. It is possible that affect experienced during an exercise bout can be quite distinct from the affective change reported from before to after exercise. For example, whereas exercise done at more moderate intensities may result in the same post-exercise affective states as more vigorous intensities, the responses during the exercise at different intensities may be very divergent. This would obviously have important implications in exercise prescription. If a person feels bad during an exercise bout, even if he feels better afterward, he might be less inclined to continue the activity. The post-exercise positive feelings might not be sufficient to "override" the negative feelings during exercise. Important theoretical implications may arise from attempts to elucidate the mechanisms underlying such affective responses. If affective responses during exercise are different from these seen following exercise, explanations for these changes need to be incorporated into theoretical models. Without such incorporation, those models are grossly incomplete and can never adequately explain the affective responses to exercise stimuli.

DOSE–RESPONSE ISSUES

The final methodological issue to be addressed before a synopsis of the literature concerns the dose–response effect. Specifically, it is currently very popular to speculate as to the intensity and duration of exercise that yields the most optimal affective response. Like the more specific depression and anxiety literatures (see Chapters 7 and 8), these parameters are poorly understood with respect to other affective responses. As in the anxiety literature, some researchers have proposed that there is a threshold of intensity and duration that must be reached before significant changes in affect can be realized (e.g., Dishman, 1986). Others (e.g., Berger, 1994) have suggested a "taxonomy" to maximize the benefits from exercise, essentially implying that one can maximize the affective benefit by exercising for a specific length of time and exercising regularly within a weekly schedule. In both cases, the recommendation has been for exercise of at least 20 to 30 minutes, duration and intensities in a "moderate" range (i.e., 70 percent of maximal aerobic capacity) in order to achieve positive psychological changes.

Numerous problems exist with deriving an optimal exercise "dosage" at this point. First, little systematic work has been done to examine duration. For example, a fairly recent review of dose–response effects found fewer than 10 studies that specifically examined duration effects (Ekkekakis & Petruzzello, 1999). From these relatively few studies it was concluded that there is "no evidence that the 'threshold' assumption has some basis in fact" (p. 354) when it comes to exercise duration.

Second, the issue of exercise intensity has also been called into question. Traditionally, intensity (again, when it has been examined at all) has been examined as a percentage of either maximal heart rate or maximal aerobic capacity. Thus, even though two individuals may have very different maximal capacities, assigning exercise workloads as a percentage of their maximal capacity relativizes the workload so that different individuals are exercising at metabolically equivalent levels. Unfortunately, this assumption appears to be inaccurate. It has been shown that individuals exercising at the same relative workload end up having very different metabolic responses. Thus, even exercise at a "moderate" intensity based on a percentage of maximal capacity results in some individuals working completely aerobically while others may require a significant contribution of anaerobic metabolism to complete the same workload. It has been proposed that an approach that accounts for individually determined metabolic landmarks may be more useful in the study of exercise intensity effects (Ekkekakis & Petruzzello, 1999). In particular, the **lactate threshold,** the point at which lactate concentrations in the blood exceed the rate at which lactate is removed from the blood, resulting in excess lactate and a shift toward anaerobic metabolism, has been suggested to be one such metabolic landmark. Although little work has utilized such metabolic landmarks, studies using the lactate threshold as a basis for prescribing exercise intensity have shown promising results (see discussion of Bixby, Spalding, & Hatfield, 2001, on page 196).

■ lactate threshold

Research on Affective Response to Exercise

This section summarizes research examining the affective responses to exercise, beyond that examining anxiety or depression responses. We emphasize studies that relate to the dose–response effect, that is, those studies that have examined varying levels of intensity, duration, or their combination. This selective review also focuses on research that has examined before and after responses (easily a larger body of research) and research that has examined in-task exercise responses.

BEFORE- AND AFTER-EXERCISE RESPONSES

Much of the early research examining the psychological responses to exercise was conducted using either the POMS or the State–Trait Anxiety Inventory (STAI; see Chapter 7). As noted by Biddle and Mutrie (2001), the relationship between exercise and mood (using the POMS) suggests a positive association between exercise and vigor and a negative association between exercise and moods like tension, anger, confusion, and fatigue. This is similar to the pattern referred to as the "iceberg profile" by Morgan (1984); see discussion later in this chapter and Exhibit 9.5. In general, research has shown that exercise seems to increase positive mood states and to reduce negative mood states.

The most interesting paradoxical effect of exercise on affect or mood is the energizing effect that is so often reported. As noted by Thayer (2001), moderate amounts of exercise usually energize the exerciser. Thayer discusses how exercise can be used to boost energy levels when one is tired or energy levels are low. He discusses the following practical self-experiment: at night while lounging around watching television, he suggests conducting a self-rating of energy (he suggests a scale from 1 to 7, with 1 being the least energy an individual usually feels and 7 being the most). He then suggests getting up and going for a 10-minute brisk walk, followed by another self-rating of energy. More often than not, feelings of energy increase. Such a practical self-regulatory technique is the result of numerous research studies where this effect has been shown. For example, in one of the first studies to document this effect, Thayer (1987) showed that 10 minutes of brisk walking significantly elevated feelings of energy for up to 120 minutes following the walk. Similar research by Saklofske, Blomme, and Kelly (1992) showed increased energy and decreased tension following walks of 4 and 10 minutes in duration. In a series of studies using both naturalistic and more controlled, laboratory settings, Ekkekakis, Hall, Van Landuyt, and Petruzzello (2000) showed that 10 to 15 minutes of walking was consistently associated with increased activation and more positive affective valence, in essence reflecting increased energy and decreased tension.

Although systematic examinations of exercise intensity beyond brisk walking have been relatively infrequent, their typical finding is that positive affect tends to increase from pre- to post-exercise following exercise intensities that are not exhaustive. Two studies are representative of these effects. First, Steptoe, Kearsley, and Walters (1993) showed, using the tension–anxiety, vigor, and depression–dejection subscales of the POMS, that vigor increased from pre- to post-exercise following cycling at both 50 percent and 70 percent of aerobic capacity; tension was decreased below pre-exercise levels by 30 minutes of recovery. In addition to these POMS subscales, Steptoe et al. used items reflective of exhilaration. Again, similar to the vigor effects, exhilaration was increased following exercise and stayed elevated during recovery. In a second study, Tate and Petruzzello (1995) examined affective responses to 30 minutes of cycling at 55 percent and 70 percent of maximal aerobic capacity. Affect was assessed using the AD ACL before, during, and following the exercise bouts. In this study, no affective changes were seen in the 55 percent intensity condition. Cycling at 70 percent resulted in significant increases in energetic arousal during and following exercise.

In general, it appears that positively valenced affective states (e.g., energy, vigor, exhilaration) are increased following moderate-intensity exercise and negatively valenced affective states (e.g., fatigue, tension) are either unchanged or reduced following moderate exercise. Following high-intensity exercise, negative affective states may be increased and positive affective states decreased, particularly in less fit individuals. However, in more fit individuals, even high-intensity exercise may result in improved positive affect (see Ekkekakis & Petruzzello, 1999).

IN-TASK EXERCISE RESPONSES

If exercise can make people feel better, either because of increased energy or decreased tension and fatigue, why don't more people exercise? As Thayer noted, "The extensive evidence about the value of exercise should have the gyms packed, the running tracks crowded, and the sidewalks filled with throngs of people walking. But they aren't" (2001, p. 32). It may very well be that even though people feel better *after* exercise, how they feel *during* exercise may be part of the problem. The work of Emmons and Diener (1986) nicely pointed out that the affect experienced during an activity is a good predictor of future engagement in that activity. A person is not likely to continue an activity that does not bring enjoyment or is not fun to do. In spite of the abundance of research examining pre- to post-exercise changes in affect, studies examining "in-task" affective responses have been rare, although there has been a recent move to change that shortcoming.

With the advent of single-item and relatively brief multi-item self-report scales for measuring affect, assessing affect during exercise has become more viable. As noted earlier, a fairly recently developed scale, the Feeling Scale (FS), has begun to get much more use in this regard. For example, Hardy and Rejeski (1989) showed that across four-minute exercise bouts of increasing intensity (30 percent, 60 percent, and 90 percent of maximal aerobic capacity), affect, as measured by the FS, became progressively more negative. Two studies by Parfitt and colleagues (Parfitt & Eston, 1995; Parfitt, Markland, & Holmes, 1994) showed similar findings. Parfitt and Eston showed that FS ratings were generally lower in a condition involving cycling at 90 percent of maximal aerobic capacity compared with 60 percent, with some additional differences between active compared with inactive participants. Parfitt et al. (1994) also showed lower FS ratings in a 90 percent intensity exercise condition relative to exercise at 60 percent.

Another interesting aspect of some of the research examining in-task affective responses has been the relationship of these responses to ongoing physiological changes. In the work of Hardy and Rejeski (1989), relationships between FS and ratings of perceived exertion became progressively more negative as intensity increased from 30 percent to 90 percent of maximal aerobic capacity. In other words, as the intensity increased, perceptions of exertion increased while FS ratings decreased, indicating more negative affect at greater exercise intensity. FS ratings were also negatively correlated with various physiological measures like ventilation, heart rate, respiratory rate, and oxygen consumption, reflecting increased negativity of affect with increasing physiological activation. Ekkekakis et al. (1997) showed similar effects in a study using cycling exercise in the heat and under conditions of dehydration: a progressive decline in affective valence (i.e., an increase in negative feelings) from beginning to end of the exercise bout.

Bixby, Spalding, and Hatfield (2001) compared cycle ergometer exercise at two different intensities, one that corresponded to the **ventilatory threshold** (VT) and another that was significantly below the ventilatory threshold. VT, which is conceptually analogous to lactate threshold, is the point at which the ventilatory equivalent for oxygen continues to increase without a concomitant increase in the ventilatory equivalent for carbon dioxide. Bixby et al. used a visual analogue mood scale, a simple rating scale in which the subject indicates current mood state by placing a mark along a horizontal line anchored with the words "worst mood" on one end and "best mood" at the other. With this instrument, Bixby et al. showed that during exercise below the VT, mood improved at 20 minutes into the exercise bout and remained elevated for the remainder of the exercise and for a period of time during recovery. In contrast, exercise performed at the VT resulted in a worsening of mood at 10 minutes into the exercise bout that remained until the recovery period.

ventilatory threshold ■

Finally, work reported by Van Landuyt, Ekkekakis, Hall, and Petruzzello (2000) highlighted the importance of in-task measures of affect in understanding how individuals might get from their pre-exercise affective state to the post-affective state. In a moderate-intensity (60 percent of predicted maximal aerobic capacity) bout of cycling, there was essentially no change in FS ratings over the course of the 30-minute bout. This lack of change was masked, however, by the fact that about half of the participants (48 percent) reported an improvement in affective valence (reflected by increased FS scores), 35 percent reported a decline in affect (decreased FS scores), and about 17 percent reported no change. In other words, the lack of change at the group level concealed the fact that some individuals actually felt better during exercise while some felt worse. This work is useful in illustrating that even moderate-intensity bouts of exercise do not necessarily result in positive affective changes *during* the activity, even though pre- to post-exercise changes with such moderate-intensity activity are generally positive.

To summarize, the general conclusion that can be derived from the available research is that affect gets progressively more negative as exercise intensity increases. Moderate-intensity exercise generally results in more positive affective changes, but this is not a universal phenomenon and individual difference factors need to be carefully examined in this regard.

A RESEARCH EXEMPLAR

As an example of how the problems described earlier can be addressed, consider the recent work of Hall, Ekkekakis, and Petruzzello (2002). Affective responses to three distinct levels of exercise intensity were examined before and after as well as during a graded treadmill protocol to the point at which the person could no longer continue. Affect was assessed using the dimensions of valence and activation contained in the circumplex model and exercise intensity was standardized across individuals. Affect was measured using both multi-item and single-item instruments. The Feeling Scale (FS) was used as a measure of affective valence, and the Felt Arousal Scale (FAS) of the Telic State Measure (Svebak & Murgatroyd, 1985) was used as a single-item measure of perceived activation. Both the FS and FAS were used to assess affect during exercise and were obtained every minute of the exercise protocol. The Activation Deactivation Adjective Check List (AD ACL) was used to provide a measure of the four quadrants of circumplex affective space discussed earlier (see Exhibit 9.3) and was completed before and at the end of the exercise as well as 10 and 20 minutes following the exercise bout. Exercise intensity was standardized by using the ventilatory threshold (VT). Once the time point at which the VT occurred was determined, the FS and FAS ratings made at the first two minutes, the minute of the VT, two minutes following the VT, the last two minutes of the bout, and during the two minutes immediately following completion of the exercise bout were selected for analysis.

The results of the study showed the following: Pre- to post-exercise responses on the AD ACL revealed beneficial affective responses, indexed

exhibit 9.4 **Affective responses to a graded exercise protocol.**

Pre- and post-exercise responses on the AD ACL.

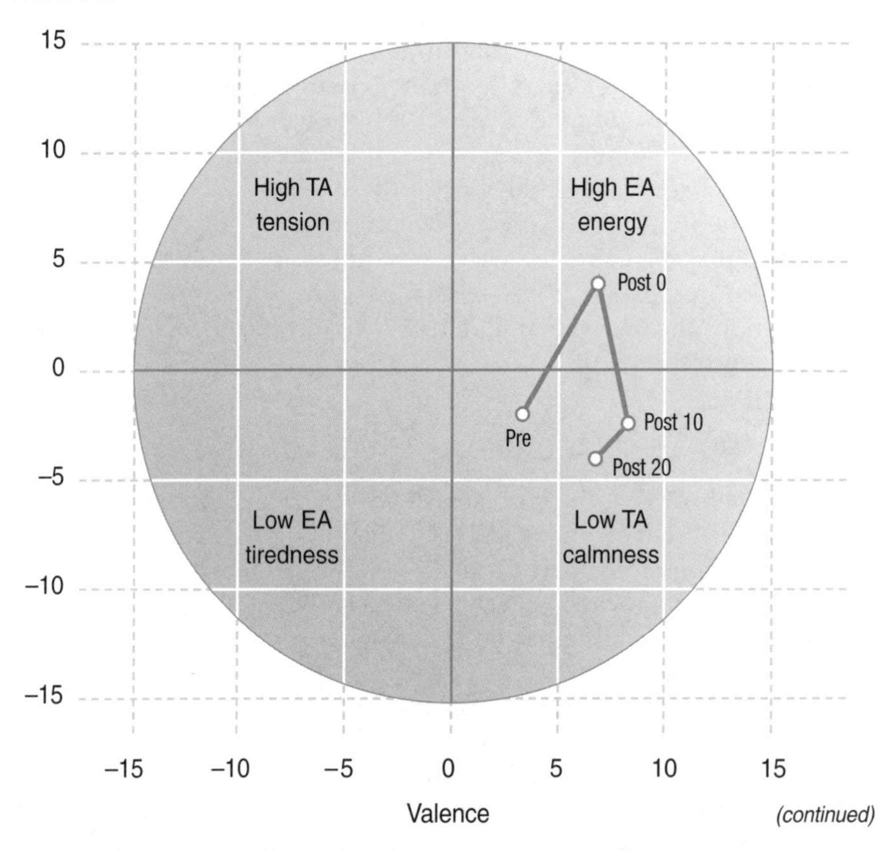

(continued)

by increased energetic arousal along with decreased tense arousal (see Exhibit 9.4, above). During exercise, however, affective valence became increasingly negative after the ventilatory threshold was reached and continued until volitional exhaustion was reached. Interestingly, this affective negativity rebounded completely when the exercise was stopped (see Exhibit 9.4, on the following page). These findings were interpreted as indicating that exercise at intensities requiring increasingly greater levels of anaerobic metabolism can have a substantial negative affective impact, albeit relatively temporary. Importantly, findings such as this could have implications for the design and implementation of exercise programs. To the extent that exercise programs can be individualized so that the exerciser does not experience negative affect during the activity, individuals might be better able to stick with their exercise regimens.

Continued. exhibit 9.4

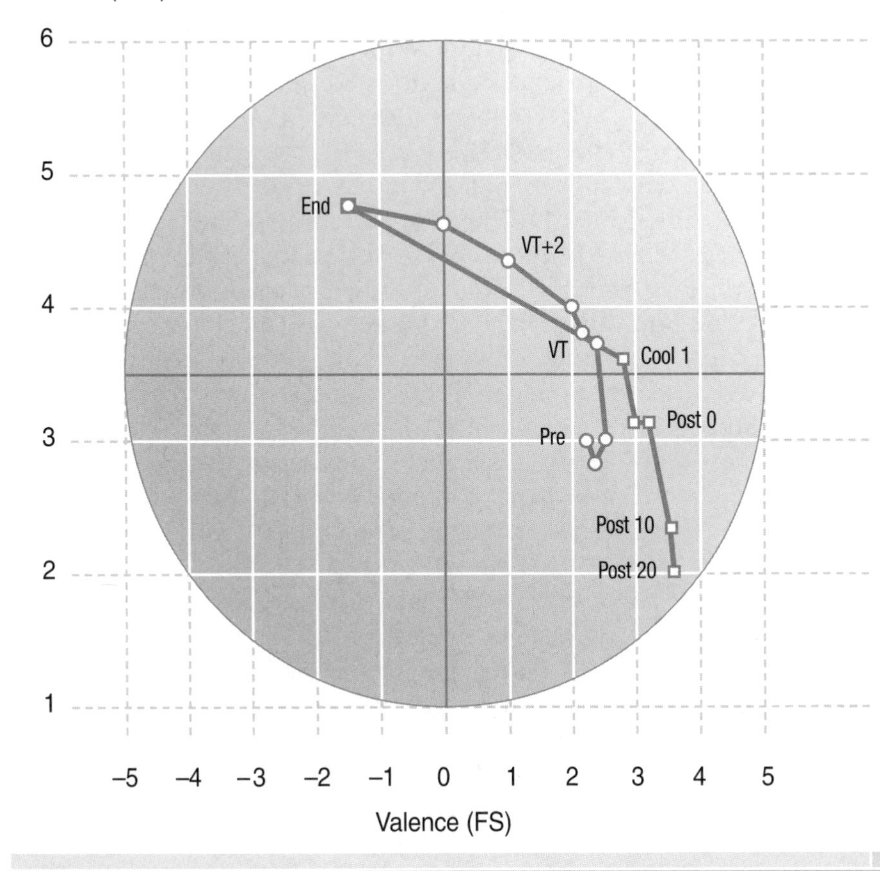

Responses across the stages of exercise, cool-down, and recovery on the FS and FAS.

Source: Hall, Ekkekakis, & Petruzzello (2002, pp. 56, 59). Reproduced with permission from *British Journal of Health Psychology.* © The British Psychological Society.

Negative Psychological Effects of Exercise on Emotional Well-Being

Although the psychological effects associated with exercise are generally regarded as positive, this is not always the case. A number of negative psychological effects can take place with extreme levels of exercise.

OVERTRAINING, THE STALENESS SYNDROME, AND DEPRESSION

It has been well documented that with overtraining in endurance athletes, the staleness syndrome often results. **Overtraining** occurs when

■ overtraining

the individual trains at a greater level than she might be accustomed to in terms of frequency, intensity, and duration. Such a pattern of training is used to help athletes adapt to greater levels of training stress so that when they reduce the amount of training in preparation for important competitions (e.g., the Olympics) their bodies respond with better performances than were achievable prior to the overtraining. One negative aspect of such overtraining is that some individuals develop the **staleness syndrome,** characterized by increased negative mental health (depression, anxiety, fatigue, reduced energy) and poorer performance. Overtraining can also lead to clinical depression in elite athletes.

staleness syndrome ■

Morgan's Mental Health Model (1984) describes the psychological profile of the elite athlete, relative to the population average, as being above average on positive factors and below average on negative factors. This has been popularly referred to as the **"iceberg profile"** because when scores from the POMS subscales are plotted on the POMS profile sheet, athletes typically have scores on the vigor subscale that fall above the 50th percentile and scores on the tension, confusion, anger, fatigue, and depression subscales that fall below the 50th percentile. Connecting the points on the profile sheet results in what looks like an iceberg (see Exhibit 9.5).

iceberg profile ■

It has been shown repeatedly that when endurance athletes move through their training cycle and increase their training workloads, the typical profile begins to flatten out and even inverts. That is, with increasing workloads, vigor scores decrease and scores on the five "negative" mood subscales increase. Such an effect is typically linked fairly tightly to the training load (Raglin & Moger, 1999), with greater increases in the negative scores and decreases in vigor as the amount of training increases. This has been known to lead to clinical levels of depression, and the only known treatment is to reduce the training load.

EXERCISE DEPENDENCE SYNDROME

exercise dependence syndrome ■

Another phenomenon that has received much more attention in the literature recently is what is referred to as the **exercise dependence syndrome.** Unfortunately, this phenomenon has been referred to by various labels, and numerous measures (see Exhibit 9.6) have been used to document its existence, all of which have led to a great deal of confusion. As defined by Hausenblas and Symons Downs (2002), exercise dependence is "a craving for leisure-time physical activity, resulting in uncontrollable excessive exercise behavior, that manifests in physiological (e.g., tolerance/withdrawal) and/or psychological (e.g., anxiety, depression) symptoms" (p. 90). One of the points raised by Hausenblas

exhibit 9.5

The iceberg profile.

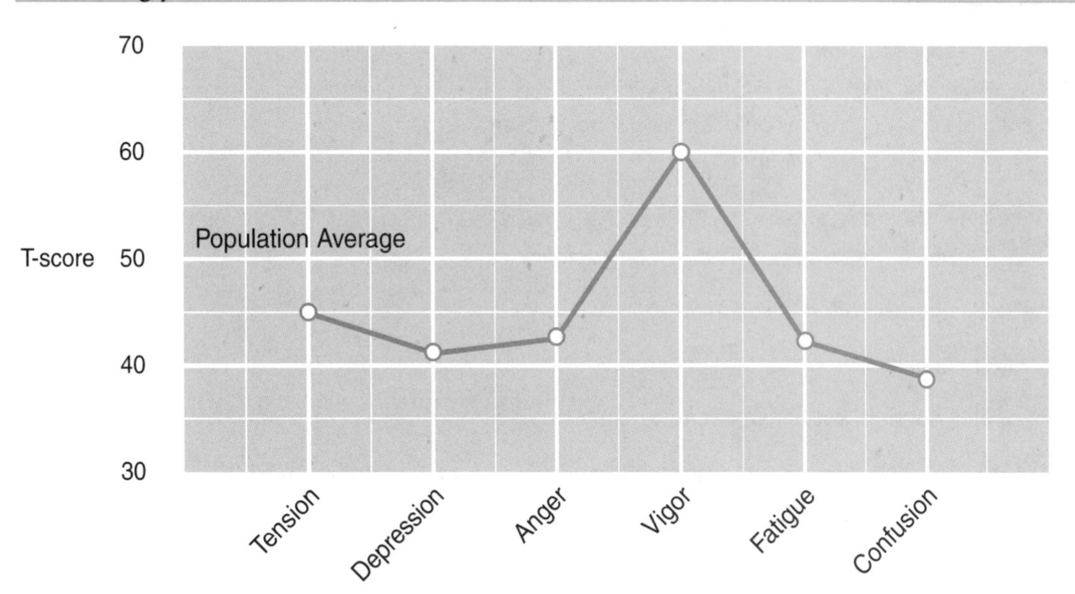

The "iceberg profile" of a selected swimmer at the outset of a macro-cycle.

Source: Morgan (1984).

exhibit 9.6

Terminology used in the study of exercise dependence .

Exercise dependence, *also* running dependence
Addiction, *also* running addiction, exercise addiction, negative addiction
Obligatory exercise
Exercise commitment
Excessive exercise
Commitment to physical activity, also excessive commitment to running
Attitudinal commitment
Compulsive runner
High-intensity running
Habitual running

Source: Hausenblas and Symons Downs (2002).

exhibit 9.7 ***Operational definitions of the multidimensional nature of exercise dependence.***

1. Tolerance
   - Need for increased amount of exercise to achieve desired effect
   - Diminished effect with continuation of same amount of exercise
2. Withdrawal
   - Withdrawal symptoms (e.g., anxiety, fatigue, disturbed sleep) when exercise is missed
   - Exercise relieves or helps avoid withdrawal symptoms
3. Intention effects: Exercise often lasts longer than was originally intended
4. Loss of control: Persistent desire and/or unsuccessful effort to control exercise (e.g., cut back)
5. Time: Lots of time spent in activities needed to obtain exercise
6. Conflict: Giving up of important social, occupational, relationship activities because of exercise
7. Continuance: Exercise is maintained in spite of knowledge that it is problematic from either physical (e.g., injury) or psychological perspectives

Source: Hausenblas & Symons Downs (2002, p. 113).

and Symons Downs in their review of the exercise dependence literature is the need for better operational definitions of exercise dependence. To that end, their suggested criteria are listed in Exhibit 9.7.

primary exercise dependence ■
secondary exercise dependence ■

It is worth noting that exercise dependence is often a part of an eating disorder. Pierce (1994) discusses the distinction between primary and secondary exercise dependence, noting that the main distinction is derived from what the objective of the exercise is for the individual. In **primary exercise dependence,** the exercise is an end in itself. Any alterations of body composition or diet are done to enhance exercise performance. In **secondary exercise dependence,** exercise is used exclusively to control body composition. Pierce also discusses a number of factors associated with exercise dependence, including psychological, behavioral, and physiological. Pierce notes that there is a positive relationship between exercise dependence and anxiety, compulsiveness, and rigidity, along with a negative association with self-esteem. Perhaps obviously, in terms of behavior, a positive association exists between exercise dependence and exercise volume (e.g., frequency, duration).

At least two different physiological factors have been proposed as explanations for exercise dependence. In the endorphin hypothesis, the individual is thought to exercise to excess because of an actual physical dependence on the chemical released during exercise, sometimes referred to as "addiction." Whether exercise dependence is an addiction is a debatable issue. Experts have not yet agreed that such addictions can actually occur with exercise, or the extent to which such dependence might occur. Endorphins are known to be released in response to stress, and exercise is certainly a form of stress. The endorphin hypothesis suggests that it is the release of those endorphins that the individual's body craves, leading to more exercise to result in more endorphin release, and the cycle repeats itself.

The psychophysiological hypothesis (also referred to as the energy conservation–sympathetic arousal hypothesis, see Thompson & Blanton, 1987) posits that because the effect of training is a decrease in sympathetic nervous system output (e.g., catecholamines—epinephrine and norepinephrine), an increase in fitness can potentially result in a state of lethargy, fatigue, and decreased arousal. This state motivates the individual to increase the training dose, thereby increasing catecholamine output and satisfying the physiological "need." This creates a vicious cycle, however, because eventually the individual adapts to the increased training load, decreasing catecholamines and increasing the negative feelings.

Although some individuals clearly exercise excessively, caution is certainly warranted at this stage of knowledge development when drawing conclusions about exercise dependence. For one thing, it is very difficult to study truly exercise-dependent individuals, if for no other reason than they are unwilling (or unable) to stop exercising and will not do so voluntarily. Thus, it is impossible to determine how their physical and psychological states vary as a function of their exercise levels and exercise withdrawal. By definition, an individual could not be dependent on exercise if there were no withdrawal symptoms upon cessation of exercise. In fact, Baekeland (1970), in his initial study attempting to examine the effects of exercise deprivation on sleep, was unable to recruit any individual who ran more than five or six days per week! In many cases it is possible to study truly dependent exercisers only when they become injured, but in those cases it is difficult to discern whether the affective responses are due to the deprivation or to the injury. Other studies purporting to examine exercise dependence by depriving exercise have made the mistake of assessing affect or mood *after* an acute bout of exercise, then depriving exercise for two or three days and assessing affect or mood again (see for example Mondin et al., 1996). This obviously confounds the acute affect-enhancing effects of exercise with whatever deprivation effects there may (or may not) be. Finally, because of the definitional and measurement problems that have plagued this area of research to this point, it is difficult to measure how serious a problem exercise dependence is in terms of its prevalence within the population.

Practical Recommendations

It would appear that one of the most reasonable things individuals can do regarding exercise and their emotional well-being is simply to become more aware of how they feel when they do or do not exercise. As Thayer (2001) outlines in his book, one way to do this is through self-study. This is a fairly simple activity, but one which could pay great dividends. As described by Thayer, self-study involves thinking about how energetic or tense you feel at different times of the day. It is also important to note how you feel before and after any exercise that you might do on a given day. You might find it advantageous to try to schedule exercise time during periods of the day when you usually experience low energy, as it has been fairly clearly shown that one of the best benefits of exercise is increased energy and decreased tension—as Nick and Stephanie discovered in the chapter-opening scenario.

As with other aspects of mental health, the amount of exercise required to achieve increased positive or decreased negative feelings is currently not known. It does seem apparent that exercise that is not excessive ("excessive" could be defined simply as activity being done every day for more than one hour at a time, particularly when it is not part of some sort of athletic training regimen) results in more positive affective responses, particularly if done below the ventilatory threshold. Perhaps the simplest rule of thumb to follow is that if you can carry on a conversation while exercising, the intensity is not too high. Such types of exercise will likely result in positive (or at least not negative) experiences during and following the exercise, thus increasing the likelihood that the exercise will be performed again (and again and again).

It is important to point out that this is a very rapidly changing area of study. Much remains to be learned about dose–response effects, and new research is being reported every week that is helping to detail these kinds of effects. It does seem clear that in addition to the reduction in depression and anxiety, exercise has much to offer that might eventually be useful in designing exercise programs that people not only engage in but also enjoy.

Conclusion

The study of the psychological outcomes of exercise is becoming increasingly recognized as an important endeavor. In spite of the relatively long history of research examining such outcomes, however, we continue to have a fairly limited knowledge of what effects exercise has and how these effects might influence exercise behavior, whether that be adherence to a regular program of activity or dropping out from such programs. Given the health benefits that accrue from exercise, a better understanding of the psychological outcomes could have a very worthwhile influence on behavior.

What Do You Know?

1. What is the definition of emotional well-being?
2. Distinguish between emotions, moods, and affect.
3. What two things led to the dissatisfaction with existing affective measures and the development of exercise-specific measures?
4. What are the two major advantages attributed to using a dimensional approach to study affect?
5. What general conclusions can be drawn regarding the before-to-after affective responses to exercise?
6. What is the metabolic landmark that seems to provide a fairly reliable indication of when, *during* exercise, affect shifts from good to bad or positive to negative?
7. Distinguish between primary and secondary exercise dependence.
8. What is the basis for the energy conservation–sympathetic arousal hypothesis?
9. Based on what is currently known, is exercise dependence a widespread problem?

Learning Activities

1. To gain a better understanding of the relationship between exercise and affect, conduct a self-experiment. Over the course of two weeks, do a simple rating of energy and tension before and after a scheduled exercise session. Use a rating from 1 to 7 for each, with 1 being none or very little and 7 being a great deal or very much. On non-exercise days, do the same ratings at approximately the same times of the day that you would exercise. After the two-week period, compare the ratings from before with after the exercise session. What differences are apparent? What happens when you compare the affect on exercise days with the affect experienced on non-exercise days?

2. Use the circumplex approach to examining affective responses. Using the circumplex diagram below, which is divided in half from side to side (this line represents activation) and from top to bottom (this line represents valence), try the following exercises. Incorporate the following time points as appropriate:

- Moderate Exercise
  - Pre-exercise
  - 5 minutes
  - 15 minutes
  - Immediately post-exercise
  - 20 minutes post-exercise
- Intense Exercise
  - Pre-exercise
  - 5 minutes
  - 15 minutes
  - Immediately post-exercise
  - 20 minutes post-exercise

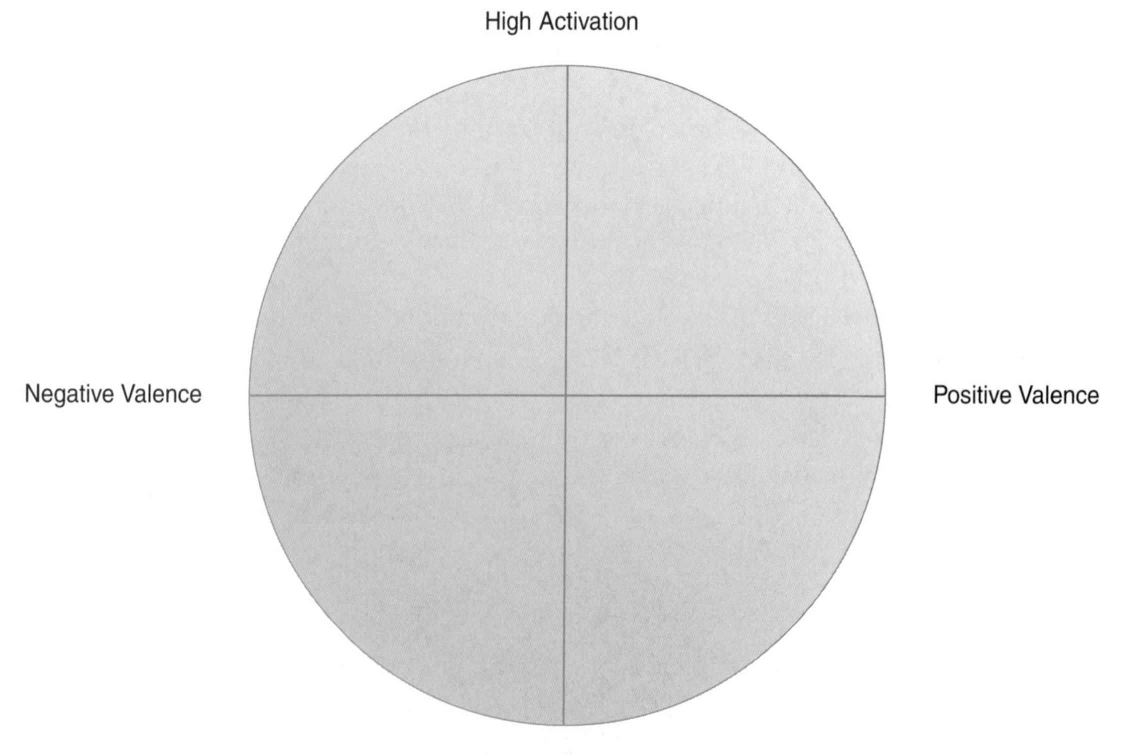

a. Describe two different intensities of exercise, noting how they differ in terms of intensity. Label one type as "moderate" and the other as "intense."

b. Draw the expected response to a 20-minute bout of the "moderate" exercise.

c. Draw the expected response to a 20-minute bout of the "intense" exercise, incorporating the same time points.

d. What are the major differences in the two drawings? Why do these differences occur?

References

Baekeland, F. (1970). Exercise deprivation: Sleep and psychological reactions. *Archives of General Psychiatry, 22,* 365–369.

Berger, B. G. (1994). Coping with stress: The effectiveness of exercise and other techniques. *Quest, 46,* 100–119.

Biddle, S. J. H., & Mutrie, N. (2001). *Psychology of physical activity: Determinants, well-being and interventions.* New York: Routledge.

Bixby, W. R., Spalding, T. W., & Hatfield, B. D. (2001). Temporal dynamics and dimensional specificity of the affective response to exercise of varying intensity: Differing pathways to a common outcome. *Journal of Sport and Exercise Psychology, 23,* 171–190.

Dishman, R. K. (1986). Mental health. In V. Seefeldt (Ed.), *Physical activity and well-being* (pp. 303–341). Reston, VA: AAHPERD.

Ekkekakis, P., Hall, E. E., Van Landuyt, L. M., & Petruzzello, S. J. (2000). Walking in (affective) circles: Can short walks enhance affect? *Journal of Behavioral Medicine, 23,* 245–275.

Ekkekakis, P., Kavouras, S. A., Casa, D. J., Herrera, J. A., Armstrong, L. E., Maresh, C. M., & Petruzzello, S. J. (1997). Affective responses to a bout of exhaustive exercise in the heat in dehydrated and rehydrated states: In search of physiological correlates. In R. Lidor & M. Bar-Eli (Eds.), *Innovations in sport psychology: Linking theory and practice* (pp. 253–254). Proceedings of the IX World Congress of Sport Psychology.

Ekkekakis, P., & Petruzzello, S. J. (1999). Acute aerobic exercise and affect: Current status, problems and prospects regarding dose–response. *Sports Medicine, 28,* 337–374.

Ekkekakis, P., & Petruzzello, S. J. (2000). Analysis of the affect measurement conundrum in exercise psychology. I. Fundamental issues. *Psychology of Sport and Exercise, 1,* 71–88.

Ekkekakis, P., & Petruzzello, S. J. (2001a). Analysis of the affect measurement conundrum in exercise psychology. II. A conceptual and methodological critique of the Exercise-Induced Feeling Inventory. *Psychology of Sport and Exercise, 2,* 1–26.

Ekkekakis, P., & Petruzzello, S. J. (2001b). Analysis of the affect measurement conundrum in exercise psychology. III. A conceptual and methodological critique of the Subjective Exercise Experiences Scale. *Psychology of Sport and Exercise, 2,* 205–232.

Ekkekakis, P., & Petruzzello, S. J. (2002). Analysis of the affect measurement conundrum in exercise psychology. IV. A conceptual case for the affect circumplex. *Psychology of Sport and Exercise, 3,* 35–63.

Emmons, R. A., & Diener, E. (1986). A goal-affect analysis of everyday situational choices. *Journal of Research in Personality, 20,* 309–326.

Gauvin, L. & Brawley, L. R. (1993). Alternative psychological models and methodologies for the study of exercise and effect. In P. Seraganian (Ed.), *Exercise psychology: The influence of physical exercise on psychological processes* (pp. 146–171). New York: John Wiley.

Gauvin L., & Rejeski, W. J. (1993). The Exercise-Induced Feeling Inventory: Development and initial validation. *Journal of Sport and Exercise Psychology, 15,* 403–423.

Gauvin, L., & Spence, J. C. (1998). Measurement of exercise-induced changes in feeling states, affect, mood, and emotions. In J. L. Duda (Ed.), *Advances in sport and exercise psychology measurement* (pp. 325–336). Morgantown, WV: Fitness Information Technology.

Hall, E. E., Ekkekakis, P., & Petruzzello, S. J. (2002). The affective beneficence of vigorous exercise revisited. *British Journal of Health Psychology, 7,* 47–66.

Hardy, C. J., & Rejeski, W. J. (1989). Not what, but how one feels: The measurement of affect during exercise. *Journal of Sport and Exercise Psychology, 11,* 304–317.

Hausenblas, H. A., & Symons Downs, D. (2002). Exercise dependence: A systematic review. *Psychology of Sport and Exercise, 3,* 89–123.

James, W. (1899). Untitled. *American Physical Education Review, 4,* 220–221.

Lox, C. L., Jackson, S., Tuholski, S. W., Wasley, D., & Treasure, D. C. (2000). Revisiting the measurement of exercise-induced feeling states: The Physical Activity Affect Scale (PAAS). *Measurement in Physical Education and Exercise Science, 4,* 79–95.

McAuley, E. (1994). Physical activity and psychosocial outcomes. In C. Bouchard, R. J. Shephard, & T. Stephens (Eds.), *Physical activity, fitness, and health: International proceedings and consensus statement* (pp. 551–568). Champaign, IL: Human Kinetics.

McAuley, E., & Courneya, K. S. (1994). The Subjective Exercise Experiences Scale (SEES): development and preliminary validation. *Journal of Sport and Exercise Psychology, 16,* 163–177.

McAuley, E., & Rudolph, D. (1995). Physical activity, aging, and psychological well-being. *Journal of Aging and Physical Activity, 3,* 67–96.

McNair, D. M., Lorr, M., & Droppleman, L. F. (1971). *Manual for the profile of mood states.* San Diego, CA: Educational and Industrial Testing Service.

Mondin, G. W., Morgan, W. P., Piering, P. N., Stegner, A. J., Stotesbury, C. L., Trine, M. R., & Wu, M. (1996). Psychological consequences of exercise deprivation in habitual exercisers. *Medicine and Science in Sports and Exercise, 28,* 1199–1203.

Morgan, W. P. (1984). Selected psychological factors limiting performance: A mental health model. *American Academy of Physical Education Papers, 18,* 70–80.

National Institutes of Health Consensus Development Panel on Physical Activity and Cardiovascular Health. (1996). Physical activity and cardiovascular health. *Journal of the American Medical Association, 276,* 241–246.

Parfitt, G., & Eston, R. (1995). Changes in ratings of perceived exertion and psychological affect in the early stages of exercise. *Perceptual and Motor Skills, 80,* 259–266.

Parfitt, G., Markland, D., & Holmes, C. (1994). Responses to physical exertion in active and inactive males and females. *Journal of Sport and Exercise Psychology, 16,* 178–186.

Pierce, E. F. (1994). Exercise dependence syndrome in runners. *Sports Medicine, 18,* 149–155.

Raglin, J. S., & Moger, L. (1999). Adverse consequences of physical activity: When more is too much. In J. M. Rippe (Ed.), *Lifestyle medicine* (pp. 998–1004). Malden, MA: Blackwell Science.

Russell, J. A. (1980). A circumplex model of affect. *Journal of Personality and Social Psychology, 39,* 1161–1178.

Russell, J. A. (1997). How shall an emotion be called? In R. Plutchik & H. R. Conte (Eds.), *Circumplex models of personality and emo-*

tions (pp. 205–222). Washington, DC: American Psychological Association.

Saklofske, D. H., Blomme, G. C., & Kelly, I. W. (1992). The effect of exercise and relaxation on energetic and tense arousal. *Personality and Individual Differences, 13,* 623–625.

Steptoe, A., Kearsley, N., & Walters, N. (1993). Acute mood responses to maximal and submaximal exercise in active and inactive men. *Psychology and Health, 8,* 89–99.

Svebak, S., & Murgatroyd, S. (1985). Metamotivational dominance: A multimethod validation of reversal theory constructs. *Journal of Personality and Social Psychology, 48,* 107–116.

Tate, A. K., & Petruzzello, S. J., (1995). Varying the intensity of acute exercise: Implications for changes in affect. *Journal of Sports Medicine and Physical Fitness, 35,* 295–302.

Thayer, R. E. (1986). Activation–deactivation adjective check list: Current overview and structural analysis. *Psychological Reports, 58,* 607–614.

Thayer, R. E. (1987). Energy, tiredness, and tension effects of a sugar snack versus moderate exercise. *Journal of Personality and Social Psychology, 52,* 119–125.

Thayer, R. E. (1989). *The biopsychology of mood and arousal.* New York: Oxford University Press.

Thayer, R. E. (2001). *Calm energy: How people regulate mood with food and exercise.* New York: Oxford University Press.

Thompson, J. K., & Blanton, P. (1987). Energy conservation and exercise dependence: A sympathetic arousal hypothesis. *Medicine and Science in Sports and Exercise, 19,* 91–99.

Van Landuyt, L. M., Ekkekakis, P., Hall, E. E., & Petruzzello, S. J. (2000). Throwing the mountains into the lakes: On the perils of nomothetic conceptions of the exercise–affect relationship. *Journal of Sport and Exercise Psychology, 22,* 208–234.

Watson, D., Clark, L. A., & Tellegen, A. (1988). Development and validation of brief measures of positive and negative affect: The PANAS scales. *Journal of Personality and Social Psychology, 54,* 1063–1070.

Watson, D., & Tellegen, A. (1985). Toward a consensual structure of mood. *Psychological Bulletin, 98,* 219–235.

Chapter 10

Self-Concept, Self-Esteem, and Exercise

KEY TERMS
- academic self-concept
- global self-esteem
- nonacademic self-concept
- perceived competence
- physical self-concept
- self-concept
- self-confidence
- self-efficacy
- self-esteem
- self-schemata
- social self-concept

Chris works for a large corporation in an office with hundreds of employees. He regularly engages in "water cooler" talk with several coworkers. He likes this particular group of individuals but feels somewhat alienated and intimidated when the conversation turns to physical activity (which it normally does). Although Chris desires to be part of this "active" group (i.e., he values exercise for a number of psychological, physical, and, mostly, social reasons), he does not maintain an image of himself as an exerciser and, furthermore, feels that he lacks the discipline needed to adhere to a physical activity regimen. This self-image causes him occasionally to think less positively about himself and his life in general than he would like.

The Significance of Self-Esteem

Recently, researchers have confirmed a notion that many in the field of psychology have long understood—that individuals who are popular, rich, and powerful are not necessarily happy. Indeed, Sheldon, Elliot, Kim, and Kasser (2001) found that these components ranked toward the bottom of psychological needs, while self-esteem topped the list of needs that bring happiness to people. This is certainly good news for those of us in the field of exercise psychology, as researchers have repeatedly stated that the greatest potential impact of physical activity may be seen in the participant's self-esteem (Folkins & Sime, 1981; Hughes, 1984; McAuley, 1994). Consider the plight of Chris in the scenario above. The image he maintains of himself as a person is, to some extent, dictated by the specific image he holds of himself as a nonexerciser. Consequently, we would expect a positive change in both his physical and overall self-concept following successful adoption and maintenance of a physical activity regimen. The findings of Sheldon et al. (2001) and researchers in the field of exercise psychology suggest that promoting the self-esteem-enhancing properties of physical activity may be a viable strategy for improving activity levels in those individuals who view self-esteem as a primary psychological need.

Self-Concept, Self-Esteem, and Related Definitions

Although the constructs of self-concept and self-esteem are closely related and are often used interchangeably, they are not the same. For the purposes of this discussion, we will consider **self-concept** simply to be the way in which we see or define ourselves ("who I am"). You may describe yourself as a son or daughter, student, or salesperson. More specifically, you might consider yourself to be a mature and hard-working student, a loyal spouse, a fitness fanatic, an extravert (outgoing, life-of-the-party type), and so on. These are just a few of the unlimited number of ways in which you might view yourself. **Self-esteem** (synonymous with self-worth) constitutes the evaluative or affective consequence of one's self-concept ("how I feel about who I am"). In other words, self-esteem is the extent to which you feel positive or negative about your self-concept. Generally, self-concept and self-esteem are considered to be global in nature. That is to say, one's self-concept and self-esteem influence, and are influenced by, all aspects of an individual's life. Although certain domains of one's life are likely to be particularly influential on self-concept and self-esteem, all domains combine to form an overall sense of each construct. In our earlier example, because Chris values physical activity, his relatively negative physical self-concept appears to be reflected in a lower-than-desired self-esteem.

Self-concept and self-esteem are distinct from other forms of self-referent thought, such as perceived competence, self-confidence, and self-efficacy, in that the latter group of constructs is primarily focused on judgments of ability and potential success in specific situations, activities or skills, or domains. For example, we might be interested in assessing an individual's level of **perceived competence** in the physical activity domain. In order to determine this, the individual would have to ask himself questions such as, "Do I consider myself to be an 'athletic' individual?" or "Can I perform most physical skills, movements, or activities capably?" **Self-confidence** in the physical activity setting is

self-concept ■

self-esteem ■

perceived competence ■

self-confidence ■

somewhat more specific in that the individual might perceive himself as capable in activities of daily living (encompassing activities such as walking up and down stairs, carrying groceries and walking) but not so capable when it comes to engaging in more complex movements (e.g., hiking, dancing, weight training). Finally, **self-efficacy** is a situation-specific form of self-confidence. In the physical activity domain, this construct generally takes the form of judgments related to a particular skill/ability in a particular situation. For instance, you could be highly self-efficacious when performing upper-body weight training but not as efficacious when performing lower-body weight training. Similarly, you might have high self-efficacy for adhering to your exercise regimen in the fall and spring months but considerably lower efficacy for adhering in the summer and winter months. In short, these related constructs are more variable than self-concept/self-esteem, but they do contribute meaningfully to an individual's self-concept and self-esteem.

■ self-efficacy

Theoretical Foundations Employed in the Physical Activity Literature

Not surprisingly, initial research investigations concerning exercise and self-concept/self-esteem were generated largely from theories and models employed in the parent discipline of psychology (social cognitive psychology to be exact). This is certainly the case with the self-concept model proposed by Shavelson, Hubner, and Stanton (1976). Later, Sonstroem and Morgan (1989) extended the Shavelson et al. model into the exercise setting. These models are the topic of the next section.

SHAVELSON, HUBNER, AND STANTON MODEL

One particular model of self-concept, introduced by Shavelson et al. (1976), has been readily adopted in the exercise psychology literature. This multifaceted model of self-concept asserts that one's general (overall) self-concept is an aggregate construct determined by judgments of self-concept in a number of domains. The model is hierarchically organized such that more situation-specific and unstable evaluations are evident at the lower levels while more global and stable evaluations are contained within the upper levels (see Exhibit 10.1).

Residing at the top of the model, general self-concept comprises two primary categories—namely, academic and nonacademic self-concept. One's **academic self-concept** encompasses the primary learning domains of English, math, history, and science. **Nonacademic self-concept** is

■ academic self-concept
■ nonacademic self-concept

exhibit 10.1 *Diagram of self-concept model.*

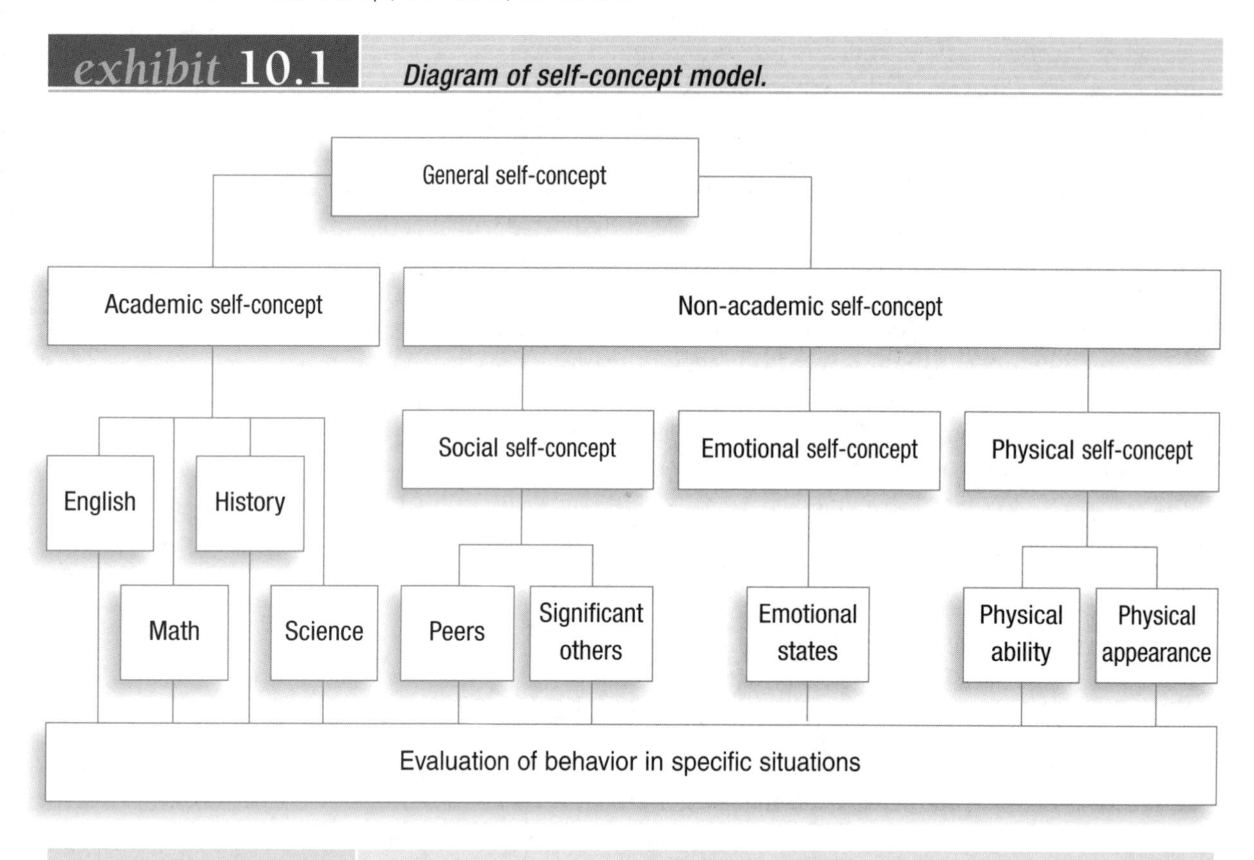

Source: Shavelson et al. (1976).

divided into social, emotional, and physical self-concept. Thus, four domains of self-concept are said to exist. With the exception of emotional self-concept, each domain is influenced by multiple subareas. For example, **physical self-concept** is dictated by the individual's judgments of both general physical abilities and physical appearance. According to the model, individuals with elevated perceptions of their physical abilities and positive feelings regarding their physical appearance would be expected to report a strong, positive physical self-concept (see Chapter 13 for more detailed discussions of body image and its impact on self-esteem and exercise behavior). Similarly, **social self-concept** would be enhanced by positive interactions with peers and significant others.

physical self-concept ■

social self-concept ■

The base level of the hierarchy is defined by the evaluation of behavior in specific situations. In regard to physical self-concept, our judgments of physical ability are generally based on our perceptions of successful and unsuccessful performances in a number of activities engaged in over a prolonged period of time. To use a mathematical analogy, each individually evaluated behavior is assigned a positive (successful) or negative (unsuccessful) number. The sum total of these evaluations indicates whether the perception of physical ability is low or high. Thus, an individual who experiences repeated success in a number of different activities would be expected to maintain a high physical self-concept.

Unfortunately, this formula is a bit simplistic. Because we value the activities we engage in to varying degrees, the formula must include "weights" for each activity. In other words, a person who places high value on physical ability related to lifetime physical activities (walking, running, strength training, etc.), but little value on physical ability related to sports (tennis, golf, softball, basketball, etc.), will maintain an overall judgment of physical ability most consistent with evaluations of behavior emanating from lifetime activities. Simply put, for such a person a disappointing string of strength training sessions will have a much greater influence on perception of physical ability than will multiple negative performances in golf.

The process is the same for physical appearance. For instance, an individual's perception of her physical appearance may be based predominantly on her body fat content. The fact that she may also possess considerable lean muscle tissue as well may be of limited consequence in her judgment. Not surprisingly, the result would be a poor evaluation of physical appearance.

SONSTROEM AND MORGAN MODEL

Building on the Shavelson et al. model, Sonstroem and Morgan (1989) proposed a model of exercise and self-esteem that also featured hierarchically organized constructs leading to predictions of **global** (overall) **self-esteem** (see Exhibit 10.2). The horizontal axis (time) lists the various assessments (two or more) that would be conducted when an intervention is presented. For example, if we were interested in the effect of a 12-month exercise program (intervention) on self-esteem, we would need to obtain a baseline (pre-program) assessment (Test 1) and at least one more assessment (Test 2) following completion of the program. Note that the model specifies an unlimited number of potential assessments beyond the second test (. . . nth test) for research designs incorporating multiple assessments over time. Thus, in the 12-month study mentioned above, it may be of interest to assess self-esteem more frequently than simply before and after the program. If this were the case, the model would expand to the right continuously until all the tests were completed, with the intervention appearing between assessments.

■ global self-esteem

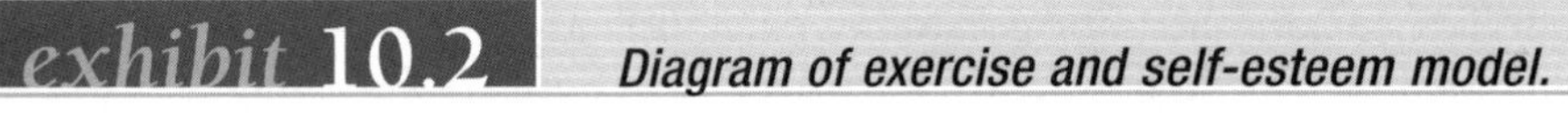

Diagram of exercise and self-esteem model.

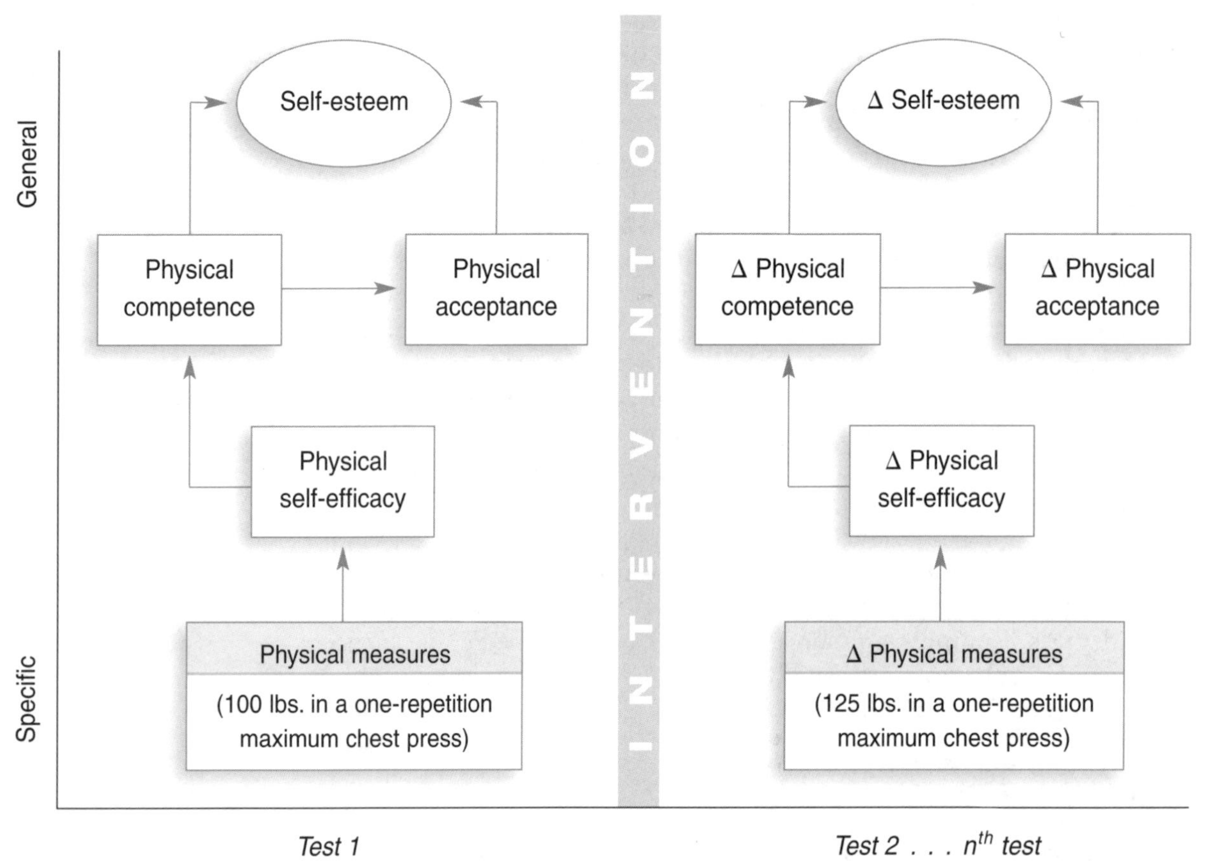

Source: Sonstroem & Morgan (1989).

The vertical axis has much the same role as in the Shavelson et al. model. The axis is anchored by specific self-perceptions at the base and general self-perception at the top. The process of altering self-esteem is initiated with physical measures located at the base of the model. Physical measures can vary tremendously, ranging from a single measure of a single variable to multiple assessments of a variety of different measures. As indicated on the vertical axis, these measures are highly specific and objective (e.g., number of pounds in a one-repetition maximum chest press). The measures are important only to the extent that they serve as a source of self-efficacy information. A composite physical self-efficacy is formed from the myriad of task-specific self-efficacies maintained by the individual. One's physical self-efficacy then informs more generalized judgments of physical competence. For example, an elderly individual who begins a cardiovascular and resistance-training exercise regimen may report substantial improvements in efficacy for these activities. Thus, his physical self-efficacy would likely be enhanced. This improved self-efficacy might also carry over and affect efficacy expectations for other "nonexercise" physical activities such as carrying heavy bags of groceries or performing yard work. The consequence is that the individual now feels relatively competent at performing most physical tasks required or experienced in his life.

As indicated in Exhibit 10.2, physical competence influences self-esteem both independently and via physical acceptance. *Physical acceptance* refers to the extent to which the individual accepts his or her level of physical competence. Thus, global self-esteem is partially driven by the extent to which the person is accepting of who she is physically. A high degree of acceptance enhances global self-esteem. If the individual is not accepting of her physical competence, global self-esteem is reduced. For example, one individual may run a 5K race at an eight-minute mile pace and be very accepting of that level of fitness. Another individual, however, may not view an eight-minute mile as an acceptable display of physical competence. Obviously, the two individuals' global self-esteem will be affected differently.

At this point in our discussion, it is necessary to discuss a critical issue related to self-esteem in general and Sonstroem and Morgan's model in particular. This issue concerns the relative contributions of objective and subjective interpretations of success to self-esteem. As alluded to in the example, different people can have different perceptions of the same performance. It is important to recognize that only the *subjective perception* of success is relevant to feelings of self-esteem. Thus, a personal trainer can tell you a hundred times that you are improving, but if you don't feel you are making improvement, your self-esteem will not improve. Conversely, a personal trainer may be concerned about the fact that you have not shown much improvement in your muscular strength. However, you may feel that the training has been a success because you have more energy and are able to perform occupational duties requiring muscular strength more easily than before you began the exercise regimen. Thus, although the objective physiological indicators of improved fitness may not be present, global self-esteem may improve because your subjective judgment of physical competence has improved. This phenomenon has been documented by Hatfield, Vaccaro, and Benedict (1985) in a study of 11 children following an eight-week exercise program. In this study, the authors reported significant improvements in global self-concept while no changes were noted in body fat percentage or cardiovascular fitness.

Measurement

Self-concept and self-esteem have traditionally been defined as unidimensional (global) constructs, and early measures designed to assess these constructs reflected this, for example, by representing self-esteem as a single score indicating a general or overall sense of esteem. Indeed, the most common self-concept/self-esteem tools used in the exercise psychology literature (e.g., Coopersmith Self-Esteem Inventory, Piers–Harris Children's Self-Concept Scale, Rosenberg Self-Esteem Scale) employed a single, global dimension (overall self-concept or self-esteem) and usually failed to address elements of physical self-concept (the Tennessee Self-Concept Scale is one exception). Fortunately, these limitations were remedied by the introduction of two physical self-concept/self-esteem inventories in the late 1980s and early 1990s.

The Physical Self-Perception Profile (PSPP; Fox & Corbin, 1989) was based largely on the notions of self-concept proposed by Shavelson et al. (1976). The 30-item battery follows a response pattern similar to that successfully employed by Harter (1985), in that two contrasting statements are presented. Respondents are asked to read each pair of statements, decide which of the two statements is most characteristic of them, and check a box denoting the extent to which the statement is characteristic of them (i.e., "sort of true for me" or "really true for me"). The instrument is divided into five subscales tapping beliefs related to sport ability, physical conditioning, body appearance/attractiveness, muscular strength, and global physical self-worth. An example of each subscale may be found in Exhibit 10.3. Although only limited empirical data currently exist, the PSPP has been shown to be a valid and reliable measure across a variety of populations including middle-aged adults, American and British college students, and overweight adults (Fox & Corbin, 1989; Fox & Dirkin, 1992; Page, Ashford, Fox, & Biddle, 1993; Sonstroem, Speliotis, & Fava, 1992).

Also based on the Shavelson et al. (1976) approach (and sharing certain subscale similarities with the PSPP), the Physical Self-Description Questionnaire (PSDQ; Marsh, Richards, Johnson, Roche, & Tremayne, 1994) is a 70-item instrument divided into nine components of physical self-concept (general health, coordination, physical activity participation, body fat, sports competence, appearance/attractiveness, muscular strength, flexibility, and cardiovascular endurance), plus two subscales assessing global physical self-concept and global self-esteem. The PSDQ consists of single-statement items and a six-point Likert scale response format ranging from 1 ("false") to 6 ("true"). An example of each subscale may be found in Exhibit 10.4. Marsh and his colleagues have

Sample items from the physical self-perception profile. exhibit 10.3

Sports Competence	"Some people feel that they are not very good when it comes to playing sports BUT others feel that they are really good at just about every sport."
Physical Condition	"Some people do not usually have a high level of stamina and fitness BUT others always maintain a high level of stamina and fitness."
Body Attractiveness	"Some people are extremely confident about the appearance of their bodies BUT others are a little self-conscious about the appearance of their bodies."
Physical Strength	"Some people feel that they are physically stronger than most people of their sex BUT others feel that they lack physical strength compared to most others of their sex."
Physical Self-Worth	"Some people feel extremely satisfied with the kind of persons they are physically BUT others sometimes feel a little dissatisfied with their physical selves."

Source: Fox & Corbin (1989).

Sample items from the physical self-description questionnaire. exhibit 10.4

Health	"I hardly ever get sick or ill."
Coordination	"I can perform movements smoothly in most physical activities."
Physical Activity	"I often do exercise or activities that make me breathe hard."
Body Fat	"I have too much fat on my body."
Sports Competence	"Most sports are easy for me."
Global Physical	"I feel good about who I am physically."
Appearance	"I am good looking."
Strength	"I am good at lifting heavy objects."
Flexibility	"I think I would perform well on a test measuring flexibility."
Endurance	"I can be physically active for a long period of time without getting tired."
Esteem	"Overall, I have a lot to be proud of."

Source: Marsh et al. (1994).

documented considerable support for the validity of the instrument in Australian adolescents (Marsh, 1996, 1997; Marsh & Redmayne, 1994), and the PSDQ appears to provide a very comprehensive assessment of physical self-concept with the added feature of global measures of both physical self-concept and self-esteem. Although this breadth in content would appear to favor the PSDQ over the PSPP, researchers should also consider the significant difference in number of questionnaire items as well as the contrasting response formats when making assessment decisions. With its more complex response format, requiring a substantial amount of reading, the PSPP may not be as "user-friendly" as the PSDQ (even though the PSPP is notably shorter). Although these issues will be largely irrelevant for most research participants, certain populations (e.g., children) may find the instrument challenging.

Selective Research

A number of outstanding reviews of the self-concept/self-esteem literature exist, and the reader is referred to these publications for extensive discussions of research findings related to these constructs (see Doan & Scherman, 1987; Fox, 2000; Gruber, 1986; McAuley, 1994; Sonstroem, 1984, 1997). Of interest are the significant number of studies that have been conducted with special populations, including older adults with and without mental retardation (Dungan, Brown, & Ramsey, 1996; Mactavish & Searle, 1992; McAuley, Mihalko, & Bane, 1997), mentally and physically healthy youth and adolescents (see Calfas & Taylor, 1994, for a review), children with learning disabilities or emotional "disturbances" (MacMahon & Gross, 1987; Politino & Smith, 1989), children with spina bifida (Andrade, Kramer, Garber, & Longmuir, 1991), obese children (Gately, Cooke, Butterly, Knight, & Carroll, 2000), adults with chronic obstructive pulmonary disease (Weaver, Richmond, & Narsavage, 1997), adults with cancer (Baldwin & Courneya, 1997), injured athletes (see Smith, 1996, for a review), clinically depressed adults (Ossip-Klein et al., 1989), and alcoholics (see Donaghy & Mutrie, 1999, for a review). In one of the earliest studies of self-concept and exercise, Collingwood and Willett (1971) enrolled five obese, teenage males in a three-week physical activity program. Participants engaged in daily aquatic and gymnasium activities for one hour with results indicating significant improvements in body weight, cardiovascular fitness, attitude toward the body and self, and self-acceptance.

McAuley, Mihalko, and Bane (1997) examined the relationships among domain-specific and global levels of self-esteem over the course of a 20-week walking program. Employing a large sample of middle- to older-age, sedentary males and females, the authors found significant improvements in both physical and global self-esteem as well as in perceptions of physical condition. Although not significant, improvements in perceptions of body attractiveness were in the hypothesized direction in spite of the fact that participants viewed body attractiveness as significantly less important following completion of the program compared with pre-program measures. The authors also sought to investigate the hierarchical structure of self-esteem as detailed in both the Shavelson et al. (1976) and Sonstroem and Morgan (1989) models. The results supported such a framework, in that perceptions of enhanced physical condition and body attractiveness influenced global self-esteem via changes in physical self-esteem. Changes in physical self-efficacy and aerobic capacity (estimated $\dot{V}O_2max$) also contributed to changes in physical self-esteem. Similar findings have been reported by Brown, Morrow, and Livingston (1982), who found that, although changes in body composition and aerobic capacity variables were significantly associated with *physical* self-concept, they were not significantly related to *overall* self-concept.

In an effort to demonstrate the long-term effects of aerobic exercise on physical and global self-concept, DiLorenzo et al. (1999) randomly assigned a large sample of healthy, middle-aged males and females to either a control group or one of two 12-week stationary bicycle exercise interventions, each of which met four times per week. Global self-concept was assessed at baseline (pre-intervention), immediately post-intervention (end of week 12), and at three, six, and twelve months following completion of the 12-week intervention. Results indicated that exercisers experienced significantly larger increases in both physical and global self-concept from pre- to post-intervention as compared with control participants. Most important, these improvements were still in effect for exercisers one year following completion of the intervention. Unfortunately, the authors failed to obtain data related to the amount of exercise that participants were engaged in between the termination of the 12-week program and the follow-up test one year later.

Addressing the variable of age, Brown and Harrison (1986) formed an exercise group and a comparison control group and subdivided each into younger and older participant samples. Participants in the control group maintained their customary sedentary lifestyles while the exercise group engaged in a 12-week weight-training program. The findings suggest that age does not exert an effect on the exercise–self-concept relationship. Specifically, older and younger exercisers improved various measures of global and physical self-concept to the same degree while the control groups showed no change.

DOSE–RESPONSE RELATIONSHIPS IN EXERCISE AND SELF-CONCEPT/SELF-ESTEEM

The current knowledge base regarding the dose–response relationship as it applies to exercise and self-concept/self-esteem is inconclusive. In fact, few studies have manipulated elements of exercise dosage in order to determine the impact on these constructs. The scant literature that does exist is generally focused on variations in exercise intensity. For example, in a study of boys with learning disabilities, MacMahon and Gross (1987) demonstrated differences in overall self-concept change over the course of a 20-week exercise program based on variations in exercise intensity. Participants were randomly assigned to one of two physical activity interventions. The aerobic intervention consisted of activities such as aerobic dance, distance running, and variants of soccer, all of which raised participants' heart rates above 160 beats per minute for 25 consecutive minutes (five days per week). The comparison group engaged in less vigorous physical activities (e.g., relay races, dodge ball, and volleyball) not requiring a sustained and elevated heart rate (i.e., below 150 beats per minute). Confirmation of intensity was obtained via the use of portable heart rate monitors. Results indicated that, although the two groups showed relatively similar improvements in cardiovascular fitness, the aerobic group (higher intensity) increased self-concept scores significantly while the comparison group (lower intensity) showed no change. Thus, overall self-concept changed independent of alterations in fitness level.

In a study reviewed earlier, DiLorenzo et al. (1999) recruited a large sample of healthy male and female adults and randomly assigned them to one of two exercise groups or a nonexercise control group. The long-duration exercise group engaged in a 48-minute bout of cycle ergometry at a *fixed* intensity (70 to 85 percent of peak heart rate reserve) for 12 weeks (four times per week). The short-duration exercise group participated in a 24-minute bout of *interval* training on the stationary bicycle at the same frequency and intensity for 12 weeks. Unfortunately, because a significant group difference in fitness improvement over the course of the 12-week program was not demonstrated, the authors collapsed the two exercise groups into one for all subsequent analyses, including those concerning both physical and overall self-concept. Such a decision fails to recognize that differences in training duration (dose) may have a discernible effect on measures of self-concept (response) irrespective of changes in fitness level.

Brown et al. (1995) recruited a large sample of sedentary middle-aged men and women and randomly assigned them to one of five 16-week interventions. The interventions consisted of a control (no exercise) group, a low-intensity walking group (45 to 55 percent of heart rate reserve, 40 to 50 minutes per session, three times per week), a low-intensity walking plus relaxation group, a moderate-intensity walking group (65 to 75 percent of heart rate reserve, 30 to 40 minutes, three times per week), and a meditative exercise group (45 minutes, three times per week). Contrary to the findings of MacMahon and Gross (1987), the results revealed no difference in self-esteem change based on variations in exercise intensity.

In a study designed to examine the relationship between frequency of physical activity and self-concept/self-esteem, Dekel, Tenenbaum, and Kudar (1996) recruited a large sample of male and female adolescents and classified them as either nonactive, moderate exercisers (two to three times per week), or high-frequency exercisers (almost every day). In addition, participants were identified as possessing either "normal" posture or were diagnosed with adolescent idiopathic scoliosis (AIS). Results revealed a significant main effect for frequency of physical activity on measures of both physical self-concept and overall self-esteem.

MECHANISMS OF CHANGE

Whereas a number of topics throughout this textbook have benefited from research that has attempted to explain the process by which exercise leads to psychological change, this is not the case for self-concept/self-esteem. In fact, other than the mastery (self-efficacy) hypothesis, no mechanism has been discussed at length in the self-concept/self-esteem literature. Nonetheless, additional explanations do exist and are presented in this section.

Mastery/Self-Efficacy

Social cognitive (self-efficacy) theory is discussed in Chapter 3; we revisit aspects of the theory here in order to demonstrate the impact of behavioral mastery on self-concept/self-esteem. Clearly, such a hypothesis is tenable given the prominent role played by self-efficacy in Sonstroem and Morgan's (1989) model of exercise and self-esteem. Recall that physical measures occupy the base of the model and directly feed physical self-efficacy. The next level of the model's hierarchy shows physical self-efficacy exerting an influence on physical self-concept. Finally, physical self-concept influences global self-esteem both independently and via physical acceptance. Returning to the example provided earlier in the chapter, let's assume that our elderly exerciser has completed a 16-week cardiovascular and resistance training exercise program. Based on the degree to which he feels he has mastered the skills required to perform the activities successfully, our participant is likely to report improvements in physical self-efficacy. This sense of accomplishment may prove to be so rewarding as ultimately to affect global self-esteem in the manner proposed by the model.

Body Image/Body Esteem

As detailed in Chapter 13, body image refers to the mental picture we form of our bodies ("what I look like"). Body esteem, then, is the emotional consequence of body image ("how I feel about what I look like"). Thus, one's perception of his or her body (image) elicits either pleasing/satisfying or displeasing/dissatisfying feelings (esteem). The attentive reader will note that these constructs are essentially self-concept and self-esteem applied to the body. It is not surprising, therefore, that body image/esteem would be implicated in a mechanism for improving overall self-concept/self-esteem.

How might this process take place? One relatively simple explanation is diagrammed in Exhibit 10.5. According to the model, prolonged participation in an exercise regimen leads to perceived improvements in body composition, muscular tone, and so forth. (independent of whether or not objective change has taken place). Positive perceptions of bodily change, in turn, serve to enhance one's body image. Finally, this improvement in body image would be expected to enhance body esteem, which, if deemed important by the individual influences global self-esteem. The proposed framework is essentially a duplicate of both the Shavelson et al. (1976) and Sonstroem and Morgan (1989) models. In the Shavelson et al. model, the physical appearance subarea of self-concept could be readily defined as body image/esteem. Similarly, the physical acceptance component of Sonstroem and Morgan's model could also be defined as body image/esteem. In all cases, the individual must consider body image/esteem important in order for it to play an influential role in global self-esteem change.

Self-Schemata

A relatively new explanation of the exercise and self-concept/self-esteem relationship involves the development of domain-specific

exhibit 10.5

Diagram of possible linkage between body image and self-esteem following chronic exercise.

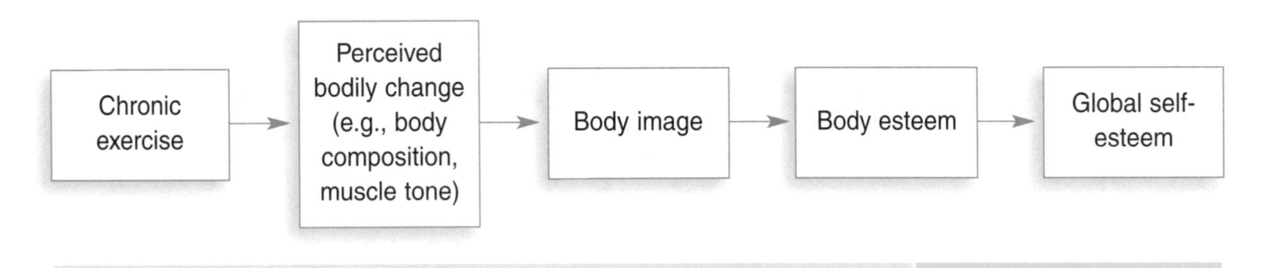

(e.g., exercise) identities known as **self-schemata.** Kendzierski (1994) has embedded this concept within the domain of exercise and determined that individuals fall into one of three categories. The first is *exerciser schematics* who describe themselves as "exercisers" and who rate this self-identification as being critical to their self-image. The second category consists of *nonexerciser schematics* who describe themselves as "nonexercisers" and who also consider the (deficient) exercise descriptor to be a significant influence on their self-image. Finally, *aschematics* describe themselves as nonexercisers but do not consider this perception to be important to their self-image.

■ self-schemata

Exhibit 10.6 suggests how exercise might affect self-concept/self-esteem via changes in exercise schema. As in the previous discussion of body image/esteem, the process is initiated by a regimen of chronic exercise. However, in this theory, we are not concerned with the potential subjective and objective changes that may occur. Instead, the important element here is that the individual merely begins to identify himself as an exerciser. Assuming that the characteristics of an exerciser are salient to the individual, the self-description will serve to enhance physical self-concept, which will, in turn, affect global self-esteem. The danger, of course, is that an individual may assign considerable importance to being an exerciser but remain unsuccessful in maintaining an exercise regimen. In this case, the impact on physical self-concept and global self-esteem would likely be negative. Clearly, other schemas exist, such as those focused on a particular religious sect, a defined role within a family (e.g., parent), or a particular occupation, company, team, or school.

exhibit 10.6 ***Diagram of possible linkage between exercise schema and self-concept/self-esteem following chronic exercise.***

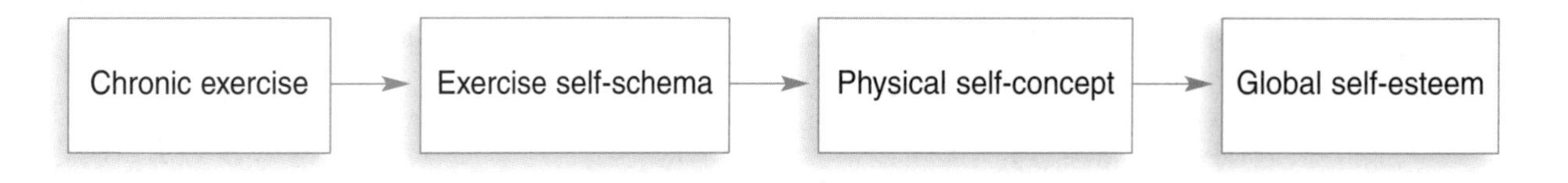

Self-Determination

Although the concept of self-determination has been a mainstay in the contemporary cognitive motivation literature, its relation to self-concept and self-esteem has not been clearly delineated. As discussed in Chapter 3, self-determination refers to an individual's drive to perform autonomously and successfully behaviors important to him or her. Self-determination has vast potential to influence self-esteem, in that perceptions of personal control have been postulated to be associated with positive self-perception while perceived lack of personal control has been hypothesized to be associated with negative self-perception (DeCharms, 1968). In an achievement setting such as exercise, the accomplishment of completing a marathon would likely lead to enhanced judgments of self-determination, because such a success requires considerable internal capabilities including self-motivation, discipline, and effort. The consequence of assuming responsibility for this successful behavior should be enhanced perceptions of one's physical self. Once again, if the outcome is deemed to be salient to the individual, physical self-concept should positively impact global self-esteem. Exhibit 10.7 details the possible linkage between self-determination and self-concept/self-esteem in the exercise domain.

exhibit 10.7 ***Diagram of possible linkage between self-determination and self-concept/self-esteem following exercise outcome.***

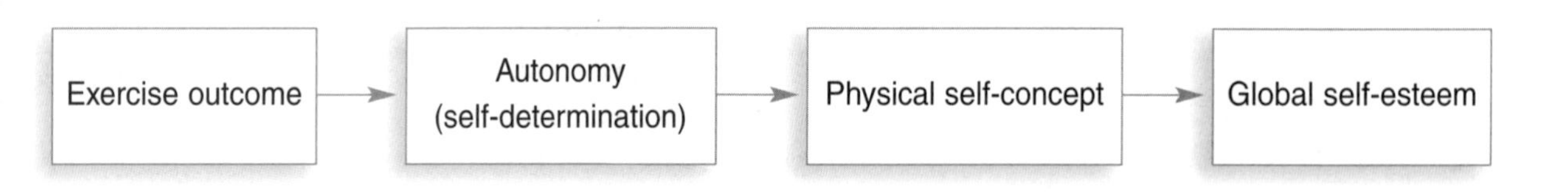

Practical Recommendations

Although there appears to be little doubt that physical activity is capable of producing substantial improvements in self-concept/self-esteem, we currently know very little about the optimal mode, intensity, or duration of activity required to do so. Nonetheless, certain steps may be taken to ensure that the activity engaged in will lead to improved self-concept/self-esteem. The first step is to determine why the individual is currently considering or participating in an exercise regimen. Generally, one's goals and objectives will provide valuable insight into the factors that are most likely to affect self-concept/self-esteem. For example, if you encounter a man who would like to improve his appearance by "getting bigger," you might prescribe a resistance-training regimen targeting increased muscular hypertrophy. Alternatively, a woman who desires to enhance her social life should be encouraged to exercise with a buddy, with a small group, or in a large class.

The second step is to conduct baseline health and fitness assessments. These could take many forms, ranging from the standard flexibility, body composition, strength, and cardiovascular endurance measures, to assessments of eating habits or ratings of satisfaction with one's current social relationships. Any additional factors that might be known to influence self-concept/self-esteem, and that may be influenced by physical activity participation, should also be included. Once the baseline measures have been obtained, repeating the assessments every eight weeks or so will provide both objective and subjective feedback regarding the progress being made in the exercise program. The exerciser can then use this information to modify self-concept/self-esteem judgments.

The third step is to ensure that the exerciser feels a sense of accomplishment and personal control from engaging in the exercise routine. Allowing the client some input into decisions regarding the program and arranging the activities in such a way as to ensure completion and a sense of success should prove helpful. Highlighting the role of personal control and accomplishment through positive verbal feedback to the client (and avoiding giving negative verbal feedback) is essential. At the same time, the exercise leader should strive to reward positive self-statements and extinguish negative self-statements made by the exerciser. A good strategy would be to highlight effort and personal improvement, as opposed to failure to obtain a goal. The key is to help the client focus on *individual* improvement rather than comparing oneself to others.

Conclusion

For many of us, the overall image that we form of ourselves (self-concept) is influenced to a large degree by the image that we form of our physical selves. This physical self-concept comprises not only our physical appearance but also the perception of our physical abilities (e.g., to exercise, play sport, perform housework or yard work). Self-esteem, synonymous with self-worth, indicates how one feels about her self-concept. These distinctions are highlighted in the seminal model of self-concept proposed by Shavelson et al. (1976) and in the context-specific model of exercise and self-esteem developed by Sonstroem and Morgan (1989). Both models are constructed in a hierarchical fashion, in which the more situation-specific and unstable evaluations (e.g., running performance) form the foundation upon which the pinnacle—a global, relatively stable judgment of self-concept or self-esteem—is built.

Recently, researchers have sought to complement the unidimensional (global) approach to measurement by positing a multidimensional philosophy whereby the myriad of domain-specific self-concepts (i.e., academic, social, emotional, physical) can be assessed individually. This chapter reviewed two measures (PSPP, PSDQ) that show promise for assessing multiple aspects of the physical self. The utility of these measures cannot be overstated, given that these subjective judgments, as opposed to objective measurements of fitness, are primarily responsible for feelings of self-esteem.

At this point, it appears that we cannot make any conclusive statements regarding dose–response relationships between exercise and self-concept/self-esteem. Indeed, little or no research exists concerning the impact of mode, frequency, or duration on these constructs, and the scant literature addressing the intensity variable has yielded inconclusive results. Clearly, exercise psychology researchers must address dose–response issues in future investigations and, furthermore, must continue to explore potential mechanisms of exercise-induced changes in self-concept/self-esteem.

What Do You Know?

1. What is the difference between self-concept and self-esteem?
2. What two factors determine physical self-concept in the Shavelson et al. model?

3. Give examples of physical measures in the Sonstroem and Morgan model.
4. What two factors primarily influence global self-esteem in the Sonstroem and Morgan model?
5. Which is most relevant to self-esteem, objective or subjective changes in fitness?
6. Why have more recent self-concept/self-esteem measures (e.g., PSPP, PSDQ) adopted a multidimensional approach rather than the traditional unidimensional approach?
7. How are the PSPP and PSDQ different? In what ways are they the same?
8. Describe the process by which mastery (self-efficacy) may influence self-concept/self-esteem in the exercise setting.
9. Describe the process by which body image/body esteem may influence self-concept/self-esteem in the exercise setting.
10. Describe the process by which self-schemata may influence self-concept/self-esteem in the exercise setting.
11. Describe the process by which self-determination may influence self-concept/self-esteem in the exercise setting.

Learning Activities

1. Obtain a copy of either the PSPP or the PSDQ (either from the appropriate reference in this chapter or from your instructor) and ask each member of the class to complete it. After properly scoring the questionnaire, ask your instructor to correlate each student's questionnaire score and activity score (from the activity in Chapter 2) and explain the results.

2. Combine the constructs from one or more of the models proposed in Exhibits 10.5, 10.6, or 10.7 with those included in the Sonstroem and Morgan (1989) model to create your own model. Feel free to be creative and to add, delete, or modify constructs according to your own theory.

3. Review the scenario at the beginning of the chapter featuring Chris. Imagine that he has asked you to design an exercise program for him. Based on the information in this chapter and in Chapter 5, what steps should you take in designing the program? Explain the rationale for your program (i.e., how will it positively affect self-concept/self-esteem?).

References

Andrade, C. K., Kramer, J., Garber, M., & Longmuir, P. (1991). Changes in self-concept, cardiovascular endurance and muscular strength of children with spina bifida aged 8 to 13 years in response to a 10-week physical-activity programme: A pilot study. *Child: Care, Health and Development, 17,* 183–196.

Baldwin, M. K., & Courneya, K. S. (1997). Exercise and self-esteem in breast cancer survivors: An application of the exercise and self-esteem model. *Journal of Sport and Exercise Psychology, 19,* 347–358.

Brown, D. R., Wang, Y., Ward, A., Ebbeling, C. B., Fortlage, L., Puleo, E., Benson, H., & Rippe, J. M. (1995). Chronic psychological effects of exercise and exercise plus cognitive strategies. *Medicine and Science in Sports and Exercise, 27,* 765–775.

Brown, E. Y., Morrow, J. R., & Livingston, S. M. (1982). Self-concept changes in women as a result of training. *Journal of Sport Psychology, 4,* 354–363.

Brown, R. D., & Harrison, J. M. (1986). The effects of a strength training program on the strength and self-concept of two female age groups. *Research Quarterly for Exercise and Sport, 4,* 315–320.

Calfas, K. J., & Taylor, W. C. (1994). Effects of physical activity on psychological variables in adolescents. *Pediatric Exercise Science, 6,* 406–423.

Collingwood, T. R., & Willett, L. (1971). The effects of physical training upon self-concept and body attitude. *Journal of Clinical Psychology, 27,* 411–412.

DeCharms, R. (1968). *Personal causation.* New York: Academic Press.

Dekel, Y., Tenenbaum, G., & Kudar, K. (1996). An exploratory study on the relationship between postural deformities and body-image and self-esteem in adolescents: The mediating role of physical activity. *International Journal of Sport Psychology, 27,* 183–196.

DiLorenzo, T. M., Bargman, E. P., Stucky-Ropp, R., Brassington, G. S., Frensch, P. A., & LaFontaine, T. (1999). Long-term effects of aerobic exercise on psychological outcomes. *Preventive Medicine, 28,* 75–85.

Doan, R. E., & Scherman, A. (1987). The therapeutic effect of physical fitness on measures of personality: A literature review. *Journal of Counseling and Development, 66,* 28–36.

Donaghy, M. E., & Mutrie, N. (1999). Is exercise beneficial in the treatment and rehabilitation of the problem drinker? A critical review. *Physical Therapy Reviews, 4,* 153–166.

Dungan, J. M., Brown, A. V., & Ramsey, M. A. (1996). Health maintenance for the independent frail older adult: Can it improve physical and mental well-being? *Journal of Advanced Nursing, 23,* 1185–1193.

Folkins, C. H., & Sime, W. E. (1981). Physical fitness training and mental health. *American Psychologist, 36,* 373–389.

Fox, K. R. (2000). Self-esteem, self-perceptions, and exercise. *International Journal of Sport Psychology, 31,* 228–240.

Fox, K. R., & Corbin, C. B. (1989). The Physical Self-Perception Profile: Development and preliminary validation. *Journal of Sport and Exercise Psychology, 11,* 408–430.

Fox, K. R., & Dirkin, G. R. (1992). Psychosocial predictors and outcomes of exercise in patients attending multidisciplinary obesity treatment. *International Journal of Obesity, 16,* 84.

Gately, P. J., Cooke, C. B., Butterly, R. J., Knight, C., & Carroll, S. (2000). The acute effects of an 8-week diet, exercise, and educational camp program on obese children. *Pediatric Exercise Science, 12,* 413–423.

Gruber, J. J. (1986). Physical activity and self-esteem development in children: A meta-analysis. *American Academy of Physical Education Papers, 19,* 30–48.

Harter, S. (1985). *Manual for the self-perception profile for children.* University of Denver, Colorado.

Hatfield, B. D., Vaccaro, P., & Benedict, G. J. (1985). Self-concept responses of children to participation in an eight-week precision jump-rope program. *Perceptual and Motor Skills, 61,* 1275–1279.

Hughes, J. R. (1984). Psychological effects of habitual aerobic exercise: A critical review. *Preventive Medicine, 13,* 66–78.

Kendzierski, D. (1994). Schema theory: An information processing focus. In R. K. Dishman (Ed.), *Advances in exercise adherence* (pp. 137–159). Champaign, IL: Human Kinetics.

MacMahon, J. R., & Gross, R. T. (1987). Physical and psychological effects of aerobic exercise in boys with learning disabilities. *Developmental and Behavioral Pediatrics, 8,* 274–277.

Mactavish, J. B., & Searle, M. S. (1992). Older individuals with mental retardation and the effect of a physical activity intervention on selected social psychological variables. *Therapeutic Recreation Journal, 1,* 38–47.

Marsh, H. W. (1996). Physical Self-Description Questionnaire: Stability and discriminant validity. *Research Quarterly for Exercise and Sport, 67,* 249–264.

Marsh, H. W. (1997). The measurement of physical self-concept: A construct validation approach. In K. R. Fox (Ed.), *The physical self: From motivation to well-being* (pp. 27–58). Champaign, IL: Human Kinetics.

Marsh, H. W., & Redmayne, R. S. (1994). A multidimensional physical self-concept and its relations to multiple components of physical fitness. *Journal of Sport and Exercise Psychology, 16,* 43–55.

Marsh, H. W., Richards, G. E., Johnson, S., Roche, L., & Tremayne, P. (1994). Physical Self-Description Questionnaire: Psychometric properties and a multitrait-multimethod analysis of relations to existing instruments. *Journal of Sport and Exercise Psychology, 16,* 270–305.

McAuley, E. (1994). Physical activity and psychosocial outcomes. In C. Bouchard, R. J. Shephard, & T. Stephens (Eds.), *Physical activity, fitness, and health* (pp. 551–568). Champaign, IL: Human Kinetics.

McAuley, E., Mihalko, S. L., & Bane, S. M. (1997). Exercise and self-esteem in middle-aged adults: Multidimensional relationships and physical fitness and self-efficacy influences. *Journal of Behavioral Medicine, 20,* 67–83.

Ossip-Klein, D. J., Doyne, E. J., Bowman, E. D., Osborn, K. M., McDougall-Wilson, I. B., & Neimeyer, R. A. (1989). Effects of running or weight lifting on self-concept in clinically depressed women. *Journal of Consulting and Clinical Psychology, 57,* 158–161.

Page, A., Ashford, B., Fox, K. R., & Biddle, S. J. H. (1993). Evidence of cross-cultural validity of the Physical Self-Perception Profile. *Personality and Individual Differences, 14,* 585–590.

Politino, V., & Smith, S. L. (1989). Attitude toward physical activity and self-concept of emotionally disturbed and normal children. *Adapted Physical Activity Quarterly, 6,* 371–378.

Shavelson, R. J., Hubner, J. J., & Stanton, G. C. (1976). Validation of construct interpretations. *Review of Educational Research, 46,* 407–441.

Sheldon, K. M., Elliot, A. J., Kim, Y., & Kasser, T. (2001). What's satisfying about satisfying events? Comparing ten candidate psychological needs. *Journal of Personality and Social Psychology, 80,* 325–339.

Smith, A. (1996). Psychological impact of injuries in athletes. *Sports Medicine, 22,* 391–405.

Sonstroem, R. J. (1984). Exercise and esteem. *Exercise and Sport Science Reviews, 12,* 123–153.

Sonstroem, R. J. (1997). Physical activity and self-esteem. In W. P. Morgan (Ed.), *Physical activity and mental health* (pp. 128–143). Washington, DC: Taylor & Francis.

Sonstroem, R. J., & Morgan, W. P. (1989). Exercise and esteem: Rationale and model. *Medicine and Science in Sports and Exercise, 21,* 329–337.

Sonstroem, R. J., Speliotis, E. D., & Fava, J. L. (1992). Perceived physical competence in adults: An examination of the Physical Self-Perception Profile. *Journal of Sport and Exercise Psychology, 14,* 207–221.

Weaver, T. E., Richmond, T. S., & Narsavage, G. L. (1997). An explanatory model of functional status in chronic obstructive pulmonary disease. *Nursing Research, 46,* 26–31.

Chapter 11

Health-Related Quality of Life

KEY TERMS

- activities of daily living (ADLs)
- control beliefs
- disease specific measures
- generic measures
- health-related quality of life (HRQL)
- individual difference factors
- objective measures
- optimism
- pessimism
- quality-adjusted life years (QALY)
- quality of life (QL)
- subjective measures

Harry is 83 years old and lives by himself in a small house in the city. He cooks and cleans for himself and walks to the corner shops a couple of times each week to buy groceries and to take care of other errands. He meets friends at a community center every Tuesday and Thursday to play cards and to participate in an exercise class for seniors. Although Harry is fairly active in his daily life, health problems prevent him from walking long distances and performing strenuous activities such as gardening. He has chronic obstructive pulmonary disease (COPD), which leaves him breathless after walking more than a block. Arthritis in his hips and shoulders makes it painful for him to do heavy lifting and bending. Fortunately, a neighbor helps out by mowing Harry's lawn in the summers and shoveling snow from his sidewalk in the winters.

Family members have offered to move Harry to a retirement facility where staff would take care of all his chores—shopping, cleaning, cooking, and so on. Harry insists, however, that despite his aches and pains, he actually feels healthiest and happiest when he is moving around the community and taking care of himself. He fears that if he no longer *had* to be physically active in his daily life, his physical functioning might decline with lack of use and he would no longer be able to stay independent and do the things that he enjoys. Harry realizes that being physically active in his daily life—even at a relatively low level—helps preserve his level of physical function, his independence, and his ability to participate in community life, and contributes to his overall health and happiness. In other words, physical activity contributes to his overall quality of life and more specifically to his health-related quality of life.

Quality of Life

quality of life (QL)

Quality of life (QL) is used to describe both subjective and objective evaluations of the "goodness" of one's life overall, and the goodness of all of the various domains that make up one's life. Subjective evaluations reflect people's own perceptions of the "goodness" or quality of their lives. Objective evaluations are typically measures of various aspects of one's life that can be made by someone other than the individual, such as a health-care worker, family member, or researcher.

Exhibit 11.1 presents the various dimensions that the World Health Organization (1993) has identified and defined as components of quality of life, along with the factors that comprise each of those dimensions.

Defining Health-Related Quality of Life (HRQL)

health-related quality of life (HRQL)

Health-related quality of life (HRQL) is a subcomponent of QL that reflects the "goodness" of those dimensions of life that can be affected by health and by health interventions, such as one's physical function, emotional well-being, and ability to fulfill family and other social roles.

Researchers and clinicians often disagree on the specific dimensions that are part of HRQL, but there is a general consensus regarding the broad, core dimensions that should be considered when measuring HRQL in most populations. These dimensions include the following:

- Physical functioning, including aerobic fitness, strength, endurance, balance, flexibility, and the ability to perform activities of daily living (ADLs) such as walking, climbing stairs, carrying heavy objects, and dressing and bathing oneself. This dimension also includes physical self-concept.
- Emotional functioning and well-being, including depression, anxiety, anger/hostility, and feelings of happiness, hope, and tranquility.
- Social functioning and ability to fulfill social roles, including involvement with community and social groups and the ability to fulfill the role of spouse, parent, employee, caregiver, and so forth.
- Cognitive functioning, including memory, attention, concentration, comprehension, problem solving, and decision making.

The World Health Organization's dimensions of quality of life. **exhibit 11.1**

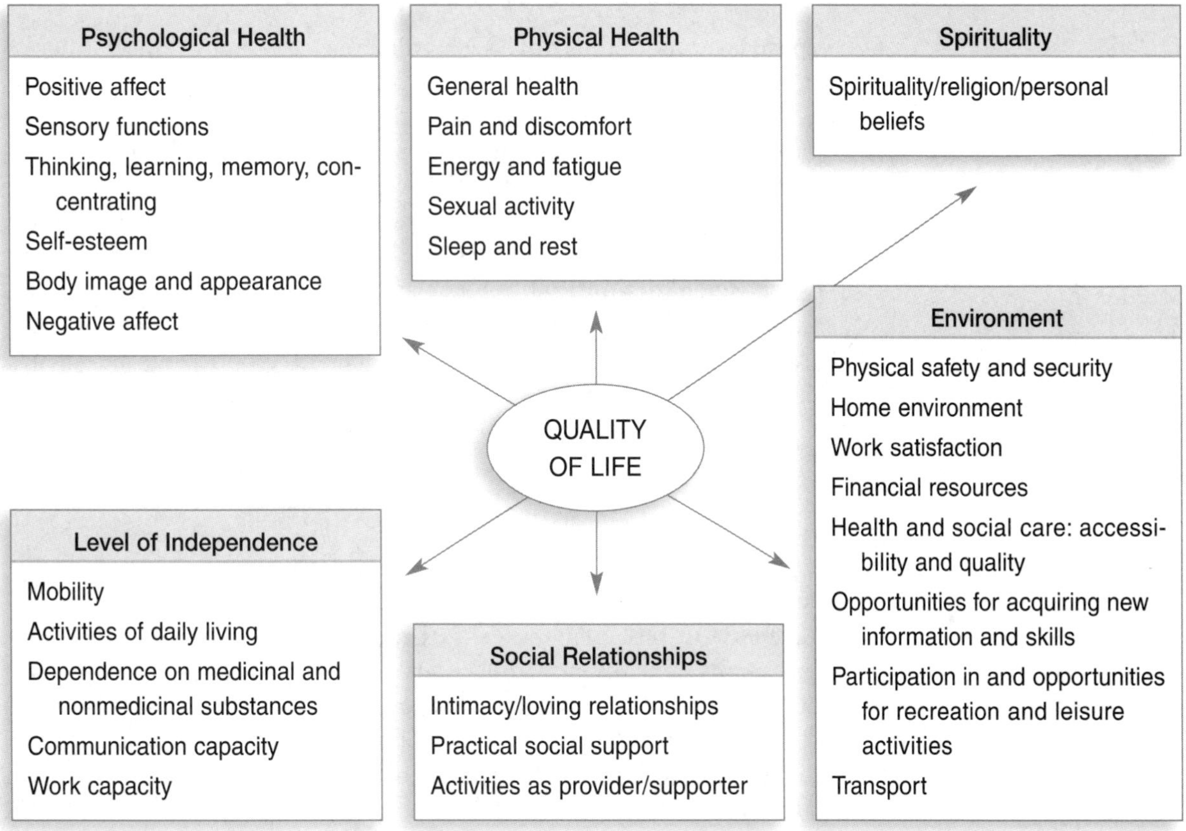

QUALITY OF LIFE

Psychological Health
- Positive affect
- Sensory functions
- Thinking, learning, memory, concentrating
- Self-esteem
- Body image and appearance
- Negative affect

Physical Health
- General health
- Pain and discomfort
- Energy and fatigue
- Sexual activity
- Sleep and rest

Spirituality
- Spirituality/religion/personal beliefs

Level of Independence
- Mobility
- Activities of daily living
- Dependence on medicinal and nonmedicinal substances
- Communication capacity
- Work capacity

Social Relationships
- Intimacy/loving relationships
- Practical social support
- Activities as provider/supporter

Environment
- Physical safety and security
- Home environment
- Work satisfaction
- Financial resources
- Health and social care: accessibility and quality
- Opportunities for acquiring new information and skills
- Participation in and opportunities for recreation and leisure activities
- Transport

- Health status, including physical health, symptoms, and states (e.g., energy, fatigue, pain, sleep).

Some researchers include other core dimensions in their definitions of HRQL, such as sexual functioning and intimacy, and work productivity. Yet unlike the dimensions listed previously, these additional dimensions may not be relevant to many populations, so we have not included them in our list of broad core dimensions. For instance, sexual functioning and intimacy would not be a relevant construct in the assessment of children. Similarly, work productivity would not be relevant to the HRQL of children, retired people, or individuals whose health status prevents them from working.

Why Is HRQL Important to Exercise Psychologists?

The past several decades have seen an increased recognition that health should not be defined simply as the absence of disability and disease (i.e., the biomedical definition of health). Rather, consistent with a biopsychosocial definition, health is now conceptualized as a positive state of physical, mental, and social well-being (World Health Organization, 1947). Previously, most interests were focused on developing interventions to improve physical health only. With acceptance of the biopsychosocial definition has come greater interest among researchers (including exercise psychologists and other exercise scientists), clinicians (physicians, physiotherapists), and patients in identifying therapeutic techniques that will enhance *all three* components of health. As a result of this shift in focus, exercise psychologists are interested in HRQL for at least three reasons:

1. HRQL IS AN IMPORTANT INDEX OF TREATMENT EFFECTIVENESS

Because HRQL reflects patients' satisfaction with all three health components—physical, mental, and social—it has become an important benchmark for determining the effectiveness of exercise interventions as well as virtually every other type of clinical intervention (e.g., pharmacological, surgical). Traditionally, clinical researchers (researchers who study the effects of clinical interventions) tended to be interested only in the effects of treatment on objective medical outcomes associated with morbidity (i.e., illness, injury) and mortality (i.e., death). Yet it is now apparent that in order to get a complete understanding of the broad range of psychological and social effects of exercise and other treatments on patients, researchers need to augment traditional medical outcome measures with measures of HRQL. Thus, most exercise intervention studies now include measures of HRQL as well as traditional measures of disability and disease. In fact, the U.S. National Institutes of Health (NIH) now mandate the inclusion of measures of HRQL in most clinical studies of therapeutic interventions. It is no longer sufficient to demonstrate that an intervention has positive physical benefits for a patient. Researchers must also demonstrate that the intervention does not have a negative effect on HRQL, as the side-effects of some treatments may be worse than the symptoms of the disease being treated.

2. IMPROVEMENTS IN HRQL ARE RECOGNIZED AS AN IMPORTANT BENEFIT OF EXERCISE

In recent years, there has been a dramatic increase in the number of studies examining exercise for the treatment of diseases such as osteoarthritis, cancer, diabetes, and heart disease, and for the prevention of physical and cognitive declines associated with aging. These studies have generated considerable knowledge regarding the therapeutic benefits of exercise. Consequently, physical activity is being used increasingly by clinicians and health promoters as a therapeutic modality for treating chronic disease and disability and for preventing age-related declines. (See Exhibit 11.2.)

For example, the Canadian Heart and Stroke Foundation recognizes exercise as an essential component of cardiac rehabilitation programs

Seniors, exercise, and quality of life. **exhibit 11.2**

Exercise is being used increasingly as a therapeutic modality to help older adults maintain their quality of life. Consequently, more and more exercise programs are being developed for seniors. These individuals belong to an exercise facility known as "The Club," which is housed in the Shalom Village long-term care facility for older adults in Ontario, Canada. The Club features group exercise classes as well as specialized weight-training equipment for older adults (e.g., weight machines that can be adjusted in one-pound increments). Anybody can join The Club. The only restriction is that you must be 75 years of age or older!

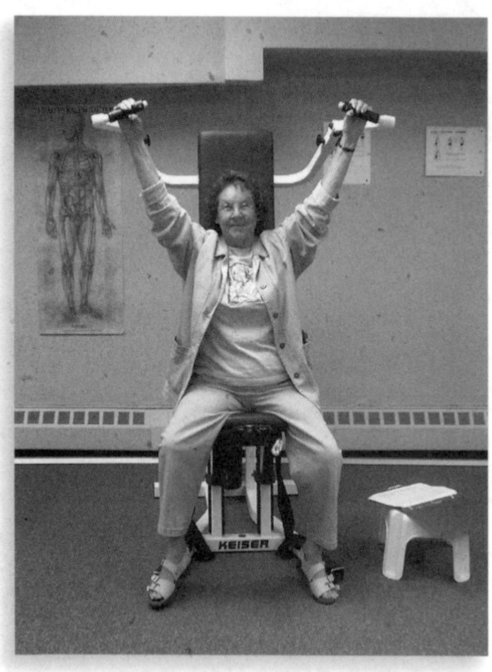

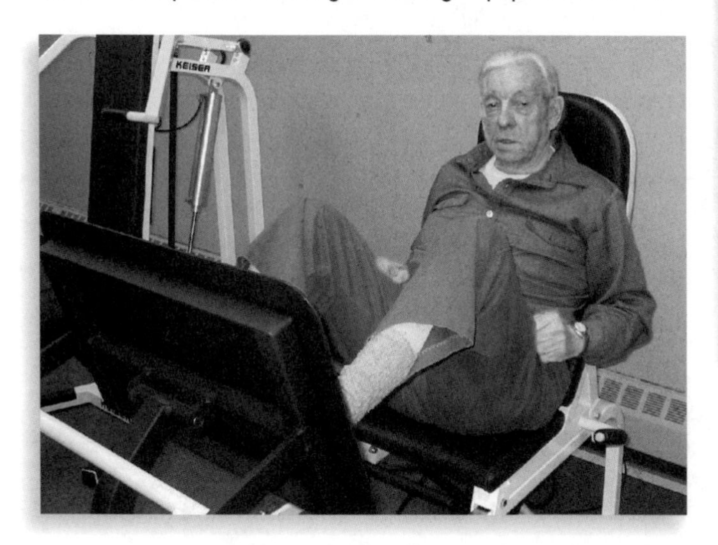

for individuals who have experienced an infarction or other cardiac event. The American Arthritis Foundation recommends exercise as a strategy for managing arthritis symptoms (e.g., pain and stiffness) and preventing further joint damage (Arthritis Foundation, 1999). The American College of Sports Medicine (1998) advocates exercise participation among older adults (including the frail elderly) and provides guidelines for prescribing exercise to this population.

Interestingly, clinicians and health promoters are not recommending exercise solely for its physical benefits; they are also endorsing the use of exercise to enhance HRQL. For example, in addition to highlighting the physical benefits of exercise to people who have had a stroke or heart attack, the Heart and Stroke Foundation also recommends exercise as a means to help these patients feel better about themselves, their physical abilities, and their lives. Specifically, the Heart and Stroke Foundation of Canada states that:

> Regular aerobic physical activity is a great asset to keeping your heart healthy and leading a healthy lifestyle. It relieves stress, speeds up the healing process, and promotes overall health and well-being.

This recommendation reflects an increasing trend toward the use of physical activity by health practitioners and promoters to improve HRQL among people with disease and disability—populations that tend to report poorer HRQL than people who are healthy (Ware, Gandek, & IQOLA, 1994; Ware et al., 1995).

3. KNOWLEDGE OF A PATIENT'S HRQL IS USEFUL FOR PRESCRIBING EXERCISE

An increased interest in HRQL among researchers and clinicians reflects a growing appreciation of the patient's thoughts and feelings with regard to prescribed treatments. How patients think and feel about the treatment (e.g., do they enjoy exercising? After exercising, do they feel better or are they completely fatigued and unable to perform activities of daily living?) is just as important as the medical outcomes derived from treatment. In fact, patients often consider the psychological and social consequences of a treatment to be *more* important than the medical consequences. By asking patients about the effects of exercise on their HRQL, we can gain an understanding of the effects of the intervention on the whole person. Such a holistic understanding allows us to make better decisions about exercise prescription. It's not enough to ask whether exercise will add years to a person's life. We must also ask whether exercise will add life to a person's years.

Measurement

As mentioned above, exercise psychologists use HRQL to assess the effectiveness of exercise interventions. But in order to use HRQL for these purposes, we must be able to measure it. There are two general approaches to measuring HRQL—the objective approach and the subjective approach.

OBJECTIVE APPROACHES TO MEASURING HRQL

In general, **objective measures** of HRQL are measures that (a) can be made by someone other than the patient, and (b) are quantitative (i.e., numeric) in nature. Objective measures can be used to assess individual HRQL components or overall HRQL. Examples of objective measures of the physical function component are the number of pounds a person can bench press and the distance he can walk in six minutes. Examples of objective measures of the health status component are the number of days a patient was confined to a hospital bed over the past month and the number of pain relief capsules the patient took over the course of a week.

■ objective measures

In addition to objective measures of individual HRQL components, there are also objective measures of overall HRQL. An example of an objective measure of one's overall HRQL is to estimate a person's life expectancy in **quality-adjusted life years** (QALY; Kaplan & Bush, 1982). The QALY approach involves calculating a numerical value that indicates the quality of one's remaining years of life. The logic behind this approach is that people with poorer health might have the same life *expectancy* as healthier individuals, but the *quality* of their remaining years may not be as good as that of a healthier person. QALY are calculated by multiplying life expectancy by the value assigned to that person's level of health (see box on the following page). QALY values can then be used to compare the HRQL of healthy people with that of individuals who have a particular disease or disability, or to compare the HRQL between groups of people with different types of disease or disability. The QALY approach can also be used to measure the effectiveness of health interventions such as exercise. For instance, among people who have incurred a spinal cord injury and who have paraplegia or quadriplegia, it has been estimated that an exercise training program could increase their QALYs by 10 percent (Noveau & Shephard, 1995). Likewise, it has been demonstrated that men who exercise consistently from the age of 35 to 65 will live more QALYs over that 30-year period than will men who are sedentary from age 35 to 65 (Hatziandreu, Koplan, Weinstein, Caspersen, & Warner, 1988).

■ quality-adjusted life years

The QALY Approach

DESCRIPTION OF HEALTH STATE	VALUATION
No problems	1.000
No problems walking about; no problems with self-care; some problems with performing usual activities; some pain or discomfort; not anxious or depressed	0.760
Some problems walking about; some problems washing or dressing self; some problems with performing usual activities; moderate pain or discomfort; moderately anxious or depressed	0.516
No problems walking about; some problems washing or dressing self; unable to perform usual activities; some pain or discomfort; not anxious or depressed	0.329
Some problems walking about; no problems with self-care; no problems with performing usual activities; moderate pain or discomfort; extremely anxious or depressed	0.222
Some problems walking about; unable to wash or dress self; unable to perform usual activities; moderate pain or discomfort; moderately anxious or depressed	0.079
Confined to bed; unable to wash or dress self; unable to perform usual activities; extreme pain or discomfort; moderately anxious or depressed	-0.429

Source: From Philips, C. & Thompson, G. (2001). *What Is a QALY?* Kent, UK: Hayward Medical Communications. Reprinted with permission.

To illustrate the concept of QALY, consider the following example. The average life expectancy for the American population is 77 years (U. S. Department of Health and Human Services, 2001). Consider two 50-year-old men living in the United States, Raj and Luis. Raj is in perfect health, but Luis has health problems that have left him with mild physical disability, some chronic pain, and feelings of depression and anxiety. Although both men have the same life expectancy—they are both expected to live 27 more years—the QALY approach suggests that given differences in their health status, the *quality* of their remaining years will be very different. Specifically, using the valuations in the table above, Raj can expect to live 27 quality-adjusted life years (27 expected years multiplied by the life quality value of 1.0). In contrast, after adjusting for the quality of his life, Luis has only 13.93 QALYs (27 expected years multiplied by the life quality value of 0.516).

The QALY approach is considered objective because it assumes all people who have similar health problems have the same "goodness" of life, regardless of how these people *feel* about their health and the impact of their health on their lives. For example, the QALY approach would consider all people who have the same symptoms as Harry (in the example at the start of this chapter) to have the same HRQL. It also assumes that better health and reduced symptomatology will automatically lead to better HRQL. This assumption is common to all objective measures of HRQL—they assume that the better the characteristics of a particular HRQL domain (e.g., the more weight a person can lift, the less pain a person experiences, the better a person's cholesterol levels), the better one's HRQL. But does improving the amount of cholesterol in one's blood, for example, necessarily mean that a person's goodness of life will improve? Of course not. And do all people with arthritis and lung disease experience the same goodness of life as Harry, who has these same conditions? Again, the answer is no. As these questions illustrate, HRQL is not simply a reflection of the actual or objective characteristics of a person's health. Rather, HRQL reflects how people think and feel about their health and the impact of their health on their lives. In other words, an individual's *subjective* perceptions of health also influence one's HRQL. A subjective approach to measuring HRQL takes these perceptions into account.

SUBJECTIVE APPROACHES TO MEASURING HRQL

■ subjective measures

Subjective measures of HRQL focus on assessing the individual's *perceptions* of the quality or goodness of the various domains that constitute HRQL. This is usually done through the administration of a questionnaire that asks patients either to rate their *level* of functioning in one or more HRQL domains, or to rate their *satisfaction* with their functioning in one or more HRQL domains. An example of a question that could be used to assess level of emotional functioning, for instance, is, "Over the past week, how happy have you felt?" An example of a question that could be used to assess satisfaction with emotional functioning is, "Over the past week, how satisfied have you been with the amount of happiness you have felt?"

Given that researchers cannot agree on how to define HRQL, you probably won't be surprised to learn that researchers also cannot agree on the best subjective measure of HRQL. Indeed, one research report noted that more than 150 different questionnaires had been used to measure HRQL in just 75 different medical studies (Gill & Feinstein, 1994)! Some of these questionnaires are designed to measure perceptions of *individual* HRQL domains, and some are designed to measure perceptions of one's *overall* HRQL. Although it is beyond the scope of this chapter to discuss HRQL measures in depth, in the following paragraphs we provide some information on two frequently used HRQL questionnaires. The first, the SF-36, is an example of a questionnaire used to assess perceived *level* of functioning across various individual HRQL domains. The second questionnaire, the PQOL, is an example of a questionnaire used to assess *satisfaction* with functioning and is a measure of one's overall HRQL.

Measuring Perceived Level of Functioning

In studies of exercise as well as virtually every other type of intervention, the most widely used measure of HRQL is the 36-item Short-Form Health Survey (Ware & Sherbourne, 1992). This questionnaire—also known as the "SF-36"—assesses patients' perceptions of their level of functioning with regard to the following dimensions of HRQL: general health, physical functioning, social functioning, mental health, bodily pain, and vitality. The SF-36 is considered a **generic measure** of HRQL because it was not designed for any particular patient population. Rather, it is considered an appropriate measure of HRQL for people with virtually any type of disease or disability. In contrast, some subjective measures of HRQL are considered **disease-specific,** because they were designed to measure HRQL only among people with a specific disease or disabling condition, such as arthritis or asthma.

generic measures ■

disease-specific measures ■

The SF-36 has been used to demonstrate the positive effects of exercise interventions on HRQL across a wide range of clinical populations, such as the frail elderly (Schectman & Ory, 2001), cardiac rehabilitation patients (Milani, Lavie, & Cassidy, 1996), women with breast cancer (Segal et al., 2001), and people with Type 2 diabetes (Kirk et al., 2001). In general, these studies have shown that exercise can improve scores on the SF-36. However, the effects of exercise on the various dimensions measured by the SF-36 tend to vary across populations. For example, when the SF-36 was used in a study of patients enrolled in a cardiac rehabilitation program, Milani and colleagues (1996) found that after a three-month exercise program, participants significantly improved on *all* HRQL dimensions. In contrast, a study of women with breast cancer found that physical functioning was the only HRQL dimension that improved after 26 weeks of training (Segal et al., 2001). Taken together, these results suggest that exercise can improve various dimensions of HRQL, as measured by the SF-36. However, researchers and clinicians should not expect to see exercise-induced improvements on all of the dimensions in all patient populations.

Measuring Satisfaction with Functioning

An example of a questionnaire that assesses *satisfaction with functioning* is the Perceived Quality of Life Scale (PQOL; Patrick, Danis, Southerland, & Hong, 1988). This 11-item generic measure of HRQL

Perceived quality of life scale. exhibit 11.3

How satisfied are you on a scale from 0 to 100 with	Not at all Satisfied										Completely Satisfied
1. The health of your body.	0	10	20	30	40	50	60	70	80	90	100
2. Your ability to think and remember.	0	10	20	30	40	50	60	70	80	90	100
3. How happy you are.	0	10	20	30	40	50	60	70	80	90	100
4. How much you see your family and friends.	0	10	20	30	40	50	60	70	80	90	100
5. The help you get from family and friends.	0	10	20	30	40	50	60	70	80	90	100
6. Your contribution to the community.	0	10	20	30	40	50	60	70	80	90	100
7. Your activities outside work.	0	10	20	30	40	50	60	70	80	90	100
8. How your income meets your needs.	0	10	20	30	40	50	60	70	80	90	100
9. How respected you are by others.	0	10	20	30	40	50	60	70	80	90	100
10. The meaning and purpose of your life.	0	10	20	30	40	50	60	70	80	90	100
11. Working/not working/retirement.	0	10	20	30	40	50	60	70	80	90	100

Source: D. L. Patrick, M. D. Danis, L. I. Southerland, & G. Hong (1988). Quality of life following intensive care. *Journal of General Internal Medicine, 3,* 218–223. The scale is scored by calculating the average rating for the 11 items.

assesses satisfaction with one's overall HRQL by asking people to rate their level of satisfaction with various aspects of life that are considered important to people with disease or disability (see Exhibit 11.3) and that are most likely to be affected by disease and treatment (i.e., health perceptions and social, cognitive, physical, and emotional functioning).

Using the PQOL, exercise has been shown to be an effective intervention for improving one's overall HRQL. For example, after 20 weeks of training, patients with osteoarthritis who were randomly assigned to an aquatic exercise class had higher PQOL scores than nonexercising patients in a control condition (Patrick et al., 2001). Similarly, in a trial of men and women with either paraplegia or quadriplegia, those assigned to an exercise training group demonstrated greater improvements on the PQOL after nine months of exercise training than those assigned to a control group. In fact, after nine months, the control group actually experienced a decrement in their PQOL scores (Hicks et al., 2003).

OBJECTIVE VERSUS SUBJECTIVE MEASURES—WHICH ARE BEST?

When treating patients with exercise, we need to ask ourselves what is more important—how *we* as researchers and health-care professionals rate their HRQL (objective approach), or how *they* perceive their own HRQL (subjective approach). The objective and subjective approaches cannot be considered equal, as there are large discrepancies between how health-care providers and family members perceive a patient's HRQL and how patients perceive their own HRQL (Bar-On & Amir, 1994). In addition, when compared to objective measures of HRQL, patients' subjective perceptions of their HRQL are usually more closely associated with important health-related outcomes such as their physical and psychological functioning, how well they adhere to treatment, and their ability to cope successfully with illness (Neill et al., 1985). Given that subjective measures are a better and more meaningful predictor of important health-related outcomes, exercise psychologists are part of a growing number of health researchers and caregivers who primarily use a subjective approach to measuring HRQL. Consequently, the vast majority of studies that have examined the effects of exercise on HRQL have used a subjective approach to HRQL measurement. Before beginning a discussion of HRQL and exercise, we first present some individual characteristics that can affect subjective perceptions of HRQL.

Effect of Individual Difference Factors on Perceptions of HRQL

Individual differences can affect people's perceptions of HRQL. For example, two people with the exact same scores on objective measures of HRQL (e.g., the same level of health and functioning, the same number of QALYs) can have very different scores on subjective measures of HRQL. The disparity between subjective and objective measures of HRQL reflects differences in how people think and feel about their lives. Three **individual difference factors** that can affect QL perceptions are personality characteristics, personal beliefs, and values.

individual difference factors ■

PERSONALITY CHARACTERISTICS

One personality characteristic that can affect HRQL perceptions is optimism. **Optimism** is a dispositional tendency to expect that good things will be plentiful in the future and that bad things will be scarce. Optimistic people have a positive orientation toward life, whereas

optimism ■

pessimism refers to people who have a negative life orientation (Scheier & Carver, 1985). To use an old adage, optimists are people who believe that the glass is "half full," whereas pessimists see the same glass as "half empty." Individuals with an optimistic personality tend to report better HRQL than those with a pessimistic personality. For example, in a study of men and women who had undergone open-heart surgery, optimistic patients reported better HRQL eight months after surgery than did pessimistic patients (Fitzgerald, Tennen, Affleck, & Pransky, 1993). Optimists may report a better HRQL than pessimists because they are more likely to take control of their health by pursuing HRQL-enriching activities such as exercise. In contrast, pessimists tend to be more passive and may be less likely actively to make changes to improve their HRQL.

■ pessimism

The personality traits of extraversion and neuroticism may also be related to HRQL. People who score high on measures of extraversion tend to be warm, socially outgoing individuals who enjoy the company of others. People who score high on the trait of neuroticism tend to be anxious individuals who worry a lot and who are prone to feelings of guilt (Eysenck & Eysenck, 1969). In their study of more than 5,000 older adults, a group of Dutch researchers found that higher levels of neuroticism were associated with lower perceptions of HRQL (Kempen, Jelicic, & Ormel, 1997). Likewise, a study of Japanese cancer patients found that higher levels of neuroticism were associated with poorer HRQL while higher levels of extraversion were associated with better HRQL (Yamaoka et al., 1998). One possible explanation for these relationships is that highly neurotic individuals experience considerable negative affect in their daily lives (after all, these are people who are worried and anxious much of the time), and their persistent negativity taints their perception of their HRQL. Conversely, extraverts experience considerable positive affect in their daily lives, and these feelings are reflected in more positive perceptions and evaluations of their HRQL.

PERSONAL BELIEFS

Among people with disease or disability, a better HRQL is associated with a stronger belief about one's level of control over aspects of the illness (e.g., beliefs about one's ability to control pain and other symptoms), its treatment (e.g., beliefs about one's ability to accept or decline a particular treatment), and the ability to care for oneself and perform activities of daily living (e.g., beliefs about one's ability to get dressed, eat, and move about without assistance). In contrast, poorer HRQL is typically reported among people who believe that they have little control over their illness and their lives, and who lack the ability to perform daily tasks (Kempen et al., 1997). Exercise may help to improve these **control beliefs.** For example, in a study of knee osteoarthritis patients, exercise was shown to enhance patients' beliefs in their ability to perform a variety of activities of daily living (Rejeski, Brawley, Ettinger, Morgan, & Thompson, 1997). Likewise, exercise has been shown to increase COPD patients' perceptions of their ability to control their breathing-related symptoms (Lacasse et al., 1996). Thus, exercise may help to improve HRQL by enhancing people's beliefs about their ability to control aspects of their lives that may be hampered by disease or illness and about their ability to control symptoms of the illness.

control beliefs

Religious and spiritual beliefs are another type of belief that appears to be related to HRQL. A review of the scientific research on health, religion, and spirituality by Larson, Sawyers, and McCullough (1997) concluded that greater religious participation is associated with more positive perceptions along the HRQL dimensions of physical, social, and psychological well-being, and with more positive perceptions of one's quality of life overall (QL). Interestingly, it seems that regardless of how religious beliefs are expressed—as church attendance and membership, praying, reading religious books, or watching religious television programs—simply having these beliefs is associated with more positive perceptions (Levin & Taylor, 1998).

Preliminary research suggests that HRQL is also associated with the *strength* of one's spiritual beliefs. The term "spirituality" refers to a belief system that focuses on self-transcendence, self-actualization, and finding integrity and meaning in one's life. People can have a sense of spirituality without ascribing to an organized religion. Although researchers are only just beginning to explore the relationship between spirituality and HRQL, the existing data indicate a positive relationship between these constructs. For instance, in a study of Hispanic and African-American cancer patients, those who scored higher on a measure of spiritual beliefs reported a greater HRQL than those who had lower scores on the measure of spiritual beliefs (Wan et al., 1999).

PERSONAL VALUES

A central determinant of HRQL perceptions is the value that one places on a particular life domain. For example, among people with similar objective levels of physical functioning, the importance that a person places on physical functioning will influence whether that person is satisfied or dissatisfied with physical functioning. For instance, in a study of older adults with knee osteoarthritis (Rejeski, Ettinger, Martin, &

Morgan, 1998), researchers identified patients who reported significant functional impairment. They then measured the value that these impaired patients placed on the HRQL domain of physical function, and their level of satisfaction with their physical function. Interestingly, impaired patients who placed high value on function reported significantly less satisfaction with their physical function than did impaired patients who placed low value on function. As this study demonstrates, when people believe that their lives lack something that they consider personally valuable (e.g., the ability to be physically active, personal relationships, a fulfilling career), this has a greater negative impact on their HRQL than when their lives lack something that they don't consider valuable.

Research on HRQL and Exercise

Our discussion of the research on HRQL focuses on two broad areas: the effects of exercise on perceptions of HRQL, and who benefits from exercise interventions.

THE EFFECTS OF EXERCISE ON PERCEPTIONS OF HRQL

So far in this textbook, we have studied exercise psychology concepts primarily within the context of understanding physical activity that is performed to improve some aspect(s) of physical fitness (i.e., what we defined in Chapter 2 as "exercise") among people who are already in relatively good general health. Yet for many people with chronic disease and disability, such as Harry, the goal of an exercise intervention is not so much to increase their physical fitness, but simply to help them regain or maintain the functional capacity (i.e., strength, endurance) to perform the activities they want or need to do in their daily lives. These activities are commonly referred to as **activities of daily living (ADLs)**. Therefore, when studying the effects of exercise training on HRQL, exercise psychologists conceptualize exercise training programs in very broad terms. These programs may include activity performed at a sufficient intensity to increase physical fitness (e.g., aerobic and strength-training programs) as well as moderate- and low-intensity activity (e.g., tai chi and some walking programs) that is not necessarily intense enough to increase fitness but can help a person maintain or attain the ability to perform activities of daily living such as shopping, climbing stairs, or doing laundry.

■ activities of daily living (ADLs)

As mentioned in the section describing the SF-36 measure of HRQL, not all dimensions of HRQL are likely to be affected by exercise. For example, sensory function—seeing, speaking, hearing—is sometimes considered an HRQL dimension (for instance, in studies of patients being treated for head and neck cancers), but it is unlikely to be improved through an exercise intervention. The following five dimensions of HRQL, however, have been identified as those most likely to be affected by exercise training programs (Rejeski, Brawley, & Shumaker, 1996):

1. Perceptions of Physical Functioning

Considerable research has shown the value of exercise training programs for improving one's perceived level of physical functioning and satisfaction with physical functioning among the elderly and patient populations such as people with arthritis, COPD, cancer, heart disease, and AIDS, to name just a few (Courneya & Friedenreich, 1999; Rejeski et al., 1996). For example, in a six-month study of older adults (with mean age of 73 years), those who had been randomly assigned to a twice weekly tai chi exercise program reported higher levels of physical functioning than those who were assigned to a control condition (Li et al., 2001). Specifically, when compared with the control group, people in the tai chi condition reported higher performance levels for vigorous and moderate physical activities as well as activities of daily living. Another study examined perceived level of physical functioning among a group of adults with arthritis (Minor, Hewett, Webel, Anderson, & Kay, 1989). Patients were randomly assigned to either a walking condition, an aerobic aquatics condition, or a control condition. After 12 weeks of training, the aquatics and walking exercise groups had more positive perceptions of their physical functioning than did the control group. The study also found that patients in the two exercise conditions had significant improvements in their physical self-concept.

Physical self-concept, which reflects how an individual feels about one's physical self in general (see Chapter 10), is also included under the HRQL domain of physical function. Although HRQL researchers have not studied physical self-concept as thoroughly as perceived level and satisfaction with physical functioning, as the above arthritis study indicates, there is evidence to suggest that people with chronic disease or disability can improve their self-concept through exercise. Further evidence comes from a study of adolescents who had been diagnosed with cancer (Keats, Courneya, Danielsen, & Whitsett, 1999). Adolescents who maintained an active lifestyle throughout the cancer experience (i.e., pre-diagnosis, during cancer treatment, and after cancer treatment) had a better physical self-concept than those who were inactive throughout the entire cancer experience or those who became inactive after diagnosis.

2. Perceptions of Health Status

Exercise training has been shown to improve perceptions of physical health and symptom severity across a wide range of populations. For example, exercise training programs have been shown to improve the perceived "goodness" of health among older adults (Wallace et al., 1998), patients with heart disease (e.g., Denollet & Brutsaert, 1995), and individuals with knee osteoarthritis (Rejeski et al., 1998). Symptom severity has also been shown to improve following exercise training. In a quantitative review of the effects of exercise training on people with COPD, exercise was shown to improve significantly patient reports of dyspnea (i.e., shortness of breath—a symptom that is particularly severe and stressful among this population) as well as patients' perceptions of their ability to *control* their dyspnea (Lacasse et al., 1996). Thus, it seems that exercise can help to alleviate some disease-related symptoms and may provide patients with a strategy for managing or controlling these symptoms.

There is also evidence to suggest that exercise can help to alleviate the uncomfortable side effects of certain disease treatments. For example, chemotherapy has severe side effects including nausea and fatigue. In a study of women undergoing chemotherapy treatment for breast cancer, Winningham and MacVicar (1988) examined the effects of exercise on nausea. Those women who were assigned to a thrice weekly program of exercise on a cycle ergometer had larger decreases in nausea than women assigned to a placebo or a control condition.

3. Perceptions of Emotional Well-Being

As described in Chapters 7, 8, and 9 exercise is associated with improvements in numerous aspects of emotional well-being among the general population, such as decreased depression and anxiety, and increased positive affect. The effects of exercise on emotional well-being have also been demonstrated in the elderly as well as various patient populations. For instance, exercise training has been shown to decrease feelings of depression and anxiety among the elderly (Wallace et al., 1998), patients with COPD (Emery, Schein, Hauck, & MacIntyre, 1998), breast cancer survivors (Segar et al., 1998), and people with spinal cord injury (Martin, Latimer, Francoeur, Hanley, & Watson, 2002; see Exhibit 11.4).

Although the majority of exercise and HRQL studies have focused on changes in negative affect, such as anxiety and depression, some studies have shown that exercise can also increase feelings of positive affect. For example, Denollet and Brutsaert (1995) measured the effects of an exercise-based cardiac rehabilitation program on the experience of

exhibit 11.4

Exercise training has been shown to significantly improve health-related quality of life among people with various types of diseases and disability.

positive mood states among men with heart disease. One group of men participated in a 12-week rehabilitation program that consisted of both group exercise classes (three times per week) and group sessions that provided education about heart disease and emotional support. A second group of men did not participate in this intervention program. The researchers reported significantly greater positive affect among men who had been part of the intervention program.

4. Perceptions of Social Functioning

The relationship between exercise and the social functioning dimension of HRQL has not yet been well-studied. Nevertheless, some evidence suggests that exercise can positively affect patient perceptions of aspects of their social lives. For instance, a review of studies of frail elderly men and women indicated that a regular exercise program can have positive effects on their perceptions of social functioning (Schechtman & Ory, 2001). Specifically, elderly individuals who were randomly assigned to an exercise program reported that their health interfered with their social activities less often than did individuals assigned to a control condition (see Exhibit 11.5).

Research involving other patient populations has also shown that exercise training programs can reduce how much a patient's health problems interfere with social activities. For example, one study examined the effects of aquatic exercise on people with fibromyalgia, a chronic condition characterized by widespread bodily pain and uncontrollable fatigue (Mannerkorpi, Nyberg, Ahlmen, & Ekdahl, 2000). Participants who exercised for six months reported that their symptoms interfered with their social activities to a lesser extent than did individuals in a no-exercise control group. Similar positive results have been found in

Studies have shown improvement in older adults' reports of their physical and social functioning and their emotional well-being following an exercise training program.

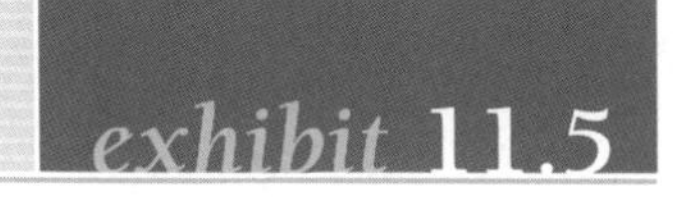

studies of other clinical populations, such as individuals with diabetes (Wiesinger et al., 2001) and clinical depression (Singh, Clements, & Fiatarone, 1997).

In addition, exercise may enhance the social confidence of people with disease and disability by reducing concerns about being perceived by others as "disabled" or "frail" (Taub, Blinde, & Greer, 1999). People with physical disabilities have reported that the physical gains made during exercise give them more confidence in social situations (Martin et al., 2002; Taub et al., 1999).

5. Perceptions of Cognitive Functioning

A relatively large body of literature exists on the topic of physical activity and objective measures of cognition. However, these studies have focused primarily on studying whether exercise can improve performance on tasks related to processing and sorting information (e.g., performing mathematical problems or sorting information into groups), or the planning and initiating of behaviors (e.g., performing a reaction time test). Exercise has been shown to improve these objective indices of cognitive performance in some special populations, such as the elderly (for a quantitative review, see Etnier et al., 1997) and people with COPD (Emery et al., 1998).

There is, however, virtually no research examining whether exercise can improve performance of the mental operations that are most meaningful to a person with disease or disability—operations that are necessary for daily functioning and social interactions. For example, it is not known whether exercise aids in the storage or recall of information that is used on a day-to-day basis, such as telephone numbers and bank machine access codes. Thus, the question remains as to whether individuals who exercise actually *perceive* improvements in their daily cognitive functioning. This latter point is critical to determining the effects of exercise on the cognitive dimension of HRQL. If a person does not perceive improved cognitive functioning, then she will not report improvement on that dimension of HRQL. In sum, there is still much to be learned about the role of exercise in improving people's perceptions of and satisfaction with their cognitive functioning.

WHO BENEFITS FROM EXERCISE INTERVENTIONS?

Rejeski and his colleagues (1996) conducted an excellent review of the physical activity and HRQL literature. Their review included studies of patient populations from three broad areas: cardiovascular disease, pulmonary disease, and arthritis. From their review, they concluded that physical activity and exercise are associated with improvements in all five components of HRQL reviewed previously. In addition, Courneya and his colleagues conducted two extensive reviews of the research examining the effects of exercise on HRQL among people who have been diagnosed with cancer (Courneya & Friedenreich, 1999; Courneya, Mackey, & Jones, 2000). They also reported significant positive effects of exercise on these five domains of HRQL. Taken together, these extensive reviews have provided compelling evidence that exercise can lead to significant improvements in the HRQL of people with a wide range of disabilities and diseases.

Exercise, however, seems to have the biggest effects among people who have the lowest levels of HRQL, primarily because these individuals have the most room for improvement. In contrast, the effects of exercise are far less dramatic among people who already have relatively high scores on a particular HRQL dimension, as it is difficult to increase HRQL further among these people. Nonetheless, for individuals who already enjoy a high level of HRQL, exercise may play an important role in maintaining this level.

Some HRQL domains may show greater improvements following an exercise intervention than others. For example, in a series of studies examining the effects of exercise on the HRQL of community-dwelling older adults, an exercise intervention was shown to have a small but significant effect on emotional functioning, an even smaller (but nonsignificant) effect on social functioning, and no effect whatsoever on health perceptions (Schectman & Ory, 2001). One reason for the differential effects of exercise on HRQL domains could be that individuals typically start out lower on some domains than others, so they have more room for improvement on certain domains. Another possibility is that exercise simply has greater effects on some domains than on others.

The Relationship Between Changes in HRQL and Objective Changes in Disease Status and Physical Fitness

The positive effects of exercise on HRQL are generally unrelated to exercise-related improvements in objective indices of disease status or physical fitness. For example, in a study of men who were HIV positive, a 12-week exercise intervention was shown to significantly improve perceptions of their emotional and physical functioning, despite no change in an objective index of disease status—the number of CD4 cells present (Lox, McAuley, & Tucker, 1995). Similarly, a study of exercise among adults with COPD showed that improvements in objective measures of physical fitness were unrelated to improvements in perceived health status and emotional well-being (Wijkstra et al., 1994). Thus, a person does not need to experience objective improvements in physical fitness in order to derive the HRQL-enhancing benefits of exercise.

The lack of an association between improvements in HRQL and improvements in objective indices of disease status and fitness may seem counterintuitive. But as emphasized throughout this chapter, HRQL is not simply a reflection of one's objective health status and level of functioning. Rather, HRQL reflects *perceptions of, and thoughts and feelings about* one's health status and functioning. Thus, in order for exercise to have an effect on HRQL, people must be able to perceive improvements in their own health and function.

The Relationship Between Changes in HRQL and Perceived Changes in Important Aspects of One's Life

How meaningful are changes in "maximal workload" or "maximal oxygen consumption" to the average older adult with COPD? Not very; most people have no idea how to interpret the results of these objective measures of physical fitness. Likewise, are changes in CD4 cell counts the only aspect of health that a person with HIV cares about? Probably not. Instead, what is often important to many people with disease and disability is changes in their ability to perform tasks that are important in their daily lives, such as climbing stairs, dealing with their emotions, and participating in family and community life (e.g., Sutherland, Lockwood, & Boyd, 1990). When exercise leads to perceived improvements in the ability to perform these important tasks, such improvements are usually more meaningful to people than are changes in objective measures of fitness or disease. As a result, when considering the impact of exercise on their HRQL, people tend to focus on whether exercise has had an impact on valued aspects of their lives.

Practical Recommendations

Based on the information provided in this chapter, we can offer several practical recommendations for designing exercise interventions to increase HRQL. First of all, in order for exercise to enhance HRQL, people must be able to *perceive* improvements in their level of functioning. Interventionists can help make people more aware of their functional gains by regularly asking them about their level of functioning in their daily lives (e.g., how many stairs can they climb, how much help do they need to get dressed or bathe, how many days were they confined to bed in the past week), or periodically testing participants' ability to perform activities of daily living (e.g., opening heavy doors, getting in and out of a car). Changes in the perceived difficulty with which these tasks are performed or the amount of help that the person needs to do these tasks can be recorded over the course of an exercise intervention and brought to the participant's attention. Often, people don't realize that they have made progress unless they are given the opportunity to see how far they have come!

Second, people must realize the *value* of exercise to their HRQL. In many cases, people may not understand how certain exercises can be of benefit to them. For example, older people may wonder why a fitness leader is asking them to perform exercises to strengthen their biceps and triceps. The exercise leader could explain how each of these exercises relate to the performance activities of daily living such as carrying a laundry basket or pushing oneself out of a bathtub. When people realize that exercise-induced strength gains result in meaningful changes to their daily functioning, exercise is more likely to have a positive effect on HRQL.

Third, people should be encouraged to engage in a variety of types of physical activity, as some types of activity may affect certain components of HRQL more than others. For example, participation in group physical activities such as a tai chi class or a lawn bowling league may provide a greater sense of improved social functioning than participation in activities that are done alone (e.g., swimming, weight training). Similarly, although *structured* exercise has been shown to enhance perceptions of physical functioning, individuals should also be encouraged to engage in short bouts of *unstructured* activity throughout the day (e.g., walking to a friend's house, gardening, grocery shopping, taking a pet for a walk). Performing these activities can increase beliefs about the level of control a person has over his or her life. As improved control beliefs may lead to increased perceptions of HRQL, it is important to encourage people to perform activities that will give them a greater sense of power over their lives. An exercise programmer might further increase control beliefs by reminding participants that by exercising, they are taking charge of an aspect of their well-being.

Conclusion

HRQL reflects the perceived goodness of the various aspects of one's life that can be affected by health and health interventions. It is a subcomponent of the broader concept of "quality of life" (QL), which reflects objective and subjective evaluations of the *overall* goodness of one's life. HRQL is considered an important benchmark for determining the effectiveness of health treatments and for making treatment decisions. As exercise is being used increasingly as a treatment for people with disease and disability, exercise psychologists are interested in determining the effects of exercise interventions on HRQL. Although researchers often disagree on how best to define and measure HRQL, there is evidence that exercise can play a role in improving at least five different dimensions of HRQL: physical function, health status, emotional well-being, social function, and cognitive function. The people who tend to make the greatest gains in HRQL following exercise interventions are those who have the lowest HRQL at the start of the intervention. Interestingly, exercise interventions do not need to cause objective improvements along dimensions such as disease status or physical fitness in order for improvements in HRQL to occur. Rather, improvements in HRQL seem to be related to perceived improvements in one's ability to perform daily activities that are considered important or meaningful to the individual.

What Do You Know?

1. What is the difference between quality of life (QL) and health-related quality of life (HRQL)?
2. Identify and briefly describe the five core dimensions of HRQL that are generally agreed upon by researchers and clinicians.
3. What is the main difference between subjective and objective measures of HRQL?
4. Give two examples of objective measures of HRQL.
5. What is meant by "quality-adjusted life years"?
6. Describe the subjective approach to measuring HRQL.
7. In studies of exercise interventions, why is the subjective approach generally considered better than the objective approach?
8. Which dimensions of HRQL are most likely to be affected by exercise training?
9. To what extent do changes in disease status and physical fitness affect HRQL?
10. Identify and describe three individual difference variables that can affect perceptions of HRQL.

Learning Activities

1. Use your knowledge of HRQL to make decisions about exercise prescription for the following two cases:

Case 1. You are studying the effects of aerobic exercise on the progression of a newly identified disease. Although blood samples reveal that exercise is curbing disease progress, patients are so fatigued after working out and experience such a big increase in pain due to exercise that they are unable to perform activities of daily living or to socialize with their families and friends. Thus, despite medical improvements, patients have significant decrements in their HRQL. Should you recommend exercise as a treatment for this disease? Defend your position.

Case 2. You have been asked to implement an exercise training program at a local nursing home where the caregivers are hoping to decrease the risk of heart disease among residents. After six months of light chair exercises (exercises performed while seated), there is no improvement in participants' cardiac risk profiles. However, participants note that since starting the exercise program, they have felt happier with their ability to walk short distances and their level of energy for participating in social activities. When their families visit, family members remark that the patients seem more positive. Do you continue the exercise program even though it is not producing any change in cardiovascular risk profile? Construct an argument defending your position to present to the director of the home.

2. Conduct a literature search to find exercise intervention studies that have used the SF-36 scale to measure changes in HRQL. Choose two studies that involved two different populations (e.g., arthritis patients and the elderly). Compare and contrast the effects of exercise on SF-36 scores for these two different groups of people.

3. Develop an exercise training program for the frail elderly that has the specific goal of improving their HRQL. Pay careful attention to:

a. the types of exercises and activities that you prescribe

b. the instructions and information that you give participants about the relationship between exercise and HRQL

c. strategies to enhance perceptions of improvement and control.

4. Choose a particular disease or disability (e.g., heart disease, hearing loss) and conduct an Internet search to find a questionnaire measuring HRQL designed specifically for people who have this particular condition. If you were to administer this measure to patients at the start of an exercise program and then three months into the exercise program, how do you think their responses to the questionnaire would change?

References

American College of Sports Medicine (1998). Position stand: Exercise and physical activity for older adults. *Medicine and Science in Sports and Exercise, 30,* 992–1008.

Arthritis Foundation (1999). *Exercise and your arthritis* [Brochure]. Atlanta, GA: Author.

Bar-On, D., & Amir, M. (1994). A new subjective measure of quality of life. *Quality of Life Newsletter, 10–11,* 6–7.

Courneya, K. S., & Friedenreich, C. M. (1999). Physical exercise and quality of life following cancer diagnosis: A literature review. *Annals of Behavioural Medicine, 21,* 171–179.

Courneya, K. S., Mackey, J. R., & Jones, L. W. (2000). Coping with cancer: Can exercise help? *Physician and Sportsmedicine, 28,* 49–51; 55–56; 66–68; 71; 73.

Denollet, J., & Brutsaert, D. L. (1995). Enhancing emotional well-being by comprehensive rehabilitation in patients with coronary heart disease. *European Heart Journal, 16,* 1070–1078.

Emery, C. F., Schein, R. L., Hauck, E. R., & MacIntyre, N. R. (1998). Psychological and cognitive outcomes of a randomized trial of exercise among patients with chronic obstructive pulmonary disease. *Health Psychology, 17,* 232–240.

Etnier, J. L., Salazar, W., Landers, D. M., Petruzzello, S. J., Han, M., & Nowell, P. (1997). The influence of physical fitness and exercise upon cognitive functioning: A meta-analysis. *Journal of Sport and Exercise Psychology, 19,* 249–277.

Eysenck, S. B., & Eysenck, H. J. (1969). Scores of three personality variables as a function of age, sex, and social class. *British Journal of Social and Clinical Psychology, 8, 69–76.*

Fitzgerald, T. E., Tennen, H., Affleck, G., & Pransky, G. S. (1993). The relative importance of dispositional optimism and control appraisals in quality of life after coronary artery bypass surgery. *Journal of Behavioural Medicine, 16,* 25–43.

Gill, T. M., & Feinstein, A. R. (1994). A critical appraisal of the quality of quality-of-life measurements. *Journal of the American Medical Association, 272,* 619–631.

Hatziandreu, E. I.,. Koplan, J. P., Weinstein, M. C., Caspersen, C. J., & Warner, K. E. (1988). A cost-effectiveness analysis of exercise as a health promotion activity. *American Journal of Public Health, 78,* 1417–1421.

Hicks, A. L., Martin, K. A., Latimer, A. E., Ditor, D. S., & McCartney, N. (2003). Long-term exercise training in persons with spinal cord injury: Effects on strength, arm ergometry performance and psychological well-being. *Spinal Cord, 41,* 29–33.

Kaplan, R. M., & Bush, J. W. (1982). Health-related quality of life measurement for evaluation research analysis. *Health Psychology, 1,* 61–80.

Keats, M. R., Courneya, K. S., Danielsen, S., & Whitsett, S. F. (1999). Leisure-time physical activity and psychosocial well-being in adolescents after cancer diagnosis. *Journal of Pediatric Oncology Nursing, 16,* 180–188.

Kempen, G. I., Jelicic, M., & Ormel, J. (1997). Personality, chronic medical morbidity, and health-related quality of life among older persons. *Health Psychology, 16, 539–546.*

Kirk, A. F., Higgins, L. A., Hughes, A. R., Fisher, B. M., Mutrie, N., Hillis, S., & MacIntyre, P. D. (2001). A randomized, controlled trial to study the effects of exercise consultation on the promotion of physical activity in people with type 2 diabetes: Pilot study. *Diabetic Medicine, 11,* 877–882.

Lacasse, Y., Wong, E., Guyatt, G. H., King, D., Cook, D. J., & Goldstein, R. S. (1996). Meta-analysis of respiratory rehabilitation in chronic obstructive pulmonary disease. *The Lancet, 348,* 1115–1119.

Larson, D. B., Sawyers, J. P., & McCullough, M. E. (1997). *Scientific research on spirituality and health: A consensus report.* Rockville, MD: National Institute for Healthcare Research.

Levin, J. S., & Taylor, R. J. (1998). Panel analyses of religious involvement and well-being in African Americans: Contemporaneous vs. longitudinal effects. *Journal of the Scientific Study of Religion, 37,* 695–709.

Li, F., Harmer, P., McAuley, E., Duncan, T. E., Duncan, S. C., Chaumeton, N., & Fisher, K. J. (2001). An evaluation of the effects of tai chi exercise on physical function among older persons: A randomized controlled trial. *Annals of Behavioural Medicine, 23,* 139–146.

Lox, C. L, McAuley, E., & Tucker, R. S. (1995). Exercise as an intervention for enhancing subjective well-being in an HIV-1 population. *Journal of Sport and Exercise Psychology, 17,* 345–362.

Mannerkorpi, K., Nyberg, B., Ahlmen, M., & Ekdahl, C. (2000). Pool exercise combined with an education program for patients with fibromyalgia syndrome: A prospective, randomized study. *Journal of Rheumatology, 10,* 2473–2481.

Martin, K. A., Latimer, A. E., Francoeur, C., Hanley, H., & Watson, K. (2002). Sustaining exercise motivation and participation among people with spinal cord injury: Lessons learned from a 9-month intervention. *Palaestra, 18,* 38–40.

Milani, R. V., Lavie, C. J., & Cassidy, M. M. (1996). Effects of cardiac rehabilitation and exercise training programs on depression in patients after major coronary events. *American Heart Journal, 132,* 726–732.

Minor, M. A., Hewett, J. E., Webel, R. R., Anderson, S. K., & Kay, D. R. (1989). Efficacy of physical conditioning exercise in patients with rheumatoid arthritis and osteoarthritis. *Arthritis and Rheumatism, 32,* 1396–1404.

Neill, W. A., Branch, L. G., De Jong, G., Smith, N. E., Hogan, C. A., Corcoran, P. J., Jette, A. M., Balasco, E. M., & Osberg, S. (1985). Cardiac disability: The impact of coronary heart disease on patients' daily activities. *Archives of Internal Medicine, 145,* 1642–1647.

Noveau, L., & Shephard, R. J. (1995). Spinal cord injury, exercise and quality of life. *Sports Medicine, 20,* 226–250.

Patrick, D. L., Danis, M., Southerland, L. I., & Hong, G. (1988). Quality of life following intensive care. *Journal of General Internal Medicine, 3,* 218–223.

Patrick, D. L., Ramsey, S. D., Spencer, A. C., Kinne, S., Belza, B., & Topolski, T. D. (2001). Economic evaluation of aquatic exercise for persons with osteoarthritis. *Medical Care, 39,* 413–424.

Philips, C., & Thompson, G. (2001). *What Is a QALY?* Kent, UK: Hayward Medical Communications.

Rejeski, W. J., Brawley, L. R., Ettinger, W., Morgan, T., & Thompson, C. (1997). Compliance to exercise therapy in older participants with knee osteoarthritis: Implications for treating disability. *Medicine & Science in Sports & Exercise, 29,* 977–985.

Rejeski, W. J., Brawley, L. R., & Shumaker, S. A. (1996). Physical activity and health-related quality of life. *Exercise and Sport Science Reviews, 24,* 71–108.

Rejeski, W. J., Ettinger, W. H., Martin, K. A., & Morgan, T. (1998). Treating disability in knee osteoarthritis with exercise therapy: A central role for self-efficacy and pain. *Arthritis Care Research, 11,* 94–101.

Rejeski, W. J., Martin, K. A., Miller, M. E., Ettinger, W. H., & Rapp, S. (1998). Perceived importance and satisfaction with physical function in patients with knee osteoarthritis. *Annals of Behavioural Medicine, 20,* 141–148.

Schectman, K. B., & Ory, M. G. (2001). The effects of exercise on the quality of life of frail older adults: A preplanned meta-analysis of the FICSIT trials. *Annals of Behavioural Medicine, 23,* 186–197.

Scheier, M. F., & Carver, C. S. (1985). Optimism, coping, and health: Assessment and implications of generalized outcome expectancies. *Health Psychology, 4,* 219–247.

Segal, R., Evans, W., Johnson, D., Smith, J., Colletta, S., Gayton, J., Woodard, S., Wells, G., & Reid, R. (2001). Structured exercise improves physical functioning in women with stages I and II breast cancer: Results of a randomized controlled trial. *Journal of Clinical Oncology, 19,* 657–665.

Segar, M. L., Katch, V. L., Roth, R. S., Weinstein Garcia, A., Portner, T. I., Glickman, S. G., Haslanger, S., & Wilkins, E. G. (1998). The effect of aerobic exercise on self-esteem and depressive and anxiety symptoms among breast cancer survivors. *Oncology Nursing Forum, 25,* 107–113.

Singh, N. A., Clements, K. M., & Fiatarone, M. A. (1997). A randomized controlled trial of progressive resistance training in depressed elders. *Journals of Gerontology: Series-A: Biological Sciences and Medical Sciences, 52A,* M27–M35.

Sutherland, H. J., Lockwood, G. A., & Boyd, N. F. (1990). Ratings of the importance of quality of life variables: Therapeutic implications for patients with metastatic breast cancer. *Journal of Clinical Epidemiology, 43,* 661–666.

Taub, D. E., Blinde, E. M., & Greer, K. R. (1999). Stigma management through participation in sport and physical activity: Experiences of male college students with physical disabilities. *Human Relations, 52,* 1469–1484.

Tsevat, J., Sherman, S. N., McElwee, J. A., Mandell, K. L., Simbarti, L. A., Sonnenberg, F. A., & Fowler, F. J. (1999). The will to live among HIV-infected patients. *Annals of Internal Medicine, 131,* 194–198.

U.S. Department of Health and Human Services. (2001). *Life expectancy hits new high in 2000; mortality declines for several leading causes of death* [On-line]. Available: www.hhs.gov/news/press/2001pres/20011010.html.

Wallace, J. I., Buchner, D. M., Grothaus, L., Leveille, S., Tyll, L., LaCroix, A. Z., & Wagner, E. H. (1998). Implementation and effectiveness of a community-based health promotion program for older adults. *Journal of Gerontology, 53A,* 301–306.

Wan, G. J., Counte, M. A., Cella, D. F., Hernandez, L., McGuire, D. B., Deasay, S., Shiomoto, G., & Hahn, E. A. (1999). The impact of socio-cultural and clinical factors on health-related quality of life reports among Hispanic and African-American cancer patients. *Journal of Outcome Measures, 3,* 200–215.

Ware, J. E., Gandek, B., IQOLA Project Group. (1994). The SF-36 Health Survey: Development and use in mental health research and the IQOLA Project. *International Journal of Mental Health, 23,* 49–73.

Ware, J. E., Kosinski, M., Bayliss, M. S., McHorney, C. A., et al. (1995). Comparison of methods for the scoring and statistical analysis of SF-36 health profile and summary measures: Summary of results from the medical outcomes study. *Medical Care, 33* (Supplement), 264–279.

Ware, J. E., & Sherbourne, C. D. (1992). The MOS 36-item short-form health survey (SF-36): I. Conceptual framework and item selection. *Medical Care, 30,* 473–483.

Wiesinger, G. F., Pleiner, J., Quittan, M., Fuchsjager-Mayrl, G., Crevanna, R., Nuhr, M. J., Francesconi, C., Seit, H. P., Francesconi, M., Fialka-Moser, V., & Wolzt, M. (2001). Health related quality of life in patients with long-standing insulin dependent (type 1) diabetes mellitus: Benefits of regular exercise training. *Wiener Klinische Wochenschrift, 113,* 670–675.

Wijkstra, P. J., Van Altena, R., Kraan, J., Otten, V., Postma, D. S., & Koeter, G. H. (1994). Quality of life in patients with chronic pulmonary obstructive disease improves after rehabilitation at home. *The European Respiratory Journal, 7,* 269–273.

Winningham, M. L., & MacVicar, M. G. (1988). The effect of aerobic exercise on patient reports of nausea. *Oncology Nursing Forum, 15,* 447–450.

World Health Organization. (1947). *Definition of health* [On-line]. Available: www.who.int/aboutwho/en/definition.html.

World Health Organization. (1993). WHOQOL Study Protocol. WHO (MNH/PSF/93.9).

Yamaoka, K., Shigehisa, T., Ogoshi, K., Haruyama, K., Watanabe, M., Hayashi, F., & Hayashi, C. (1998). Health-related quality of life varies with personality types: A comparison among cancer patients, non-cancer patients and healthy individuals in a Japanese population. *Quality of Life Research, 6,* 535–544.

Chapter 12

Social Influences on Exercise

In just two months, Lakeisha will be turning 30. To celebrate, Lakeisha and her girlfriends are planning to take a tropical vacation together. This trip, of course, has led to endless talks about bathing suits and how to look good in them. Consequently, at a recent doctor's appointment, Lakeisha asked her family physician to put her on a diet so that she could shed a few pounds. Instead of prescribing a diet, the doctor prescribed an exercise program. Like most people, Lakeisha *knows* that exercise is essential to weight loss—in fact, when she and her friends first started planning their trip, she joined a gym and went to her first aerobics class. Unfortunately, Lakeisha hated the class and vowed never to return. The aerobics instructor seemed to comment on every mistake she made, which embarrassed Lakeisha and made her feel that everyone was watching her. Working out in the weight training center of the gym was even worse—she felt out of place with so many men in the center, all of whom could lift 10 times the weight she could. Having given up on aerobics and the gym, Lakeisha is feeling the pressure to go on a "quick fix" crash diet. When she mentions this to her doctor, the doctor suggests Lakeisha find a workout partner, and that they exercise in a place where Lakeisha is comfortable. Now Lakeisha and her exercise buddy work out five days a week to an exercise video in the privacy of her living room. They depend on each other for motivation and support, and Lakeisha is sticking to their program partly because she doesn't want to let her partner down. Now that she's feeling more confident about her exercise abilities, Lakeisha and her girlfriends have agreed to meet twice a week at the gym to lift weights together. With her best friends by her side, Lakeisha is actually looking forward to going back to the gym!

KEY TERMS

- behavioral reactance
- companionship support
- emotional support
- group cohesion
- group composition
- informational support
- instrumental support
- norm
- osteoporosis
- overprotectiveness
- social control
- social facilitation
- social influence
- social support
- stereotypes
- validation

Defining Social Influence

social influence ■

Social influence is defined as "real or imagined pressure to change one's behavior, attitudes, or beliefs" (Alcock, Carment, & Sadava, 1991, p. 195). Within the context of exercise and physical activity, people such as doctors, fitness leaders, and family members can exert social influence. Sometimes, the effects of social influence are negative, as when Lakeisha quit the aerobics class because the instructor embarrassed her. Other times, social influence can be positive, as when Lakeisha resumed exercising after her doctor encouraged her.

Exercise psychologists are interested in understanding why social influence has an effect on exercise and other forms of physical activity, and the conditions under which it has its greatest effects. Answers to these questions may lead to the development of interventions that use social influence to increase physical activity participation. In this chapter, we examine how people exert social influence over others' exercise-related thoughts, feelings, and behaviors.

Defining Social Support

social support ■

Social support is probably the most important type of social influence in exercise and other physical activity settings. In general, the term **social support** refers to the perceived comfort, caring, assistance, and information that a person receives from others. Exercise psychologists are interested in the role that social support plays in influencing exercise behavior. Although there are many studies of social support in the exercise psychology literature, there has been little agreement among researchers as to how social support should be operationally defined.

SIZE OF THE SOCIAL NETWORK

In some exercise studies, social support has been operationally defined as the size of one's social network—that is, the number of social relationships one has. When social support is defined this way, it is typically measured as the number of groups or individuals that an exerciser can turn to for support (e.g., exercise class members, family, doctors, friends, fitness leader, colleagues from work, and so on). This approach, however, does not take into account the quality or type of support provided. Exercisers may have many social contacts, but that doesn't necessarily mean that they are receiving adequate comfort, caring, assistance, or information from these contacts to facilitate them to exercise.

AMOUNT AND TYPE OF SUPPORT PROVIDED

Another approach to operationally defining social support is to assess how much of a particular *type* of support is perceived by the exerciser. There are five main types of social support (Wills & Shinar, 2000), each of which serves a different function. A description of these functions as they apply in exercise settings follows.

- **Instrumental support** involves providing tangible, practical assistance that will help a person achieve exercise goals. Examples of instrumental support include spotting a weightlifter at the gym, driving your father to his cardiac rehabilitation exercise class, or taking care of a friend's baby while she exercises.

▪ instrumental support

- **Emotional support** occurs through the expression of encouragement, caring, empathy, and concern toward a person. Praising an exerciser for her efforts, encouraging her to work harder, and sympathizing with her when she complains about aching muscles are all examples of emotional support. This type of support enhances self-esteem, reduces anxiety, and gives the person a sense of comfort, acceptance, and reassurance of self-worth.

▪ emotional support

- **Informational support** includes giving directions, advice, or suggestions about how to exercise and providing feedback regarding the exerciser's progress. Lakeisha received informational support about exercise when she went to see her family physician. Health practitioners and fitness trainers are formal sources of informational support for exercise, but informal sources such as family and friends can also provide informational support by sharing their own exercise experiences and by providing tips for maintaining an active lifestyle.

▪ informational support

- **Companionship support** reflects the availability of persons with whom one can exercise, such as a friend, family member, or exercise group. Lakeisha received companionship support from her exercise buddy. Companionship support produces positive affect and may distract people from negative exercise-related feelings (e.g., fatigue, pain, boredom) that might interfere with exercise enjoyment and ultimately cause the individual to quit exercising.

▪ companionship support

- **Validation** involves comparing oneself with others in order to gauge progress and to confirm (or "validate") that one's thoughts, feelings, problems, and experiences are "normal." For example, many people with chronic health conditions such as heart disease or obesity say that exercising in groups of people similar to themselves gives them the feeling that "if they can do it, so can I," and provides a sense that they are not alone in their struggle to adhere to the exercise regimen.

▪ validation

Research on the Relationship Between Social Support and Physical Activity

Evidence shows that a relationship exists between social support and physical activity regardless of whether social support is conceptualized and measured in terms of the *number* of social contacts or the amount and type of support received.

NUMBER OF SOCIAL CONTACTS

With regard to the importance of the number of social contacts, a study of more than 2,600 adults demonstrated that those who had more available support sources (e.g., close friends, neighbors, spouse) reported greater levels of physical exertion during leisure-time physical activities than those with fewer support sources (Hibbard, 1988).

AMOUNT AND TYPE OF SOCIAL SUPPORT

The importance of receiving adequate amounts of social support for physical activity has also been demonstrated. In a study of nearly 3,000 Australian college students, participants were asked to indicate the amount of companionship support and emotional support for exercise that they received from family and friends, and the amount of physical activity that they had performed in the past two weeks. Among those who were classified as receiving low levels of social support, only 50 percent of the women and 60 percent of the men were sufficiently physically active for good health. In contrast, among those who were classified as receiving high levels of social support, about 65 percent of the women and 80 percent of the men were considered sufficiently active (Leslie et al., 1999).

Greater amounts of emotional support were also associated with greater levels of physical activity in a study of middle-aged and older women in the United States, even after adjusting for race/ethnicity, marital status, age, income and education (Eyler et al., 1999). Specifically, women who reported that their family and friends gave them little or no encouragement to exercise (a form of emotional support) were much more likely to be sedentary (defined as no participation in exercise, sports, or physically active hobbies in the past two weeks) than were women who reported medium or high levels of encouragement.

Few studies have looked at multiple types of social support for physical activity and then compared the influence of one type versus another. Thus little is known about the types of social support that are most related to physical activity participation.

In one study, however, multiple types of perceived social support were measured across an 18-week exercise program for middle-aged and older adults and then each type was examined in relation to participants' adherence to the program (Duncan, McAuley, Stoolmiller, & Duncan, 1993). The researchers found that as perceptions of emotional support increased (specifically, support that increased feelings of self-esteem and belongingness), so did adherence to the program. In contrast, greater perceptions of instrumental support (specifically, having someone to turn to for exercise information and advice) were not associated with greater adherence to the program. The authors also noted that the relationship between the different types of social support and adherence fluctuated over the course of the study. For example, emotional support was more strongly related to adherence toward the end of the program than at the beginning of the program. These results suggest that as exercisers' needs and coping abilities fluctuate over time, so do their social support requirements.

Another study compared the effects of instrumental and emotional support on exercise performance among patients who reported chronic pain (Patrick & D'Eon, 1996). In this study, spouses were asked to support and motivate their partners (i.e., the patients) while they performed an exercise bout on a stationary bicycle. The spouses' behavior was video-recorded and subsequently analyzed to determine the amount of emotional support (defined as expressions of caring such as smiling and touching) and instrumental support (defined as behaviors designed to facilitate the patient's optimal performance, such as monitoring the duration of the exercise bout) provided. Analyses revealed that the more emotional support a patient received while exercising, the longer he or she was able to continue cycling. There was no association between the amount of instrumental support received and exercise duration. Moreover, most patients said that they did not consider expressions of instrumental support to be positive, perhaps because they did not like to be reminded of how long they had been exercising. These results suggest that exercisers with chronic pain need emotional support more than they need instrumental support.

Based on the limited research comparing specific types of social support for exercise, it seems that the most effective type of support depends upon the exerciser's needs at a given point in time. These needs may vary as a function of changes in the exerciser's thoughts and feelings (e.g., changes in self-efficacy for exercising or changes in mood states) or changes in biophysical factors such as pain and disability. There is even some evidence to suggest that gender is related to exercisers' social support needs. In an exercise setting, self-esteem support may be more important to women than it is to men (Duncan, Duncan, & McAuley, 1993).

In short, a relationship between social support and physical activity has been demonstrated in a wide variety of populations (e.g., men and women, people of different ages, with varying racial and ethnic backgrounds) and using a wide variety of social support measures (e.g., number of social contacts, amount of encouragement, amount of companionship support). This suggests that the relationship between social support and physical activity is a powerful one.

Research on Individual and Group Influences on Exercise

In this section, we examine individuals and groups who provide social support as well as other forms of social influence over exercise. To determine the extent of different individual and group social influences on exercise, Carron, Hausenblas, and Mack (1996) conducted a quantitative review of 87 studies. From these studies, they identified four categories of people who could potentially affect thoughts, feelings, and behaviors relating to exercise. The four categories were: family (e.g., spouse, children), important others (e.g., non–family members such as physicians, friends, work colleagues), fitness instructors or other professionals within the exercise environment, and other exercise participants. The results of the reviewed studies were statistically combined to determine the overall effects (or "effect sizes") of social influence on exercise behavior, intentions to exercise, exercise attitudes and satisfaction, and self-efficacy. A summary of some of the results is presented in Exhibit 12.1. Guidelines for interpreting effect sizes are that .20, .50, and .80 represent small, medium, and large effect sizes (Cohen, 1992). As the exhibit shows, all of the effect sizes fell in the small to medium range, indicating that family members, important others, exercise class leaders, and class members do exert a modest amount of social influence over various aspects of exercise. In this chapter, we discuss these four sources of support and influence, along with the influence of co-exercisers and observers, as well as society.

THE FAMILY

Spousal Support

Among adults, the positive effects of a supportive spouse or partner on exercise behavior have been consistently demonstrated. For example, healthy married adults who joined a fitness program with their spouse

Selected results from Carron et al.'s (1996) quantitative analysis of the effects of important others, family members, class members, and the class leader on exercise-related behavior, thoughts, and feelings.

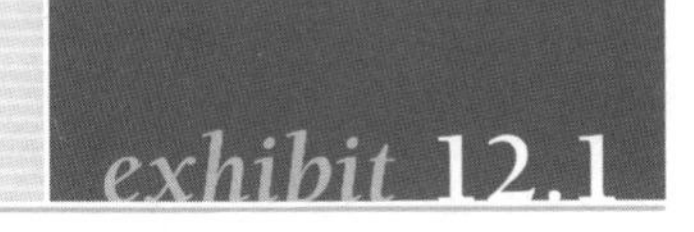

VARIABLES	NUMBER OF STUDIES	EFFECT SIZE
The influence of important others on		
Exercise adherence	21	.44
Exercise intentions	6	.44
Exercise attitudes and satisfaction	5	.63
The influence of family members on		
Exercise adherence	53	.36
Exercise intentions	27	.49
Exercise efficacy	3	.40
The influence of class members on		
Exercise adherence	22	.32
The influence of the exercise leader on		
Exercise adherence	9	.31

Source: Values are based on data presented by Carron et al. (1996).

had significantly better attendance and were less likely to drop out of the program than married people who joined without their spouse (Wallace, Raglin, & Jastremski, 1995). Another demonstration of the impact of spousal support comes from a landmark study in which exercise compliance and dropout rates were tracked for participants in a cardiac rehabilitation program (Erling & Oldridge, 1985). As is typical in the exercise compliance literature, approximately 48 percent of patients dropped out within their first six months of joining the program. However, an interesting phenomenon occurred when the exercise program opened its doors to the spouses of the cardiac patients, inviting them to exercise along with their husbands and wives at the rehabilitation center. Six months later, among those patients who had a spouse exercising with them, dropout rates had plummeted to 10 percent. Among those patients who had a spouse who did not exercise with them, the dropout rate was 33 percent. The large difference in dropout rates (10 percent vs. 33 percent) probably reflects the fact that patients who exercised with their spouses had more social support for exercise (emotional support and companionship support) than did those who did not exercise with their spouses.

Parental Support

Among children and youth, social support from parents and other family members has been identified as one of the most important determinants of participation in all forms of physical activity (e.g., competitive and recreational sports, structured exercise, active leisure; U.S. Department of Health and Human Services, 1996). Parental support is important to children's activity levels because parents can provide so many different types of instrumental support (e.g., organizing physical activities, providing transportation and equipment, paying activity fees), emotional support (e.g., encouraging their children), informational support (e.g., giving instruction on how to perform a new physical activity), and companionship support (e.g., playing with their children). Physically active parents may even provide validation support and influence activity patterns by serving as role models for their children, thus establishing norms for a physically active lifestyle.

The most common and most important types of family and parental support probably differ depending on the child's gender and age. Nonetheless, support from one's family is crucial to physical activity participation among boys and girls of all ages. Sallis, Prochaska, Taylor, Hill, and Geraci (1999) surveyed a national sample of 1,500 parents and children in Grades 4 through 12. In this cross-sectional study, they found that family support for physical activity was one of the strongest predictors of both boys' and girls' level of physical activity at all grade levels.

Thus far, we have talked about the effects of parental support on children's participation in various types of *physical activity,* rather than the effects of parental support on children's participation in *structured exercise.* Our discussion of physical activity (as opposed to exercise) reflects the fact that children tend to engage in physical activity through involvement in sports or active games (e.g., tag, skipping) rather than through structured exercise bouts. However, some children are prescribed exercise for the treatment or management of a medical condition. For these children, parental involvement and support can play a very important role in compliance with the prescription. For

THE BUCKETS © UFS. Reprinted by permission.

instance, a series of experiments examined the long-term effects of different diet and exercise interventions on childhood obesity (Epstein, Valoski, Wing, & McCurley, 1994). After 10 years, children who were part of a treatment that targeted their parents' eating and exercise behaviors as well as their own lost more weight than did children whose treatment targeted only their own behaviors. Presumably, children's compliance was best when their parents took part in the intervention with them because these children perceived the greatest amount of social support.

The Downside of Family Support

Sometimes, family support can deter physical activity. When family members pressure or pester their loved one to exercise, or make him or her feel guilty for not exercising, the person may actually respond in the opposite direction and exercise less (Lewis & Rook, 1999). The phenomenon whereby people respond in a direction opposite to the direction being advocated is known as **behavioral reactance.** Behavioral reactance may occur when individuals perceive significant others to be exerting social control, rather than providing social support. Because people generally do not like to be controlled by others (but they do like to be supported), they may try to reestablish a sense of control by doing the opposite of what is being asked of them. For example, a woman who likes to jog short distances for exercise might feel pressured by her husband to run faster and longer. If she perceives this pressure negatively—that her husband is trying to control and change her exercise regimen—she may react by doing the opposite of

■ behavioral reactance

her husband's request and give up jogging altogether. This would be an example of behavioral reactance. Of course, she could also perceive this pressure positively—that her husband is providing her with emotional support (encouragement) to work harder—and increase the intensity and duration of her workouts. Whether the woman considers the pressure to be **social control** or social support hinges on how she interprets and perceives the situation.

social control

overprotectiveness

Overprotectiveness is another example of the potential negative effects of social support on physical activity. We say that a person is being "overprotective" when he goes overboard in trying to protect another person from harm. Often, the overprotective person is perceived as being intrusive and controlling. For example, a person with a chronic disease or disability may have overprotective family members who insist on doing activities that the person can and should do for herself (e.g., walking to the store, doing light housework). By refusing to let the patient do these activities, they undermine her self-efficacy to be active in future situations (Berkhuysen, Nieuwland, Buunk, Sanderman, & Rispens, 1999), thus leading to a vicious cycle of inactivity and further physical decline.

Likewise, overprotective parents may limit their children's participation in physical activities that are perceived to have a high risk of injury due to physical contact (e.g., hockey, football), falls (e.g., in-line skating, snowboarding), and other potential hazards (e.g., cycling amid other vehicles). Some parents may be so concerned about their child's well-being that they discourage participation in these types of activities. A few parents may be so overprotective that they prevent their children from engaging in everyday physical activities such as jumping rope or climbing monkey bars, because they consider the potential for injury to be too great. On the other hand, we have all heard of parents who are *overly* encouraging and supportive of their children's sport and physical activity participation—signing them up for countless classes and lessons, yelling and screaming from the sidelines. Unfortunately, children often perceive such strong encouragement as parental pressure. A dislike of pressure has been cited as a reason for children's dropping out of physical activity programs (Gould, Feltz, Horn, & Weiss, 1982).

THE PHYSICIAN

Physicians and other health professionals have been identified as important sources of information support for people wishing to become more physically active. For example, in a survey of 2,300

Australians, those who were inactive were asked to choose their preferred source of advice on how to become more physically active. Advice from a doctor or health professional was preferred over all other listed sources, which included books, videotapes, and exercise groups (Booth, Bauman, Owen, & Gore, 1997). Similarly, in a population study of Canadians, nearly a quarter of those surveyed indicated that they looked to health professionals for advice on how to become physically active (CFLRI, 2000).

An increasing number of physicians are discussing the benefits of physical activity with their patients. Nonetheless, many still do not view exercise as a critical discussion topic—probably because exercise is not perceived as a treatment that has immediate effects on illness. Other physicians may recognize the importance of exercise, but they don't discuss it with their patients because they feel unqualified to perform exercise counseling and prescription (Pinto, Goldstein, DePue, & Milan, 1998). Even among physicians who do prescribe exercise, few spend more than three to five minutes on physical activity counseling (Lewis, Clancy, Leake, & Schwartz, 1991). Given the complexity of prescribing exercise and the many questions that patients may have regarding the prescription, five minutes is certainly not enough time to provide adequate information.

It is unfortunate that not all physicians counsel their patients to exercise. Just as Lakeisha took her physician's advice to exercise, many patients are willing to try exercising when it is recommended to them by a health-care professional. The impact of physician recommendations to exercise was examined in Project PACE (Patient-Centered Assessment and Counseling for Exercise). This study looked at the effects of brief physical activity counseling delivered to sedentary adults by physicians during a scheduled office visit (Calfas, Long, Sallis, Oldenburg, & French, 1996). Self-reported physical activity was measured before the office visit and four to six weeks later. At follow-up, patients who received PACE counseling increased their minutes of weekly walking by 38.1 compared with 7.5 among the control group. Additionally, 52 percent of the patients who received PACE counseling adopted "some" physical activity compared with just 12 percent of the control group.

Project PACE looked at the short-term effects of physician-based activity counseling. Subsequent studies have demonstrated that exercise advice from a family physician can also have longer-term effects on activity participation. For example, an Australian study found that adults who received verbal advice from a family physician regarding physical activity were more likely to be doing some physical activity at

6- and 12-month follow-ups than adults who did not receive advice (e.g., Bull & Jamrozik, 1998). As well, physician-based counseling may be particularly effective for promoting physical activity among older adults [for reference, see the PAL project, referred to in Pinto et al. (1998)], as older adults may be more inclined to heed a physician's advice than are younger adults (Rhodes et al., 1999).

THE EXERCISE CLASS LEADER

Exercise class leaders and other fitness professionals (e.g., personal trainers, fitness consultants) can have a powerful social influence on participants. Indeed, fitness leaders are often cited as the single most important determinant of an exerciser's continued participation in an exercise program (Franklin, 1988). The potent influence of fitness leaders is largely due to their ability to provide multiple types of social support. Fitness leaders are in a position to provide informational support regarding what exercises to do and how to do them, as well as emotional support (e.g., providing encouragement and praise), instrumental support (e.g., organizing fitness classes), and companionship support (e.g., a fitness instructor can distract exercisers from feelings of pain, fatigue, and boredom).

The social influence of personal trainers was demonstrated in a study of obese men and women. Participants in one group were each assigned a personal trainer who scheduled exercise sessions, made reminder phone calls to the participant before each session, and attended each session, working out alongside the participant. Another group of study participants was given the same exercise prescription, but not a personal trainer. At the end of the 18-month study, participants who had been assigned a personal exercise trainer attended more than twice as many exercise sessions as those who did not have a personal trainer (Jeffery, Wing, Thorson, & Burton, 1998).

The Importance of Leadership Style

A good exercise leader can have a positive social influence on exercisers and can contribute to increases in their self-efficacy, enjoyment, and motivation to exercise. Conversely, as Lakeisha found out at the start of this chapter, a bad leader can have a negative social influence on exercisers and may ultimately cause them to drop out of a fitness program. Given the potential effects of fitness professionals on exercise behavior, it is important to identify the characteristics that make a good exercise leader. To this end, exercise psychologists have conducted a series of experiments comparing the effects of two different exercise leadership styles (Fox, Rejeski, & Gauvin, 2000; Martin & Fox, 2001; Turner, Rejeski, & Brawley, 1997).

In these experiments, a single exercise instructor was trained to conduct one exercise class using a socially supportive leadership style, and to conduct another class using a socially bland leadership style. The supportive leadership style was characterized by the instructor providing exercisers with lots of social support in the form of encouragement, verbal reinforcement, and praise, and showing interest in the participants by addressing them by name and engaging them in casual conversation before and after the exercise session. In contrast, the bland leadership style was characterized by an absence of social support. In this condition, the leader verbally criticized exercisers who made mistakes, did not provide encouragement or praise, failed to address participants by name, and did not interact with them before or after the class.

These experiments showed that when compared with participants who experienced the bland leadership style, participants who experienced the socially supportive leadership style reported the following:

- Greater exercise self-efficacy
- More energy and enthusiasm
- Less post-exercise fatigue
- Less concern about embarrassing themselves and trying new things during the exercise class
- More enjoyment of the exercise class
- Stronger intentions to join an exercise class in the future

These results indicate that a socially supportive instructor can have very positive effects on participants' psychological responses to a *single* exercise class. Presumably, a socially supportive instructor would have similar positive effects on participants' long-term responses to exercise training *programs* and should promote better adherence to exercise than would an unsupportive instructor.

Although no studies have yet examined the effects of different leadership styles on adherence, preliminary research suggests that better instructors do promote better adherence. Bray and his colleagues (Bray, Gyurcsik, Culos-Reed, Dawson, & Martin, 2001) found that exercise initiates who were highly confident in their fitness instructor's communication, teaching, and motivating skills attended more classes in a 10-week fitness program than those who were not very confident in their instructor's skills. Characteristics that instilled confidence in participants included the leader's ability to provide appropriate and timely verbal cues that warned participants about upcoming moves (i.e., a form of informational support) and to provide exercisers with a good, intense workout (i.e., a form of instrumental support).

The Fitness Instructor as Role Model

Many people consider fitness professionals to be reliable sources of health and fitness information. Moreover, many exercisers, particularly those who are just starting an exercise program, look to fitness professionals as role models for their own health and fitness goals (Worsley, 1989). Given their potential social influence, fitness instructors must be aware of how their actions can affect other people. For example, instructors who exercise even when they are ill, or who spend exorbitant amounts of time at the gym, are sending a message to class members that it is okay to exercise excessively (see Chapter 9 for a discussion of exercise addiction). This certainly is not the message that fitness professionals should be conveying. Rather, they should be using their influence to promote healthy attitudes toward exercise.

To promote healthy exercise attitudes, a fitness instructor can

- Emphasize the importance of getting adequate rest between workouts and taking the time to fully recuperate when sick or injured
- Emphasize fitness and fun during exercise classes as opposed to fat and calorie burning
- Encourage participants to set realistic fitness and weight loss goals.

In addition, instructors need to know that for some exercisers, a few words of praise can be a powerful reinforcement that determines whether that person adheres or drops out of an exercise program. Thus, instructors should take the time to reinforce participants for improved exercise ability (e.g., increased intensity and duration) and regular program attendance (Martin & Hausenblas, 1998).

THE EXERCISE GROUP

A growing body of literature indicates that various aspects of exercise groups can serve to promote or to undermine exercise-related thoughts, feelings, and behavior. In this section we look at three aspects of the exercise group and their effects on exercise. These three aspects are group cohesion, group size, and group composition.

Group Cohesion

group cohesion

Group cohesion is defined as "a dynamic process reflected in the tendency of a group to stick together and remain united in the pursuit of its instrumental objectives and/or for the satisfaction of member affective needs" (Carron et al., 1998, p. 212). The Group Environment Questionnaire (GEQ; Carron, Brawley, & Widmeyer, 1998) and the Physical Activity Environment Questionnaire (PAEQ, see Exhibit 12.2; Estabrooks & Carron, 2000b) are the most frequently used measures of group cohesion in exercise and physical activity settings. These questionnaires measure how group members feel about social aspects of the group (e.g., their liking of group members, the extent to which they interact with members outside of the exercise setting) as well as task-related aspects of the group (e.g., their liking of group goals and activities). The GEQ and PAEQ assess group members' level of attraction to the social and task-related aspects of the group and group members' perceptions regarding how integrated they think the group is in terms of its social and task-related activities (see Exhibit 12.3 for a model of cohesion). From this standpoint, a cohesive exercise group would be one in which members are drawn to a common goal and are integrated around the pursuit of that goal and satisfying social interactions and communication.

Not surprisingly, cohesive exercise groups foster greater exercise adherence than do less cohesive exercise groups (Carron, Widmeyer, & Brawley, 1988). For example, in university-based exercise classes, members who score high on the GEQ measure of attractions to group-task (ATG-T) have been shown to attend more exercise classes and to be less likely to drop out of the program than members who score low on ATG-T (Spink & Carron, 1992, 1993, 1994). Furthermore, most of these university-based studies have found that ATG-T is the only GEQ dimension to distinguish between those who adhere and those who drop out. University-based studies have typically found no difference between adherers and dropouts on the other three GEQ dimensions, attractions to group-social (ATG-S), group integration-social (GI-S), and group integration-task (GI-T). In contrast, in a study conducted at a private health club, the two social dimensions of the GEQ (ATG-S and GI-S) were the only dimensions to distinguish adherers from dropouts (Spink & Carron, 1994). There were no differences between these two groups on the task-related dimensions of the GEQ (ATG-T, GI-T). Thus, whereas task cohesion plays a more important role than social cohesion in adherence to university-based exercise programs, the opposite may be true in private fitness clubs. These differences may reflect different motives for joining university versus private fitness centers. People who join private fitness clubs may be more motivated

exhibit 12.2 ***The Physical Activity Environment Questionnaire.***

Physical Activity Environment Questionnaire

PART A

The following questions are designed to assess your feelings about *your personal involvement* with your physical activity group. Using the following scale, please fill in a number from 1 to 9 to indicate your level of agreement with each of the statements. If you neither agree nor disagree, respond by using the number 5.

1	2	3	4	5	6	7	8	9
Very strongly disagree	*Strongly disagree*	*Disagree*		*Neither agree nor disagree*		*Agree*	*Strongly agree*	*Very strongly agree*

1. I like the amount of physical activity I get in this program.	① ② ③ ④ ⑤ ⑥ ⑦ ⑧ ⑨
2. This physical activity group is an important social unit for me.	① ② ③ ④ ⑤ ⑥ ⑦ ⑧ ⑨
3. I enjoy my social interactions within this physical activity group.	① ② ③ ④ ⑤ ⑥ ⑦ ⑧ ⑨
4. This physical activity group provides me with a good opportunity to improve in areas of fitness I consider important.	① ② ③ ④ ⑤ ⑥ ⑦ ⑧ ⑨
5. I like meeting the people who come to this physical activity group.	① ② ③ ④ ⑤ ⑥ ⑦ ⑧ ⑨
6. I am happy with the intensity of the physical activity in this program.	① ② ③ ④ ⑤ ⑥ ⑦ ⑧ ⑨
7. I like the program of physical activities done in this group.	① ② ③ ④ ⑤ ⑥ ⑦ ⑧ ⑨
8. If this program were to end, I would miss my contact with the other participants.	① ② ③ ④ ⑤ ⑥ ⑦ ⑧ ⑨
9. I enjoy new exercises done in this physical activity group.	① ② ③ ④ ⑤ ⑥ ⑦ ⑧ ⑨
10. In terms of the social experiences in my life, this physical activity group is very important.	① ② ③ ④ ⑤ ⑥ ⑦ ⑧ ⑨
11. This physical activity group provides me with good opportunities to improve my personal fitness.	① ② ③ ④ ⑤ ⑥ ⑦ ⑧ ⑨
12. The social interactions I have in this physical activity group are important to me.	① ② ③ ④ ⑤ ⑥ ⑦ ⑧ ⑨

Items 1, 4, 6, 7, 9, and 11 measure Attractions to Group-Task (ATG-T) Items 2, 3, 5, 8, 10, nd 12 measure Attractions to Group-Social (ATG-S).

The Physical Activity Environment Questionnaire is scored by calculating the average rating given for each of the subscales (i.e., for ATG-T, ATG-S, GI-T, and GI-S).

Continued. exhibit 12.2

Physical Activity Environment Questionnaire

PART B

The following questions are designed to assess your feelings about *your physical activity group as a whole.* Using the following scale, indicate your level of agreement with each of the statements. If you neither agree nor disagree, respond by using the number 5.

1	2	3	4	5	6	7	8	9
Very strongly disagree	*Strongly disagree*	*Disagree*		*Neither agree nor disagree*		*Agree*	*Strongly agree*	*Very strongly agree*

1. Members of our physical activity group often socialize during exercise time.	① ② ③ ④ ⑤ ⑥ ⑦ ⑧ ⑨
2. Our group is united in its beliefs about the benefits of the physical activities offered in this program.	① ② ③ ④ ⑤ ⑥ ⑦ ⑧ ⑨
3. Members of our physical activity group would likely spend time together if the program were to end.	① ② ③ ④ ⑤ ⑥ ⑦ ⑧ ⑨
4. Our group is in agreement about the program of physical activities that should be offered.	① ② ③ ④ ⑤ ⑥ ⑦ ⑧ ⑨
5. Members of our group are satisfied with the intensity of physical activity in this program.	① ② ③ ④ ⑤ ⑥ ⑦ ⑧ ⑨
6. Members of our group sometimes socialize together outside of activity time.	① ② ③ ④ ⑤ ⑥ ⑦ ⑧ ⑨
7. We spend time socializing with each other before or after our activity sessions.	① ② ③ ④ ⑤ ⑥ ⑦ ⑧ ⑨
8. Members of our group enjoy helping if work needs to be done to prepare for the activity sessions.	① ② ③ ④ ⑤ ⑥ ⑦ ⑧ ⑨
9. We encourage each other in order to get the most out of the program.	① ② ③ ④ ⑤ ⑥ ⑦ ⑧ ⑨

Items 2, 4, 5, 8, and 9 measure Group Integration-Task (GI-T). Items 1, 3, 6, and 7 measure Group Integration-Social (GI-S). The Physical Activity Environment Questionnaire is scored by calculating the average rating given for each of the four subscales (i.e., for ATG-T, ATG-S, GI-T, and GI-S).

Source: Estabrooks, P. A., & Carron, A. V. The physical activity group cohesion in exercise classes. *Group Dynamics, 4,* 230–243.

exhibit 12.3 *Conceptual model of group cohesion as measured by the GEQ and PAEQ.*

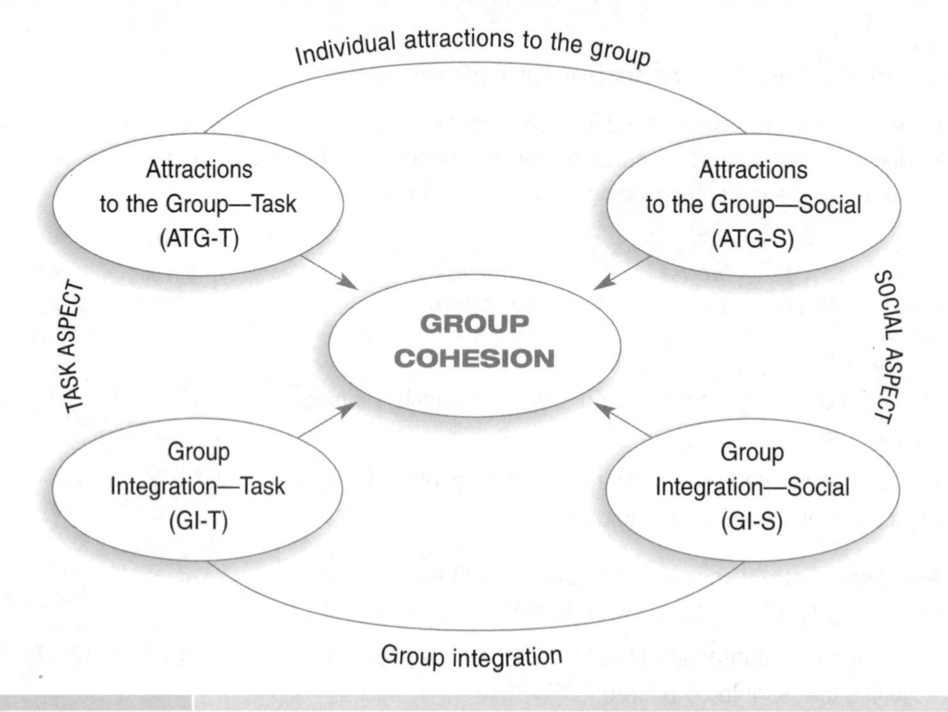

to exercise by the opportunity to meet new people and to socialize with others than are university-based exercisers.

Different types of cohesion (i.e., task vs. social) may be more or less important in different exercise settings (e.g., a university setting vs. a private health club). In any case, it is clear that feelings of cohesion are related to whether an individual adheres to an exercise program. Interestingly, Carron, Hausenblas, and Mack (1996) have noted that task cohesion may be a more important influence on exercise adherence than all of the sources listed in Exhibit 12.1. Carron et al. (1996) calculated the overall effects of task cohesion on exercise adherence across six different studies and obtained an effect size of .62. This effect size is larger than any of the effect sizes shown in Exhibit 12.1. When they calculated the effect of social cohesion across four different studies, the effect size was much smaller—only .25. These results suggest that given the potent effects that cohesion—particularly task cohesion—has on adherence, interventions that increase feeling of group cohesion among exercisers could go a long way in improving exercise adherence. In the discussion that follows, we present what studies have shown regarding three important questions concerning group cohesion.

1. How can feelings of cohesion be increased in exercise classes? Carron and Spink (1993) developed a team-building intervention to improve cohesion among exercise class participants. The intervention utilized five group dynamics principles that have been shown to increase group cohesiveness:

a. *Develop feelings of distinctiveness among group members.* Creating a group name or group uniform can help to create a sense of group identity and a sense of "we" among group members that makes them feel distinct from non–group members.

b. *Assign group roles and/or positions.* Giving group members responsibilities for particular tasks (e.g., distributing equipment) fosters greater interdependence among group members. Also, having members choose their own spot in which to stand during the class, or using specific places in the class for low-, medium-, and high-impact exercisers contributes to the development of a more stable group structure.

c. *Establish group norms.* The establishment of group norms includes adopting a common goal (e.g., completing 20 minutes of continuous aerobic activity) and a common work ethic among group members (such as, "We keep our feet moving even if we are too tired to keep up with the exercise"). Essentially, the group develops a common set of behavioral expectations for group members. The establishment of group norms, combined with a stable group structure, contributes to a stronger sense of "we," greater conformity, and ultimately greater cohesiveness.

d. *Provide opportunities to make sacrifices for the group.* When individuals make sacrifices to the group, such as agreeing to shorten the aerobic workout time on some days so that the group may have a longer abdominal workout, their commitment to the group increases and their cohesiveness is enhanced.

e. *Provide opportunities for interaction.* Increasing task and social interactions during the class leads to increased perceptions of cohesion. Task interactions can consist of exercises that require participants to "buddy up" with a partner. Examples of social interactions would be introducing class members to one another or asking participants to "high-five" the person next to them at the end of the class.

2. What are the benefits of the team-building intervention? The preceding intervention was developed in collaboration with a group of university program fitness instructors who then applied the strategies in their exercise classes (Carron & Spink, 1993). Eight weeks later, the GEQ was administered to exercisers in these classes (experimental condition), as well as to exercisers whose instructors did not apply the intervention (control condition). Exercisers who were part of the experimental condition had significantly greater ATG-Task scores than did exercisers who were part of the control group. There were no significant differences on any of the other GEQ subscale scores. When Spink and Carron (1993) implemented their team-building intervention in another university fitness setting, there were fewer dropouts in the experimental group (20 percent) than in the control group (33 percent). Carron and Spink's team-building intervention has also been used with exercise classes for older adults, where similar positive effects on exercise adherence have been found (Brawley, Rejeski, & Fox, 2000; Estabrooks & Carron, 1999). Taken together, these results indicate that a team-building intervention implemented by the class instructor provides an easy and effective way to improve exercise adherence among people of all ages.

3. How does cohesion foster adherence? The exact mechanisms by which cohesion enhances adherence are not known, however, some possible mechanisms have been suggested. One possibility is that more cohesive groups foster more positive attitudes toward class attendance (Courneya & McAuley, 1995); people may simply feel more positively about exercising in cohesive groups because these groups provide greater social support and interaction than do less cohesive groups. According to the theory of planned behavior (see Chapter 3), more positive attitudes should spur stronger exercise intentions, and ultimately greater exercise participation.

A second possibility is that more cohesive groups generate greater self-efficacy in their group members than do less cohesive groups (Estabrooks & Carron, 2000a). For example, highly cohesive exercise groups may provide their members with more efficacy-enhancing verbal persuasion (such as encouraging comments like "You can do it!"). As discussed in Chapter 3, verbal persuasion is a source of self-efficacy. People who have greater exercise self-efficacy adhere better to exercise programs than do those who have low exercise self-efficacy.

Group Size

As the number of people in an exercise class increases, perceptions of group cohesiveness decrease (Carron & Spink, 1995), as does satisfaction with the exercise experience (Carron, Brawley, & Widmeyer, 1990). Presumably, bigger exercise groups result in more crowding and fewer opportunities for participants to interact with one another. Hence, enjoyment and cohesion are diminished.

Physical Environment Influences

In this chapter we examine the role of *social* influences on exercise-related thoughts, feelings, and behaviors. To supplement this discussion, let's take a look at some *environmental* influences on exercise.

Temperature: There are probably few people who would enthusiastically choose to exercise in extreme heat. Studies of swimmers have shown that as the temperature of the pool increases, ratings of enjoyment decrease (Berger & Owen, 1992). Similarly, warmer room temperatures have been associated with reports of greater tension, fatigue, and negative mood during exercise (Hansen, Stevens, & Coast, 2001).

Music: Many people say that they enjoy exercising to music. No wonder—research suggests that music can enhance positive feelings derived from the physical activity experience—except when the exercise is of a very high intensity (Brownley, McMurray, & Hackney, 1995; Steptoe & Cox, 1988).

Mirrors: Mirror, mirror, on the wall, who's the fittest of them all? Gym mirrors can help people to perfect their technique when lifting weights or trying new aerobics moves. Highly active women report greater feelings of exercise self-efficacy after exercising in front of a mirror than after exercising without a mirror (Katula & McAuley, 2001). However, for inexperienced exercisers, exercising in front of a mirror may actually lead to an increase in negative mood (Martin, Jung, & Gauvin, in press).

Odors: Some smells in the gym may actually improve your performance. The application of peppermint odor in an exercise environment has been shown to reduce exercisers' perceptions of effort and frustration (Raudenbush, Meyer, Eppich, 2002). Inhaling peppermint may also improve performance on tasks requiring strength, such as pushups and sprinting (Raudenbush, Corley, Eppich, 2001).

Perceptions of the instructor can also be affected by group size. The same aerobics instructor taught a large class (150 to 200 participants), a medium-sized class (50 to 80), and a small class (20 to 30) using the exact same routine, music, instructions, and level of enthusiasm (Prossin & Carron, 1989). At the end of each class, participants rated the instructor on several dimensions including her effectiveness as a role model, her personableness, her use of feedback, and her general teaching style. Although a panel of fitness instructors observed and confirmed that the aerobic instructor's behavior was exactly the same across all three classes, participants in the medium-sized class rated the instructor less favorably than did participants in the other two classes.

To explain this curvilinear relationship between class size and instructor evaluation, Carron (1990) suggested that the instructor's role is clearest—for both the instructor and the participant—in the largest and the smallest classes. In large classes, participants expect the leader to use a group-oriented approach (i.e., instructors address and reinforce the group as a whole, rather than individual members), and this is the approach that most instructors do indeed use with large classes. In small classes, participants expect, and usually receive, a more individual-oriented approach (i.e., addressing and reinforcing individual members within the group rather than the group as a whole). In medium-sized classes, however, it may be unclear whether a group- or individual-oriented approach is best. Thus, there may be discrepancies between the approach expected by participants and the approach used by the instructor. Perception of these discrepancies could manifest as dissatisfaction with the instructor. In addition, because instructors may be unsure about how to approach a medium-sized class, they may use both styles inconsistently. Such inconsistency in leadership style could also contribute to dissatisfaction with the instructor.

Group Composition

The effects of group composition on exercise-related thoughts, feelings, and behaviors are not as well studied as other aspects of the exercise group, such as size and cohesion. Nonetheless, there is some evidence to suggest that characteristics of the people who make up the exercise group can affect responses to the exercise experience.

Gender makeup. Gender makeup is one group composition factor that can affect an exerciser's comfort level. Like Lakeisha, women often report that they feel uncomfortable in exercise centers where male exercisers are in the majority. Women in cardiac rehabilitation programs, for example, have reported that they feel out of place and a "curiosity" in exercise programs that are dominated by men (Benson, Arthur, & Rideout, 1997). In response to these feelings, some hospitals have established separate programs for female cardiac patients. Similarly, many private health clubs offer fitness classes for women only. We are unaware of any studies that have examined men's level of comfort in exercise classes that are dominated by women (e.g., aerobic dance classes). However, we wonder if there are men who would *like* to participate in aerobic dance and other predominantly female exercise classes, but who avoid them because they don't want to be seen as an "oddity."

Similarity of oneself to other group members. Whether one feels similar to other group members can affect comfort level and motivation. Obese people, for example, indicate that they prefer to exercise in groups of other obese people (Bain, Wilson, & Chaikind, 1989), and their adherence may be compromised if they are required to exercise with non-obese individuals (Treasure, Lox, & Lawton, 1998). Likewise, people generally want to exercise with others of similar ability. Feeling markedly less competent than other group members can deplete an exerciser's self-confidence and motivation.

Group member enthusiasm. The enthusiasm of group members can affect responses to the exercise experience. Fox et al. (2000) randomly assigned people who had never done step aerobics before to exercise in a class comprised of participants who were either enthusiastic, encouraging of one another, and socially interactive (enriched condition), or unenthused, not encouraging of one another, and not socially interactive (bland condition). Not surprisingly, after the exercise class, participants in the enriched condition reported greater enjoyment of the exercise bout and stronger future intentions to join an exercise group than those in the bland condition.

However, participants in the enriched condition also reported greater worries about embarrassing themselves and being evaluated by members of the exercise group (Martin & Fox, 2001). Among these first-time exercisers, it seems that encouragement and attention from other group members elicited feelings of self-consciousness and anxiety. These findings suggest that exercise initiates may be more comfortable when the presence of other exercisers is downplayed. Thus, in the early stages of an exercise program for novices, it may be beneficial to focus on helping the exerciser to master exercise skills before introducing any type of team-building intervention that would draw attention to individual participants, such as having exercisers "buddy up" and work out together. As exercisers become more confident in their physical abilities, worries about social evaluation and attention probably dissipate, and an interactive, supportive exercise environment becomes an appealing and welcome feature.

CO-EXERCISERS AND OBSERVERS

Even when people are not part of an actual exercise group or class, other individuals in their exercise environment (e.g., the person riding a stationary bike next to them at the gym, the people they pass while jogging through a park) can influence exercise behavior. In this section, we look at the influence of co-exercisers (i.e., people we exercise with) and observers on exercise effort and exertion.

Actual Effort

In a clever study, Worringham and Messick (1983) secretly timed solitary joggers as they ran alone along a path. Unknown to the joggers, the researchers had asked a young woman to stand alongside the jogging path. In one condition, the young woman was instructed to watch as the jogger ran by. In the other condition, she was instructed to turn her back when the jogger came by. It was found that both male and female joggers increased their speed when the woman was watching them, but did not increase their speed when the woman had her back turned to them.

social facilitation ■

The phenomenon in which people increase their effort and performance when others are watching them is known as **social facilitation.** Numerous explanations have been put forth to explain social facilitation. In this context, a likely explanation is that the joggers picked up their pace because they wanted to make a good impression on the female observer.

Self-Reported Effort

The presence of others and the desire to make a good impression can influence an exerciser's self-reported effort. For instance, people report lower ratings of perceived exertion (RPE) when they exercise next to a person who gives the impression that the exercise is very easy than when they exercise alone (Hardy, Hall, & Prestholdt, 1986). Presumably, people want to create the impression that they are just as fit as the people exercising around them. Hence, they may be reluctant to admit that they find a workout to be more strenuous than does the person next to them. Similarly, in exercise-testing situations involving very heavy workloads, men have been shown to report lower RPEs when a woman conducts the test than when a man conducts the test (Boutcher, Fleischer-Curtian, & Gines, 1988). The desire to impress the opposite sex is probably what prompts these men to claim that an objectively hard workout does not actually *feel* all that difficult.

Of course there are dangers associated with trying to create good impressions in exercise settings, whether through putting forth extra effort or claiming that a workout isn't very strenuous when it really is. Some people may exert themselves too strenuously when others are watching, resulting in exhaustion, muscle strain, heat stroke, or even death. People have indeed injured themselves by lifting too much weight at the gym, and in one study these injured parties subsequently indicated that they overlifted because they were concerned that others would perceive them as weak if they reduced the amount of weight already set on a machine or bench (Martin & Leary, 2001). Similarly, in his paper on impression management in sport and exercise, Leary (1992) tells of an acquaintance who died of heat-related complications during a 10K race. The runner refused to quit, arguing that because he had boasted to his friends and coworkers of running in the race, he could not face them if he didn't finish. In this case, his concerns about making a good impression literally killed him.

SOCIETY

Broadly conceived, the term "society" refers to a group of people who form a single community on the basis of sharing some common characteristic, such as living in the same geographical region (e.g., "western society"), having the same occupation (e.g., "The Law Society of Upper Canada") or sharing the same leisure interests (e.g., "The Dead Poets Society"). The term "culture" refers to the values, customs, norms, rules, and beliefs that are held by members of a particular society. With regard to physical activity, two aspects of culture that represent social influences on physical activity are *norms* and *stereotyped beliefs*.

Norms for Physical Activity

■ norm

A **norm** is a pattern of behaviors or beliefs generally held by members of a particular group (or "society"). Within a given society, norms for physical activity can be reflected by a variety of factors, such as the value that members place on physical activity (e.g., do they believe that it is important to be physically active?), the amount of resources dedicated to helping people be physically active (e.g., the availability of public exercise facilities), and the visibility of physically active individuals (e.g., is it typical or "normal" to see people outside exercising?). According to the theory of planned behavior (see Chapter 3), norms have an impact on exercise behavior through their effect on behavioral intentions. That is, people will have greater intentions to be physically active if they perceive societal or cultural expectations and encouragement to be active, than if they do not.

An excellent example of the impact of cultural norms on physical activity can be seen by comparing physical activity rates of older adults living in North America with those of older adults living in China. In Canada and the United States, cultural norms for physical activity among the elderly are not particularly positive. Physical activity among older adults is often considered inappropriate, without benefit, or even dangerous (O'Brien Cousins, 2000). Although efforts have been made

exhibit 12.4

In China, cultural norms for older exercisers are very positive.

in recent years to change these normative beliefs, American and Canadian surveys still indicate that less than a third of men and women over the age of 65 are sufficiently active to derive health benefits (Canadian Fitness and Lifestyle Research Institute, 2000; U.S. Department of Health and Human Services, 1996). In China, however, nearly 40 percent of men and women aged 66 to 75 are considered physically active (China National Sports Council, 1997). This difference in participation rates between North American and Chinese elderly may reflect differences in norms for physical activity among the aged. Unlike North Americans, the Chinese have a long tradition of exercise and physical activity among older adults. Every morning, in cities and towns across China, large groups of older adults can be seen performing tai chi quan (a traditional form of Chinese exercise) and other exercises in public parks and squares, on streets and sidewalks—virtually anywhere that provides sufficient space (see Exhibit 12.4). In addition, more than 200,000 elderly physical activity associations throughout China provide physical activity opportunities for older people, including swimming, dancing, and tai chi quan (Hong & Lu, 1999). Clearly, the Chinese have more positive normative beliefs about the appropriateness of exercise for the elderly than do North Americans. These differences are reflected in the higher physical activity participation rates seen in Chinese society.

Stereotyped Beliefs

stereotypes ■ **Stereotypes** are beliefs—true or false—about the characteristics of people who belong to a particular group. They represent our general expectations or preconceptions for people in that group and are generalized to almost all of the group's members. With regard to physical activity and exercise, stereotypes about the type of people who engage in certain activities can shape our attitudes and our intentions regarding participation in those activities. For example, the stereotyped belief that weight training is a "man's activity" has been cited as a deterrent to older women's participation in strength training (Khoury-Murphy & Murphy, 1992). This is unfortunate because strength training has been identified as an important strategy for reducing the risk of fractures associated with **osteoporosis** (American College of Sports Medicine, 1995)—a disease that afflicts one in three women over the age of 50 and is characterized by low bone mass and deterioration of bone tissue (National Osteoporosis Society, 2000). Some exercise programmers have noted that they must first change women's stereotyped beliefs about strength training before they can convince them to adopt a strength-training regimen. Such changes have been accomplished through strategies that involve challenging inaccurate beliefs about strength training (such as, "weight training will masculinize my body," "weight training is done by sweaty men in sweaty gyms"), and "feminizing" the exercise training environment (e.g., by decorating the fitness center in soft colors and using pastel colored weights; Khoury-Murphy & Murphy, 1992).

■ osteoporosis

In addition to having stereotyped beliefs about the people who engage in specific activities, members of different societal groups may have stereotypes about exercisers and nonexercisers in general. Indeed, studies have shown that North American university students hold very negative stereotypes for nonexercisers and consider them to be lazy and sloppy, with poor self-control (Martin & Leary, in press; Martin, Sinden, & Fleming, 2000). In contrast, university students hold highly positive stereotypes for exercisers, and consider them to be very attractive people who are also intelligent, highly sociable, and hard working. We should note that these stereotypes may be unique to predominantly Caucasian, middle-class university students. People who belong to other segments of society (e.g., older adults, those with less education or who are less affluent) may not hold the same stereotypes for exercisers and nonexercisers. Nonetheless, it has been suggested that for those people who do hold these stereotypes, some of them may be motivated to exercise simply to avoid the negative stereotypes associated with being a "couch potato."

Practical Recommendations

This chapter has provided information regarding how people can influence one another's physical activity behavior. This information can be applied to promote both the initiation and long-term maintenance of a physical activity program in a number of ways.

First, exercisers should be encouraged to seek out support from others. Keeping in mind that there are different types of social support, exercisers should be encouraged to identify people in their lives who can provide them with the types of support that they need most (e.g., informational support, companionship support). It is important to note that some people find it difficult to ask others for help, either because they are afraid the other person will say no, or because they do not want to burden the other person. In such cases, these people could be encouraged to find a buddy who also wants help in changing a health habit (e.g., exercising, quitting smoking). Knowing that they are *giving* support to someone may make these people more comfortable about *seeking* support from that person.

Second, people who are in a position of social influence should take every opportunity to encourage and promote physical activity, as their words and actions can have a potent effect on others' activity behavior. For instance, ideally, all family physicians (as well as chiropractors, osteopaths, physiotherapists, and so on) should discuss and prescribe physical activity with each and every patient. Likewise, parents should act as positive role models and be physically active with their children on a regular basis. There is, of course, a fine balance between encouraging and pressuring a person to become physically active. When exerting social influence, it is important not to belittle people or make them feel guilty for not exercising. These actions could result in the person giving up exercise altogether.

Third, interventionists can apply several strategies to improve the social aspects of the exercise environment. For instance, the fitness leader can work to develop a positive, socially supportive leadership style. Attending leadership seminars, seeking out feedback from class participants and fitness leaders, or videotaping and reviewing oneself teaching an exercise class can help in this effort. The social environment may also be improved through the team-building techniques discussed in this chapter to build a more cohesive group. The use of these strategies can help to create a more comfortable group exercise environment that may prevent exercisers like Lakeisha from quitting group exercise programs.

Finally, if physical activity is to become commonplace among all members of society, then there is a need to change some of the cultural norms and stereotypes associated with it. For example, there needs to be a shift from viewing exercise programs for seniors as "unusual," as this normative belief creates the impression that exercise is not a normal part of an older person's lifestyle. If every community had a seniors fitness program in place (like the Chinese model), physical activity among seniors would be seen as the norm, and more older people would likely be physically active.

Conclusion

Researchers have identified several sources of social support and other types of social influence on physical activity. These sources include the family, the physician (and other health-care professionals), the exercise class leader, the exercise group, co-exercisers and observers, and society. For better or for worse, these groups and individuals can have a potent impact on our own exercise behavior.

On the positive side, people such as family members and health-care professionals may provide social support. This support can take many forms, including instrumental support, emotional support, informational support, companionship support, and validation. Other people within the exercise context, such as the fitness leader and other exercisers, can also exert a positive social influence by building a supportive, cohesive exercise environment. All of these constructive behaviors can lead to more positive exercise-related thoughts, feelings, and behaviors.

On the negative side, people who are trying to be socially supportive may actually come across as controlling, overprotective, or exerting excessive pressure. When supportive behavior is perceived in this negative light, the recipient of the behavior may react by decreasing his level of physical activity or quitting an activity program altogether. Likewise, aspects of the fitness leader's behavior—such as being overly critical—and characteristics of the exercise group—such as poor cohesion—may result in more negative thoughts and feelings toward exercise participation, and ultimately poorer adherence.

What Do You Know?

1. Briefly describe two ways in which social support can be operationalized.
2. Identify and describe the five main types of social support.
3. Describe two factors that may influence the type of social support an exerciser needs.
4. What is "behavioral reactance"?
5. Why might physician-based activity counseling be a particularly effective way of promoting physical activity among adults?
6. Describe the characteristics of a socially supportive leadership style and three benefits that exercisers experience from being exposed to this style.

7. Define group cohesion.
8. Describe three strategies that can be used to increase perceptions of group cohesion in an exercise class.
9. What is the relationship between group size and exercise adherence?
10. Describe two aspects of group composition that can affect exercise-related thoughts, feelings, and behaviors.
11. Provide an example of the social facilitation phenomenon in group exercise settings.
12. How might cultural norms affect physical activity behavior?

Learning Activities

1. Create a table with six columns. In the first column, list all of the sport, recreation, and exercise programs, clubs, and activities that you have participated in throughout your life. At the top of the remaining five columns, write down the five main types of social support. Now, for each activity you listed, indicate the people who provided you with each type of social support and the things that they did or said to give you that support. Do you see any patterns in the table? Have you needed certain types of support more than others? Has one individual provided more support than others? Have your needs for certain types of support changed over time?

2. Imagine that you are in charge of 50 students living in a college residence. You have been asked to develop a "Get Fit, Stay Active" program for these students. Given what you now know about social influences and physical activity, devise a plan to use social influence to get your students physically active.

3. Test the social influence effects of co-exercisers. In a quiet part of a gym, ask 10 classmates to perform as many sit-ups as they can in a 60-second period. Be sure that each person performs the task without anyone else observing. After all 10 people have completed the task, calculate the average number of sit-ups performed, but do not tell this number to your classmates. Now, ask 10 additional classmates to do the 60-second sit-up task all together, in a group. Calculate the average number of sit-ups that were performed by members of this group. Is there a difference in the two results?

References

Alcock, J. E., Carment, D. W., & Sadava, S. W. (1991). *A textbook of social psychology* (2nd ed.). Scarborough, ON: Prentice Hall.

American College of Sports Medicine. (1995). Osteoporosis and exercise. *Medicine and Science in Sport and Exercise, 27,* 1–7.

Bain, L. L., Wilson, T., & Chaikind, E. (1989). Participant perceptions of exercise programs for overweight women. *Research Quarterly for Exercise and Sport, 60,* 134–143.

Benson, G., Arthur, H., & Rideout, E. (1997). Women and heart attack: A study of women's experiences. *Canadian Journal of Cardiovascular Nursing, 8,* 16–23.

Berger, B. G., & Owen, D. R. (1992). Preliminary analysis of a causal relationship between swimming and stress reduction: Intense exercise may negate the effects. *International Journal of Sport Psychology, 23,* 70–85.

Berkhuysen, M. A., Nieuwland, W., Buunk, B. P., Sanderman, R., & Rispens, P. (1999). Change in self-efficacy during cardiac rehabilitation and the role of perceived overprotectiveness. *Patient Education and Counseling, 38,* 21–32.

Booth, M. L., Bauman, A., Owen, N., & Gore, C. J. (1997). Physical activity preferences, preferred sources of assistance, and perceived barriers to increased activity among physically inactive Australians. *Preventive Medicine, 26,* 131–137.

Boutcher, S. H., Fleischer-Curtian, L. A., & Gines, S. D. (1988). The effects of self-presentation on perceived exertion. *Journal of Sport and Exercise Psychology, 10,* 270–280.

Brawley, L. R., Rejeski, W. J., & Fox, L. D. (2000). A group mediated cognitive-behavioural intervention for increasing adherence to physical activity in older adults. *Journal of Applied Biobehavioural Research, 5,* 47–65.

Bray, S. R., Gyurcsik, N. C., Culos-Reed, S. N., Dawson, K. A., & Martin, K. A. (2001). An exploratory investigation of the relationship between proxy efficacy, self-efficacy and exercise attendance. *Journal of Health Psychology, 6,* 425–434.

Brownley, K. A., McMurray, R. G., & Hackney, A. C. (1995). Effects of music on physiological and affective responses to graded treadmill exercise in trained and untrained runners. *International Journal of Psychophysiology, 19,* 193–201.

Bull, F. C., & Jamrozik, K. (1998). Advice on exercise from a family physician can help sedentary patients to become active. *American Journal of Preventive Medicine, 15,* 85–94.

Calfas, K. J., Long, B. J., Sallis, J. F., Oldenburg, B., & French, M. (1996). Mediators of change in physical activity following an intervention in primary care: PACE. *Preventive Medicine, 26,* 73–81.

Canadian Fitness and Lifestyle Research Institute. (1999). *Physical Activity Monitor.* Ottawa, ON. Author.

Carron, A. V. (1990). Group size in sport and physical activity: Social psychological and performance consequences. *International Journal of Sport Psychology, 21,* 286–304.

Carron, A. V., Brawley, L. R., & Widmeyer, W. N. (1990). The impact of group size in an exercise setting. *Journal of Sport and Exercise Psychology, 12,* 376–387.

Carron, A. V., Brawley, L. R., & Widmeyer, W. N. (1998). The measurement of cohesiveness in sports groups. In J. L. Duda (Ed.), *Advances in sport and exercise psychology measurement* (pp. 213–226). Morgantown, WV: Fitness Information Technology.

Carron, A. V., Hausenblas, H. A., & Mack, D. (1996). Social influence and exercise: A meta-analysis. *Journal of Sport and Exercise Psychology, 18,* 1–16.

Carron, A. V., & Spink, K. S. (1993). Team building in an exercise setting. *The Sport Psychologist, 7,* 8–18.

Carron, A. V., & Spink, K. S. (1995). The group size-cohesion relationship in minimal groups. *Small Group Research, 26,* 86–105.

Carron, A. V., Widmeyer, W. N., & Brawley, L. R. (1988). Group cohesion and individual adherence to physical activity. *Journal of Sport and Exercise Psychology, 10,* 127–138.

China National Sports Council. (1997). *Report on China mass sports survey.* Beijing: Author.

Cohen, J. (1992). A power primer. *Psychological Bulletin, 112,* 155–159.

Courneya, K. S., & McAuley, E. (1995). Cognitive mediators of the social influence–exercise adherence relationship: A test of the theory of planned behaviour. *Journal of Behavioural Medicine, 18,* 499–515.

Duncan, T. E., Duncan, S. C., & McAuley, E. (1993). The role of domain and gender-specific provisions of social relations in adherence to a prescribed exercise regimen. *Journal of Sport and Exercise Psychology, 15,* 220–231.

Duncan, T. E., McAuley, E., Stoolmiller, M., & Duncan, S. C. (1993). Serial fluctuations in exercise behaviour as a function of social support and efficacy cognitions. *Journal of Applied Social Psychology, 23,* 1498–1522.

Epstein, L. H., Valoski, A., Wing, R. R., & McCurley, J. (1994). Ten-year outcomes of behavioural family-based treatment for childhood obesity. *Health Psychology, 13,* 373–383.

Erling, J., & Oldridge, N. B. (1985). Effect of a spousal-support program on compliance with cardiac rehabilitation. *Medicine and Science in Sports and Exercise, 17,* 284.

Estabrooks, P. A., & Carron, A. V. (1999). Group cohesion in older adult exercisers: Prediction and intervention effects. *Journal of Behavioural Medicine, 22,* 575–588.

Estabrooks, P. A., & Carron, A. V. (2000a). Predicting self-efficacy in elderly exercisers: The role of task cohesion. *Journal of Aging and Physical Activity, 8,* 41–50.

Estabrooks, P. A., & Carron, A. V. (2000b). The physical activity group environment questionnaire: An instrument for the assessment of cohesion in exercise classes. *Group Dynamics, 4,* 230–243.

Eyler, A. A., Brownson, R. C., Donatelle, R. J., King, A. C., Brown, D., & Sallis, J. F. (1999). Physical activity social support and middle- and older-aged minority women: Results from a U.S. survey. *Social Science and Medicine, 49,* 781–789.

Fox, L. D., Rejeski, W. J., & Gauvin, L. (2000). Effects of leadership style and group dynamics on enjoyment of physical activity. *American Journal of Health Promotion, 14,* 277–283.

Franklin, B. A. (1988). Program factors that influence exercise adherence: Practical adherence skills for the clinical staff. In R. K. Dishman (Ed.), *Exercise adherence: Its impact on public health* (pp. 237–258). Champaign, IL: Human Kinetics.

Gould, D., Feltz, D., Horn, T., & Weiss, M. (1982). Reasons for attrition in competitive youth swimming. *Journal of Sport Behaviour, 5,* 155–165.

Hansen, C. J., Stevens, L. C., & Coast, J. R. (2001). Exercise duration and mood state: How much is enough to feel better? *Health Psychology, 20,* 267–275.

Hardy, C. J., Hall, E. G., & Presholdt, P. H. (1986). The mediational role of social influence in the perception of exertion. *Journal of Sport Psychology, 8,* 88–104.

Hibbard, J. H. (1988). Age, social ties and health behaviors: An exploratory study. *Health Education Research, 3,* 131–139.

Hong, Y., & Lu, Y. (1999). Physical activity and health among older adults in China. *Journal of Aging and Physical Activity, 7,* 247–250.

Jeffery, R. W., Wing, R. R., Thorson, C., & Burton, L. R. (1998). Use of personal trainers and financial incentives to increase exercise in a behavioural weight-loss program. *Journal of Consulting and Clinical Psychology, 66,* 777–783.

Katula, J. A., & McAuley, E. (2001). The mirror does not lie: Acute exercise and self-efficacy. *Journal of Behavioral Medicine, 8,* 319–326.

Khoury-Murphy, M., & Murphy, M. D. (1992). Southern (bar)belles: The cultural problematics of implementing a weight training program among older Southern women. *Play and Culture, 5,* 409–419.

Leary, M. R. (1992). Self-presentational processes in exercise and sport. *Journal of Sport and Exercise Psychology, 14,* 339–351.

Leslie, E., Owen, N., Salmon, J., Bauman, A., Sallis, J. F., & Lo, S. K. (1999). Insufficiently active Australian college students: Perceived personal, social, and environmental influences. *Preventive Medicine, 28,* 20–27.

Lewis, C. E., Clancy, C., Leake, B., & Schwartz, J. S. (1991). The counseling practices of internists. *Annals of Internal Medicine, 114,* 54–58.

Lewis, M. A., & Rook, K. S. (1999). Social control in personal relationships: Impact on health behaviours and psychological distress. *Health Psychology, 18,* 63–71.

Martin, K. A., & Fox, L. D. (2001). Group and leadership effects on social anxiety experienced during an exercise class. *Journal of Applied Social Psychology, 31,* 1000–1016.

Martin, K. A., & Hausenblas, H. A. (1998). Psychological commitment to exercise and eating disorder symptomatology among female aerobic instructors. *The Sport Psychologist, 12,* 180–190.

Martin, K. A., Jung, M. E., & Gauvin, L. (in press). To see or not to see: The effects of exercising in mirrored and unmirrored environments on women's mood states. *Health Psychology.*

Martin, K. A., & Leary, M. R. (2001). Self-presentational determinants of health risk behaviour among college freshmen. *Psychology and Health, 16,* 17–27.

Martin, K. A., & Leary, M. R. (in press). Single, female, physically active: Effects of exercise status and body weight on stereotyped perceptions of young women. *Journal of Personality and Social Behavior, 16.*

Martin, K. A., Sinden, A. R., & Fleming, J. C. (2000). Inactivity may be hazardous to your image: The effects of exercise participation on impression formation. *Journal of Sport and Exercise Psychology, 22,* 283–291.

National Osteoporosis Society. (2000). Osteoporosis [On-line]. Available: www.nos.org.uk/default.asptends.

O'Brien Cousins, S. (2000). My heart couldn't take it: Older women's beliefs about exercise benefits and risks. *Journals of Gerontology, 55B,* 283–294.

Patrick, L., & D'Eon, J. (1996). Social support and functional status in chronic pain patients. *Canadian Journal of Rehabilitation, 9,* 195–201.

Pinto, B. M., Goldstein, M. G., DePue, J. D., & Milan, F. B. (1998). Acceptability and feasibility of physician-based activity counseling: The PAL project. *American Journal of Preventive Medicine, 15,* 95–102.

Prossin, A. J., & Carron, A. V. (1989). *The effects of fitness class size on the participants' perception of the leader.* Unpublished manuscript, University of Western Ontario.

Raudenbush, B., Corley, N., & Eppich, W. (2001). Enhancing athletic performance through the administration of peppermint odor. *Journal of Sport and Exercise Psychology, 23,* 156–160.

Raudenbush, B., Meyer, B., & Eppich, W. (2002). The effects of odors on objective and subjective measures of athletic performance. *International Sports Journal, 6,* 14–27.

Rhodes, R. E., Martin, A. D., Taunton, J. E., Rhodes, E. C., Donnelly, M., & Elliot, J. (1999). Factors associated with exercise adherence among older adults: An individual perspective. *Sports Medicine, 28,* 397–411.

Sallis, J. M., Prochaska, J. J., Taylor, W. C., Hill, J. O., & Geraci, J. C. (1999). Correlates of physical activity in a national sample of girls and boys in grades 4 through 12. *Health Psychology, 18,* 410–415.

Spink, K. S., & Carron, A. V. (1992). Group cohesion and adherence in exercise classes. *Journal of Sport and Exercise Psychology, 14,* 78–86.

Spink, K. S., & Carron, A. V. (1993). The effects of team building on the adherence patterns of female exercise participants. *Journal of Sport and Exercise Psychology, 15,* 39–49.

Spink, K. S., & Carron, A. V. (1994). Group cohesion effects in exercise classes. *Small Group Research, 25,* 26–42.

Steptoe, A., & Cox, S. (1988). Acute effects of aerobic exercise on mood. *Health Psychology, 7,* 329–340.

Treasure, D. C., Lox, C. L., & Lawton, B. R. (1998). Determinants of physical activity in a sedentary, obese female population. *Journal of Sport and Exercise Psychology, 20,* 218–224.

Turner, E. E., Rejeski, W. J., & Brawley, L. R. (1997). Psychological benefits of activity are influenced by the social environment. *Journal of Sport and Exercise Psychology, 19,* 119–130.

U.S. Department of Health and Human Services. (1996). *Physical activity and health: A report of the Surgeon General.* McLean, VA: International Medical Publishing.

Wallace, J. P., Raglin, J. S., & Jastremski, C. A. (1995). Twelve month adherence of adults who joined a fitness program with a spouse vs. without a spouse. *Journal of Sports Medicine and Physical Fitness, 35,* 206–213.

Wills, T. A., & Shinar, O. Measuring perceived and received social support. In S. Cohen, L. G. Underwood, & B. H. Gottlieb (Eds.), *Social support measurement and intervention* (pp. 86–135). New York: Oxford University Press.

Worringham, C. J., & Messick, D. M. (1983). Social facilitation of running: An unobtrusive study. *Journal of Social Psychology, 121,* 23–29.

Worsley, A. (1989). Perceived reliability of sources of health information. *Health Education, 4,* 367–376.

Chapter 13

Body Image and Exercise

June is 19 years old and a college sophomore. Until she went away to college, June trained and competed in dance and gymnastics. An attractive girl, June was often told that much of her success in these activities was due to the appeal of her "all-American good looks." Since retiring from competition two years ago, June has gained 10 pounds, but she is still of average weight for her 5 foot, 2 inch frame. Nonetheless, whenever she looks in the mirror, June sees herself as overweight. She is constantly saying things to herself like "I hate my body," and "My hips are too fat," and "What good are you anyway?" Some days, she feels so bad about herself that it takes all of her effort just to get out of bed. Although June's favorite outfits used to consist of fitted jeans and t-shirts, lately she prefers to wear baggy sweat suits that hide the shape of her body. One of June's friends suggests that she might feel better if she exercised more regularly. However, June feels too embarrassed about her body to put on shorts and a t-shirt and attend an exercise class.

June's story is typical of a woman with a poor or disturbed body image. Historically, body image and body image disturbance have been considered issues that affect only young women. Yet today, body image disturbance is on the rise among both men and women of all ages. This is a significant health concern, because body image disturbance may be associated with poorer psychological well-being (e.g., increased risk for depression and eating disorders) and a greater likelihood of engaging in behaviors that put one's physical health at risk (e.g., smoking, over-exercising, or not exercising at all). Given these health concerns, exercise psychologists are interested in understanding how exercise interventions help to improve body image, and how body image can affect physical activity participation.

KEY TERMS

- affective/emotional dimension
- avoidance behaviors
- behavioral dimension
- body composition
- body ideal
- body image
- body image disturbance
- body reality
- bulimia nervosa
- cognitive dimension
- healthy body image
- lifestyle behaviors
- perceptual dimension

Body Image Defined

body image ■ **Body image** is a multidimensional construct that reflects how we see our own body, and how we think, feel, and act toward it. Thus, body image is generally defined in terms of four dimensions—perceptual, cognitive, affective, and behavioral.

perceptual dimension ■ The **perceptual dimension** reflects the picture of our own body that we form in our mind. It is how we see our bodies when we look in a mirror and how we imagine ourselves to look—thin or fat, short or tall, muscular or lean, and so on. How we perceive or think that we look is not necessarily the same as how we actually look. As June's story demonstrates, some people may perceive themselves as overweight when they look in a mirror even though they are actually of average weight or even underweight.

cognitive dimension ■ The **cognitive dimension** of body image reflects how we think about or evaluate our body in terms of both its appearance and function. This includes beliefs regarding the attractiveness, strength, and fitness of the body and its various parts, the extent to which we focus on our bodies, and the things we say to ourselves about our bodies.

affective/emotional dimension ■ The **affective** or **emotional dimension** of body image reflects feelings experienced in relation to the body's appearance and function. People may experience positive feelings about the body such as comfort and pride, or negative feelings such as anxiety, shame, and disgust.

behavioral dimension ■ Finally, the **behavioral dimension** represents things we do that reflect our positive or negative perceptions, thoughts, and feelings about our bodies, such as the types of clothing we wear and the activities we choose to engage in.

Healthy Body Image Versus Body Image Disturbance

healthy body image ■ A **healthy body image** is reflected in positive self-evaluations along the four body image dimensions. Individuals with a healthy body image have accurate perceptions about their body shape and size, have thoughts and feelings about their body that are predominately positive, and behave in ways that reflect these positive evaluations. In contrast, body image disturbance ■ **body image disturbance** is evidenced when the individual has negative self-evaluations along any or all of the body image dimensions. Along the perceptual dimension, body image disturbance is indicated when perceptions of one's body shape and size differ from one's actual shape and size. Along the cognitive and affective dimensions, negative thoughts and feelings about one's body are indicative of disturbance. And along the behavioral dimension, actions performed to hide or change the body would be evidence of body image disturbance.

Traditionally, body image disturbance has been seen as a "women's issue." However, times are changing. In 1973, *Psychology Today* magazine reported that 15 percent of men and 25 percent of women were dissatisfied with their appearance. In 1986, it reported that 34 percent of men and 38 percent of women were dissatisfied. In the magazine's 1997 survey, 43 percent of men and 56 percent of women were dissatisfied with their appearance. These data indicate that body image dissatisfaction has increased dramatically among both genders and that over the past three decades, body image disturbance has become almost as common among men as it is among women.

FACTORS IN BODY IMAGE FORMATION AND DISTURBANCE

Body image reflects an interplay between our body reality and our body ideal. **Body reality** refers to our actual physical characteristics—height, weight, body fat, lean body mass, bone structure, fitness, strength, disease, and so on. **Body ideal** refers to how we think our body should look and function. When people's body reality and body ideal are the same or very similar, they usually have a positive, healthy body image. But when people perceive their body reality to be worse than their body ideal—for example, when they judge their bodies to be fatter than they think they should be—this judgment often results in negative thoughts, feelings, perceptions, and behaviors that are indicative of body image disturbance.

- body reality
- body ideal

Where do body ideals come from? A healthy body ideal is derived from a recognition that human bodies naturally come in a wide range of shapes and sizes and that genetic factors are instrumental in determining one's weight and shape. Because there are limits to how much one can override genetic predispositions for body shape and size, and limits to how much one can reshape the body through diet and exercise (Brownell, 1991), it would be absurd for everyone to have the same body ideal. Rather, each individual's body ideal should reflect a realistic level of health and fitness for one's own unique and personal body shape.

Media Influence

Unfortunately, in our society personal body ideals tend to be displaced by media-driven body ideals. Instead of celebrating a range of body ideals, the media promotes a very strict and narrowly defined image of the ideal

FOR BETTER OR FOR WORSE © UFS. Reprinted by permission.

body, particularly for women and increasingly so for men. Many people fail to realize that these ideals are unrealistic and unattainable for the vast majority of the population. The predominance of "perfect" bodies in television, magazines, movies, and videos perpetuates the misconception that the bodies of fashion models and movie stars are the norm.

Cultural Influences

Cultural body ideals generally reflect those glamorized in the media. However, people who are part of ethnic groups that reject the media ideal have healthier body images than do those who belong to groups that endorse the media ideal. Indeed, studies have shown that although African American women are, on average, heavier than Caucasian American women, African Americans have less of a discrepancy between their perceived and ideal body size and less body dissatisfaction than their Caucasian counterparts (Harris, 1994; Rucker & Cash, 1992). These differences are probably the result of differences in culture-bound values regarding the relative importance of thinness and the acceptance of heavier, more rounded body shapes. Such positive values result in a healthier and more realistic body ideal and ultimately, better body image among women who identify with African American culture than among those who identify with Caucasian American culture (Abrams, Allen, & Gray, 1993).

Activity Participation

The activities that we choose to participate in can influence body image by altering perceptions of the body ideal. For example, women who participate in bodybuilding have a greater acceptance of bulkier, more muscular female body shapes, despite the divergence of these shapes from cultural body ideals (Furnham, Titman, & Sleeman, 1994). Likewise, men who participate in bodybuilding have a body ideal that is considerably more hypertrophic (i.e., has greater muscle mass) than the ideal of men who participate in other sports (Blouin & Goldfield, 1995). Whether these ideals are a cause or an effect of participating in bodybuilding is unclear. Nonetheless, continued participation in activities that endorse a particular body ideal can lead the participant to adopt the ideal for that activity and to reject the media or cultural ideal. If the new ideal is more realistic than the media ideal, body image can improve as the discrepancy between body ideal and body reality becomes narrower. However, if the new ideal is even *less* realistic and *less* attainable, the gap between body ideal and reality will widen and body image disturbance will increase. For example, male bodybuilders—who have a very unnatural, hypertrophic body ideal—were found to be more dissatisfied with their bodies than men who participated in sports where the body ideal was closer to that of the media ideal (see Blouin & Goldfield).

Changes to Body Reality

Across the lifespan, the body grows and alters in size, shape, proportion, and function. These changes can have a profound effect on feelings about oneself and one's body. For example, the growth of facial hair may be a source of pride for a pubescent boy who is eager to take on the appearance of a man. In contrast, a woman who undergoes a mastectomy as part of cancer treatment may be devastated by the loss of her breast, and feel that she is no longer attractive and womanly. Among older adults, age-related changes in body reality—such as the graying of hair and the wrinkling of skin—can also affect body image (Martin, Leary, & Rejeski, 2000). Thus, not surprisingly, body image is important to people of all ages (Pliner, Chaiken, & Flett, 1990)—not just young adults.

GENDER DIFFERENCES IN BODY IMAGE DISSATISFACTION

Men and women who are dissatisfied with their bodies usually have opposite reasons for their dissatisfaction. Most women are dissatisfied because they want to be thinner in terms of their overall body weight. Most men who are dissatisfied want to be heavier in terms of having more lean muscle mass.

Gender differences in body dissatisfaction reflect differences between the male and female body image ideals that are glamorized by the media and endorsed by Westernized culture. These ideals set the standard of female bodily attractiveness as ultra-thin, shapely, toned, and firm. The male standard is considered the V-shaped physique: broad, muscular shoulders, toned "six-pack" abdominals, a narrow waist, and muscular legs. What many people don't realize, however, is that these two "ideals" are physiologically unattainable for a vast majority of the population (Brownell, 1991). Moreover, for women in

Range of actual and desired body weight of male college sample compared to cultural and medical standards.

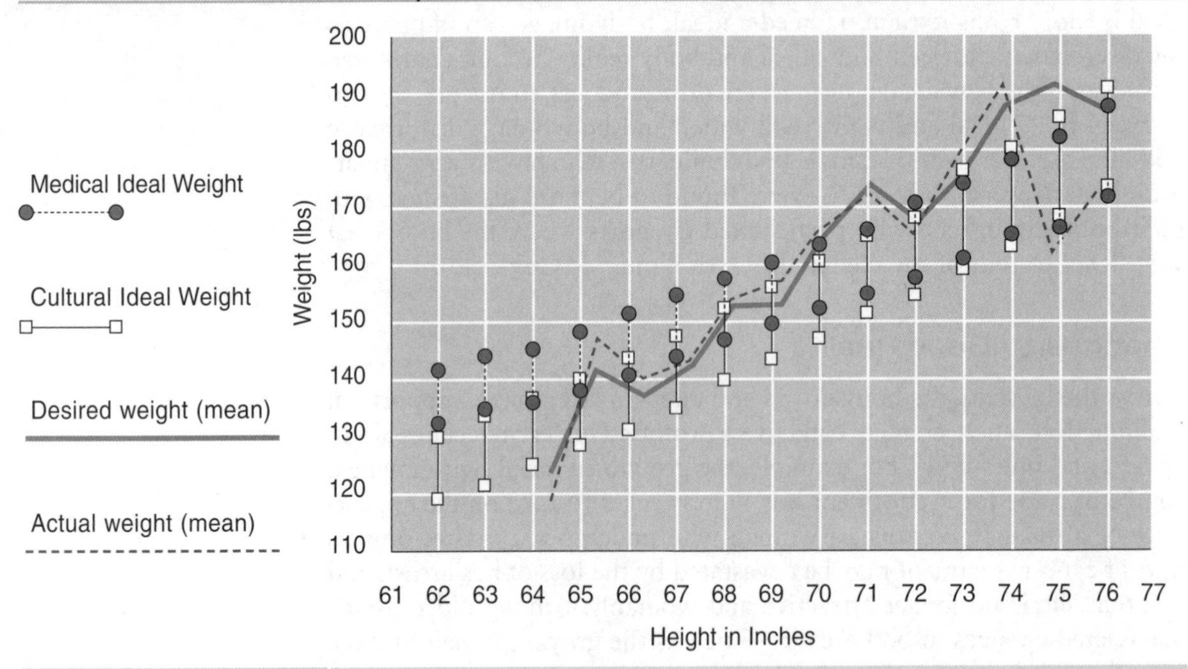

Range of actual and desired body weight of female college sample compared to cultural and medical standards. exhibit 13.2

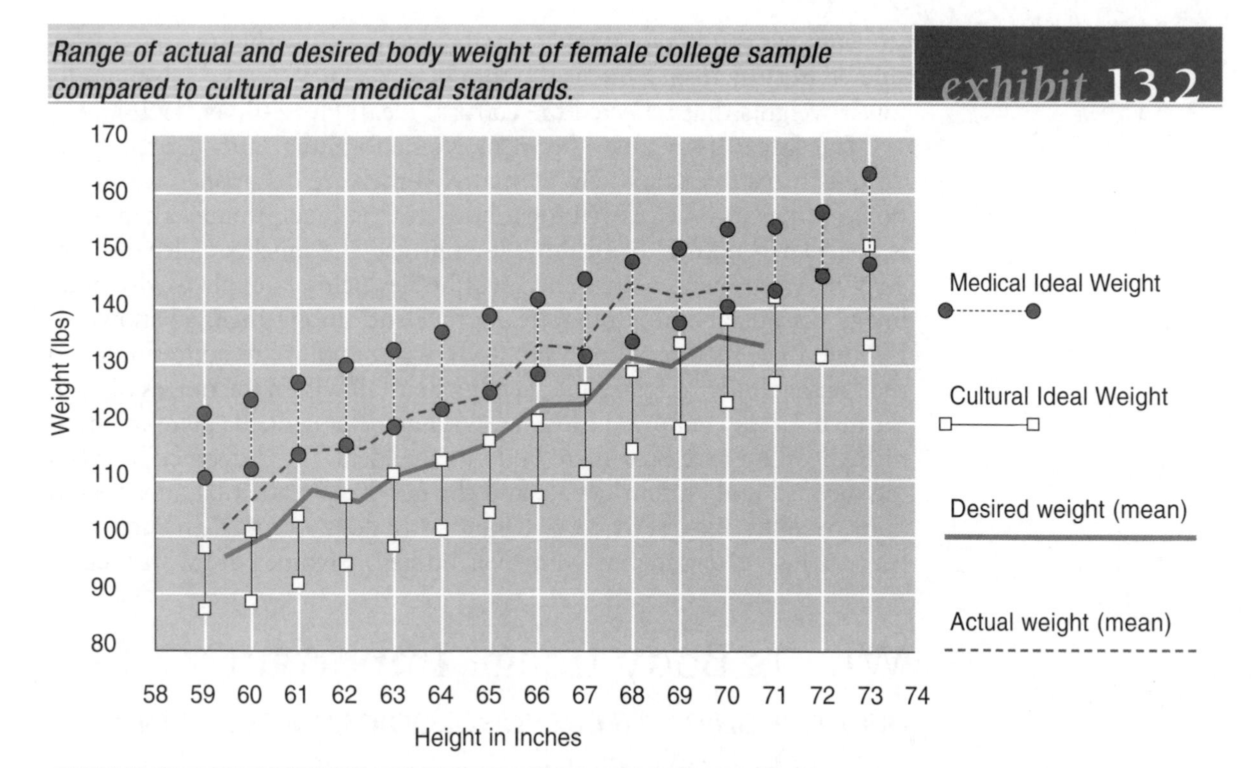

From *Am I Thin Enough Yet? The Cult of Thinness and the Commercialization of Identity* by Sharlene Hesse-Biber, copyright © 1996 by Oxford University Press, Inc. Used by permission of Oxford University Press, Inc.

particular, the ultra-thin ideal is very much in opposition to the medical ideal of what constitutes a healthy body (Hesse-Biber, 1996).

Exhibits 13.1 and 13.2 show the discrepancy between the cultural and medical body ideals, and how actual and desired weights compare to these ideals. The values signifying the cultural ideal represent the desirable or "ideal" weights recommended by commercial diet centers in the United States for people with an average-sized frame. The values signifying the medical ideal were drawn from the Metropolitan Life Insurance Company's 1983 height and weight charts for men and women (Metropolitan Life Insurance Company, 2001). They represent the weights at which mortality rates are the lowest for a person with a medium-sized frame. Exhibit 13.1 shows that for men, there is very little difference between the cultural and medical ideals, although the cultural ideal weighs slightly less. But Exhibit 13.2 shows that for women, there is virtually no overlap between the medical and the cultural weight ideals—the cultural ideal weighs less. Furthermore, the solid and dotted lines on Exhibit 13.2 show that in a sample of college students, women's *actual* body weights were well within the range considered healthy from a medical standpoint, yet they *desired* substantially lower weights that reflected the cultural ideal (Hesse-Biber, 1996).

The large discrepancy between women's actual and desired body weights helps to explain why so many women are dissatisfied with their bodies; many women yearn for a body that is much thinner than what is considered natural or healthy. In contrast, the much smaller discrepancy between men's actual and ideal bodies helps to explain why body image dissatisfaction is not yet as prevalent among men; as shown in Exhibit 13.1, men tend to desire body weights that are quite similar to their actual body weights, and weights that fall within the ranges of both the medical and cultural ideals. Yet with increasing media glamorization of the lean and well-cut male body image ideal, the difference between the medical and cultural ideals and the gap between actual and desired body weights may start to widen. If this does occur, then men may become just as dissatisfied with their bodies as women are with theirs.

Why Is Body Image Important?

RELATIONSHIP WITH PSYCHOLOGICAL WELL-BEING

A healthy body image is related to better psychological well-being in at least two ways: better self-esteem and lowered risk for depression and anxiety.

Self-Esteem

Numerous studies have shown a positive correlation between body image satisfaction and self-esteem (Miller & Downey, 1999), indicating that people who feel better about their bodies tend to feel better about themselves overall. This relationship is much stronger for women than it is for men, as a woman's feelings of self-worth are more strongly influenced by her perceived physical attractiveness than are a man's (Rodin, Silberstein, & Striegel-Moore, 1985).

Depression and Anxiety

A poor body image has been associated with greater anxiety and depressive symptomatology (Cohen & Esther, 1993; Kirkcaldy, Eysenck, Furnham, & Siefen, 1998), particularly among women. Specifically, depressed and anxious individuals view their appearance more negatively than do nondepressed and nonanxious individuals, despite no differences between these groups' actual body shape or size. It is unknown, however, whether depression and anxiety lead to body image disturbance, or whether body image disturbance leads to depression and anxiety.

RELATIONSHIP TO PHYSICAL WELL-BEING

Body image is also related to physical well-being, insofar as it can affect one's tendency to engage in health-damaging and health-promoting behaviors.

Health-Damaging Behaviors

Eating disorders and unhealthy weight control strategies. Body image disturbance has been identified as a risk factor for the development of eating disorders and is a key feature of eating disorder symptomatology (Polivy & Herman, 2002). A review of more than 60 studies found that women diagnosed with eating disorders reported greater body image dissatisfaction and more distorted body image perceptions than the general population (Cash & Deagle, 1997). Body image disturbance is also a risk factor for relapse after successful eating disorder treatment. In one study, patients who were successfully treated for **bulimia nervosa** (an eating disorder characterized by binge eating and excessive compensatory behaviors) but who retained negative attitudes toward their body shape and weight were more likely to relapse over a one-year period than were those who developed a more positive body image (Fairburn, Peveler, Jones, & Hope, 1993).

"Before you try on any bathing suit, you're required to sign this waiver releasing us from liability should you incur permanent damage to your self-esteem."

CLOSE TO HOME © 1996 John McPherson. Reprinted with permission of Universal Press Syndicate.

■ bulimia nervosa

Body image disturbance can also lead to dieting and other unhealthy weight-loss methods such as fasting, purging, excessive exercising, the use of laxatives and diet pills, and steroid use among men who want to increase their lean muscle mass. A study conducted at the Centers for Disease Control in Atlanta, Georgia, reported that in 1997, 3.7 percent of young men in Grades 9 to 12 had used steroids at least once. Although nearly half of these men were using steroids to improve their sports performance, just as many were using steroids to change their physical appearance (Centers for Disease Control, 1997).

Smoking. Many smokers (particularly women and adolescents) report that they smoke to maintain or lose weight. Thus, body image concerns may lead some people to start smoking or to continue smoking (Wiseman, Turco, Sunday, & Halmi, 1998). However, a longitudinal study of nearly 4,000 men and women between the ages of 18 and 30 found that over a seven-year period, smokers and nonsmokers gained the same amount of weight (Klesges et al., 1998). Apparently, smoking is not as effective a weight management strategy as many people believe.

Health-Promoting Behaviors

On the positive side, body image concerns may prompt people to take better care of their health (Heinberg, Thompson, & Matzon, 2001). A diet or exercise program may be initiated for the primary goal of changing one's body reality and body image, but a secondary benefit may be health improvements associated with eating more healthfully and being more physically active.

Measurement

Exercise psychologists are interested in understanding the relationship between exercise behavior and body image. But in order to study this relationship, we need valid and reliable measures of all four dimensions of body image (i.e., perceptual, cognitive, affective, and behavioral). Although many more body image measures exist than can be discussed in this chapter, some of the most common approaches to measuring body image are described next. For an excellent overview of body image measures used by exercise psychologists, see Bane and McAuley (1998).

PERCEPTUAL MEASURES

Perceptual measures of body image assess the level of accuracy of judgments about the size of one's body parts or the body as a whole. Body-part procedures require individuals to indicate the perceived width of a particular body part. For example, with the adjustable light beam apparatus approach (Thompson & Thompson, 1986), four light beams are projected simultaneously onto a wall. Respondents are then asked to adjust the light beams to match the *perceived* width of their cheeks, waist, hips, and thighs. The *actual* width of the respondent's body parts is then measured. A ratio is calculated comparing actual width with perceived width. This ratio indicates the degree to which the person overestimates or underestimates his or her body size and reflects the accuracy of the body image perceptions. Body-part estimation can also be done by simply asking participants to mark their body widths on a sheet of paper attached to a wall. Again, perceived widths are compared with actual body-part widths and the ratio of over- or underestimation is calculated.

For assessing whole-body perceptions, a commonly used technique requires individuals to view a range of real-life photographic or videotaped images of themselves that have been morphed (modified) to appear larger or smaller than actual body size. From the array of images, respondents are asked to choose the one that best represents their actual body size. The difference between what people think they look like and what they actually look like represents the accuracy of their body-size perception. For both the body-part and the whole-body perception tests, when individuals perceive themselves to be different from their actual size, this is evidence of body image disturbance.

COGNITIVE MEASURES

Of the four dimensions of body image, there are more measures of the cognitive dimension than any other. Measures of the cognitive dimension typically consist of questionnaires that assess the degree of satisfaction with one's body shape, size, and function, and attitudes, beliefs, and thoughts about one's body shape, size, and function.

Degree of satisfaction is usually measured by presenting respondents with a list of various body parts (chest, legs, etc.) or aspects of physical function (energy level, strength, etc.) and asking them to rate their level of satisfaction or dissatisfaction with each item on the list. The Body Esteem Scale (Franzoi & Shields, 1984) is an example of this type of measure.

Another way in which satisfaction is measured is by presenting respondents with a series of drawings that represent a range of possible body shapes and sizes, from very thin to very overweight, such as the drawings presented in Exhibit 13.3. Respondents are asked to choose the drawing they think best represents their current size and the drawing that best represents their ideal size. The discrepancy between the two chosen figures is taken as an indication of body size dissatisfaction.

Attitudes, beliefs, and thoughts about one's body are typically measured using a series of questionnaire items. The Multidimensional Body–Self Relations Questionnaire (MBSRQ; Cash, Winstead, & Janda, 1986) is an excellent example of this type of measure. The most comprehensive cognitive measure of body image, the MBSRQ consists of 10 subscales that assess body image cognitions related to the body's appearance, health, and physical functioning.

exhibit 13.3 ***Line drawings used as a cognitive measure of body image.***

Respondents are asked to choose the drawing they think best represents their current size and the drawing that best represents their ideal size. The discrepancy between the two chosen figures is taken as an indication of body size dissatisfaction.

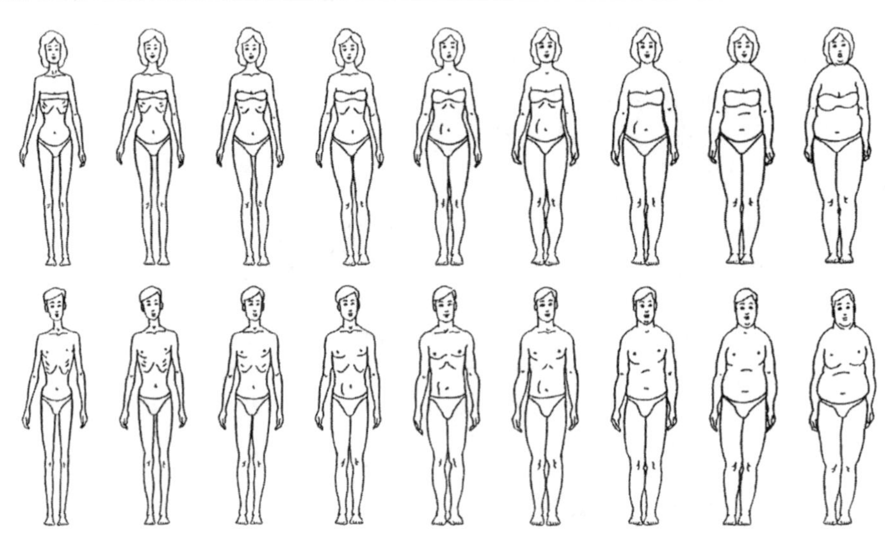

Source: From Thompson, M. A. and Gray, J. J. (1995) Development and validation of a new body assessment scale. *Journal of Body Assessment,* 64(2), 263. Reprinted with permission of Lawrence Erlbaum Associates, Inc.

AFFECTIVE MEASURES

In contrast to the multitude of cognitive and perceptual measures of body image that are available, there are relatively few measures of the affective dimension. Affective measures assess feelings such as worry, shame, anxiety, comfort, embarrassment, and pride in relation to the body. Greater negative feelings are associated with greater body image disturbance. An example of an affective measure is the Body Shape Questionnaire (BSQ; Cooper, Taylor, Cooper, & Fairburn, 1987), which assesses how often people feel concerned or worried about their body. The questionnaire contains items such as "How often do you feel fat after eating?" and "How often do you cry because you dislike your body?" The Social Physique Anxiety Scale (SPAS; Hart, Leary, & Rejeski, 1989), another affective measure of body image that has been used extensively in exercise psychology research, is a questionnaire that assesses the level of anxiety that people experience when other people evaluate or "check out" their body. The nine-item version of the SPAS is shown in Exhibit 13.4.

Another affective aspect of body image—body comfort—can be measured using a body focus procedure (Butters & Cash, 1987). This procedure requires participants to examine their body in a full-length, three-panel mirror for 30 seconds and then to indicate their level of comfort.

Social Physique Anxiety Scale (nine-item version).

exhibit 13.4

Read each of the following statements carefully and indicate the degree to which the statement is characteristic or true of you, according to the following scale:

1 = Not at all characteristic of me

2 = Slightly characteristic of me

3 = Moderately characteristic of me

4 = Very characteristic of me

5 = Extremely characteristic of me

1. I wish I wasn't so uptight about my physique/figure.	① ② ③ ④ ⑤
2. There are times when I am bothered by thoughts that other people are evaluating my weight or muscular development negatively.	① ② ③ ④ ⑤
3. Unattractive features of my physique/figure make me nervous in certain social settings.	① ② ③ ④ ⑤
4. In the presence of others, I feel apprehensive about my physique/figure.	① ② ③ ④ ⑤
5. I am comfortable with how fit my body appears to others.	① ② ③ ④ ⑤
6. It would make me uncomfortable to know others were evaluating my physique/figure.	① ② ③ ④ ⑤
7. When it comes to displaying my physique/figure to others, I am a shy person.	① ② ③ ④ ⑤
8. I usually feel relaxed when it is obvious that others are looking at my physique/figure.	① ② ③ ④ ⑤
9. When in a bathing suit, I often feel nervous about the shape of my body.	① ② ③ ④ ⑤

(*Note:* The SPAS is scored by reverse-scoring items 5 and 8 and then summing the scores for all items. Higher scores indicate greater social physique anxiety.)

Adapted from E. A. Hart, M. R. Leary, and W. J. Rejeski, 1989. The measurement of social physique anxiety, *Journal of Sport & Exercise Psychology, 11*(1), 98. Reprinted with permission.

BEHAVIORAL MEASURES

Of the four dimensions of body image, the behavioral dimension has the fewest measures. Measures of the behavioral component assess the frequency with which one engages in activities that might be indicative of body image disturbance. These activities fall into two general categories: avoidance behaviors and lifestyle behaviors (Rosen, Srebnik, Saltzberg, & Wendt, 1991).

avoidance behaviors

Avoidance behaviors are actions performed to divert attention away from the body or to prevent other people from seeing one's body. Examples include wearing baggy clothes, shunning social events, and avoiding physical or sexual intimacy.

lifestyle behaviors

Lifestyle behaviors are actions performed with the goal of altering the body or that reflect extensive body image concern. Examples include restrained eating or dieting, excessive exercising, exercising only for the purpose of losing weight (as opposed to improving health), using steroids, weighing oneself repeatedly, and seeking out cosmetic surgery to alter one's appearance.

Both categories of behavior are generally measured using questionnaires that ask participants to self-report the frequency with which they engage in these behaviors. Sometimes, it may also be possible to obtain direct measures (rather than self-report measures) of these activities. For example, it may be possible to observe and record the type of clothing that a person wears to an aerobics class as a direct behavioral index of that person's body image. However, there has been very little development of valid and reliable direct approaches to measure these behaviors.

Research on Body Image and Exercise

Given the importance of body image to psychological and physical well-being, it is important to develop strategies to improve body image. Exercise psychologists can play an important role in this endeavor by studying the effects of exercise on body image and using this information to develop body image–enhancing exercise interventions.

EXERCISE CAN IMPROVE BODY IMAGE

In a comprehensive review of exercise interventions, Martin and Lichtenberger (2002) concluded that exercise training can lead to significant improvements in body image. Although both aerobic exercise (e.g., jogging, swimming) and weight training have been shown to improve body image, weight training seems to have more potent effects. Differences in

Exercise Versus Psychological Interventions for Improving Body Image

Cognitive behavior therapy (CBT), a type of psychological intervention, has been used successfully to improve body image (Butters & Cash, 1987; Grant & Cash, 1995). In general, CBT consists of strategies such as relaxation training, cognitive restructuring, stress management, and desensitization procedures that individuals are trained to use to improve their thoughts, feelings, perceptions, and behaviors toward their bodies.

One study has shown that exercise may be just as effective as CBT for improving body image. Fifty-four women who scored very low on a measure of body satisfaction were randomly assigned to either a CBT treatment group, an exercise treatment group, or a control group (Fisher & Thompson, 1994). Those assigned to the CBT group participated in six one-hour sessions of therapy over a six-week period. Those assigned to the exercise group participated in a one-hour exercise class each week for six weeks, and were also instructed to exercise on their own at least two additional times per week. Participants in the control group did not receive any intervention. Over the six-week study, the CBT and exercise groups showed significant and similar improvements along the cognitive and affective dimensions of body image. The control group showed no improvement. These findings suggest that exercise is just as good as psychological interventions for improving body image. Of course, unlike psychological interventions, exercise interventions have the added bonus of improving people's health and physical fitness at the same time as they improve body image.

the impact of these two training modalities were demonstrated in a study by Tucker and Mortell (1993). These researchers randomly assigned 30 women to a weight-training program and 30 to a walking program. Both programs were held three times per week. Body satisfaction was measured at the start of the study and again 12 weeks later. Upon completion of the exercise program, both groups showed significant improvements in body image, but those assigned to the weight-training intervention showed greater improvements than did the walkers.

An interesting question is whether exercise is as effective as traditional psychological approaches to improving body image. Unfortunately, this issue has not been well studied. Nonetheless, the results of one experiment have provided encouraging results (Fisher & Thompson, 1994). You can read about this study in the box above.

MECHANISMS OF CHANGE

Exhibit 13.5 shows three proposed mechanisms by which exercise may improve body image: improved physical fitness, increased awareness of physical capabilities, and increased self-efficacy.

exhibit 13.5 *Three proposed mechanisms by which exercise may improve body image.*

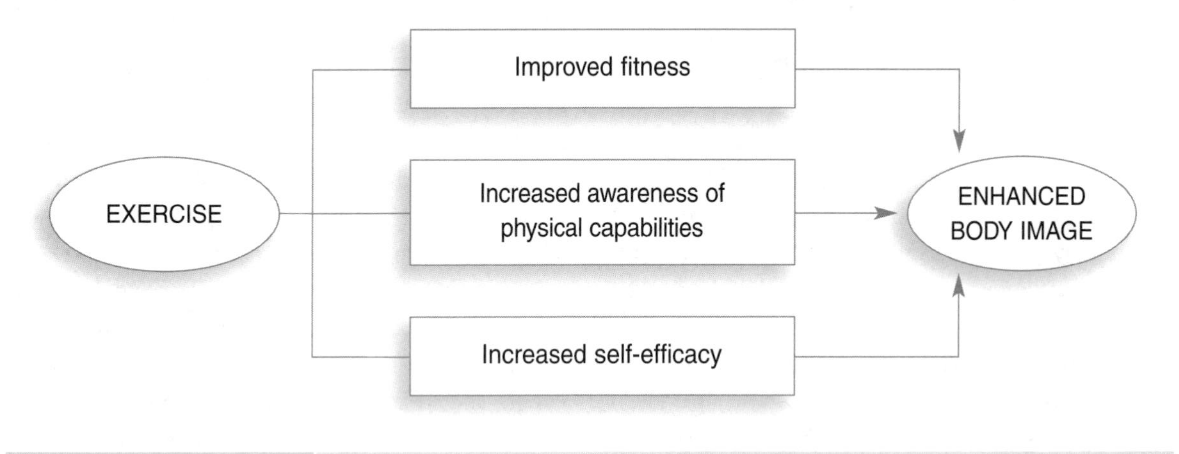

Improved Physical Fitness

Fitness reflects one's level of cardiorespiratory endurance (or aerobic fitness), muscular strength and endurance, flexibility, body composition, and ability to perform functional activities such as those associated with daily living. The vast majority of exercise intervention studies have examined body image change in relation to change in just a *single* fitness component—**body composition** (the relative amount of lean body mass vs. fat in the body). Some of these studies have shown that changes in body composition are significantly related to the amount of body image change experienced during an exercise intervention, with larger decreases in body fat and body weight leading to greater improvements in body image (McAuley, Bane, Rudolph, & Lox, 1995; Tucker & Maxwell, 1992). However, the effects of improved body composition are fairly modest and generally account for less than 10 percent of the total change in body image. Moreover, in some exercise training studies, participants have significantly improved their body image, but have shown very little or no significant change in body composition (e.g., Tucker & Mortell, 1993). These findings suggest that greater decreases in body weight are not necessarily associated with greater improvements in body image, and that relatively small alterations in body composition can lead to considerably large improvements in body image.

body composition ■

A few studies have examined the relationship between changes in the strength and endurance aspects of physical fitness and changes in body image. As with improvements in body composition, improvements in strength and endurance seem to account for only modest amounts of change in body image. For example, one study found that changes in strength across a 12-week weight-training program accounted for just 12 percent of the variability in body image change (Tucker & Mortell, 1993). These results suggest that other variables account for much of the effects of exercise on body image.

Even if changes in strength and endurance do account for some of the variability in body image change, it is unknown whether actual improvements in *fitness* explain the fitness–body image relationship, or whether *perceived* improvements in physical appearance that are caused by fitness change (e.g., improved muscle tone, clothing fits better) trigger improvements in body image. In other words, is it actual changes in strength and endurance that make people feel better about their bodies? Or is it the changes in physical appearance that *accompany* improved fitness that make people feel better about their bodies? The answers to these questions are not yet known.

Increased Awareness of Physical Capabilities

If changes in body composition do not fully explain the positive effects of exercise on body image, then what does? Perhaps exercise improves body image by making people more aware of their physical capabilities, while reducing focus on their physical appearance. This shift in awareness may be particularly relevant to women, who, unlike men, tend to place greater value on physical appearance than on physical capabilities or function and, hence, are more inclined to start exercising primarily to change their appearance (McDonald & Thompson, 1992). (Men's motivation to start exercising generally focuses on improving physical function; see Ashford, Biddle, & Goudas, 1993.) Because it is virtually impossible for most women to achieve the cultural body image ideal through exercise, those who embark on an exercise program with the goal of attaining this ideal are setting themselves up for inevitable failure and continued body dissatisfaction.

It is possible, however, for most women to improve their physical functioning and conditioning through exercise training. When women exercise to improve nonappearance aspects of body image (such as satisfaction with physical function), they are more likely to experience success and satisfaction than when they exercise for appearance-related reasons. This may explain why women who exercise for fitness-related motives express greater body satisfaction than those who exercise for appearance-related motives. Because our culture and the media do not have strictly defined ideals for fitness (i.e., in terms of how fast a woman should be able to run, or how much weight she should be able to lift), women who focus on improving along fitness dimensions are not constantly comparing themselves with an unattainable standard (Martin & Lichtenberger, 2002).

Increased Self-Efficacy

When exercisers pay attention to their physical capabilities and see themselves improving, it is likely that their physical self-efficacy also improves. Such changes in self-efficacy may lead to changes in body image. This hypothesis is consistent with the exercise and self-esteem model (see Chapter 9), which suggests that exercise-related improvements in physical self-efficacy can lead to more positive feelings about one's body. Indeed, Baldwin and Courneya (1997) found that among a sample of breast cancer survivors, greater exercise participation was associated with greater physical self-efficacy, which was in turn related to greater body image satisfaction. Although self-efficacy was only modestly associated with body image, these results do suggest that self-efficacy may account for at least some of exercise's effects on body image.

WHO BENEFITS MOST FROM EXERCISE INTERVENTIONS?

Exercise interventions have the greatest impact on the people who have the poorest body image. In Tucker and Mortell's study (1993), for example, the women who had the poorest body image at the start of the study showed the greatest improvements over the course of the study. It follows, then, that exercise training could be particularly beneficial to people whose body image may be threatened by disease or illness (Martin & Lichtenberger, 2002). Indeed, exercise training has been associated with increased body image satisfaction among women recovering from breast cancer (Baldwin & Courneya, 1997), men and women with paraplegia and quadriplegia (Hicks et al., 2003), adolescents with postural deformities (Dekel, Tenenbaum, & Kudar, 1996), and obese women (Foster, Wadden, & Vogt, 1997). These findings speak to the robustness of exercise for improving body image across a variety of special populations.

It is important to note, however, that studies of the effects of exercise on body image have involved mostly Caucasian, well-educated women between the ages of 17 and 65. There have been a few studies of exercise training among men, but most of these investigations have involved middle-aged individuals. Consequently, little is known about the effects of exercise training on younger men and people drawn from other ethnic groups or socioeconomic strata. Also, little is known about the effects of exercise interventions on children's body image. Yet given that sports participation has been associated with better body image among children (Statistics Canada, 2001), it is suspected that structured exercise interventions could have a similar positive effect. In support of this idea, a case study of six obese children demonstrated that thrice weekly exercise with a personal trainer resulted in improvements in body image (see O'Brien & Martin, 1998).

INFLUENCE OF BODY IMAGE ON EXERCISE BEHAVIOR

Exercise Motivation

As discussed earlier in this chapter, body image concerns can be a powerful motivator for starting an exercise program. Indeed, a survey of exercise participation motives among adult men and women indicated that the desire to lose weight or increase muscle tone are primary motives for starting an exercise program (Rodgers & Gauvin, 1994).

Over time, however, most people who start an exercise program to change their appearance gradually shift their motives toward exercising for continued physical and psychological well-being (Ingledew, Markland, & Medley, 1998). In fact, long-term maintenance of an exercise program is generally associated with endorsement of physical and psychological motives for exercise, rather than motives related to improving appearance. This shift in motives probably occurs when exercise initiates begin to see and value the fitness and mood-related benefits associated with being active. Among some people, however, the desire for weight loss and a toned physique continues to be the top priority. This desire may lead to exercise dependence (Davis, 2000), as discussed in Chapter 10.

Body image can also have demotivating effects on exercise. As was the case with June—the girl portrayed in the story at the start of this chapter—body image dissatisfaction can cause some people to avoid exercise completely. Sometimes, people may refuse to exercise because they are worried about looking overweight, uncoordinated, weak, or unfit (Leary, 1992). This phenomenon was demonstrated in a study of Irish adolescents that found that among teenagers who did not exercise regularly, body image concerns were cited as a major reason for avoiding exercise (Martin, Leary, & O'Brien, 2001).

Likewise, people who are severely overweight or obese frequently indicate that they avoid signing up for exercise programs and joining gyms because they are embarrassed or ashamed of their appearance (Bain, Wilson, & Chaikind, 1989). Unfortunately, even when obese people do take the first step and sign up for exercise programs, concerns about their appearance may prevent them from adhering. For example, in a study of obese women who were part of a walking group, those who had greater anxiety about their body's appearance (i.e., greater social physique anxiety) had poorer attendance than those who were not so anxious about their appearance (Treasure, Lox, & Lawton, 1998).

Exercise Setting and Attire Preferences

Exercise setting preferences appear to be influenced by body image concerns. For example, Spink (1992) administered the Social Physique Anxiety Scale (SPAS) to a sample of young women and asked them where they typically exercised. Women who had high scores on the SPAS (that is, women who reported that they experienced very high levels of anxiety when other people evaluated their bodies) were more likely to exercise in private settings (alone at home) than were women who had low scores on the SPAS (women who reported little or no anxiety when other people evaluated their bodies).

Body image concerns may also influence preferences for certain types of exercise attire. Crawford and Eklund (1994) conducted a study that required women to watch a videotaped exercise class in which class members wore conservative aerobics attire (shorts and t-shirts) and a second tape in which participants wore revealing aerobics attire (tights and thong leotards). After watching each tape, women completed a questionnaire that assessed their feelings toward that particular exercise class. The questionnaire included items such as "I would be comfortable exercising with this class" and "I would feel out of place in this exercise class." Analyses revealed a significant correlation between social physique anxiety and feelings about the exercise classes. Higher levels of social physique anxiety were associated with more negative feelings toward the class that wore the revealing attire and more positive feelings toward the class that wore the conservative attire.

Practical Recommendations

Given what is known about the effects of body image on exercise participation and the effects of exercise training on body image, several issues should be kept in mind when promoting exercise and developing exercise interventions to improve body image. First, with regard to exercise promotion, it is important that promotional materials show a wide range of body shapes, sizes, and physical abilities. Exercise campaigns that show only ultra-fit models send an inaccurate message that a fit appearance is a prerequisite for joining a gym or starting an exercise program. Consequently, people who are dissatisfied with their bodies may avoid joining a fitness program because they believe that they "don't look good enough" to be seen exercising in public.

Exercise programs should also focus on improving physical function, strength, and endurance rather than on changing physical appearance. Programs that help people to set realistic and attainable goals and that teach people how to monitor progress in terms of functional fitness improvements should have a more positive impact on body image than programs with an emphasis on "building buns of steel" and "fighting flabby abs." In short, to achieve body image change, exercise programs should focus on what people *can* realistically change, rather than draw attention to what they cannot. Granted, many people start exercising to improve their body image, but effort should be directed toward educating or orienting these individuals to the other physical and mental benefits of exercise. Fitness instructors can go one step further in de-emphasizing physical appearance by encouraging participants to wear loose-fitting, comfortable exercise attire, and donning such attire themselves (Martin & Hausenblas, 1998).

With regard to developing interventions to improve body image, the results of some studies suggest that in order to see significant gains in body image, exercise intensity and duration should be moderate to high (Ready, Fitzpatrick, Boreskie, & Hrycaiko, 1991; Tucker & Mortell, 1993)—perhaps because this level of exercise is most likely to generate the greatest improvements in physical function, fitness, appearance, and self-efficacy. In addition, as stated previously, weight training seems to be the type of exercise most conducive to body image change, perhaps because it tends to result in faster, more obvious physical changes (e.g., increased muscle tone and improved body composition) than aerobic activities such as walking. *Seeing* these changes in body composition can make one feel better about one's body (Tucker & Maxwell, 1992).

There is also some evidence to suggest that people who enjoy their workouts the most show the biggest exercise-related improvements in body image. Tucker and Mortell's (1993) study found that among women assigned to the weight-training group, the better they felt at the conclusion of each training session, the more they tended to gain in body image across the three-month program. Perhaps the cumulative effects of mood-enhancing exercise bouts lead to better psychological well-being in general (i.e., less depression and anxiety, greater self-esteem), which translates into more positive feelings about one's body.

It may also be that people who enjoy their workouts exercise harder and adhere better than do those who don't enjoy exercising, thus reaping greater improvements in fitness, function, and appearance.

Conclusion

The most recent data suggest that an increasingly large proportion of men and women are dissatisfied with their bodies. For some people, body dissatisfaction can be a powerful incentive to exercise, and for others it can be a potent deterrent to exercise. Exercise psychologists are interested in studying the relationship between body image and exercise-related thoughts, feelings, and behaviors. They are also interested in determining whether exercise can be used to improve body image. Although the research to date has been limited primarily to studies of Caucasian women, the results of these studies suggest that exercise—particularly strength training—can significantly improve body image. Given the importance of body image to mental and physical well-being, it is encouraging to note that exercise can be a highly effective intervention for alleviating body image disturbance.

What Do You Know?

1. Identify and describe the four dimensions of body image.
2. Describe two factors that can influence body image formation and disturbance.
3. How do men and women differ in terms of discrepancies between their medical and cultural body image ideals and their body realities?
4. Give two reasons why body image is important to psychological and physical well-being.
5. Describe one type of measurement strategy for each of the four dimensions of body image.
6. Describe three ways in which exercise may improve body image.
7. How might body image have a motivating effect on exercise behavior?
8. How might body image have a demotivating effect on exercise behavior?

9. Why might exercise be particularly useful for improving the body image of people with disease or disability?
10. What type of exercise would you recommend to a woman who wanted to improve her body image?

Learning Activities

1. Examine how exercise and body image are portrayed for men and women by the media. Choose one popular women's magazine and one popular men's magazine (not fitness magazines). Compare the following across the two magazines:

   a. the number of references to exercise as a way to lose weight and change physical appearance
   b. the number of references to exercise as a way to improve one's health
   c. the number of advertisements and articles on diets and diet products
   d. the number of models whose bodies could be considered typical or representative of the general population
   e. the number of models whose bodies represent the ultra-trim and ultra-fit cultural ideal

2. Take a large piece of paper and draw an outline of your body. Try to make the drawing as accurate as possible in terms of height, width, shape, and so forth. Now, think about how you feel about the following parts of your body:

Shoulders	Upper arms	Buttocks
Chest	Lower arms	Upper legs
Stomach	Hips	Lower legs

Mark on your diagram your feelings about each of these parts. On the parts that you like to show off, draw a star. On the parts that you want to hide, draw a blanket. On the parts that you feel neutral about, draw a balanced scale. On the parts you are simply content with, draw a happy face.

Discuss any patterns you see in the symbols shown on your diagram, the body parts you work out most during exercise, and the types of clothes you like to wear.

Now, lie down on your drawing and have a friend trace the outline of your body. Are there any differences between how you drew your body and how it is actually shaped?

3. The transition from middle school to high school is a big one for both boys and girls. Lots of things are changing in their lives, including their bodies. Design an intervention program for young teenagers (ages 13 to 15) with the objective of improving or maintaining a healthy body image.

4. Imagine that you are an instructor at a fitness club. You have been asked to design an exercise program for obese people. Taking into account what you now know about body image and exercise, design a program in which obese people will feel comfortable, and that will also lead to changes in their body image.

References

Abrams, K. K., Allen, L. R., & Gray, J. J. (1993). Disordered eating attitudes and behaviors, psychological adjustment and ethnic identity: A comparison of black and White female college students. *International Journal of Eating Disorders, 14,* 49–57.

Ashford, B., Biddle, S., & Goudas, M. (1993). Participation in community sports centres: motives and predictors of enjoyment. *Journal of Sports Sciences, 11,* 249–256.

Bain, L. L., Wilson, T., & Chaikind, E. (1989). Participant perceptions of exercise programs for overweight women. *Research Quarterly for Exercise and Sport, 60,* 134–143.

Baldwin, M. K., & Courneya, K. S. (1997). Exercise and self-esteem in breast cancer survivors: An application of the exercise and self-esteem model. *Journal of Sport and Exercise Psychology, 19,* 347–358.

Bane, S., & McAuley, E. (1998). Body image and exercise. In J. L. Duda (Ed.), *Advances in sport and exercise psychology measurement* (pp. 311–324). Morgantown, WV: Fitness Information Technology.

Blouin, A. G., & Goldfield, G. S. (1995). Body image and steroid use in male bodybuilders. *International Journal of Eating Disorders, 18,* 159–165.

Brownell, K. D. (1991). Dieting and the search for the perfect body: Where physiology and culture collide. *Behavior Therapy, 22,* 1–12.

Butters, J. W., & Cash, T. F. (1987). Cognitive-behavioral treatment of women's body image satisfaction: A controlled-outcome study. *Journal of Consulting and Clinical Psychology, 55,* 889–897.

Cash, T. F., & Deagle, E. A. (1997). The nature and extent of body-image disturbance in anorexia nervosa and bulimia nervosa: A meta-analysis. *International Journal of Eating Disorders, 22,* 107–125.

Cash, T. F., Winstead, B. A., & Janda, L. H. (1986). The great American shape-up. *Psychology Today, 20*(4), 30–37.

Centers for Disease Control. (2001). *Youth risk behavior survey, 1997* [On-line]. Available: www.cdc.gov

Cohen, T., & Esther, M. (1993). Depressed mood and concern with weight and shape in normal young women. *International Journal of Eating Disorders, 14,* 223–227.

Cooper, P. J., Taylor, M. J., Cooper, Z., & Fairburn, C. G. (1987). The development and validation of the body shape questionnaire. *International Journal of Eating Disorders, 6,* 485–494.

Crawford, S., & Eklund, R. C. (1994). Social physique anxiety, reasons for exercise, and attitudes toward exercise settings. *Journal of Sport and Exercise Psychology, 16,* 70–82.

Davis, C. (2000). Exercise abuse. *International Journal of Sport Psychology, 31,* 278–289.

Dekel, Y., Tenenbaum, G., & Kudar, K. (1996). An exploratory study on the relationship between postural deformities and body-image and self-esteem in adolescents: The mediating role of physical activity. *International Journal of Sport Psychology, 27,* 183–196.

Fairburn, C. G., Peveler, R. C., Jones, R., & Hope, R. A. (1993). Predictors of a 12-month outcome in bulimia nervosa and the influence of attitudes to shape and weight. *Journal of Consulting and Clinical Psychology, 61,* 696–698.

Fisher, E., & Thompson, J. K. (1994). A comparative evaluation of cognitive behavior therapy (CBT) versus exercise therapy (ET) for the treatment of body image disturbance. *Behavior Modification, 18,* 171–185.

Foster, G. D., Wadden, T. A., & Vogt, R. A. (1997). Body image in obese women before, during, and after weight loss treatment. *Health Psychology, 16,* 226–229.

Franzoi, S. L., & Shields, S. A. (1984). The body esteem scale: Multidimensional structure and sex differences in a college population. *Journal of Personality Assessment, 48,* 173–178.

Furnham, A., Titman, P., & Sleeman, E. (1994). Perception of female body shapes as a function of exercise. *Journal of Social Behavior and Personality, 9,* 335–352.

Grant, J. R., & Cash, T. F. (1995). Cognitive-behavioral body image therapy: Comparative efficacy of group and modest-contact treatments. *Behaviour Therapy, 26,* 69–84.

Harris, S. M. (1994). Racial differences in predictors of college women's body image attitudes. *Women and Health, 21,* 89–104.

Hart, E. A., Leary, M. R., & Rejeski, W. J. (1989). The measurement of social physique anxiety. *Journal of Sport and Exercise Psychology, 11,* 94–104.

Heinberg, L. J., Thompson, J. K., & Matzon, J. L. (2001). Body image dissatisfaction as a motivator for healthy lifestyle change: Is some distress beneficial? In R. H. Striegel-Moore & L. Smolak (Eds.), *Eating disorders: Innovative directions in research and practice* (pp. 215–232). Washington, DC: American Psychological Association.

Hesse-Biber, S. (1996). *Am I thin enough yet?* New York: Oxford University Press.

Hicks, A. L., Martin, K. A., Latimer, A. E., Ditor, D. S., & McCartney, N. (2003). Long-term exercise training in persons with spinal cord injury: effects on strength, arm ergometry performance and psychological well-being. *Spinal Cord, 41,* 29–33.

Ingledew, D., Markland, D., & Medley, A. R. (1998). Exercise motives and stages of change. *Journal of Health Psychology, 3,* 477–489.

Kirkcaldy, B. D., Eysenck, M., Furnham, A. F., & Siefen, G. (1998). Gender, anxiety and self-image. *Personality and Individual Differences, 24,* 677–684.

Klesges, R. C., Ward, K. D., Ray, J. W., Cutter, G., Jacobs, D. R., & Wagenknecht, L. E. (1998). The prospective relationships between smoking and weight in a young, biracial cohort: The coronary artery risk development in young adults study. *Journal of Consulting and Clinical Psychology, 66,* 987–993.

Leary, M. R. (1992). Self-presentational processes in exercise and sport. *Journal of Sport and Exercise Psychology, 14,* 339–351.

Martin, K. A., & Hausenblas, H. A. (1998). Psychological commitment to exercise and eating disorder symptomatology among female aerobic instructors. *The Sport Psychologist, 12,* 180–190.

Martin, K. A., Leary, M. R., & O'Brien, J. (2001). The role of self-presentation in the health practices of a sample of Irish adolescents. *Journal of Adolescent Health, 28,* 259–262.

Martin, K. A., Leary, M. R., & Rejeski, W. J. (2000). Self-presentational concerns in older adults: Implications for health and well-being. *Basic and Applied Social Psychology, 22,* 169–179.

Martin, K. A., & Lichtenberger, C. M. (2002). Fitness enhancement and body image change. In T. F. Cash & T. Pruzinsky (Eds.), *Body images: A handbook of theory, research, and clinical practice.* New York: Guilford Press.

Martin, K. A., Rejeski, W. J., Leary, M. R., McAuley, E., & Bane, S. (1997). Is the Social Physique Anxiety Scale really multidimensional? Conceptual and statistical arguments for a unidimensional model. *Journal of Sport & Exercise Psychology, 19,* 360–368.

McAuley, E., Bane, S. M., Rudolph, D., & Lox, C. (1995). Physique anxiety and exercise in middle-aged adults. *Journal of Gerontology, 50B,* 229–235.

McDonald, K., & Thompson, J. K. (1992). Eating disturbance, body image dissatisfaction, and reasons for exercising: Gender differences and correlational findings. *International Journal of Eating Disorders, 11,* 289–292.

Metropolitan Life Insurance Company. (2001). *Height and weight tables, 1993* [On-line]. Available: www.metlife.com

Miller, C. T., & Downey, K. T. (1999). A meta-analysis of heavyweight and self-esteem. *Personality and Social Psychology Review, 31,* 68–84.

O'Brien, J., & Martin, K. A. (1998). Up and running: Interventions in exercise psychology. *Irish Journal of Psychology, 19,* 439–446.

Pliner, P., Chaiken, S., & Flett, G. L. (1990). Gender differences in concern with body weight and physical appearance over the life span. *Personality and Social Psychology Bulletin, 16,* 263–273.

Polivy, J., & Herman, C. P. (2002). Causes of eating disorders. *Annual Review of Psychology, 53,* 187–213.

Ready, A. E., Fitzpatrick, D. W., Boreskie, S. L., & Hrycaiko, D. W. (1991). The response of obese females to low impact exercise and diet counseling. *The Journal of Sports Medicine and Physical Fitness, 31,* 587–595.

Rodgers, W. M., & Gauvin, L. (1994). *Contributions and comparisons of personal strivings and outcome expectancies in the understanding of participation motives and exercise adherence* (University of Alberta, Department of Physical Education and Sport Studies Rep. No. 922R010).

Rodin, J., Silberstein, L. R., & Striegel-Moore, R. H. (1985). Women and weight: A normative discontent. In T. B. Sonderegger (Ed.), *Nebraska Symposium on Motivation: Vol. 32. Psychology and Gender.* Lincoln: University of Nebraska.

Rosen, J. C., Srebnik, D., Saltzberg, E., & Wendt, S. (1991). Development of a body image avoidance questionnaire. *Psychological Assessment, 8,* 32–37.

Rucker, C. E., & Cash, T. F. (1992). Body images, body-size perceptions, and eating behaviors among African-American and white college women. *International Journal of Eating Disorders, 12,* 291–299.

Spink, K. S. (1992). Relation of anxiety about social physique to location of participation in physical activity. *Perceptual and Motor Skills, 74,* (Spec. Issue), 1075–1078.

Statistics Canada (2001). *Canadian social trends: children's participation in sports, 2001* [Online]. Available: www.statcan.ca

Thompson, J. K., Coovert, M. D., Richards, K. J., & Johnson, S. (1995). Development of body image, eating disturbance, and general psychological functioning in female adolescents: Covariance structure modeling and longitudinal investigations. *International Journal of Eating Disorders, 18,* 221–236.

Thompson, J. K., & Thompson, C. M. (1986). Body size distortion and self-esteem in asymptomatic normal weight males and females. *International Journal of Eating Disorders, 5,* 1061–1068.

Treasure, D. C., Lox, C. L., & Lawton, B. R. (1998). Determinants of physical activity in a sedentary, obese female population. *Journal of Sport and Exercise Psychology, 20,* 218–224.

Tucker, L. A., & Maxwell, K. (1992). Effects of weight training on the emotional well-being and body image of females: Predictors of greatest benefit. *American Journal of Health Promotion, 6,* 338–344, 371.

Tucker, L. A., & Mortell, R. (1993). Comparison of the effects of walking and weight training programs on body image in middle-aged women: An experimental study. *American Journal of Health Promotion, 8,* 34–42.

Wiseman, C. V., Turco, R. M., Sunday, S. R., & Halmi, K. A. (1998). Smoking and body image concerns in adolescent girls. *International Journal of Eating Disorders, 24,* 429–433.

Glossary

abstinence violation effect In behavior change, when a single lapse in behavior causes an individual to give up trying to change a behavior, resulting in a full relapse.

academic self-concept One of the two primary categories of general self-concept, encompassing the primary learning domains of English, math, history, and science.

acquired immune deficiency syndrome (AIDS) An infectious disease caused by the HIV virus (human immunodeficiency virus), which damages the body's immune system, leaving the person vulnerable to a large number of illnesses.

action stage Stage at which a person is exercising at optimal levels for health and fitness.

acute Short-term, temporary.

adherence Maintaining an exercise regimen for a prolonged period of time.

adoption The beginning stage of an exercise regimen.

affect A general, valenced response to a stimulus that does not require thought processes to precede it.

affective dimension of body image Feelings experienced in relation to the body's appearance and function.

affective states Psychological states relating to feelings or emotions.

agoraphobia An anxiety disorder characterized by severe, pervasive anxiety when in situations perceived to be difficult to escape from, or complete avoidance of certain situations.

agreeableness In the Five Factor Model, compatibility with others.

all-cause mortality rates Death by any cause.

amotivation The absence of motivation and/or lack of intention to engage in a behavior.

androgynous Term that refers to an individual who scores high on both the expressive and instrumental personality dimensions.

antecedent cue A cue that precedes a behavior in classical conditioning.

anthropological hypothesis An explanation for the link between physical activity and depression based on evolutionary theory.

anxiety disorders A category of mental health disorders characterized by excessive or inappropriate expression of anxiety.

anxiolytic Anxiety reducing.

arthritis A category of more than 100 conditions that involve inflammation of the joints, pain, stiffness, and sometimes swelling.

attitude An individual's positive or negative thoughts concerning a performance or behavior.

autonomic nervous system A branch of the nervous system which controls physiological functioning relatively automatically (e.g., heart rate, blood pressure, respiration).

avoidance behaviors Actions performed to divert attention away from the body or to prevent other people from seeing one's body.

behavioral dimension Things we do that reflect our positive or negative perceptions, thoughts, and feelings about our bodies.

behavioral economics A model of behavior that integrates stimulus–response theory with research on cognitive psychology and decision making in order to understand how people allocate time and effort to various options.

behavioral processes Behaviors that a person undertakes in order to change aspects of the environment that can affect exercise participation.

behavioral reactance The phenomenon whereby people respond in a direction opposite to the direction being advocated.

bipolar disorder A mood disorder characterized by one or more episodes of mania or mixed episodes of mania and depression.

biopsychosocial approach The belief that the body, mind, and social environment influence one another and, ultimately, behavior.

body composition The relative amount of lean body mass versus fat in the body.

body ideal An individual's perception of how his or her body should look and function.

body image A multidimensional construct that reflects how one sees, thinks, feels, and behaves toward one's own body; includes perceptual, cognitive, affective, and behavioral dimensions.

body image disturbance Negative self-evaluations along any or all of the body image dimensions.

body-part procedures A perceptual measurement based on the perceived width of a particular body part.

body reality An individual's *actual* physical characteristics, such as height, weight, strength, and disease. When body reality is the same or similar to body ideal, this is usually indicative of a healthy body image. When body reality is dissimilar to body ideal, there may be body image disturbance.

bulimia nervosa An eating disorder characterized by binge eating and dramatic behaviors to compensate for overeating (e.g., self-induced vomiting, strenuous exercise, inappropriate use of diuretics and/or laxatives).

cancer A disease of the cells characterized by unrestricted cell growth that usually results in the formation of a tumor. Cancer is the second most frequent cause of death in North America.

categorical approach An approach that assumes that affective states are distinct and have unique properties and antecedents.

cerebretonia Sheldon's term for the tense, introverted, socially restrained, and inhibited personality associated with the ectomorph somatype.

chronic Long-term, relatively permanent.

chronic obstructive pulmonary disease (COPD) Respiratory disease characterized by permanently reduced airflow; includes both emphy- sema and chronic bronchitis. One of the five leading causes of death in North America; 80 percent of cases in the United States are related to smoking.

circumplex model A model that describes affective states along the perimeter of a circle defined by the dimension of affective valence and activation.

classical conditioning A theory that a reflexive behavior can be elicited through repeated pairings of the behavior with an antecedent cue.

clinical anxiety Having enough anxiety symptoms at a sufficient enough intensity to meet criteria for a clinical disorder requiring some form of therapeutic intervention (e.g., psychotherapy, medication).

cognitive behavior therapy (CBT) A form of psychotherapy whereby individuals are trained to use strategies (such as relaxation training and stress management) to replace negative thought patterns with thoughts that will lead to positive feelings and behaviors.

cognitive dimension How we think about or evaluate our body in terms of both its appearance and function.

cognitive restructuring The process of changing how one thinks about a situation or event.

conscientiousness In the Five Factor Model, the number of goals an individual is focused on and the level of self-discipline used to accomplish those goals.

consciousness raising Increasing one's awareness and memory of the benefits of physical activity.

constitutional theory A theory that individuals possess certain body types (somatypes) that determine personality.

contemplation stage The stage in which a person intends to start exercising within the next six months.

contextual motivation A relatively stable pattern of motivation experienced in a particular context.

core The portion of personality that includes our perceptions of the external world and our self, and our basic attitudes, values, interests and motives.

cues-to-action Stimuli in the environment or within the person that prompt a particular behavior.

cues-to-decision Stimuli that initiate a process of deciding whether or not to perform a behavior.

cultural body ideal In Western society, the rigidly defined ideal body weight/type glamorized by the media (also called *media ideal*).

cyclothymia A mood disorder characterized by manic and depressive states, but of insufficient intensity/duration to diagnose as bipolar or major depressive disorder.

decisional balance A model that reflects how people perceive the pros and cons of changing their behavior.

depressive disorder A mental illness characterized by one or more of the following: sustained feelings of sadness, feelings of guilt or worthlessness, disturbances in appetite, disturbances in sleep patterns, lack of energy, difficulty concentrating, loss of interest in all or most activities, problems with memory, thoughts of suicide, hallucinations.

descriptive studies Exercise research that describes the differences between people in the different TM stages.

diabetes A disease in which the body is unable properly to use and store glucose, leading to a buildup of glucose in the bloodstream, or hyperglycemia.

dimensional approach An approach that assumes that affective states are inter-related and can be accurately captured by a small number of dimensions.

dispositional approach A perspective on personality that emphasizes the person; examples include biological theories and trait theories.

distraction/time-out hypothesis A hypothesis that suggests that the anxiety-reducing effects of exercise are due to the distraction it provides from the normal routine.

double-blind experiments Experiments in which neither the subjects nor the experimenters know which subjects are receiving a drug or a placebo.

dysthymia Chronic form of depression.

ectomorph A body type characterized by linearity, tallness, and leanness; in constitutional theory, individuals with this body type are characterized as tense, introverted, socially restrained, and inhibited.

effect size Estimates of magnitude of an effect.

emotional dimension See *affective dimension.*

emotions States of feeling elicited following an appraisal in which an object (a person or event) is determined to impact on the well-being of the individual.

endomorph A body type characterized by plumpness, fatness, and roundedness; in constitutional theory, this body type is linked with affection, sociability, relaxation, and joviality.

endorphin hypothesis An explanation for depression reducing effects of exercise based on the body's production of endorphins during exercise.

energetic arousal (EA) A dimension of the AD ACL characterized by feelings ranging from energy, vigor, and liveliness to feeling of fatigue and tiredness.

epidemic Anything that affects a large number of people; the study of patterns of disease, injury, and disability, and their risk factors and causes.

epidemiology The study of epidemics, dealing with the incidence, distribution, and control of disease in a population.

exercise A form of leisure physical activity (as opposed to occupational or household physical activity) that is undertaken in order to achieve a particular objective (e.g., improved appearance, improved cardiorespiratory fitness, reduced stress).

exercise dependence syndrome A craving for leisure-time physical activity, resulting in uncontrollable excessive exercise behavior that manifests in physiological and/or psychological symptoms.

expectancy value approach A theory that motivation is predicated on the individual's expected behavioral outcome and the value placed on the predicted outcome.

experiential processes Techniques for increasing a person's awareness of, and changing their thoughts and feelings about, themselves and their exercise behavior.

expressive personality A personality characterized by such traits as understanding, sympathy, affection, and compassion.

external regulation The process of engaging in a behavior for the purpose of obtaining an external reward or avoiding an externally applied punishment.

extinction Withholding a positive stimulus after a behavior in order to decrease the likelihood of that behavior happening in the future.

extraversion–introversion dimension In Eysenck's personality theory, the dimension of the personality driven by the level of arousal in the cortex of the brain.

extraverts In Eysenck's personality theory, individuals with low base levels of cortical arousal who seek opportunities for additional stimulation.

extrinsic motivation Motivation that is induced by a force outside the individual.

fibromyalgia A chronic condition characterized primarily by widespread pain throughout the body and uncontrollable fatigue.

functional capacity An individual's physical ability to perform the daily activities that she or he wants or needs to do.

generalized anxiety disorder An anxiety disorder characterized by worry lasting more than six months, along with multiple symptoms (e.g., muscle tension, poor concentration, insomnia, irritability).

generic measures of HRQL Measures designed to assess multiple aspects of HRQL across a wide range of patient populations (e.g., the SF-36).

global motivation The degree of motivation normally experienced by an individual across most behavioral domains.

global self-esteem An individual's overall self-esteem based on his or her self-esteem in the various domains of life.

group cohesion The tendency of a group to stick together and remain united in pursuit of its objectives.

hardiness A personality construct defined as a sense of control over events; commitment, dedication, or involvement in everyday life; and a tendency to perceive life events as challenges and opportunities rather than as stressors.

health-damaging behaviors Behaviors that could lead to a state of illness or injury, such as steroid use, smoking, or using illicit drugs.

health-promoting behaviors Behaviors that may lead to improvements in health or that help to maintain an existing state of good health, such as exercising regularly, eating a well-balanced diet, and getting sufficient sleep.

health-related quality of life (HRQL) Subjective perceptions of the "goodness" of those aspects of life that can be affected by health and health interventions.

healthy body ideal A realistic goal for health and fitness for one's unique and personal body shape.

healthy body image Positive self-evaluations in the perceptual, cognitive, affective, and behavioral dimensions.

heart disease (also coronary heart disease) Illnesses that result from the narrowing and blocking of the coronary arteries that enmesh the heart and supply it with oxygen-rich blood; the leading cause of death in North America.

iceberg profile Psychological profile of elite athletes based on various mood states.

identified regulation The process of engaging in behavior motivated by personal goals.

imagery A behavior performed in the mind using some or all of the body's senses (sight, sound, touch, taste, smell).

instrumental conditioning A principle that states that a new behavior can be learned, or an existing behavior can be changed by pairing that behavior with a subsequent consequence. A positive consequence will increase the likelihood of the behavior occurring again in the future. A negative consequence will decrease its probability of occurring in the future.

instrumental personality A personality characterized by traits such as risk-taking, independence, aggression, and competitiveness.

integrated regulation The process of engaging in a behavior in order to confirm one's sense of self.

interactionist perspective A behavioral model that views both the individual and the situation in which the individual is involved as important in determining behavior.

intervention studies Research that uses the TM to develop exercise interventions.

intrinsic motivation Motivation that emanates from within a person.

introjected regulation The process of engaging in a behavior in response to a self-imposed source of pressure.

introverts In Eysenck's personality theory, individuals with higher base levels of cortical activation, who tend to augment incoming stimulation to avoid further arousal.

knee osteoarthritis A form of arthritis characterized by the degeneration of the cartilage that covers the knee joint, resulting in painful areas of the joint where bone rubs against bone.

lactate threshold The point at which lactate concentrations in the blood exceed the rate at which lactate is removed from the blood, resulting in excess lactate and a shift toward anaerobic metabolism.

lapse A brief period of inactivity (session, week) that precedes resumption of the regular exercise regimen.

learning approaches Theories about personality that focus on the environment; includes condition or behaviorist theories and social learning theories.

learning theory A theory that explains how people learn new behaviors.

lifestyle behaviors Actions performed with the goal of altering the body or that reflect extensive body image concern.

limbic system The collection of brain structures responsible for emotional responding.

longitudinal studies Study design that allows researchers to monitor changes in behavior across a relatively long period of time (i.e., years) in the same group of people.

maintenance stage The stage at which a person has been exercising at optimal levels for six months.

major depressive disorder A mood disorder not driven by physiological causes characterized by depressed mood most of the day nearly every day and loss of interest or pleasure in all or most activities.

mastery The process of accomplishing or completing a goal; the thorough learning and performance of a skill, technique, or behavior.

mastery hypothesis A hypothesis that explains the effect of exercise on depression by positing that these effects are derived from the sense of accomplishment or mastery felt upon completion of a task.

medical body ideal The body weight at which mortality rates are lowest for a person of a given height.

medical model The use of traditional forms of medicine (e.g., pharmacology) for improving physical and/or mental health.

mental disorders Health conditions characterized by alterations in thinking, mood, or behavior associated with distress and/or impaired functioning.

mental health According to the Surgeon General, a state of successful performance of mental function, resulting in productive activities, fulfilling relationships with other people, and the ability to adapt to change and to cope with adversity.

mental health problems Signs and symptoms of insufficient intensity or duration to meet the criteria for mental disorders, but sufficient to potentially warrant active efforts in health promotion, prevention, and treatment.

mental illness The term used to refer to all diagnosable mental disorders.

mesomorph A body type characterized by wide muscular shoulders and narrow hips—the classic athletic body type; in constitutional theory, individuals with this body type are thought to be adventurous, risk-taking, dominant, aggressive, and leaders.

meta-analyses Quantitative reviews of research studies.

moderating factors Variables that could influence treatment effects.

monamine hypothesis An explanation for the effect of exercise on depression based on the alteration of brain neurotransmitters such as serotonin, norepinephrine, and dopamine.

moods Subjective states of feeling that have a cognitive basis and that can enhance or interfere with purposive behavior.

morbidity Disease.

motivation The degree of determination, drive, or desire with which an individual approaches or avoids a behavior.

negative reinforcers Unpleasant or aversive stimuli that, when withdrawn after a behavior, will increase the frequency of that behavior in the future.

neuroticism A personality trait associated with activity of the limbic system and the autonomic nervous system and characterized by more labile and longer-lasting autonomic reactions.

neuroticism–stability dimension In Eysenck's personality theory, the dimension associated with limbic system activity and the autonomic nervous system.

non-academic self-concept One of the two primary categories of general self-concept, comprising social, emotional, and physical self-concept.

noncompliance Failure to maintain an exercise regimen prescribed by a health-care professional.

norm A pattern of behaviors or beliefs common to members of a particular group or society.

obsessive-compulsive disorder An anxiety disorder characterized by obsessions, such as recurrent thoughts or images perceived as inappropriate or forbidden, that elicit anxiety and compulsions, including behaviors or thoughts, that reduce the anxiety associated with obsessions.

openness to experience In the Five Factor Model, the ability to adjust ideas and/or activities when presented with new ideas or situations.

optimism A general personal tendency to expect more good experiences than bad experiences in one's own life.

osteoporosis A disease characterized by low bone mass and deterioration of bone tissue.

overprotectiveness The quality of going to extremes in trying to protect another person from harm.

overtraining Training at a greater level than an individual is accustomed to in terms of frequency, intensity, and duration.

panic disorder An anxiety disorder characterized by intense fear and discomfort associated with physical and mental symptoms, including sweating, trembling, shortness of breath, chest pain, nausea, fear of dying, or loss of control of emotions.

past performance accomplishments The degree of success perceived by an individual who has previously engaged in activities similar to, or the same as, the current behavior.

perceived behavioral control (PBC) The degree of personal control an individual perceives he or she has over a behavior.

perceived competence An individual's judgment of his or her abilities and potential success in specific situations, activities, skills, or domains.

perceptual dimension The picture of our own body that we form in our mind.

personality The underlying, relatively stable, psychological structures and processes that organize human experience and shape a person's actions and reactions to the environment.

pessimism A general personal tendency to expect more bad than good experiences in one's own life.

phobia An anxiety disorder characterized by an exaggerated, irrational fear of an object or class of objects.

physical activity Bodily movements that cause increases in physical exertion beyond that which occurs during normal activities of daily living.

physical activity epidemiology The study of the "epidemic" of physical inactivity concerned with the five "W's" of exercise (who exercises; where, when, and why they do so; and what they do).

physical self-concept An individual's judgments of his or her general physical abilities and physical appearance.

physiological toughness model A psychological model that postulates that exposure to stressors can lead to psychological coping and emotional stability.

positive reinforcer Any intrinsic or extrinsic reward that increases the likelihood of a person repeating a behavior.

post-traumatic stress disorder An anxiety disorder characterized by anxiety and behavioral disturbances following exposure to extreme trauma (e.g., combat, physical assault) that persist for more than one month.

precontemplation stage A stage in which a person has no intention to start exercising in the foreseeable future.

predictive studies Exercise research that has attempted to predict future exercise behavior.

preparation stage The stage at which a person performs tasks (such as getting medical clearance or buying exercise equipment) that will prepare them for starting an exercise program.

primary exercise dependence A psychological condition in which exercise is an end in itself.

psychobiological model A model of behavior that advocates considering both biological and psychological factors.

psychoticism–superego dimension In Eysenck's personality theory, the dimension of personality that is driven by hormonal function.

public policy Government statements or rules that are meant to influence people's behavior.

punishment An unpleasant or uncomfortable stimulus after a behavior that serves to decrease the probability of that behavior happening in the future.

quality-adjusted life years (QALY) An objective, numerical measure of QL that represents the number of years a person is expected to live, adjusted for (or taking into account) health problems that may affect the quality of those remaining years.

quality of life (QL) The overall "goodness" of a person's life; includes both subjective and objective evaluations of all the factors that contribute to one's life.

Rating of Perceived Exertion Scale A scale on which an individual rates how intense she thinks an activity is.

rehabilitation psychology An area of psychology that deals with the relationship between psychological factors and the physical rehabilitation process.

reinforcement management The process of developing strategies for rewarding or reinforcing oneself when exercise goals are met.

relapse Failure to resume regular exercise following a lapse in activity.

role-related behaviors Variable, daily behaviors influence by the particular context in which we find ourselves.

secondary exercise dependence A psychological condition in which exercise is used exclusively to control body composition.

sedentary Chronic (long-term) pattern of inactivity.

self-concept The way in which we see or define ourselves.

self-confidence Confidence in one's self and in one's powers and abilities. In the physical activity setting an individual's perception of his or her ability to perform certain physical activities.

self-determination Autonomous, self-dependent behavior.

self-efficacy The extent to which individuals feel they will be successful in performing the desired behavior given the abilities they possess and the situation in which they find themselves.

self-esteem The evaluative or affective consequence of one's self-concept.

self-motivation A generalized, non-specific tendency to persist in absence of extrinsic reinforcement.

self reevaluation The process by which individuals consider how they feel about their exercise behavior.

self-schemata An individual's domain-specific identities, e.g., exercise identity.

sense of subjective norm A construct that focuses on the degree to which the individual feels social pressure to perform a behavior.

situational motivation Motivation experienced in a particular activity at a specific point in time.

social cognitive approach A psychological approach that views exercise behavior as being influenced by human cognition and external stimuli.

social ecological models A model that takes the approach that individual-level factors are only one of multiple levels of influence on behavior.

social facilitation The phenomenon by which people increase their effort and performance when others are watching them.

social influence Real or imagined pressure to change one's behavior, attitudes, or beliefs.

social interaction hypothesis A hypothesis that proposes that the reason exercise reduces depression is that it provides an opportunity for the individual to interact with others.

social persuasion Verbal and nonverbal tactics used by others in an attempt to increase a person's self-efficacy.

social self-concept An individual's judgment of his or her general ability to interact positively with others.

social support The degree of perceived comfort, caring, assistance, and information that a person receives from others.

somatotonia Sheldon's term for the adventurous, risk-taking, dominant, and aggressive personality he associated with the ectomorph somatype.

Specific Measures of HRQL Measures designed to measure the most valued domains of HRQL among people with a particular disease or disability.

spinal cord injury (SCI) Neurological damage in the spine that results in the loss of motor control, sensation, and reflexes. The damage may be caused by disease or an injury.

staleness syndrome An aspect of overtraining characterized by increased negative mental health.

state anxiety A noticeable but transient emotional state characterized by feelings of apprehension and heightened autonomic nervous system activity.

stereotypes A set of beliefs—true or false—about the characteristics of people who belong to a particular group.

stimulus control The process of placing cues in the environment that will remind people to be more physically active.

stress The physical and emotional tension we feel when we face challenges in our lives.

subsequent reinforcement A reward that follows a behavior.

tai chi A Chinese martial art characterized by soft, slow, flowing movements that emphasize force rather than strength.

tense arousal (TA) A dimension of the AD ACL characterized by feelings ranging from subjective tension to placidity, quietness, and stillness.

theory An explanation about why a behavior or phenomenon occurs.

thermogenic hypothesis A hypothesis that states that elevated body temperature resulting from exercise can also lead to psychological changes such as reduced anxiety.

trait anxiety A general predisposition to respond across many situations with apprehension, worry, and nervousness.

traits Relatively enduring, highly consistent internal attributes.

transtheoretical model (TM) A behavioral model that integrates elements from across a variety of theories and models of behavior.

Type A behavior pattern (TABP) A personality type marked by anger, hostility, and sense of urgency which has been implicated in cardiovascular disease; sometimes called coronary-prone personality.

typical responses Our fairly predictable behaviors and ways of reacting to our environment.

vicarious experiences The process of experiencing a sensation, situation, or behavior via imagined participation in another individual's encounter.

visceratonia Sheldon's term for the affectionate, sociable, relaxed, and jovial personality he associated with the endomorph somatype.

Author Index

Subject Index